TWENTIETH-CENTURY AMERICAN POETRY

Edited, and with a Preface, by
Conrad Aiken

Modern Library
New York

THE MODERN LIBRARY
is published by
RANDOM HOUSE, INC.

BENNETT CERF • DONALD S. KLOPFER

Manufactured in the United States of America

ACKNOWLEDGMENTS

My thanks are due the following poets, publishers and agents for permission to reprint poems copyrighted by them:

THE AMERICAN PRESS—for "The Wind's Head" by John L. Sweeney, reprinted from *America.*

ROBERT BAGG—for "'Laine" and "Ronald Wyn" by Robert Bagg, copyright 1957, 1960 by Robert Bagg, from *Madonna of the Cello,* published by Wesleyan University Press.

R. P. BLACKMUR—for "All Things Are a Flowing," "Half-Tide Ledge" and "Scarabs for the Living" by R. P. Blackmur.

BONI & LIVERIGHT—for poems by H. D. from *Collected Poems.*

BRANDT AND BRANDT—for "On Hearing a Symphony of Beethoven" by Edna St. Vincent Millay, from *The Buck in the Snow,* published by Harper & Brothers, copyright, 1928, by Edna St. Vincent Millay; "What Lips My Lips Have Kissed," from *The Harp Weaver,* published by Harper & Brothers, copyright 1920, by Edna St. Vincent Millay—for "Preludes to Attitude" and "Preludes to Definition" by Conrad Aiken, from *Preludes to Memnon,* published by Charles Scribner's Sons, copyright, 1930, 1931 by Conrad Aiken;—and for "My Father Moved Through Dooms of Love," "Anyone Lived in a Pretty How Town" and "As Freedom Is a Breakfastfood" by E. E. Cummings, from *Fifty Poems,* published by Duell, Sloan and Pearce, copyright, 1939, 1940, by E. E. Cummings; "Always Before Your Voice My Soul," from *Tulips and Chimneys* by E. E. Cummings, published by Thomas Seltzer, copyright, 1923, by Thomas Seltzer, and "Somewhere I Have Never Travelled Gladly Beyond," from *Collected Poems* by E. E. Cummings, published by Harcourt, Brace & Co., copyright, 1923, 1925, 1931, 1935, 1938, by E. E. Cummings.

NICHOLAS L. BROWN—for poems by Alfred Kreymborg, from *Blood of Things.*

KENNETH BURKE—for "Enigma," "The Wrens," "The Conspirators," "Mercy Killing" and "Stout Affirmation," reprinted by permission of the author, from *Book of Moments: Poems 1915-54* (Hermes Publications, Los Altos, California).

JOHN CIARDI—for "Elegy Just in Case," by John Ciardi, copyright 1947, 1955, reprinted by permission of the author.

HORATIO COLONY—for "The Gold That Fell on the Danae," "Autumnal," "Summer Lightning," "Thunder Over Earth" and "The Young Prince" from *A Brook of Leaves* by Horatio Colony, copyright 1935, by Horatio Colony.

MALCOLM COWLEY—for "Stone Horse Shoals," "The Long Voyage" and "Eight Melons," by Malcolm Cowley, from *The Dry Season,* copyright, 1941.

JOHN DAY COMPANY—for "Country Summer" and "Sundown" by Leonie Adams.

REUEL DENNEY—for "McSorley's Bar," by Reuel Denney, published in *Poetry.*

DIAL PRESS, INC.—for "Family Screams," by Hy Sobiloff, reprinted from *In the Deepest Aquarium,* copyright 1959, by Hy Sobiloff.

EDWARD DORO—for "To a Lad Who Would Wed Himself to Music" and "Open Letter to John Doe" by Edward Doro, from *The Boar & Shibboleth,* copyright, 1932, by Edward Doro.

DOUBLEDAY & COMPANY, INC.—for "Ajanta" by Muriel Rukeyser, from *Beast in View;*—for poems by Theodore Roethke from *Words for the Wind:* "The Lost Son," copyright 1947, by Theodore Roethke; "I Knew a Woman," copyright 1954, by Theodore Roethke; "Elegy for Jane," copyright 1950, by Theodore Roethke;—and for poems by Delmore Schwartz from *Summer Knowledge:* "Conclusion," copyright © 1959, by Delmore Schwartz; "At a Solemn Musick," copyright © 1958 by Delmore Schwartz.

FARRAR, STRAUS AND CUDAHY, INC.—for "Mother's Table," "Little Girl Cat" and "Painting of a Lobster by Picasso" by Hy Sobiloff, from *Dinosaurs and Violins,* copyright 1954, by Hy Sobiloff;—and for "Homage to Mistress Bradstreet" by John Berryman from *Homage to Mistress Bradstreet,* copyright 1956, by John Berryman.

HORACE GREGORY—for "Fortune for Mirabel," "The Passion of M'Phail IV" and "Chorus for Survival XIV" by Horace Gregory, from *Poems: 1930-40,* published by Harcourt, Brace & Co., 1941.

HARCOURT, BRACE & WORLD, INC.—for "Jazz Fantasia" and "Wind Song" by Carl Sandburg, from *Smoke and Steel;*—for "Animula," "Marina," "Ash-Wednesday" and "Burnt Norton" by T. S. Eliot, from *Collected Poems of T. S. Eliot;*—for "The Quaker Graveyard in Nantucket," and "A Drunken Fisherman" by Robert Lowell, from *Lord Weary's Castle,* and "Falling Asleep Over the Aeneid" by Robert Lowell, from *The Mills of the Kavanaughs;*—for "Mind," "Exeunt," "Love Calls Us to the Things of This World," "Beasts," and "An Event" by Richard Wilbur, from *Things of This World,* and "The Death of a Toad" by Richard Wilbur, from *Ceremony and Other Poems,* and "Potato" by Richard Wilbur, from *The Beautiful Changes;*—for "In an Iridescent Time," "In a Liberal Arts Building," "Orchard" and "The Pear" by Ruth Stone, from *In an Iridescent Time;*—and for "L'Annunciazione" and "Myth" by Ned O'Gorman, from *The Night of the Hammer.*

HARPER & ROW—for "Renascence" by Edna St. Vincent Millay;—and for "Pictures by Vuillard," "Annotation for an Epitaph," "The Celebration in the Plaza," "Lucifer in the Train" and "Recorders in Italy" by Adrienne Cecile Rich, reprinted from *The Diamond Cutters,* copyright, 1952, 1953, 1954, 1955, by Adrienne Rich Conrad.

HOLT, RINEHART AND WINSTON, INC.—for poems by Robert Frost, from *North of Boston* and *A Boy's Will,* and "My November Guest," "Mowing," "To Earthward," "Fire and Ice," "Stopping by Woods on a Snowy Evening," "Bereft" and "Desert Places" by Robert

Frost, from *Complete Poems of Robert Frost,* copyright, 1923, 1928, 1934 by Holt, Rinehart and Winston, Inc., copyright 1936, by Robert Frost, copyright renewed 1951, © 1956, 1962 by Robert Frost;—for "The Centaur," "The Red Bird Tapestry" and "The School of Desire" by May Swenson, from *A Cage of Spines,* copyright 1956, 1958 by May Swenson.

HOUGHTON MIFFLIN CO.—for poems by Amy Lowell;—for poems by John Gould Fletcher;—"L'An Trentiesme de Mon Eage," "The Too-Late Born," "Einstein," "You, Andrew Marvell," "Memorial Rain" and "Ars Poetica" by Archibald MacLeish, from *Collected Poems;*—for "Kind Sir: These Woods," "Said the Poet to the Analyst," "Where I Live in This Honorable House of Laurel Tree" and "Her Kind" by Anne Sexton from *To Bedlam and Part Way Back;*—for "Rain Over a Continent," "Promontory Moon" and "The Supper After the Last" by Galway Kinnell, from *What a Kingdom It Was;*—and for "The Fish" and "Invitation to Miss Marianne Moore" by Elizabeth Bishop, from *Poems North and South.*

THE HUDSON REVIEW—for "Hannah Dustin" by Louis O. Coxe, copyright 1954, by the Hudson Review, Inc.

INDIANA UNIVERSITY PRESS—for "Murder Mystery" and "To My Friend Whose Parachute Did Not Open" by David Wagoner, from *A Place to Stand.*

MARGOT JOHNSON AGENCY—for "Dandelions" and "The First Leaf" by Howard Nemerov, from *The Salt Garden,* copyright 1954, by Howard Nemerov.

JOHN KEES—for poems of Weldon Kees, copyright 1947 and 1954 by Weldon Kees.

ALFRED A. KNOPF, INC.—for poems by Wallace Stevens, and "Sea Surface Full of Clouds," "To the One of Fictive Music," "Cortège for Rosenbloom" and "The Comedian as the Letter C" by Wallace Stevens, from *Collected Poems,* copyright 1931, 1954 by Wallace Stevens;—for "Bells for John Whiteside's Daughter," "Lady Lost," "Blue Girls," "Here Lies a Lady," "Captain Carpenter," "Husband Betrayed" and "Little Boy Blue" by John Crowe Ransom;—for poems by T. S. Eliot; —and RUPERT HART-DAVIS LTD., for "White Goat, White Ram," "Two Horses" and "Blue Cockerel" by W. S. Merwin, reprinted from *Green with Beasts,* published in 1956 by Alfred A. Knopf;—and for poems by James Merrill, reprinted from *The Country of a Thousand Years of Peace,* copyright 1951 by James Merrill.

LITTLE, BROWN & COMPANY—for poems by Emily Dickinson, from *Poems: First Series; Poems: Second Series; Poems: Third Series* and *The Single Hound;*—and for poems by Stanley Kunitz, from *Selected Poems:* "Lovers Relentlessly," copyright © 1957 by Stanley Kunitz; "Foreign Affairs," copyright © 1958 by Stanley Kunitz; "Deciduous Branch," copyright © 1954 by Stanley Kunitz.

LIVERIGHT PUBLISHING CORPORATION—for "The Tree," "The Tomb at Akr Çaar," "Portrait d'une Femme," "Apparuit," "A Virginal," "The Return," "The River-Merchant's Wife: A Letter," "Dance Figure," "Ité," "Lament of the Frontier Guard" and "Taking Leave of a Friend" by Ezra Pound;—and for "Voyages II," "The River," "The Dance," "Indiana," and "Atlantis," from *The Bridge* by Hart Crane, and "Paraphrase," "In Shadow," "Legend" and "Voyages VI" by Hart Crane.

MACMILLAN COMPANY—for poems by Edwin Arlington Robinson from *Collected Poems;*—for "Poems About the Moon" and "The Eagle That Is Forgotten" by Vachel Lindsay, from *Collected Poems;*—for "The Monkeys," "The Fish" and "Poetry" by Marianne Moore, and "The Mind Is an Enchanting Thing," "England" and "Part of a Novel, Part of a Poem, Part of a Play" by Marianne Moore, from *Collected Poems,* copyright 1951 by Marianne Moore;—for "The Aunt," "Everything That Is," "Here the Stem Rises" and "Haydn: The Horn" by Daniel Berrigan, from *Time Without Number,* copyright 1952, 1957 by Daniel Berrigan;—for poems by Theodore Weiss, from *Outlanders:* "Barracks Apt. 14" and "Homecoming," copyright 1957, by Theodore Weiss, and "Hayseed," copyright 1952 by Theodore Weiss;—and for "The White Dress" and "Lightning for Atmosphere" by Marya Zaturenska, from *Listening Landscape.*

CLAIRE MCALLISTER—for "Mystery" (from *Boetteghe Oscure,* Spring 1960), "Daphne" (from *Poetry London-NewYork,* Winter 1956), and "A Dedication" (from *Poetry London-New York,* March 1956), by Claire McAllister.

THE NEW YORKER—for "The Gardener" by John Hall Wheelock, copyright 1957 by *The New Yorker.*

NEW DIRECTIONS—for "Song," "A Reason for Writing" and "Spring Song" by Theodore Spencer;—for "Heracles," "Sonnet to the Moon" and "Sir Gawaine and the Green Knight" by Yvor Winters;—for "Train Ride" and "Fish Food" by John Wheelwright;—for "A Letter from the Country" by Howard Baker;—for "End of Season," "Revelation" and "Pursuit" by Robert Penn Warren;—for "Canto II" from *The Cantos of Ezra Pound,* copyright 1934, 1948 by Ezra Pound, and "The Alchemist" by Ezra Pound, from *Personae,* copyright 1926, 1954 by Ezra Pound;—for "Tract," "The Yachts," "Gulls," "Portrait of a Lady" by William Carlos Williams, from *The Complete Collected Poems of William Carlos Williams,* copyright 1938, by William Carlos Williams; and "Burning The Christmas Greens" by William Carlos Williams, from *The Collected Later Poems of William Carlos Williams,* copyright 1944, 1948, 1950 by William Carlos Williams;—for "In the Naked Bed, in Plato's Cave," "At This Moment of Time," "Socrates' Ghost Must Haunt Me Now" and "Mentrechè il Vento, Come Fa, Si Tace" by Delmore Schwartz, and "Starlight Like Intuition Pierced the Twelve" by Delmore Schwartz, from *Vaudeville for a Princess,* copyright 1950, by New Directions;—and for "From This There's No Returning" and "Homage to Ghosts" by Jean Garrigue, from *The Ego and the Centaur,* copyright 1947, by New Directions.

THE NEW REPUBLIC—for "The Last Supper" by Oscar Williams.

OXFORD UNIVERSITY PRESS, and CHATTO AND WINDUS LTD.—for "The Groundhog" and "1934" by Richard Eberhart, from *Collected Poems 1930-1960,* © 1960 by Richard Eberhart.

CHARLES PHILBRICK—for "New England Suite" by Charles Philbrick, copyright 1959, by Charles Philbrick, reprinted from *The Beloit Poetry Journal,* Volume IX, Number 4, Summer 1959.

RANDOM HOUSE, INC.—for "Continent's End," "Birds," "Love the Wild Swan" and "Apology for Bad Dreams" by Robinson Jeffers;—for "Ballad of a Sweet Dream of Peace" by Robert Penn Warren, from *Promises: Poems 1954-1956,* © copyright 1957 by Robert Penn Warren;—and for "Praising Poets of That Country" and "The Ecstasies of Dialectic" by Howard Nemerov, from *Guide to the Ruins,* copyright 1950, by Howard Nemerov.

REYNAL & HITCHCOCK, INC.—for "Nostalgia," "The Fly," "Epitaph for John and Richard," "Travelogue for Exiles," "The Twins," "Poet" and "Waitress" by Karl Shapiro.

CHARLES SCRIBNER'S SONS—for "Hasbrouck and the Rose," "Hymn to Chance" and "About Women" by H. Phelps Putnam;—for "Old Countryside" and "Summer Wish" by Louise Bogan;—for "A Recollection," "Fiametta," "Admonition" and "The Return" by John Peale Bishop; and "Speaking of Poetry" by John Peale Bishop, from *Now with His Love,* copyright 1933, by Charles Scribner's Sons; and "Ode" by John Peale Bishop, copyright 1932 by the New Republic, Inc.;—for "The Poet's Testament" by George Santayana, copyright 1952 by Time, Inc. from *The Poet's Testament,* first published as "Santayana's Testament";—and for "Ode to the Confederate Dead" by Allen Tate; and "Shadow and Shade," copyright 1933 by the New Republic, Inc.; "The Mediterranean," copyright 1933 by the Yale University Press; "Idiot," "Last Days of Alice," and "The Robber Bridegroom," all from *Poems 1922-47* by Allen Tate, copyright 1948.

GEORGE STARBUCK—for Part II of the "Poems from a First Year in Boston" by George Starbuck, from *Bone Thoughts.*

HELEN FRITH STICKNEY—for poems by Trumbull Stickney.

ALAN SWALLOW—for "The Metaphysical Amorist," "To a Friend, on Her Examination for the Doctorate in English" and "Agnosco Veteris Vestigia Flammae" by J. V. Cunningham, from *The Exclusions of a Rhyme, Poems and Epigrams,* copyright 1947, 1960, by J. V. Cunningham.

JOHN L. SWEENEY—for "Separation" and "Exaction" by John L. Sweeney.

THE TITLE—for "His Shield" by Marianne Moore.

UNIVERSITY OF MICHIGAN PRESS—for "Despair in Seascape" and "Voyage of Discovery: 1935" by Richmond Lattimore, from *Poems,* Ann Arbor 1957, copyright by the University of Michigan.

UNIVERSITY OF MINNESOTA PRESS—for "Autumnal" by Louis O. Coxe, from *The Second Man,* copyright 1955 by the University of Minnesota.

VIKING PRESS, INC.—for "Boy with His Hair Cut Short" by Muriel Rukeyser;—for "There Came You Wishing Me," "Be Beautiful, Noble, Like the Antique Ant," "God Said, 'I Made a Man,' " "Now, If You Will Look in My Brain," "My Mouth Is Very Quiet," "The Way My

Ideas Think Me," "Saw God Dead, but Laughing" and "Mostly Are We Mostless" by José Garcia Villa.

WESLEYAN UNIVERSITY PRESS—for poems by Donald Justice, from *The Summer Anniversaries:* "The Poet at Seven" © 1959 by Donald Justice, "Ladies by Their Windows" copyright 1954 by Donald Justice, "Southern Gothic" © 1958 by Donald Justice, and "Tales from a Family Album" © 1957 by Donald Justice.

REED WHITTEMORE—for "The Old Lecher" by Louis O. Coxe.

OSCAR WILLIAMS—for "Star," "In Common," "Elegy for Gordon Barber" and "With God Conversing" by Gene Derwood, from *The Poems of Gene Derwood,* published by Clarke & Way, Inc., copyright 1942, 1943, 1944, 1955 by Oscar Williams;—and for "The Leg in the Subway," "Dinner Guest" and "The Man Coming Toward You" by Oscar Williams, from *Selected Poems* (Charles Scribner's Sons 1946, and Clarke & Way 1958), copyright, 1940, 1946 by Oscar Williams.

WILLIAM CARLOS WILLIAMS—for "The Wanderer" by William Carlos Williams.

JAMES WRIGHT and BOETTEGHE OSCURE—for "The Avenger" by James Wright.

YALE UNIVERSITY PRESS—for Parts I, III, and IV of "Poems from a First Year in Boston" by George Starbuck, from *Bone Thoughts;*—for "Elegy in a Firelit Room," "Lament for My Brother on a Hayrake" and "On the Skeleton of a Hound" by James Wright, from *The Green Wall;*—and for "The Connecticut River" by Reuel Denney, from *The Connecticut River and Other Poems.*

CONTENTS

PREFACE

When this anthology was first compiled, it was with a very specific purpose: it was primarily designed for publication in England, and in the pious hope of enlightening that country, then singularly uninformed about American literature, as to the state of contemporary American poetry. With this end in view, the editor quite avowedly made no attempt, as he put it, "to cover the entire field" of American poetry, but rather, as seemed to promise a more effective introduction, "to compile an anthology in which fewer poets might figure, and in which, therefore, they might more generously and identifiably be represented." For this purpose, fourteen poets were selected, and with them Emily Dickinson, the latter because she was at that time wholly unknown in England, and because, as the editor observed it, "seemed wise to include in an anthology of the contemporary, one poet of an earlier generation." The little book justified itself, if modestly. The English critics were properly irritated, and made their first annoyed and surprised acquaintance with, among others, Robinson and Stevens.

In the five years which passed before the book came out in America, it did not seem to the editor that the poetic "scene" had sufficiently altered, in its main features, to warrant any great change in its contents. Accordingly, it remained pretty much the same book that the English had known; and in fact it has remained the same ever since. The depression came and went, and the New Deal, and the Writers' Project. And the war came. Indeed, a generation, and more, had passed and quite suddenly it appeared that where before there was one poet, now there were fifty. To the twenty years of twentieth-century American poetry in the original volume, there were now twenty more to be added; and what had in those days seemed at best a very promising beginning was now secure and brilliant in accomplishment. "The best English poetry being written today" —an anonymous American writer made the remark a few years ago to an anonymous English writer—"is being written by Americans." It was quite true, and it is still quite true. The half century of American poetry which begins with Emily Dickinson is so varied, so rich and so new, as to compare favorably with any but the greatest similar spans in the whole history of English poetry. For the first time, English poetry is really being revitalized on the western shores of the Atlantic. For the first time, American poetry is assured, mature and easy, in an unforced awareness of its wonderful bilateral tradition, its unique inheritance of two separate but complementary cultures. "The European who has settled in America"—the editor noted in his earlier volume—"and who has become the American, uses the English language; but one must bear it constantly in mind that although he has worked few outward changes in the language, he has none the less begun very distinctly to charge it anew with emotional and temperamental and tactile significances, which arise naturally out of his adjustment to a new scene." Mr. T. S. Eliot once observed that the American had one very great cultural advantage over the European: he could, if he wished, *become* European; in that process of "becoming," or acquiring, he could actually possess more than the European, possess it with a fuller awareness. May one not say similarly that the English language, whether as it crossed the Atlantic in the *Mayflower,* or as it passes the New York customs barrier today, has one great advantage over the English language of Whitechapel or Canterbury or Parliament Square or the Banbury Road? It is the English language becoming American.

So said the editor in his introduction to the third edition of this book, in 1944; and it is if anything truer now than it was then. But let the poets speak for themselves. Here are eighty-one where before were fifty-five, and of these twenty-three now appear in an anthology for the first time. As in the earlier editions, the editor has when possible preferred to include such poets as could best be represented by a group of poems, and, with few exceptions, to avoid the one-poem poet. Emily Dickinson has again been permitted to remain, both as forerunner and touchstone, and so has Trumbull Stickney, the natural link between Dickinson and the twentieth-century "thing." If Auden is not present, it is simply because he is no more an American poet than Eliot is an English one. For the rest, it is enough to say that here is a body of work that, for variety and brilliance, is unsurpassed anywhere during this period.

CONRAD AIKEN

Brewster, Massachusetts

TWENTIETH-CENTURY AMERICAN POETRY

THE POET'S TESTAMENT

I give back to the earth what the earth gave,
All to the furrow, nothing to the grave,
The candle's out, the spirit's vigil spent;
Sight may not follow where the vision went.

I leave you but the sound of many a word
In mocking echoes haply overheard,
I sang to heaven. My exile made me free,
From world to world, from all worlds carried me.

Spared by the Furies, for the Fates were kind,
I paced the pillared cloisters of the mind;
All times my present, everywhere my place,
Nor fear, nor hope, nor envy saw my face.

Blow what winds would, the ancient truth was mine,
And friendship mellowed in the flush of wine,
And heavenly laughter, shaking from its wings
Atoms of light and tears for mortal things.

To trembling harmonies of field and cloud,
Of flesh and spirit was my worship vowed.
Let form, let music, let all-quickening air
Fulfil in beauty my imperfect prayer.

GEORGE SANTAYANA

EMILY DICKINSON

"In Winter"

I

In Winter, in my room,
I came upon a worm,
Pink, lank, and warm.
But as he was a worm
And worms presume,
Not quite with him at home—
Secured him by a string
To something neighbouring,
And went along.

A trifle afterward
A thing occurred,
I'd not believe it if I heard—
But state with creeping blood;
A snake, with mottles rare,
Surveyed my chamber floor,
In feature as the worm before,
But ringed with power.
The very string
With which I tied him, too,
When he was mean and new,
That string was there.

I shrank—"How fair you are!"
Propitiation's claw—

"Afraid," he hissed,
"Of me?
No cordiality?"
He fathomed me.

Then to a rhythm slim
Secreted in his form,
As patterns swim,
Projected him.

That time I flew,
Both eyes his way,
Lest he pursue—
Nor ever ceased to run,
Till in a distant town,
Towns on from mine—
I sat me down;
This was a dream.

II

I died for beauty, but was scarce
Adjusted in the tomb,
When one who died for truth was lain
In an adjoining room.

He questioned softly why I failed?
"For beauty," I replied.
"And I for truth—the two are one;
We brethren are," he said.

And so, as kinsmen met a-night,
We talked between the rooms,
Until the moss had reached our lips,
And covered up our names.

III

I've seen a dying eye
Run round and round a room
In search of something, as it seemed,
Then cloudier become;
And then, obscure with fog,
And then be soldered down,
Without disclosing what it be,
'Twere blessed to have seen.

IV

The Chariot

Because I could not stop for Death,
He kindly stopped for me;
The carriage held but just ourselves
And Immortality.

We slowly drove, he knew no haste,
And I had put away
My labour, and my leisure too,
For his civility.

We passed the school where children played,
Their lessons scarcely done;
We passed the fields of gazing grain,
We passed the setting sun.

We paused before a house that seemed
A swelling on the ground;
The roof was scarcely visible,
The cornice but a mound.

Since then 'tis centuries; but each
Feels shorter than the day
I first surmised the horses' heads
Were toward eternity.

V

If I shouldn't be alive
When the robins come,
Give the one in red cravat
A memorial crumb.

If I couldn't thank you,
Being just asleep,
You will know I'm trying
With my granite lip!

VI

Safe in their alabaster chambers,
Untouched by morning and untouched by noon,
Sleep the meek members of the resurrection,
Rafter of satin, and roof of stone.

Light laughs the breeze in her castle of sunshine;
Babbles the bee in a stolid ear;
Pipe the sweet birds in ignorant cadence—
Ah, what sagacity perished here!

Grand go the years in the crescent above them;
Worlds scoop their arcs, and firmaments row,
Diadems drop and Doges surrender,
Soundless as dots on a disk of snow.

VII

The Wind

Of all the sounds despatched abroad,
There's not a charge to me
Like that old measure in the boughs,
That phraseless melody

The wind does, working like a hand
Whose fingers brush the sky,
Then quiver down, with tufts of tune
Permitted gods and me.

When winds go round and round in bands,
And thrum upon the door,
And birds take places overhead,
To bear them orchestra,

I crave him grace, of summer boughs,
If such an outcast be,
He never heard that fleshless chant
Rise solemn in the tree,

As if some caravan of sound
On deserts, in the sky,
Had broken rank,
Then knit, and passed
In seamless company.

VIII

In the Garden

A bird came down the walk:
He did not know I saw;
He bit an angle-worm in halves
And ate the fellow, raw.

And then he drank a dew
From a convenient grass,
And then hopped sidewise to the wall
To let a beetle pass.

He glanced with rapid eyes
That hurried all abroad—

They looked like frightened beads, I thought;
He stirred his velvet head

Like one in danger; cautious,
I offered him a crumb,
And he unrolled his feathers
And rowed him softer home

Than oars divide the ocean,
Too silver for a seam,
Or butterflies, off banks of noon,
Leap, plashless, as they swim.

IX

The Snake

A narrow fellow in the grass
Occasionally rides;
You may have met him—did you not,
His notice sudden is.

The grass divides as with a comb,
A spotted shaft is seen;
And then it closes at your feet
And opens further on.

He likes a boggy acre,
A floor too cool for corn.
Yet when a child, and barefoot,
I more than once, at morn,

Have passed, I thought, a whip-lash
Unbraiding in the sun—
When, stooping to secure it,
It wrinkled, and was gone.

Several of nature's people
I know, and they know me;
I feel for them a transport
Of cordiality;

But never met this fellow,
Attended or alone,
Without a tighter breathing,
And zero at the bone.

X

The Storm

There came a wind like a bugle;
It quivered through the grass,
And a green chill upon the heat
So ominous did pass
We barred the windows and the doors
As from an emerald ghost;
The doom's electric moccasin
That very instant passed.
On a strange mob of panting trees,
And fences fled away,
And rivers where the houses ran
The living looked that day.
The bell within the steeple wild
The flying tidings whirled.
How much can come
And much can go,
And yet abide the world!

XI

It was not death, for I stood up,
And all the dead lie down;
It was not night, for all the bells
Put out their tongues, for noon.

It was not frost, for on my flesh
I felt siroccos crawl—
Nor fire, for just my marble feet
Could keep a chancel cool.

And yet it tasted like them all;
The figures I have seen
Set orderly for burial,
Reminded me of mine,

As if my life were shaven
And fitted to a frame,
And could not breathe without a key;
And 'twas like midnight, some,

When everything that ticked has stopped,
And space stares, all around,
Or grisly frosts, first autumn morns,
Repeal the beating ground.

But most like chaos—stopless, cool—
Without a chance or spar,
Or even a report of land
To justify despair.

XII

Parting

My life closed twice before its close;
It yet remains to see
If Immortality unveil
A third event to me,

So huge, so hopeless to conceive,
As these that twice befell.
Parting is all we know of heaven,
And all we need of hell.

XIII

To my quick ear the leaves conferred;
The bushes they were bells;
I could not find a privacy
From Nature's sentinels.

In cave if I presumed to hide,
The walls began to tell;
Creation seemed a mighty crack
To make me visible.

XIV

Not any sunny tone
From any fervent zone
Finds entrance there.
Better a grave of Balm
Toward human nature's home,
And Robins near,
Than a stupendous Tomb
Proclaiming to the gloom
How dead we are.

XV

A Snake

Sweet is the swamp with its secrets,
Until we meet a snake;
'Tis then we sigh for houses,
And our departure take
At that enthralling gallop
That only childhood knows,
A snake is summer's treason,
And guile is where it goes.

XVI

I have a king who does not speak;
So, wondering, through the hours meek
  I trudge the day away—
Half glad when it is night and sleep,
If, haply, through a dream to peep
  In parlours shut by day.

And if I do, when morning comes
It is as if a hundred drums
  Did round my pillow roll,
And shouts fill all my childish sky,
And bells keep saying 'victory'
  From steeples in my soul!

And if I don't, the little Bird
Within the orchard is not heard,
  And I omit to pray,
'Father, Thy will be done' today,
For my will goes the other way,
  And it were perjury!

XVII

Evening

The cricket sang,
And set the sun,
And workmen finished, one by one
Their seam the day upon.

The low grass loaded with the dew,
The twilight stood as strangers do
With hat in hand, polite and new,
To stay as if, or go.

A vastness, as a neighbour, came—
A wisdom without face or name,

A peace, as hemispheres at home—
And so the night became.

XVIII

Aurora

Of bronze and blaze
The north, to-night!
So adequate its forms,
So preconcerted with itself,
So distant to alarms—
An unconcern so sovereign
To universe, or me,
It paints my simple spirit
With tints of majesty,
Till I take vaster attitudes,
And strut upon my stem,
Disdaining men and oxygen,
For arrogance of them.
My splendours are menagerie;
But their competeless show
Will entertain the centuries
When I am, long ago,
An island in dishonoured grass,
Whom none but daisies know.

XIX

Immortality

It is an honourable thought,
And makes one lift one's hat,
As one encountered gentlefolk
Upon a daily street,

That we've immortal place,
Though pyramids decay,

And kingdoms, like the orchard,
Flit russetly away.

XX

Trying to Forget

Bereaved of all, I went abroad,
No less bereaved to be
Upon a new peninsula—
The grave preceded me,

Obtained my lodgings ere myself,
And when I sought my bed,
The grave it was, reposed upon
The pillow for my head.

I waked, to find it first awake,
I rose—it followed me;
I tried to drop it in the crowd,
To lose it in the sea,

In cups of artificial drowse
To sleep its shape away—
The grave was finished, but the spade
Remained in memory.

XXI

I felt a funeral in my brain,
And mourners, to and fro,
Kept treading, treading, till it seemed
That sense was breaking through.

And when they all were seated,
A service like a drum
Kept beating, beating, till I thought
My mind was going numb.

And then I heard them lift a box,
  And creak across my soul
With those same boots of lead, again.
  Then space began to toll

As all the heavens were a bell,
  And Being but an ear,
And I am silence some strange race,
  Wrecked, solitary, here.

XXII

Dying

I heard a fly buzz when I died;
  The stillness round my form
Was like the stillness in the air
  Between the heaves of storm.

The eyes beside had wrung them dry,
  And breaths were gathering sure
For that last onset, when the king
  Be witnessed in his power.

I willed my keepsakes, signed away
  What portion of me I
Could make assignable—and then
  There interposed a fly,

With blue, uncertain, stumbling buzz,
  Between the light and me;
And then the windows failed, and then
  I could not see to see.

XXIII

A clock stopped—not the mantel's;
  Geneva's farthest skill

Can't put the puppet bowing
  That just now dangled still.

An awe came on the trinket!
  The figures hunched with pain,
Then quivered out of decimals
  Into degreeless noon.

It will not stir for doctors,
  This pendulum of snow;
The shopman importunes it,
  While cool, concernless No

Nods from the gilded pointers,
  Nods from the seconds slim,
Decades of arrogance between
  The dial life and him.

EDWIN ARLINGTON ROBINSON

Ben Jonson Entertains a Man from Stratford

You are a friend then, as I make it out,
Of our man Shakespeare, who alone of us
Will put an ass's head in Fairyland
As he would add a shilling to more shillings,
All most harmonious—and out of his
Miraculous inviolable increase
Fills Ilion, Rome, or any town you like
Of olden time with timeless Englishmen;
And I must wonder what you think of him—
All you down there where your small Avon flows
By Stratford, and where you're an Alderman.
Some, for a guess, would have him riding back

To be a farrier there, or say a dyer;
Or maybe one of your adept surveyors;
Or like enough the wizard of all tanners.
Not you—no fear of that; for I discern
In you a kindling of the flame that saves—
The nimble element, the true caloric;
I see it, and was told of it, moreover,
By our discriminate friend himself, no other.
Had you been one of the sad average,
As he would have it—meaning, as I take it,
The sinew and the solvent of our Island,
You'd not be buying beer for this Terpander's
Approved and estimated friend Ben Jonson;
He'd never foist it as a part of his
Contingent entertainment of a townsman
While he goes off rehearsing, as he must,
If he shall ever be the Duke of Stratford.
And my words are no shadow on your town—
Far from it; for one town's as like another
As all are unlike London. Oh, he knows it—
And there's the Stratford in him; he denies it,
And there's the Shakespeare in him. So, God help him!
I tell him he needs Greek; but neither God
Nor Greek will help him. Nothing will help that man.
You see the fates have given him so much,
He must have all or perish—or look out
Of London, where he sees too many lords.
They're part of half what ails him: I suppose
There's nothing fouler down among the demons
Than what it is he feels when he remembers
The dust and sweat and ointment of his calling
With his lords looking on and laughing at him.
King as he is, he can't be king *de facto,*
And that's as well, because he wouldn't like it;
He'd frame a lower rating of men then
Than he has now; and after that would come
An abdication or an apoplexy.
He can't be king, not even king of Stratford—
Though half the world, if not the whole of it,

May crown him with a crown that fits no king
Save Lord Apollo's homesick emissary:
Not there on Avon, or on any stream
Where Naiads and their white arms are no more
Shall he find home again. It's all too bad.
But there's a comfort, for he'll have that House—
The best you ever saw; and he'll be there
Anon, as you're an Alderman. Good God!
He makes me lie awake o' nights and laugh.

And you have known him from his origin,
You tell me; and a most uncommon urchin
He must have been to the few seeing ones—
A trifle terrifying, I dare say,
Discovering a world with his man's eyes,
Quite as another lad might see some finches,
If he looked hard and had an eye for Nature.
But this one had his eyes and their foretelling,
And he had you to fare with, and what else?
He must have had a father and a mother—
In fact I've heard him say so—and a dog,
As a boy should, I venture; and the dog,
Most likely, was the only man who knew him.
A dog, for all I know, is what he needs
As much as anything right here to-day,
To counsel him about his disillusions,
Old aches, and parturitions of what's coming—
A dog of orders, an emeritus,
To wag his tail at him when he comes home,
And then to put his paws up on his knees
And say, "For God's sake, what's it all about?"

I don't know whether he needs a dog or not—
Or what he needs. I tell him he needs Greek;
I'll talk of rules and Aristotle with him,
And if his tongue's at home he'll say to that,
"I have your word that Aristotle knows,
And you mine that I don't know Aristotle."
He's all at odds with all the unities,

And what's yet worse it doesn't seem to matter;
He treads along through Time's old wilderness
As if the tramp of all the centuries
Had left no roads—and there are none, for him;
He doesn't see them, even with those eyes—
And that's a pity, or I say it is.
Accordingly we have him as we have him—
Going his way, the way that he goes best,
A pleasant animal with no great noise
Or nonsense anywhere to set him off—
Save only divers and inclement devils
Have made of late his heart their dwelling-place.
A flame half ready to fly out sometimes
At some annoyance may be fanned up in him,
But soon it falls, and when it falls goes out;
He knows how little room there is in there
For crude and futile animosities,
And how much for the joy of being whole,
And how much for long sorrow and old pain.
On our side there are some who may be given
To grow old wondering what he thinks of us
And some above us, who are, in his eyes,
Above himself—and that's quite right and English.
Yet here we smile, or disappoint the gods
Who made it so; the gods have always eyes
To see men scratch; and they see one down here
Who itches, manor-bitten, to the bone,
Albeit he knows himself—yes, yes, he knows—
The lord of more than England and of more
Than all the seas of England in all time
Shall ever wash. D'ye wonder that I laugh?
He sees me, and he doesn't seem to care;
And why the devil should he? I can't tell you.
I'll meet him out alone of a bright Sunday,
Trim, rather spruce, and quite the gentleman.
"What, ho, my lord!" say I. He doesn't hear me;
Wherefore I have to pause and look at him.
He's not enormous, but one looks at him.
A little on the round if you insist,

For now, God save the mark, he's growing old;
He's five and forty, and to hear him talk
These days you'd call him eighty; then you'd add
More years to that. He's old enough to be
The father of a world, and so he is.
"Ben, you're a scholar, what's the time of day?"
Says he; and there shines out of him again
An aged light that has no age or station—
The mystery that's his—a mischievous
Half-mad serenity that laughs at fame
For being won so easy, and at friends
Who laugh at him for what he wants the most,
And for his dukedom down in Warwickshire;—
By which you see we're all a little jealous. . . .
Poor Greene! I fear the colour of his name
Was even as that of his ascending soul;
And he was one where there are many others—
Some scrivening to the end against their fate,
Their puppets all in ink and all to die there;
And some with hands that once would shade an eye
That scanned Euripides and Æschylus
Will reach by this time for a pot-house mop
To slush their first and last of royalties.
Poor devils! and they all play to his hand;
For so it was in Athens and old Rome.
But that's not here or there; I've wandered off.
Greene does it, or I'm careful. Where's that boy?

Yes, he'll go back to Stratford. And we'll miss him?
Dear sir, there'll be no London here without him.
We'll all be riding, one of these fine days,
Down there to see him—and his wife won't like us;
And then we'll think of what he never said
Of women—which, if taken all in all
With what he did say, would buy many horses.
Though nowadays he's not so much for women:
"So few of them," he says, "are worth the guessing."
But there's a worm at work when he says that,
And while he says it one feels in the air

A deal of circumambient hocus-pocus.
They've had him, dancing till his toes were tender,
And he can feel 'em now, come chilly rains.
There's no long cry for going into it,
However, and we don't know much about it.
But you in Stratford, like most here in London,
Have more now in the *Sonnets* than you paid for;
He's put one there with all her poison on,
To make a singing fiction of a shadow
That's in his life a fact, and always will be.
But she's no care of ours, though Time, I fear,
Will have a more reverberant ado
About her than about another one
Who seems to have decoyed him, married him,
And sent him scuttling on his way to London—
With much already learned, and more to learn,
And more to follow. Lord! how I see him now,
Pretending, maybe trying, to be like us.
Whatever he may have meant, we never had him;
He failed us, or escaped, or what you will—
And there was that about him (God knows what—
We'd flayed another had he tried it on us)
That made as many of us as had wits
More fond of all his easy distances
Than one another's noise and clap-your-shoulder.
But think you not, my friend, he'd never talk!
Talk? He was eldritch at it; and we listened—
Thereby acquiring much we knew before
About ourselves, and hitherto had held
Irrelevant, or not prime to the purpose.
And there were some, of course, and there be now,
Disordered and reduced amazedly
To resignation by the mystic seal
Of young finality the gods had laid
On everything that made him a young demon;
And one or two shot looks at him already
As he had been their executioner;
And once or twice he was, not knowing it—
Or knowing, being sorry for poor clay

And saying nothing . . . Yet, for all his engines,
You'll meet a thousand of an afternoon
Who strut and sun themselves and see around 'em
A world made out of more that has a reason
Than his, I swear, that he sees here to-day;
Though he may scarcely give a Fool an exit
But we mark how he sees in everything
A law that, given that we flout it once too often,
Brings fire and iron down on our naked heads.
To me it looks as if the power that made him,
For fear of giving all things to one creature,
Left out the first—faith, innocence, illusion,
Whatever 'tis that keeps us out o' Bedlam—
And thereby, for his too consuming vision,
Empowered him out of nature; though to see him,
You'd never guess what's going on inside him.
He'll break out some day like a keg of ale
With too much independent frenzy in it;
And all for cellaring what he knows won't keep,
And what he'd best forget—but that he can't.
You'll have it, and have more than I'm foretelling;
And there'll be such a roaring at the Globe
As never stunned the bleeding gladiators.
He'll have to change the colour of its hair
A bit, for now he calls it Cleopatra.
Black hair would never do for Cleopatra.
But you and I are not yet two old women,
And you're a man of office. What he does
Is more to you than how it is he does it—
And that's what the Lord God has never told him.
They work together, and the Devil helps 'em;
They do it of a morning, or if not,
They do it of a night; in which event
He's peevish of a morning. He seems old;
He's not the proper stomach or the sleep—
And they're two sovran agents to conserve him
Against the fiery art that has no mercy
But what's in that prodigious grand new House.
I gather something happening in his boyhood

Fulfilled him with a boy's determination
To make all Stratford 'ware of him. Well, well,
I hope at last he'll have his joy of it,
And all his pigs and sheep and bellowing beeves,
And frogs and owls and unicorns, moreover,
Be less than hell to his attendant ears.
Oh, past a doubt we'll all go down to see him.

He may be wise. With London two days off,
Down there some wind of heaven may yet revive him;
But there's no quickening breath from anywhere
Shall make of him again the young poised faun
From Warwickshire, who'd made, it seems, already
A legend of himself before I came
To blink before the last of his first lightning.
Whatever there be, there'll be no more of that;
The coming on of his old monster Time
Has made him a still man; and he has dreams
Were fair to think on once, and all found hollow.
He knows how much of what men paint themselves
Would blister in the light of what they are;
He sees how much of what was great now shares
An eminence transformed and ordinary;
He knows too much of what the world has hushed
In others, to be loud now for himself;
He knows now at what height low enemies
May reach his heart, and high friends let him fall;
But what not even such as he may know
Bedevils him the worst: his lark may sing
At heaven's gate how he will, and for as long
As joy may listen, but *he* sees no gate,
Save one whereat the spent clay waits a little
Before the churchyard has it, and the worm.
Not long ago, late in an afternoon,
I came on him unseen down Lambeth way,
And on my life I was afear'd of him:
He gloomed and mumbled like a soul from Tophet,
His hands behind him and his head bent solemn.
"What is it now," said I, "another woman?"

That made him sorry for me, and he smiled.
"No, Ben," he mused; "it's Nothing. It's all Nothing.
We come, we go; and when we're done, we're done;
Spiders and flies—we're mostly one or t'other—
We come, we go; and when we're done, we're done;"
"By God, you sing that song as if you knew it!"
Said I, by way of cheering him; "what ails ye?"
"I think I must have come down here to think,"
Says he to that, and pulls his little beard;
"Your fly will serve as well as anybody,
And what's his hour? He flies, and flies, and flies,
And in his fly's mind has a brave appearance;
And then your spider gets him in her net,
And eats him out, and hangs him up to dry.
That's Nature, the kind mother of us all.
And then your slattern housemaid swings her broom,
And where's your spider? And that's Nature, also.
It's Nature, and it's Nothing. It's all Nothing.
It's all a world where bugs and emperors
Go singularly back to the same dust,
Each in his time; and the old, ordered stars
That sang together, Ben, will sing the same
Old stave to-morrow."

When he talks like that,
There's nothing for a human man to do
But lead him to some grateful nook like this
Where we be now, and there to make him drink.
He'll drink, for love of me, and then be sick;
A sad sign always in a man of parts,
And always very ominous. The great
Should be as large in liquor as in love—
And our great friend is not so large in either:
One disaffects him, and the other fails him;
Whatso he drinks that has an antic in it,
He's wondering what's to pay in his insides;
And while his eyes are on the Cyprian
He's fribbling all the time with that damned House.
We laugh here at his thrift, but after all

It may be thrift that saves him from the devil;
God gave it, anyhow—and we'll suppose
He knew the compound of His handiwork.
To-day the clouds are with him, but anon
He'll out of 'em enough to shake the tree
Of life itself and bring down fruit unheard-of—
And, throwing in the bruised and whole together,
Prepare a wine to make us drunk with wonder;
And if he live, there'll be a sunset spell
Thrown over him as over a glassed lake
That yesterday was all a black wild water.

God send he live to give us, if no more,
What now's a-rampage in him, and exhibit,
With a decent half-allegiance to the ages
An earnest of at least a casual eye
Turned once on what he owes to Gutenberg,
And to the fealty of more centuries
Than are as yet a picture in our vision.
"There's time enough—I'll do it when I'm old,
And we're immortal men," he says to that;
And then he says to me, "Ben, what's 'immortal'?
Think you by any force of ordination
It may be nothing of a sort more noisy
Than a small oblivion of component ashes
That of a dream-addicted world was once
A moving atomy much like your friend here?"
Nothing will help that man. To make him laugh,
I said then he was a mad mountebank—
And by the Lord I nearer made him cry.
I could have eat an eft then, on my knees,
Tails, claws, and all of him; for I had stung
The king of men, who had no sting for me,
And I had hurt him in his memories;
And I say now, as I shall say again,
I love the man this side idolatry.
He'll do it when he's old, he says. I wonder.
He may not be so ancient as all that.
For such as he the thing that is to do

Will do itself—but there's a reckoning;
The sessions that are now too much his own,
The roiling inward of a still outside,
The churning out of all those blood-fed lines,
The nights of many schemes and little sleep,
The full brain hammered hot with too much thinking,
The vexed heart over-worn with too much aching—
This weary jangling of conjoined affairs
Made out of elements that have no end,
And all confused at once, I understand,
Is not what makes a man to live forever.
O, no, not now! He'll not be going now:
There'll be time yet for God knows what explosions
Before he goes. He'll stay awhile. Just wait:
Just wait a year or two for Cleopatra,
For she's to be a balsam and a comfort;
And that's not all a jape of mine now, either.
For granted once the old way of Apollo
Sings in a man, he may then, if he's able,
Strike unafraid whatever strings he will
Upon the last and wildest of new lyres;
Nor out of his new magic, though it hymn
The shrieks of dungeoned hell, shall he create
A madness or a gloom to shut quite out
A cleaving daylight, and a last great calm
Triumphant over shipwreck and all storms.
He might have given Aristotle creeps,
But surely would have given him his *katharsis.*
He'll not be going yet. There's too much yet
Unsung within the man. But when he goes,
I'd stake ye coin o' the realm his only care
For a phantom world he sounded and found wanting
Will be a portion here, a portion there,
Of this or that thing or some other thing
That has a patent and intrinsical
Equivalence in those egregious shillings.
And yet he knows, God help him! Tell me, now,
If ever there was anything let loose
On earth by gods or devils heretofore

Like this mad, careful, proud, indifferent Shakespeare!
Where was it, if it ever was? By heaven,
'Twas never yet in Rhodes or Pergamon—
In Thebes or Nineveh, a thing like this!
No thing like this was ever out of England;
And that he knows. I wonder if he cares.
Perhaps he does. . . . O Lord, that House in Stratford!

Eros Turannos

She fears him, and will always ask
  What fated her to choose him;
She meets in his engaging mask
  All reasons to refuse him;
But what she meets and what she fears
Are less than are the downward years,
Drawn slowly to the foamless weirs
  Of age, were she to lose him.

Between a blurred sagacity
  That once had power to sound him,
And Love, that will not let him be
  The Judas that she found him,
Her pride assuages her almost,
As if it were alone the cost.—
He sees that he will not be lost,
  And waits and looks around him.

A sense of ocean and old trees
  Envelops and allures him;
Tradition, touching all he sees,
  Beguiles and reassures him;
And all her doubts of what he says
Are dimmed with what she knows of days—
Till even prejudice delays
  And fades, and she secures him.

The falling leaf inaugurates
  The reign of her confusion;

The pounding wave reverberates
  The dirge of her illusion;
And home, where passion lived and died,
Becomes a place where she can hide,
While all the town and harbour side
  Vibrate with her seclusion.

We tell you, tapping on our brows,
  The story as it should be—
As if the story of a house
  Were told, or ever could be;
We'll have no kindly veil between
Her visions and those we have seen—
As if we guessed what hers have been,
  Or what they are or would be.

Meanwhile we do no harm; for they
  That with a god have striven,
Not hearing much of what we say,
  Take what the god has given;
Though like waves breaking it may be,
Or like a changed familiar tree,
Or like a stairway to the sea
  Where down the blind are driven.

The Gift of God

Blessed with a joy that only she
  Of all alive shall ever know,
She wears a proud humility
  For what it was that willed it so—
That her degree should be so great
  Among the favoured of the Lord
That she may scarcely bear the weight
  Of her bewildering reward.

As one apart, immune, alone,
  Or featured for the shining ones,

And like to none that she has known
  Of other women's other sons—
The firm fruition of her need,
  He shines anointed; and he blurs
Her vision, till it seems indeed
  A sacrilege to call him hers.

She fears a little for so much
  Of what is best, and hardly dares
To think of him as one to touch
  With aches, indignities, and cares;
She sees him rather at the goal,
  Still shining; and her dream foretells
The proper shining of a soul
  Where nothing ordinary dwells.

Perchance a canvass of the town
  Would find him far from flags and shouts,
And leave him only the renown
  Of many smiles and many doubts;
Perchance the crude and common tongue
  Would havoc strangely with his worth;
But she, with innocence unwrung,
  Would read his name around the earth.

And others, knowing how this youth
  Would shine, if love could make him great,
When caught and tortured for the truth
  Would only writhe and hesitate;
While she, arranging for his days
  What centuries could not fulfil,
Transmutes him with her faith and praise,
  And has him shining where she will.

She crowns him with her gratefulness,
  And says again that life is good;
And should the gift of God be less
  In him than in her motherhood,

His fame, though vague, will not be small
As upward through her dream he fares,
Half clouded with a crimson fall
Of roses thrown on marble stairs.

For a Dead Lady

No more with overflowing light
Shall fill the eyes that now are faded,
Nor shall another's fringe with night
Their woman-hidden world as they did.
No more shall quiver down the days
The flowing wonder of her ways,
Whereof no language may requite
The shifting and the many-shaded.

The grace, divine, definitive,
Clings only as a faint forestalling;
The laugh that love could not forgive
Is hushed, and answers to no calling;
The forehead and the little ears
Have gone where Saturn keeps the years;
The breast where roses could not live
Has done with rising and with falling.

The beauty, shattered by the laws
That have creation in their keeping,
No longer trembles at applause,
Or over children that are sleeping;
And we who delve in beauty's lore
Know all that we have known before
Of what inexorable cause
Makes Time so vicious in his reaping.

The Man Against the Sky

Between me and the sunset, like a dome
Against the glory of a world on fire,

Now burned a sudden hill,
Bleak, round, and high, by flame-lit height made higher,
With nothing on it for the flame to kill
Save one who moved and was alone up there
To loom before the chaos and the glare
As if he were the last god going home
Unto his last desire.
Dark, marvellous, and inscrutable he moved on
Till down the fiery distance he was gone,
Like one of those eternal, remote things
That range across a man's imaginings
When a sure music fills him and he knows
What he may say thereafter to few men—
The touch of ages having wrought
An echo and a glimpse of what he thought
A phantom or a legend until then;
For whether lighted over ways that save,
Or lured from all repose,
If he go on too far to find a grave,
Mostly alone he goes.
Even he, who stood where I had found him,
On high with fire all round him,
Who moved along the molten west,
And over the round hill's crest
That seemed half ready with him to go down,
Flame-bitten and flame-cleft,
As if there were to be no last thing left
Of a nameless unimaginable town—
Even he who climbed and vanished may have taken
Down to the perils of a depth not known,
From death defended, though by men forsaken,
The bread that every man must eat alone;
He may have walked while others hardly dared
Look on to see him stand where many fell;
And upward out of that as out of hell,
He may have sung and striven
To mount where more of him shall yet be given,
Bereft of all retreat,
To sevenfold heat—

As on a day when three in Dura shared
The furnace, and were spared
For glory by that king of Babylon
Who made himself so great that God, who heard,
Covered him with long feathers, like a bird.
Again, he may have gone down easily,
By comfortable altitudes, and found,
As always, underneath him solid ground
Whereon to be sufficient and to stand
Possessed already of the promised land,
Far stretched and fair to see:
A good sight, verily,
And one to make the eyes of her who bore him
Shine glad with hidden tears.
Why question of his ease of who before him,
In one place or another where they left
Their names as far behind them as their bones,
And yet by dint of slaughter, toil, and theft,
And shrewdly sharpened stones,
Carved hard the way for his ascendancy
Through deserts of lost years?
Why trouble him now who sees and hears
No more than what his innocence requires,
And therefore to no other height aspires
Than one at which he neither quails nor tires?
He may do more by seeing what he sees
Than others eager for iniquities;
He may, by seeing all things for the best,
Incite futurity to do the rest.
Or with an even likelihood,
He may have met with atrabilious eyes
The fires of time on equal terms and passed
Indifferently down, until at last
His only kind of grandeur would have been,
Apparently, in being seen.
He may have had for evil or for good
No argument; he may have had no care
For what without himself went anywhere
To failure or to glory, and least of all

For such a stale, flamboyant miracle;
He may have been the prophet of an art
Immovable to old idolatries;
He may have been a player without a part,
Annoyed that even the sun should have the skies
For such a flaming way to advertise;
He may have been a painter sick at heart
With Nature's toiling for a new surprise;
He may have been a cynic, who now, for all
Of anything divine that his effete
Negation may have tasted,
Saw truth in his own image, rather small,
Forbore to fever the ephemeral,
Found any barren height a good retreat
From any swarming street,
And in the sun saw power superbly wasted;
And when the primitive old-fashioned stars
Came out again to shine on joys and wars
More primitive, and all arrayed for doom,
He may have proved a world a sorry thing
In his imagining,
And life a lighted highway to the tomb.
Or, mounting with unfirm unsearching tread,
His hopes to chaos led,
He may have stumbled up there from the past,
And with an aching strangeness viewed the last
Abysmal conflagration of his dreams—
A flame where nothing seems
To burn but flame itself, by nothing fed;
And while it all went out,
Not even the faint anodyne of doubt
May then have eased a painful going down
From pictured heights of power and lost renown,
Revealed at length to his outlived endeavour
Remote and unapproachable forever;
And at his heart there may have gnawed
Sick memories of a dead faith foiled and flawed
And long dishonoured by the living death
Assigned alike by chance

To brutes and hierophants;
And anguish fallen on those he loved around him
May once have dealt the last blow to confound him,
And so have left him as death leaves a child,
Who sees it all too near;
And he who knows no young way to forget
May struggle to the tomb unreconciled.
Whatever suns may rise and set
There may be nothing kinder for him here
Than shafts and agonies;
And under these
He may cry out and stay on horribly;
Or, seeing in death too small a thing to fear,
He may go forward like a stoic Roman
Where pangs and terrors in his pathway lie—
Or, seizing the swift logic of a woman,
Curse God and die.

Or maybe there, like many another one
Who might have stood aloft and looked ahead,
Black-drawn against wild red,
He may have built unawed by fiery gules
That in him no commotion stirred,
A living reason out of molecules
Why molecules occurred,
And one for smiling when he might have sighed
Had he seen far enough,
And in the same inevitable stuff
Discovered an odd reason too for pride
In being what he must have been by laws
Infrangible and for no kind of cause.
Deterred by no confusion or surprise
He may have seen with his mechanic eyes
A world without a meaning, and had room,
Alone amid magnificence and doom,
To build himself an airy monument
That should, or fail him in his vague intent,
Outlast an accidental universe—
To call it nothing worse—

Or, by the burrowing guile
Of Time disintegrated and effaced,
Like once-remembered mighty trees go down
To ruin, of which by man may now be traced
No part sufficient even to be rotten,
And in the book of things that are forgotten
Is entered as a thing not quite worth while.
He may have been so great
That satraps would have shivered at his frown,
And all he prized alive may rule a state
No larger than a grave that holds a clown;
He may have been a master of his fate,
And of his atoms—ready as another
In his emergence to exonerate
His father and his mother;
He may have been a captain of a host,
Self-eloquent and ripe for prodigies,
Doomed here to swell by dangerous degrees,
And then give up the ghost.
Nahum's great grasshoppers were such as these,
Sun-scattered and soon lost.

Whatever the dark road he may have taken,
This man who stood on high
And faced alone the sky,
Whatever drove or lured or guided him—
A vision answering a faith unshaken,
An easy trust assumed by easy trials,
A sick negation born of weak denials,
A crazed abhorrence of an old condition,
A blind attendance on a brief ambition—
Whatever stayed him or derided him,
His way was even as ours;
And we, with all our wounds and all our powers,
Must each await alone at his own height
Another darkness or another light;
And there, of our poor self dominion reft,
If inference and reason shun
Hell, Heaven, and Oblivion,

May thwarted will (perforce precarious,
But for our conservation better thus)
Have no misgivings left
Of doing yet what here we leave undone?
Or if unto the last of these we cleave,
Believing or protesting we believe
In such an idle and ephemeral
Florescence of the diabolical—
If, robbed of two fond old enormities,
Our being had no onward auguries,
What then were this great love of ours to say
For launching other lives to voyage again
A little farther into time and pain,
A little faster in a futile chase
For a kingdom and a power and a Race
That would have still in sight
A manifest end of ashes and eternal night?
Is this the music of the toys we shake
So loud—as if there might be no mistake
Somewhere in our indomitable will?
Are we no greater than the noise we make
Along our blind atomic pilgrimage
Whereon by crass chance billeted we go
Because our brains and bones and cartilage
Will have it so?
If this we say, then let us all be still
About our share in it, and live and die
More quietly thereby.

Where was he going, this man against the sky?
You know not, nor do I.
But this we know, if we know anything:
That we may laugh and fight and sing
And of our transience here make offering
To an orient Word that will not be erased,
Or, save in incommunicable gleams
Too permanent for dreams,
Be found or known.
No tonic or ambitious irritant

Of increase or of want
Has made an otherwise insensate waste
Of ages overthrown
A ruthless, veiled, implacable foretaste
Of other ages that are still to be
Depleted and rewarded variously
Because a few, by fate's economy,
Shall seem to move the world the way it goes;
No soft evangel of equality,
Safe-cradled in a communal repose
That huddles into death and may at last
Be covered well with equatorial snows—
And all for what, the devil only knows—
Will aggregate an inkling to confirm
The credit of a sage or of a worm,
Or tell us why one man in five
Should have a care to stay alive
While in his heart he feels no violence
Laid on his humour and intelligence
When infant Science makes a pleasant face
And waves again that hollow toy, the Race;
No planetary trap where souls are wrought
For nothing but the sake of being caught
And sent again to nothing will attune
Itself to any key of any reason
Why man should hunger through another season
To find out why 'twere better late than soon
To go away and let the sun and moon
And all the silly stars illuminate
A place for creeping things,
And those that root and trumpet and have wings,
And herd and ruminate,
Or dive and flash and poise in rivers and seas,
Or by their loyal tails in lofty trees
Hang screeching lewd victorious derision
Of man's immortal vision.
Shall we, because Eternity records
Too vast an answer for the time-born words
We spell, whereof so many are dead that once

In our capricious lexicons
Were so alive and final, hear no more
The Word itself, the living word
That none alive has ever heard
Or ever spelt,
And few have ever felt
Without the fears and old surrenderings
And terrors that began
When Death let fall a feather from his wings
And humbled the first man?
Because the weight of our humility,
Wherefrom we gain
A little wisdom and much pain,
Falls here too sore and there too tedious,
Are we in anguish or complacency,
Not looking far enough ahead
To see by what mad couriers we are led
Along the roads of the ridiculous,
To pity ourselves and laugh at faith
And while we curse life bear it?
And if we see the soul's dead end in death,
Are we to fear it?
What folly is here that has not yet a name
Unless we say outright that we are liars?
What have we seen beyond our sunset fires
That lights again the way by which we came?
Why pay we such a price, and one we give
So clamouringly, for each racked empty day
That leads one more last human hope away,
As quiet fiends would lead past our crazed eyes
Our children to an unseen sacrifice?
If after all that we have lived and thought,
All comes to Nought—
If there be nothing after Now,
And we be nothing anyhow,
And we know that—why live?
'Twere sure but weaklings' vain distress
To suffer dungeons where so many doors
Will open on the cold eternal shores

That look sheer down
To the dark tideless floods of Nothingness
Where all who know may drown.

TRUMBULL STICKNEY

Be Still. The Hanging Gardens Were a Dream

Be still. The Hanging Gardens were a dream
That over Persian roses flew to kiss
The curlèd lashes of Semiramis.
Troy never was, nor green Skamander stream.
Provence and Troubadour are merest lies,
The glorious hair of Venice was a beam
Made within Titian's eye. The sunsets seem,
The world is very old and nothing is.
Be still. Thou foolish thing, thou canst not wake,
Nor thy tears wedge thy soldered lids apart,
But patter in the darkness of thy heart.
Thy brain is plagued. Thou art a frighted owl
Blind with the light of life thou'ldst not forsake,
And error loves and nourishes thy soul.

Live Blindly

Live blindly and upon the hour. The Lord,
Who was the Future, died full long ago.
Knowledge which is the Past is folly. Go,
Poor child, and be not to thyself abhorred.
Around thine earth sun-wingèd winds do blow
And planets roll; a meteor draws his sword;
The rainbow breaks his seven-coloured chord

And the long strips of river-silver flow:
Awake! Give thyself to the lovely hours.
Drinking their lips, catch thou the dream in flight
About their fragile hairs' aërial gold.
Thou art divine, thou livest,—as of old
Apollo springing naked to the light,
And all his island shivered into flowers.

He Said: "If in His Image I Was Made"

He said: "If in his image I was made,
I am his equal and across the land
We two should make our journey hand in hand
Like brothers dignified and unafraid."
And God that day was walking in the shade.
To whom he said: "The world is idly planned,
We cross each other, let us understand
Thou who thou art, I who I am," he said.
Darkness came down. And all that night was heard
Tremendous clamour and the broken roar
Of things in turmoil driven down before.
Then silence. Morning broke, and sang a bird.
He lay upon the earth, his bosom stirred;
But God was seen no longer any more.

On Some Shells Found Inland

These are my murmur-laden shells that keep
A fresh voice tho' the years lie very gray.
The wave that washed their lips and tuned their lay
Is gone, gone with the faded ocean sweep,
The royal tide, gray ebb and sunken neap
And purple midday,—gone! To this hot clay
Must sing my shells, where yet the primal day,
Its roar and rhythm and splendour will not sleep.
What hand shall join them to their proper sea
If all be gone? Shall they forever feel

Glories undone and worlds that cannot be?—
'T were mercy to stamp out this agèd wrong,
Dash them to earth and crunch them with the heel
And make a dust of their seraphic song.

In Ampezzo

Only once more and not again—the larches
Shake to the wind their echo, "Not again,"—
We see, below the sky that over-arches
Heavy and blue, the plain

Between Tofana lying and Cristallo
In meadowy earths above the ringing stream:
Whence interchangeably desire may follow,
Hesitant as in dream,

At sunset, south, by lilac promontories
Under green skies to Italy, or forth
By calms of morning beyond Lavinores
Tyrolward and to north:

As now, this last of latter days, when over
The brownish field by peasants are undone
Some widths of grass, some plots of mountain clover
Under the autumn sun,

With honey-warm perfume that risen lingers
In mazes of low heat, or takes the air,
Passing delicious as a woman's fingers
Passing amid the hair;

When scythes are swishing and the mower's muscle
Spans a repeated crescent to and fro,
Or in dry stalks of corn the sickles rustle,
Tangle, detach and go,

Far thro' the wide blue day and greening meadow
Whose blots of amber beaded are with sheaves,
Whereover pallidly a cloud-shadow
Deadens the earth and leaves:

Whilst high around and near, their heads of iron
Sunken in sky whose azure overlights
Ravine and edges, stand the gray and maroon
Desolate Dolomites,—

And older than decay from the small summit
Unfolds a stream of pebbly wreckage down
Under the suns of midday, like some comet
Struck into gravel stone.

Faintly across this gold and amethystine
September, images of summer fade;
And gentle dreams now freshen on the pristine
Viols, awhile unplayed,

Of many a place where lovingly we wander,
More dearly held that quickly we forsake,—
A pine by sullen coasts, an oleander
Reddening on the lake.

And there, each year with more familiar motion,
From many a bird and windy forestries,
Or along shaking fringes of the ocean
Vapours of music rise.

From many easts the morning gives her splendour;
The shadows fill with colours we forget;
Remembered tints at evening grow tender,
Tarnished with violet.

Let us away! soon sheets of winter metal
On this discoloured mountain-land will close,
While elsewhere Spring-time weaves a crimson petal,
Builds and perfumes a rose.

Away! for here the mountain sinks in gravel.
Let us forget the unhappy site with change,
And go, if only happiness be travel
After the new and strange:—

Unless 'twere better to be very single,
To follow some diviner monotone,
And in all beauties, where ourselves commingle,
Love but a love, but one,

Across this shadowy minute of our living,
What time our hearts so magically sing,
To mitigate our fever, simply giving
All in a little thing?

Just as here, past yon dumb and melancholy
Sameness of ruin, while the mountains ail,
Summer and sunset-coloured autumn slowly
Dissipate down the vale;

And all these lines along the sky that measure,
Sorapis and the rocks of Mezzodi
Crumble by foamy miles into the azure
Mediterranean sea:

Whereas to-day at sunrise, under brambles,
A league above the moss and dying pines
I picked this little—in my hand that trembles—
Parcel of columbines.

Now in the Palace Gardens

Now in the palace gardens warm with age,
On lawn and flower-bed this afternoon
The thin November-coloured foliage
Just as last year unfastens lilting down,

And round the terrace in gray attitude
The very statues are becoming sere
With long presentiment of solitude.
Most of the life that I have lived is here,

Here by the path and autumn's earthy grass
And chestnuts standing down the breadths of sky:
Indeed I know not how it came to pass,
The life I lived here so unhappily.

Yet blessing over all! I do not care
What wormwood I have ate to cups of gall;
I care not what despairs are buried there
Under the ground, no, I care not at all.

Nay, if the heart have beaten, let it break!
I have not loved and lived but only this
Betwixt my birth and grave. Dear Spirit, take
The gratitude that pains so deep it is.

When Spring shall be again, and at your door
You stand to feel the mellower evening wind,
Remember if you will my heart is pure,
Perfectly pure and altogether kind;

How much it aches to linger in these things!
I thought the perfect end of love was peace
Over the long-forgiven sufferings.
But something else, I know not what it is,

The words that came so nearly and then not,
The vanity, the error of the whole,
The strong cross-purpose, oh, I know not what
Cries dreadfully in the distracted soul.

The evening fills the garden, hardly red;
And autumn goes away, like one alone.
Would I were with the leaves that thread by thread
Soften to soil, I would that I were one.

Fidelity

Not lost or won but above all endeavour
Thy life like heaven circles around mine;
Thy eyes it seems upon my eyes did shine
        Since forever.

For aught he summon up his earliest hour
No man remembers the surprise of day,
Nor where he saw with virgin wonder play
        The first flower.

And o'er the imagination's last horizon
No brain has leaning descried nothing more:
Still there are stars and in the night before
        More have arisen.

Not won or lost is unto thee my being;
Our eyes were always so together met.
If mine should close, if ever thine forget,
        Time is dying.

At Sainte-Marguerite

The gray tide flows and flounders in the rocks
Along the crannies up the swollen sand.
Far out the reefs lie naked—dunes and blocks
Low in the watery wind. A shaft of land
Going to sea thins out the western strand.

It rains, and all along and always gulls
Career sea-screaming in and weather-glossed.
It blows here, pushing round the cliff; in lulls
Within the humid stone a motion lost
Ekes out the flurried heart-beat of the coast.

It blows and rains a pale and whirling mist
This summer morning. I that hither came—
Was it to pluck this savage from the schist.
This crazy yellowish bloom without a name,
With leathern blade and tortured wiry frame?

Why here alone, away, the forehead pricked
With dripping salt and fingers damp with brine,
Before the offal and the derelict
And where the hungry sea-wolves howl and whine
Like human hours? now that the columbine

Stands somewhere shaded near the fields that fall
Great starry sheaves of the delighted year,
And globing rosy on the garden wall
The peach and apricot and soon the pear
Drip in the teasing hand their sugared tear.

Inland a little way the summer lies.
Inland a little and but yesterday
I saw the weary teams, I heard the cries
Of sicklemen across the fallen hay,
And buried in the sunburned stacks I lay

Tasting the straws and tossing, laughing soft
Into the sky's great eyes of gold and blue
And nodding to the breezy leaves aloft
Over the harvest's mellow residue.
But sudden then—then strangely dark it grew.

How good it is, before the dreary flow
Of cloud and water, here to lie alone
And in this desolation to let go
Down the ravine one with another, down
Across the surf to linger or to drown

The loves that none can give and none receive,
The fearful asking and the small retort,
The life to dream of and the dream to live!

Very much more is nothing than a part,
Nothing at all and darkness in the heart.

I would my manhood now were like the sea.—
Thou at high-tide, when compassing the land
Thou find'st the issue short, questioningly
A moment poised, thy floods then down the strand
Sink without rancour, sink without command,

Sink of themselves in peace without despair,
And turn as still the calm horizon turns,
Till they repose little by little nowhere
And the long light unfathomable burns
Clear from the zenith stars to the sea-ferns.

Thou art thy Priest, thy Victim and thy God.
Thy life is bulwarked with a thread of foam,
And of the sky, the mountains and the sod
Thou askest nothing, evermore at home
In thy own self's perennial masterdom.

Leave Him Now Quiet

Leave him now quiet by the way
To rest apart.
I know what draws him to the dust alway
And churns him in the builder's lime:
He has the fright of time.

I heard it knocking in his breast
A minute since;
His human eyes did wince,
He stubborned like the massive slaughter beast
And as a thing o'erwhelmed with sound
Stood bolted to the ground.

Leave him, for rest alone can cure—
If cure there be—
This waif upon the sea.

He is of those who slanted the great door
And listened—wretched little lad—
To what they said.

Near Helikon

By such an all-embalming summer day
As sweetens now among the mountain pines
Down to the cornland yonder and the vines,
To where the sky and sea are mixed in gray,
How do all things together take their way
Harmonious to the harvest, bringing wines
And bread and light and whatsoe'er combines
In the large wreath to make it round and gay.
To me my troubled life doth now appear
Like scarce distinguishable summits hung
Around the blue horizon: places where
Not even a traveller purposeth to steer,—
Whereof a migrant bird in passing sung,
And the girl closed her window not to hear.

In Ampezzo (II)

In days of summer let me go
Up over fields, at afternoon,
And, lying low against my stone
On slopes the scythe has pain to mow,
Look southward a long hour alone.

For evening there is lovelier
Than vision or enchanted tale:
When wefts of yellow vapour pale,
And green goes down to lavender
On rosy cliffs, shutting the vale

Whose smoke of violet forest seeks
The steep and rock, where crimson crawls,

And drenched with carmine fire their walls
Go thinly smouldering to the peaks,
High, while the sun now somewhere falls;

Except a cloud-caught ochre spark
In one last summit,—and away
On lazy wings of mauve and gray,
Away and near, like memory, dark
Is bluish with the filmy day,

What time the swallows flying few
Over uncoloured fields become
Small music thro' the shining dome;
And sleepy leaves are feeling dew
Above the crickets' under-hum,

In bye-tone to a savage sound
Of waters that with discord smite
The frigid wind and lurking light,
And swarm behind the gloom, and bound
Down sleepy valleys to the night:

And thoughts delicious of the whole,
Gathering over all degrees,
Yet sad for something more than these,
Across low meadow-lands of soul
Grow large, like north-lights no one sees.

I care not if the painter wrought
The tinted dream his spirit hid,
When rich with sight he saw, amid
A jarring world, one tone, and caught
The colour passing to his lid.

Be still musician and thy choir!
Where trumpets blare and the bow stings
In symphony a thousand strings
To cry of wood-wind and desire
Of one impassioned voice that sings.

Nay, silence have the poet's mode
And southern vowels all! let die,
So ghostly-vague, the northern cry!—
This world is better than an ode
And evening more than elegy.—

Yet what shall singing do for me?
How shall a verse be crimsoned o'er?
I ever dream one art the more;
I who did never paint would see
The colour painters languish for,

And wisely use the instruments
That earlier harmony affords;
I dream a poesy of chords
Embroidered very rich in tints:
'Tis not enough, this work of words.

A wilder thing inflames our hearts.
We do refuse to sift and share.
For we would musically bear
The burden of the gathered arts
Together which divided were,

And, passing Knowledge, highly rear
Upon her iron architrave
These airy images we crave,—
Lest wholly vain and fallen sheer
Our vision dress us for the grave.

Mnemosyne

It's autumn in the country I remember.

How warm a wind blew here about the ways!
And shadows on the hillside lay to slumber
During the long sun-sweetened summer-days.

It's cold abroad the country I remember.

The swallows veering skimmed the golden grain
At midday with a wing aslant and limber;
And yellow cattle browsed upon the plain.

It's empty down the country I remember.

I had a sister lovely in my sight:
Her hair was dark, her eyes were very sombre;
We sang together in the woods at night.

It's lonely in the country I remember.

The babble of our children fills my ears,
And on our hearth I stare the perished ember
To flames that show all starry thro' my tears.

It's dark about the country I remember.

AMY LOWELL

Little Ivory Figures Pulled with String

Is it the tinkling of mandolins which disturbs you?
Or the dropping of bitter-orange petals among the coffee-cups?
Or the slow creeping of the moonlight between the olive-trees?
Drop! drop! the rain
Upon the thin plates of my heart.

String your blood to chord with this music,
Stir your heels upon the cobbles to the rhythm of a dance-tune.
They have slim thighs and arms of silver;
The moon washes away their garments;

They make a pattern of fleeing feet in the branch shadows,
And the green grapes knotted about them
Burst as they press against one another.
The rain knocks upon the plates of my heart,
They are crumpled with its beating.

Would you drink only from your brains, Old Man?
See, the moonlight has reached your knees,
It falls upon your head in an accolade of silver.
Rise up on the music,
Fling against the moon-drifts in a whorl of young light bodies:
Leaping grape-clusters,
Vine leaves tearing from a grey wall.
You shall run, laughing, in a braid of women,
And weave flowers with the frosty spines of thorns.
Why do you gaze into your glass,
And jar the spoons with your finger-tapping?
The rain is rigid on the plates of my heart.
The murmur of it is loud—loud.

The City of Falling Leaves

Leaves fall,
Brown leaves,
Yellow leaves streaked with brown.
They fall,
Flutter,
Fall again.
The brown leaves,
And the streaked yellow leaves,
Loosen on their branches
And drift slowly downwards.
One,
One, two, three,
One, two, five.
All Venice is a falling of Autumn leaves—
Brown,
And yellow streaked with brown.

"That sonnet, *Abate,*
Beautiful,
I am quite exhausted by it.
Your phrases turn about my heart
And stifle me to swooning.
Open the window, I beg.
Lord! What a strumming of fiddles and mandolins!
'Tis really a shame to stop indoors.
Call my maid, or I will make you lace me yourself.
Fie, how hot it is, not a breath of air!
See how straight the leaves are falling.
Marianna, I will have the yellow satin caught up with silver
fringe,
It peeps out delightfully from under a mantle.
Am I well painted to-day, *caro Abate mio?*
You will be proud of me at the *Ridotto,* hey?
Proud of being *Cavalier Servente* to such a lady?"
"Can you doubt it, *Bellissima Contessa?*
A pinch more rouge on the right cheek,
And Venus herself shines less . . ."
"You bore me, *Abate,*
I vow I must change you!
A letter, Achmet?
Run and look out of the window, *Abate.*
I will read my letter in peace."
The little black slave with the yellow satin turban
Gazes at his mistress with strained eyes.
His yellow turban and black skin
Are gorgeous—barbaric.
The yellow satin dress with its silver flashings
Lies on a chair
Beside a black mantle and a black mask.
Yellow and black,
Gorgeous—barbaric.
The lady reads her letter,
And the leaves drift slowly
Past the long windows.
"How silly you look, my dear *Abate,*
With that great brown leaf in your wig.

Pluck it off, I beg you,
Or I shall die of laughing."
A yellow wall
Aflare in the sunlight,
Chequered with shadows,
Shadows of vine leaves,
Shadows of masks.
Masks coming, printing themselves for an instant,
Then passing on,
More masks always replacing them.
Masks with tricorns and rapiers sticking out behind
Pursuing masks with plumes and high heels,
The sunlight shining under their insteps.
One,
One, two,
One, two, three,
There is a thronging of shadows on the hot wall,
Filigreed at the top with moving leaves.
Yellow sunlight and black shadows,
Yellow and black,
Gorgeous—barbaric.
Two masks stand together,
And the shadow of a leaf falls through them,
Marking the wall where they are not.
From hat-tip to shoulder-tip,
From elbow to sword-hilt,
The leaf falls.
The shadows mingle,
Blur together,
Slide along the wall and disappear.
Gold of mosaics and candles,
And night blackness lurking in the ceiling beams.
Saint Mark's glitters with flames and reflections.
A cloak brushes aside,
And the yellow of satin
Licks out over the coloured inlays of the pavement.
Under the gold crucifixes
There is a meeting of hands
Reaching from black mantles.

Sighing embraces, bold investigations,
Hide in confessionals,
Sheltered by the shuffling of feet.
Gorgeous—barbaric
In its mail of jewels and gold,
Saint Mark's looks down at the swarm of black masks;
And outside in the palace gardens brown leaves fall,
Flutter,
Fall.
Brown.
And yellow streaked with brown.
Blue-black, the sky over Venice,
With a pricking of yellow stars.
There is no moon,
And the waves push darkly against the prow
Of the gondola,
Coming from Malamocco
And streaming toward Venice.
It is black under the gondola hood,
But the yellow of a satin dress
Glare out like the eye of a watching tiger.
Yellow compassed about with darkness,
Yellow and black,
Gorgeous—barbaric.
The boatman sings,
It is Tasso that he sings;
The lovers seek each other beneath their mantles,
And the gondola drifts over the lagoon, aslant to the coming dawn.
But at Malamocco in front,
In Venice behind,
Fall the leaves,
Brown,
And yellow streaked with brown.
They fall,
Flutter,
Fall.

ROBERT FROST

The Road Not Taken

Two roads diverged in a yellow wood,
And sorry I could not travel both
And be one traveller, long I stood
And looked down one as far as I could
To where it bent in the undergrowth;

Then took the other, as just as fair,
And having perhaps the better claim,
Because it was grassy and wanted wear;
Though as for that the passing there
Had worn them really about the same,

And both that morning equally lay
In leaves no step had trodden black.
Oh, I kept the first for another day!
Yet knowing how way leads on to way,
I doubted if I should ever come back.

I shall be telling this with a sigh
Somewhere ages and ages hence:
Two roads diverged in a wood, and I—
I took the one less travelled by,
And that has made all the difference.

Home Burial

He saw her from the bottom of the stairs
Before she saw him. She was starting down,
Looking back over her shoulder at some fear.

She took a doubtful step and then undid it
To raise herself and look again. He spoke
Advancing toward her: "What is it you see
From up there always—for I want to know."
She turned and sank upon her skirts at that,
And her face changed from terrified to dull.
He said to gain time: "What is it you see?"
Mounting until she cowered under him,
"I will find out now—you must tell me, dear."
She, in her place, refused him any help
With the least stiffening of her neck and silence.
She let him look, sure that he wouldn't see,
Blind creature; and a while he didn't see.
But at last he murmured, "Oh," and again, "Oh."
"What is it—what?" she said.

"Just that I see."
"You don't," she challenged. "Tell me what it is."

"The wonder is I didn't see at once.
I never noticed it from here before.
I must be wonted to it—that's the reason.
The little graveyard where my people are!
So small the window frames the whole of it.
Not so much larger than a bedroom, is it?
There are three stones of slate and one of marble,
Broad-shouldered little slabs there in the sunlight
On the sidehill. We haven't to mind *those*.
But I understand: it is not the stones,
But the child's mound——"

"Don't, don't, don't, don't," she cried.
She withdrew shrinking from beneath his arm
That rested on the banister, and slid downstairs;
And turned on him with such a daunting look,
He said twice over before he knew himself:
"Can't a man speak of his own child he's lost?"

"Not you! Oh, where's my hat? Oh, I don't need it!
I must get out of here. I must get air.
I don't know rightly whether any man can."

"Amy! Don't go to someone else this time.
Listen to me. I won't come down the stairs."
He sat and fixed his chin between his fists.
"There's something I should like to ask you, dear."

"You don't know how to ask it."

"Help me, then."

Her fingers moved the latch for all reply.

"My words are nearly always an offence.
I don't know how to speak of anything
So as to please you. But I might be taught
I should suppose. I can't say I see how.
A man must partly give up being a man
With women-folk. We could have some arrangement
By which I'd bind myself to keep hands off
Anything special you're a mind to name.
Though I don't like such things 'twixt those that love.
Two that don't love can't live together without them.
But two that do can't live together with them."
She moved the latch a little. "Don't, don't go.
Don't carry it to someone else this time.
Tell me about it if it's something human.
Let me into your grief. I'm not so much
Unlike other folks as your standing there
Apart would make me out. Give me my chance,
I do think, though, you overdo it a little.
What was it brought you up to think it the thing
To take your mother-loss of a first child
So inconsolably—in the face of love.
You'd think his memory might be satisfied—"

"There you go sneering now!"
"I'm not, I'm not!
You make me angry. I'll come down to you.
God, what a woman! And it's come to this,
A man can't speak of his own child that's dead."

"You can't because you don't know how.
If you had any feelings, you that dug
With your own hand—how could you?—his little grave;
I saw you from that very window there,
Making the gravel leap and leap in air,
Leap up, like that, like that, and land so lightly
And roll back down the mound beside the hole.
I thought, who is that man? I don't know you.
And I crept down the stairs and up the stairs
To look again, and still your spade kept lifting.
Then you came in. I heard your rumbling voice
Out in the kitchen, and I don't know why,
But I went near to see with my own eyes.
You could sit there with the stains on your shoes
Of the fresh earth from your own baby's grave
And talk about your everyday concerns.
You had stood the spade up against the wall
Outside there in the entry, for I saw it."

"I shall laugh the worst laugh I ever laughed.
I'm cursed. God, if I don't believe I'm cursed."
"I can repeat the very words you were saying.
'Three foggy mornings and one rainy day
Will rot the best birch fence a man can build.'
Think of it, talk like that at such a time!
What had how long it takes a birch to rot
To do with that was in the darkened parlour.
You *couldn't* care! The nearest friends can go
With anyone to death, comes so far short
They might as well not try to go at all.
No, from the time when one is sick to death,
One is alone, and he dies more alone.

Friends make pretence of following to the grave,
But before one is in it, their minds are turned
And making the best of their way back to life
And living people, and things they understand.
But the world's evil. I won't have my grief so
If I can change it. Oh, I won't, I won't!"

"There, you have said it all and you feel better.
You won't go now. You're crying. Close the door.
The heart's gone out of it: why keep it up.
Amy! There's someone coming down the road!"
"*You*—oh, you think the talk is all. I must go—
Somewhere out of this house. How can I make you—"
"If—you—do!" She was opening the door wider.
"Where do you mean to go? First tell me that.
I'll follow and bring you back by force. I *will!*—"

The Wood-Pile

Out walking in the frozen swamp one grey day
I paused and said, "I will turn back from here.
No, I will go on farther—and we shall see."
The hard snow held me, save where now and then
One foot went down. The view was all in lines
Straight up and down of tall slim trees
Too much alike to mark or name a place by
So as to say for certain I was here
Or somewhere else: I was just far from home.
A small bird flew before me. He was careful
To put a tree between us when he lighted,
And say no word to tell me who he was
Who was so foolish as to think what *he* thought.
He thought that I was after him for a feather—
The white one in his tail; like one who takes
Everything said as personal to himself:
One flight out sideways would have undeceived him.
And then there was a pile of wood for which
I forgot him and let his little fear

Carry him off the way I might have gone,
Without so much as wishing him good-night.
He went behind it to make his last stand.
It was a cord of maple, cut and split
And piled—and measured, four by four by eight.
And not another like it could I see.
No runner tracks in this Year's snow looped near it.
And it was older sure than this year's cutting,
Or even last year's or the year's before.
The wood was grey and the bark warping off it
And the pile somewhat sunken. Clematis
Had wound strings round and round it like a bundle.
What held it though on one side was a tree
Still growing, and on one a stake and prop,
These latter about to fall. I thought that only
Someone who lived in turning to fresh tasks
Could so forget his handiwork on which
He spent himself, the labour of his axe,
And leave it there far from a useful fireplace
To warm the frozen swamp as best it could
With the slow smokeless burning of decay.

The Fear

A lantern light from deeper in the barn
Shone on a man and woman in the door
And threw their lurching shadows on a house
Near by, all dark in every glossy window.
A horse's hoof pawed once the hollow floor,
And the back of the gig they stood beside
Moved in a little. The man grasped a wheel,
The woman spoke out sharply, "Whoa, stand still!
I saw it just as plain as a white plate,"
She said, "as the light on the dashboard ran
Along the bushes at the roadside—a man's face.
You *must* have seen it too."

"I didn't see it.

Are you sure——"
"Yes, I'm sure!"
"——it was a face?"

"Joel, I'll have to look. I can't go in,
I can't, and leave a thing like that unsettled.
Doors locked and curtains drawn will make no difference.
I always have felt strange when we came home
To the dark house after so long an absence,
And the key rattled loudly into place
Seemed to warn someone to be getting out
At one door as we entered at another.
What if I'm right, and someone all the time—
Don't hold my arm!"
"I say it's someone passing."

"You speak as if this were a travelled road.
You forget where we are. What is beyond
That he'd be going to or coming from
At such an hour of night, and on foot too.
What was he standing still for in the bushes?"

"It's not so very late—it's only dark.
There's more in it than you're inclined to say.
Did he look like——?"
"He looked like anyone.
I'll never rest to-night unless I know.
Give me the lantern."
"You don't want the lantern."

She pushed past him and got it for herself.
"You're not to come," she said. "This is my business.
If the time's come to face it, I'm the one
To put it the right way. He'd never dare—
Listen! He kicked a stone. Hear that, hear that!

He's coming towards us. Joel, *go* in—please.
Hark!—I don't hear him now. But please go in."

"In the first place you can't make me believe it's——"

"It is—or someone else he's sent to watch.
And now's the time to have it out with him
While we know definitely where he is.
Let him get off and he'll be everywhere
Around us, looking out of trees and bushes
Till I shan't dare to set a foot outdoors.
And I can't stand it. Joel, let me go!"

"But it's nonsense to think he'd care enough."

"You mean you couldn't understand his caring.
Oh, but you see he hadn't had enough—
Joel, I won't—I won't—I promise you.
We mustn't say hard things. You mustn't either."
"I'll be the one, if anybody goes!
But you give him the advantage with this light
What couldn't he do to us standing here!
And if to see was what he wanted, why
He has seen all there was to see and gone."

He appeared to forget to keep his hold,
But advanced with her as she crossed the grass.
"What do you want?" she cried to all the dark.
She stretched up tall to overlook the light
That hung in both hands hot against her skirt.

"There's no one; so you're wrong," he said.
"There is—
What do you want?" she cried, and then herself
Was startled when an answer really came.

"Nothing." It came from well along the road.
She reached a hand to Joel for support:

The smell of scorching woollen made her faint.
"What are you doing round this house at night?"

"Nothing." A pause: there seemed no more to say.
And then the voice again: "You seem afraid.
I saw by the way you whipped up the horse.
I'll just come forward in the lantern light
And let you see."

"Yes, do—Joel, go back!"
She stood her ground against the noisy steps
That came on, but her body rocked a little.

"You see," the voice said.

"Oh." She looked and looked.
"You don't see—I've a child here by the hand."

"What's a child doing at this time of night—?"

"Out walking. Every child should have the memory
Of at least one long-after-bedtime walk.
What, son?"

"Then I should think you'd try to find
Somewhere to walk——"

"The highway as it happens—
We're stopping for the fortnight down at Dean's."
"But if that's all—Joel—you realize—
You won't think anything. You understand?
You understand that we have to be careful.
This is a very, very lonely place.
Joel!" She spoke as if she couldn't turn.
The swinging lantern lengthened to the ground,
It touched, it struck, it clattered and went out.

Birches

When I see birches bend to left and right
Across the lines of straighter darker trees,
I like to think some boy's been swinging them.
But swinging doesn't bend them down to stay.
Ice-storms do that. Often you must have seen them
Loaded with ice a sunny winter morning
After a rain. They click upon themselves
As the breeze rises, and turn many-coloured
As the stir cracks and crazes their enamel.
Soon the sun's warmth makes them shed crystal shells
Shattering and avalanching on the snowcrust—
Such heaps of broken glass to sweep away
You'd think the inner dome of heaven had fallen.
They are dragged to the withered bracken by the load,
And they seem not to break; though once they are bowed
So low for long, they never right themselves:
You may see their trunks arching in the woods
Years afterwards, trailing their leaves on the ground
Like girls on hands and knees that throw their hair
Before them over their heads to dry in the sun.
But I was going to say when Truth broke in
With all her matter-of-fact about the ice-storm
(Now am I free to be poetical?)
I should prefer to have some boy bend them
As he went out and in to fetch the cows—
Some boy too far from town to learn baseball,
Whose only play was what he found himself,
Summer or winter, and could play alone.
One by one he subdued his father's trees
By riding them down over and over again
Until he took the stiffness out of them,
And not one but hung limp, not one was left
For him to conquer. He learned all there was
To learn about not launching out too soon
And so not carrying the tree away

Clear to the ground. He always kept his poise
To the top branches, climbing carefully
With the same pains you use to fill a cup
Up to the brim, and even above the brim.
Then he flung outward, feet first, with a swish,
Kicking his way down through the air to the ground.
So was I once myself a swinger of birches.
And so I dream of going back to be.
It's when I'm weary of considerations,
And life is too much like a pathless wood
Where your face burns and tickles with the cobwebs
Broken across it, and one eye is weeping
From a twig's having lashed it open,
I'd like to get away from earth a while
And then come back to it and begin over.
May no fate wilfully misunderstand me
And half grant what I wish and snatch me away
Not to return. Earth's the right place for love:
I don't know where it's likely to go better.
I'd like to go by climbing a high birch tree,
And climb black branches up a snow-white trunk
Toward heaven, till the tree could bear no more,
But dipped its top and set me down again.
That would be good both going and coming back.
One could do worse than be a swinger of birches.

The Sound of the Trees

I wonder about the trees.
Why do we wish to bear
Forever the noise of these
More than another noise
So close to our dwelling place?
We suffer them by the day
Till we lose all measure of pace,
And fixity in our joys,
And acquire a listening air.

They are that that talks of going
But never gets away;
And that talks no less for knowing,
As it grows wiser and older,
That now it means to stay.
My feet tug at the floor
And my head sways to my shoulder
Sometimes when I watch trees sway,
From the window or the door.
I shall set forth for somewhere,
I shall make the reckless choice
Some day when they are in voice
And tossing so as to scare
The white clouds over them on.
I shall have less to say,
But I shall be gone.

Hyla Brook

By June our brook's run out of song and speed.
Sought for much after that, it will be found
Either to have gone groping underground
(And taken with it all the Hyla breed
That shouted in the mist a month ago,
Like ghost of sleigh-bells in a ghost of snow)—
Or flourished and come up in jewel-weed,
Weak foliage that is blown upon and bent
Even against the way its waters went.
Its bed is left a faded paper sheet
Of dead leaves stuck together by the heat—
A brook to none but who remember long.
This as it will be seen is other far
Than with brooks taken otherwhere in song.
We love the things we love for what they are.

The Oven Bird

There is a singer everyone has heard,
Loud, a mid-summer and a mid-wood bird,
Who makes the solid tree trunks sound again.
He says that leaves are old and that for flowers
Mid-summer is to spring as one to ten.
He says the early petal-fall is past
When pear and cherry bloom went down in showers
On sunny days a moment overcast;
And comes that other fall we name the fall.
He says the highway dust is over all.
The bird would cease and be as other birds
But that he knows in singing not to sing.
The question that he frames in all but words
Is what to make of a diminished thing.

My November Guest

My Sorrow, when she's here with me,
    Thinks these dark days of autumn rain
Are beautiful as days can be;
She loves the bare, the withered tree;
    She walks the sodden pasture lane.

Her pleasure will not let me stay.
    She talks and I am fain to list:
She's glad the birds are gone away,
She's glad her simple worsted grey
    Is silver now with clinging mist.

The desolate, deserted trees,
    The faded earth, the heavy sky,
The beauties she so truly sees,
She thinks I have no eye for these,
    And vexes me for reason why.

Not yesterday I learned to know
    The love of bare November days
Before the coming of the snow,
But it were vain to tell her so,
    And they are better for her praise.

Mowing

There was never a sound beside the wood but one,
And that was my long scythe whispering to the ground.
What was it it whispered? I knew not well myself;
Perhaps it was something about the heat of the sun,
Something, perhaps, about the lack of sound—
And that was why it whispered and did not speak.
It was no dream of the gift of idle hours,
Or easy gold at the hand of fay or elf:
Anything more than the truth would have seemed too weak
To the earnest love that laid the swale in rows,
Not without feeble-pointed spikes of flowers
(Pale orchises), and scared a bright green snake.
The fact is the sweetest dream that labor knows.
My long scythe whispered and left the hay to make.

To Earthward

Love at the lips was touch
As sweet as I could bear;
And once that seemed too much;
I lived on air

That crossed me from sweet things,
The flow of—was it musk
From hidden grapevine springs
Down hill at dusk?

I had the swirl and ache
From sprays of honeysuckle

That when they're gathered shake
Dew on the knuckle.

I craved strong sweets, but those
Seemed strong when I was young;
The petal of the rose
It was that stung.

Now no joy but lacks salt
That is not dashed with pain
And weariness and fault;
I crave the stain

Of tears, the aftermark
Of almost too much love,
The sweet of bitter bark
And burning clove.

When stiff and sore and scarred
I take away my hand
From leaning on it hard
In grass and sand,

The hurt is not enough:
I long for weight and strength
To feel the earth as rough
To all my length.

Fire and Ice

Some say the world will end in fire,
Some say in ice.
From what I've tasted of desire
I hold with those who favor fire.
But if it had to perish twice,
I think I know enough of hate

To say that for destruction ice
Is also great
And would suffice.

Stopping by Woods on a Snowy Evening

Whose woods these are I think I know.
His house is in the village though;
He will not see me stopping here
To watch his woods fill up with snow.

My little horse must think it queer
To stop without a farmhouse near
Between the woods and frozen lake
The darkest evening of the year.

He gives his harness bells a shake
To ask if there is some mistake.
The only other sound's the sweep
Of easy wind and downy flake.

The woods are lovely, dark and deep.
But I have promises to keep,
And miles to go before I sleep,
And miles to go before I sleep.

Bereft

Where had I heard this wind before
Change like this to a deeper roar?
What would it take my standing there for,
Holding open a restive door,
Looking down hill to a frothy shore?
Summer was past and day was past.
Sombre clouds in the west were massed.
Out in the porch's sagging floor,

Leaves got up in a coil and hissed,
Blindly struck at my knee and missed.
Something sinister in the tone
Told me my secret must be known:
Word I was in the house alone
Somehow must have gotten abroad,
Word I was in my life alone,
Word I had no one left but God.

Desert Places

Snow falling and night falling fast oh fast
In a field I looked into going past,
And the ground almost covered smooth in snow,
But a few weeds and stubble showing last.

The woods around it have it—it is theirs.
All animals are smothered in their lairs.
I am too absent-spirited to count;
The loneliness includes me unawares.

And lonely as it is that loneliness
Will be more lonely ere it will be less—
A blanker whiteness of benighted snow
With no expression, nothing to express.

They cannot scare me with their empty spaces
Between stars—on stars where no human race is.
I have it in me so much nearer home
To scare myself with my own desert places.

CARL SANDBURG

Cool Tombs

When Abraham Lincoln was shoveled into the tombs, he forgot
the copperheads and the assassin . . . in the dust, in the
cool tombs.

And Ulysses Grant lost all thought of con men and Wall Street,
cash and collateral turned ashes . . . in the dust, in the cool
tombs.

Pocahontas' body, lovely as a poplar, sweet as a red haw in
November or a pawpaw in May, did she wonder? does she
remember? . . . in the dust, in the cool tombs?

Take any streetful of people buying clothes and groceries, cheer-
ing a hero or throwing confetti and blowing tin horns . . .
tell me if the lovers are losers . . . tell me if any get more
than the lovers . . . in the dust . . . in the cool tombs.

Jazz Fantasia

Drum on your drums, batter on your banjos, sob on the long
cool winding saxophones. Go to it, O jazzmen.

Sling your knuckles on the bottoms of the happy timpans, let
your trombones ooze, and go husha-husha-hush with the
slippery sandpaper.

Moan like an autumn wind high in the lonesome treetops, moan
soft like you wanted somebody terrible, cry like a racing car
slipping away from a motorcycle-cop, bang-bang! you jazz-

men, bang altogether drums, traps, banjos, horns, tin cans—make two people fight on the top of a stairway and scratch each other's eyes in a clinch tumbling down the stairs.

Can the rough stuff . . . Now a Mississippi steamboat pushes up the night river with a hoo-hoo-hoo-oo . . . and the green lanterns calling to the high soft stars . . . a red moon rides on the humps of the low river hills . . . Go to it, O jazzmen.

Wind Song

Long ago I learned how to sleep,
In an old apple orchard where the wind swept by counting its money and throwing it away,
In a wind-gaunt orchard where the limbs forked out and listened or never listened at all,
In a passel of trees where the branches trapped the wind into whistling, "Who, who are you?"
I slept with my head in an elbow on a summer afternoon and there I took a sleep lesson.
There I went away saying: I know why they sleep, I know how they trap the tricky winds.
Long ago I learned how to listen to the singing wind and how to forget and how to hear the deep whine,
Slapping and lapsing under the day blue and the night stars:
Who, who are you?

Who can ever forget
listening to the wind go by
counting its money
and throwing it away?

Gone

Everybody loved Chick Lorimer in our town
Far off.
Everybody loved her.

So we all love a wild girl keeping a hold
    On a dream she wants.
Nobody knows now where Chick Lorimer went.
Nobody knows why she packed her trunk . . . a few old things
And is gone,
        Gone with her little chin
        Thrust ahead of her
        And her soft hair blowing careless
        From under a wide hat,
Dancer, singer, a laughing passionate lover.

Were there ten men or a hundred hunting Chick?
Were there five men or fifty with aching hearts?
    Everybody loved Chick Lorimer.
        Nobody knows where she's gone.

VACHEL LINDSAY

The Eagle That Is Forgotten

(John P. Altgeld. Born December 30, 1847; died March 12, 1902)

Sleep softly . . . eagle forgotten . . . under the stone.
Time has its way with you there, and the clay has its own.
"We have buried him now," thought your foes, and in secret rejoiced.
They made a brave show of their mourning, their hatred unvoiced,
They had snarled at you, barked at you, foamed at you, day after day,
Now you were ended. They praised you, . . . and laid you away.

The others that mourned you in silence and terror and truth,
The widow bereft of her pittance, the boy without youth,
The mocked and the scorned and the wounded, the lame and
the poor
That should have remembered forever, . . . remember no more.

Where are those lovers of yours, on what name do they call
The lost, that in armies wept over your funeral pall?
They call on the names of a hundred high-valiant ones,
A hundred white eagles have risen, the sons of your sons,
The zeal in their wings is a zeal that your dreaming began
The valor that wore out your soul in the service of man.

Sleep softly, . . . eagle forgotten, . . . under the stone,
Time has its way with you there, and the clay has its own.
Sleep on, O brave-hearted, O wise man, that kindled the flame—
To live in mankind is far more than to live in a name,
To live in mankind, far, far more . . . than to live in a name.

Poems about the Moon

I. Euclid

Old Euclid drew a circle
On a sand-beach long ago.
He bounded and enclosed it
With angles thus and so.
His set of solemn greybeards
Nodded and argued much
Of arc and of circumference,
Diameter and such.
A silent child stood by them
From morning until noon
Because they drew such charming
Round pictures of the moon.

II. *Yet Gentle Will the Griffin Be*

(What Grandpa Told the Children)

The moon? It is a griffin's egg,
Hatching to-morrow night.
And how the little boys will watch
With shouting and delight
To see him break the shell and stretch
And creep across the sky.
The boys will laugh. The little girls,
I fear, may hide and cry.
Yet gentle will the griffin be,
Most decorous and fat,
And walk up to the milky way
And lap it like a cat.

III. *A Sense of Humour*

No man should stand before the moon
To make sweet song thereon,
With dandified importance,
His sense of humour gone.

Nay, let us don the motley cap,
The jester's chastened mien,
If we would woo that looking-glass
And see what should be seen.

O mirror on fair Heaven's wall,
We find there what we bring.
So, let us smile in honest part
And deck our souls and sing.

Yea, by the chastened jest alone
Will ghosts and terrors pass,

And fays, or suchlike friendly things,
Throw kisses through the glass.

IV. What Semiramis Said

The moon's a steaming chalice
Of honey and venom-wine.
A little of it sipped by night
Makes the long hours divine.
But oh, my reckless lovers,
They drain the cup and wail,
Die at my feet with shaking limbs
And tender lips all pale.
Above them in the sky it bends
Empty and grey and dread.
To-morrow night 'tis full again,
Golden, and foaming red.

V. The Scissors-Grinder

(*What the Tramp Said*)

The old man had his box and wheel
For grinding knives and shears.
No doubt his bell in village streets
Was joy to children's ears.
And I bethought me of my youth
When such men came around,
And times I asked them in, quite sure
The scissors should be ground.
The old man turned and spoke to me,
His face at last in view.
And then I thought those curious eyes
Were eyes that once I knew.

"The moon is but an emery-wheel
To whet the sword of God,"

He said. "And here beside my fire
I stretch upon the sod
Each night, and dream, and watch the stars
And watch the ghost-clouds go.
And see that sword of God in Heaven
A-waving to and fro.
I see that sword each century, friend,
It means the world-war comes
With all its bloody, wicked chiefs
And hate-inflaming drums.
Men talk of peace, but I have seen
That emery-wheel turn round.
The voice of Abel cries again
To God from out the ground.
The ditches must flow red, the plague
Go stark and screaming by
Each time that sword of God takes edge
Within the midnight sky.
And those that scorned their brothers here
And sowed a wind of shame
Will reap the whirlwind as of old
And face relentless flame."

And thus the scissors-grinder spoke,
His face at last in view.
And there beside the railroad bridge
I saw the Wandering Jew.

VI. Aladdin and the Jinn

"Bring me soft song," said Aladdin.
"This tailor-shop sings not at all.
Chant me a word of the twilight,
Of roses that mourn in the fall.
Bring me a song like hashish
That will comfort the stale and the sad,
For I would be mending my spirit,
Forgetting these days that are bad,

Forgetting companions too shallow,
Their quarrels and arguments thin,
Forgetting the shouting Muezzin:"—
"I AM YOUR SLAVE," said the Jinn.

"Bring me old wines," said Aladdin.
"I have been a starved pauper too long.
Serve them in vessels of jade and of shell,
Serve them with fruit and with song:—
Wines of pre-Adamite Sultans
Digged from beneath the black seas:—
New-gathered dew from the heavens
Dripped down from Heaven's sweet trees,
Cups from the angels' pale tables
That will make me both handsome and wise,
For I have beheld her, the princess,
Firelight and starlight her eyes.
Pauper I am, I would woo her.
And—let me drink wine, to begin,
Though the Koran expressly forbids it."
"I AM YOUR SLAVE," said the Jinn.

"Plan me a dome," said Aladdin,
"That is drawn like the dawn of the MOON,
When the sphere seems to rest on the mountains,
Half-hidden, yet full-risen soon.
Build me a dome," said Aladdin,
"That shall cause all young lovers to sigh,
The fullness of life and of beauty,
Peace beyond peace to the eye—
A palace of foam and of opal,
Pure moonlight without and within,
Where I may enthrone my sweet lady."
"I AM YOUR SLAVE," said the Jinn.

WALLACE STEVENS

The Comedian as the Letter C

I

The World without Imagination

Nota: man is the intelligence of his soil,
The sovereign ghost. As such, the Socrates
Of snails, musician of pears, principium
And lex. Sed quæritur: is this same wig
Of things, this nincompated pedagogue,
Preceptor to the sea? Crispin at sea
Created, in his day, a touch of doubt.
An eye most apt in gelatines and jupes,
Berries of villages, a barber's eye,
An eye of land, of simple salad-beds,
Of honest quilts, the eye of Crispin, hung
On porpoises, instead of apricots,
And on silentious porpoises, whose snouts
Dibbled in waves that were mustachios,
Inscrutable hair in an inscrutable world.
One eats one pâté, even of salt, quotha.
It was not so much the lost terrestrial,
The snug hibernal from that sea and salt,
That century of wind in a single puff.
What counted was mythology of self,
Blotched out beyond unblotching. Crispin,
The lutanist of fleas, the knave, the thane,
The ribboned stick, the bellowing breeches, cloak
Of China, cap of Spain, imperative haw
Of hum, inquisitorial botanist,
And general lexicographer of mute

And maidenly greenhorns, now beheld himself,
A skinny sailor peering in the sea-glass.
What word split up in clickering syllables
And storming under multitudinous tones
Was name for this short-shanks in all that brunt?
Crispin was washed away by magnitude.
The whole of life that still remained in him
Dwindled to one sound strumming in his ear,
Ubiquitous concussion, slap and sigh,
Polyphony beyond his baton's thrust.

Could Crispin stem verboseness in the sea,
The old age of a watery realist,
Triton, dissolved in shifting diaphanes
Of blue and green? A wordy, watery age
That whispered to the sun's compassion, made
A convocation, nightly, of the sea-stars,
And on the clopping foot-ways of the moon
Lay grovelling. Triton incomplicate with that
Which made him Triton, nothing left of him,
Except in faint, memorial gesturings,
That were like arms and shoulders in the waves,
Here, something in the rise and fall of wind
That seemed hallucinating horn, and here,
A sunken voice, both of remembering
And of forgetfulness, in alternate strain.
Just so an ancient Crispin was dissolved.
The valet in the tempest was annulled.
Bordeaux to Yucatan, Havana next,
And then to Carolina. Simple jaunt.
Crispin, merest minuscule in the gales,
Dejected his manner to the turbulence.
The salt hung on his spirit like a frost,
The dead brine melted in him like a dew
Of winter, until nothing of himself
Remained, except some starker, barer self
In a starker, barer world, in which the sun
Was not the sun because it never shone
With bland complaisance on pale parasols,

Beetled, in chapels, on the chaste bouquets.
Against his pipping sounds a trumpet cried
Celestial sneering boisterously. Crispin
Became an introspective voyager.

Here was the veritable ding an sich, at last,
Crispin confronting it, a vocable thing,
But with a speech belched out of hoary darks
Noway resembling his, a visible thing,
And excepting negligible Triton, free
From the unavoidable shadow of himself
That lay elsewhere around him. Severance
Was clear. The last distortion of romance
Forsook the insatiable egotist. The sea
Severs not only lands but also selves.
Here was no help before reality.
Crispin beheld and Crispin was made new.
The imagination, here, could not evade,
In poems of plums, the strict austerity
Of one vast, subjugating, final tone.
The drenching of stale lives no more fell down.
What was this gaudy, gusty panoply?
Out of what strict destruction did it spring?
It was caparison of wind and cloud
And something given to make whole among
The ruses that were shattered by the large.

II

Concerning the Thunderstorms of Yucatan

In Yucatan, the Maya sonneteers
Of the Caribbean amphitheatre,
In spite of hawk and falcon, green toucan
And jay, still to the night-bird made their plea,
As if raspberry tanagers in palms,
High up in orange air, were barbarous.
But Crispin was too destitute to find

In any commonplace the sought-for aid.
He was a man made vivid by the sea,
A man come out of luminous traversing,
Much trumpeted, made desperately clear,
Fresh from discoveries of tidal skies,
To whom oracular rockings gave no rest.
Into a savage color he went on.

How greatly had he grown in his demesne,
This auditor of insects! He that saw
The stride of vanishing autumn in a park
By way of decorous melancholy; he
That wrote his couplet yearly to the spring,
As dissertation of profound delight,
Stopping, on voyage, in a land of snakes,
Found his vicissitudes had much enlarged
His apprehension, made him intricate
In moody rucks, and difficult and strange
In all desires, his destitution's mark.
He was in this as other freemen are,
Sonorous nutshells rattling inwardly.
His violence was for aggrandizement
And not for stupor, such as music makes
For sleepers halfway waking. He perceived
That coolness for his heat came suddenly,
And only, in the fables that he scrawled
With his own quill, in its indigenous dew,
Of an æsthetic tough, diverse, untamed,
Incredible to prudes, the mint of dirt,
Green barbarism turning paradigm.
Crispin foresaw a curious promenade
Or, nobler, sensed an elemental fate,
And elemental potencies and pangs,
And beautiful barenesses as yet unseen,
Making the most of savagery of palms,
Of moonlight on the thick, cadaverous bloom
That yuccas breed, and of the panther's tread.
The fabulous and its intrinsic verse
Came like two spirits parleying, adorned

In radiance from the Atlantic coign,
For Crispin and his quill to catechize.
But they came parleying of such an earth,
So thick with sides and jagged lops of green,
So intertwined with serpent-kin encoiled
Among the purple tufts, the scarlet crowns,
Scenting the jungle in their refuges,
So streaked with yellow, blue and green and red
In beak and bud and fruity gobbet-skins,
That earth was like a jostling festival
Of seeds grown fat, too juicily opulent,
Expanding in the gold's maternal warmth.

So much for that. The affectionate emigrant found
A new reality in parrot-squawks.
Yet let that trifle pass. Now, as this odd
Discoverer walked through the harbor streets
Inspecting the cabildo, the façade
Of the cathedral, making notes, he heard
A rumbling, west of Mexico, it seemed,
Approaching like a gasconade of drums.
The white cabildo darkened, the façade,
As sullen as the sky, was swallowed up
In swift, successive shadows, dolefully.
The rumbling broadened as it fell. The wind,
Tempestuous clarion, with heavy cry,
Came bluntly thundering, more terrible
Than the revenge of music on bassoons.
Gesticulating lightning, mystical,
Made pallid flitter. Crispin, here, took flight.
An annotator has his scruples, too.
He knelt in the cathedral with the rest,
This connoisseur of elemental fate,
Aware of exquisite thought. The storm was one
Of many proclamations of the kind,
Proclaiming something harsher than he learned
From hearing signboards whimper in cold nights
Or seeing the midsummer artifice
Of heat upon his pane. This was the span

Of force, the quintessential fact, the note
Of Vulcan, that a valet seeks to own,
The thing that makes him envious in phrase.

And while the torrent on the roof still droned
He felt the Andean breath. His mind was free
And more than free, elate, intent, profound
And studious of a self possessing him,
That was not in him in the crusty town
From which he sailed. Beyond him, westward, lay
The mountainous ridges, purple balustrades,
In which the thunder, lapsing in its clap,
Let down gigantic quavers of its voice,
For Crispin to vociferate again.

III

Approaching Carolina

The book of moonlight is not written yet
Nor half begun, but, when it is, leave room
For Crispin, fagot in the lunar fire,
Who, in the hubbub of his pilgrimage
Through sweating changes, never could forget
That wakefulness or meditating sleep,
In which the sulky strophes willingly
Bore up, in time, the somnolent, deep songs.
Leave room, therefore, in that unwritten book
For the legendary moonlight that once burned
In Crispin's mind above a continent.
America was always north to him,
A northern west or western north, but north,
And thereby polar, polar-purple, chilled
And lank, rising and slumping from a sea
Of hardy foam, receding flatly, spread
In endless ledges, glittering, submerged
And cold in a boreal mistiness of the moon.
The spring came there in clinking pannicles

Of half-dissolving frost, the summer came,
If ever, whisked and wet, not ripening,
Before the winter's vacancy returned.
The myrtle, if the myrtle ever bloomed,
Was like a glacial pink upon the air.
The green palmettoes in crepuscular ice
Clipped frigidly blue-black meridians,
Morose chiaroscuro, gauntly drawn.

How many poems he denied himself
In his observant progress, lesser things
Than the relentless contact he desired;
How many sea-masks he ignored; what sounds
He shut out from his tempering ear; what thoughts,
Like jades affecting the sequestered bride;
And what descants, he sent to banishment!
Perhaps the Arctic moonlight really gave
The liaison, the blissful liaison,
Between himself and his environment,
Which was, and is, chief motive, first delight,
For him, and not for him alone. It seemed
Illusive, faint, more mist than moon, perverse,
Wrong as a divagation to Peking,
To him that postulated as his theme
The vulgar, as his theme and hymn and flight,
A passionately niggling nightingale.
Moonlight was an evasion, or, if not,
A minor meeting, facile, delicate.

Thus he conceived his voyaging to be
An up and down between two elements,
A fluctuating between sun and moon,
A sally into gold and crimson forms,
As on this voyage, out of goblinry,
And then retirement like a turning back
And sinking down to the indulgences
That in the moonlight have their habitude.
But let these backward lapses, if they would,
Grind their seductions on him, Crispin knew

It was a flourishing tropic he required
For his refreshment, an abundant zone,
Prickly and obdurate, dense, harmonious,
Yet with a harmony not rarefied
Nor fined for the inhibited instruments
Of over-civil stops. And thus he tossed
Between a Carolina of old time,
A little juvenile, an ancient whim,
And the visible, circumspect presentment drawn
From what he saw across his vessel's prow.

He came. The poetic hero without palms
Or jugglery, without regalia.
And as he came he saw that it was spring,
A time abhorrent to the nihilist
Or searcher for the fecund minimum.
The moonlight fiction disappeared. The spring,
Although contending featly in its veils,
Irised in dew and early fragrancies,
Was gemmy marionette to him that sought
A sinewy nakedness. A river bore
The vessel inward. Tilting up his nose,
He inhaled the rancid rosin, burly smells
Of dampened lumber, emanations blown
From warehouse doors, the gustiness of ropes,
Decays of sacks, and all the arrant stinks
That helped him round his rude æsthetic out.
He savored rankness like a sensualist.
He marked the marshy ground around the dock,
The crawling railroad spur, the rotten fence,
Curriculum for the marvelous sophomore.
It purified. It made him see how much
Of what he saw he never saw at all.
He gripped more closely the essential prose
As being, in a world so falsified,
The one integrity for him, the one
Discovery still possible to make,
To which all poems were incident, unless
That prose should wear a poem's guise at last.

IV

The Idea of a Colony

Nota: his soil is man's intelligence.
That's better. That's worth crossing seas to find.
Crispin in one laconic phrase laid bare
His cloudy drift and planned a colony.
Exit the mental moonlight, exit lex,
Rex and principium, exit the whole
Shebang. Exeunt omnes. Here was prose
More exquisite than any tumbling verse:
A still new continent in which to dwell.
What was the purpose of his pilgrimage,
Whatever shape it took in Crispin's mind,
If not, when all is said, to drive away
The shadow of his fellows from the skies,
And, from their stale intelligence released,
To make a new intelligence prevail?
Hence the reverberations in the words
Of his first central hymns, the celebrants
Of rankest trivia, tests of the strength
Of his æsthetic, his philosophy,
The more invidious, the more desired.
The florist asking aid from cabbages,
The rich man going bare, the paladin
Afraid, the blind man as astronomer,
The appointed power unwielded from disdain.
His western voyage ended and began.
The torment of fastidious thought grew slack,
Another, still more bellicose, came on.
He, therefore, wrote his prolegomena,
And, being full of the caprice, inscribed
Commingled souvenirs and prophecies.
He made a singular collation. Thus:
The natives of the rain are rainy men.
Although they paint effulgent, azure lakes,
And April hillsides wooded white and pink,
Their azure has a cloudy edge, their white

And pink, the water bright that dogwood bears.
And in their music showering sounds intone.
On what strange froth does the gross Indian dote,
What Eden sapling gum, what honeyed gore,
What pulpy dram distilled of innocence,
That streaking gold should speak in him
Or bask within his images and words?
If these rude instances impeach themselves
By force of rudeness, let the principle
Be plain. For application Crispin strove,
Abhorring Turk as Esquimau, the lute
As the marimba, the magnolia as rose.

Upon these premises propounding, he
Projected a colony that should extend
To the dusk of a whistling south below the south,
A comprehensive island hemisphere.
The man in Georgia waking among pines
Should be pine-spokesman. The responsive man,
Planting his pristine cores in Florida,
Should prick thereof, not on the psaltery,
But on the banjo's categorical gut,
Tuck, tuck, while the flamingoes flapped his bays.
Sepulchral señors, bibbling pale mescal,
Oblivious to the Aztec almanacs,
Should make the intricate Sierra scan.
And dark Brazilians in their cafés,
Musing immaculate, pampean dits,
Should scrawl a vigilant anthology,
To be their latest, lucent paramour.
These are the broadest instances. Crispin,
Progenitor of such extensive scope,
Was not indifferent to smart detail.
The melon should have apposite ritual,
Performed in verd apparel, and the peach,
When its black branches came to bud, belle day,
Should have an incantation. And again,
When piled on salvers its aroma steeped
The summer, it should have a sacrament

And celebration. Shrewd novitiates
Should be the clerks of our experience.
These bland excursions into time to come,
Related in romance to backward flights,
However prodigal, however proud,
Contained in their afflatus the reproach
That first drove Crispin to his wandering.
He could not be content with counterfeit,
With masquerade of thought, with hapless words
That must belie the racking masquerade,
With fictive flourishes that preordained
His passion's permit, hang of coat, degree
Of buttons, measure of his salt. Such trash
Might help the blind, not him, serenely sly.
It irked beyond his patience. Hence it was,
Preferring text to gloss, he humbly served
Grotesque apprenticeship to chance event,
A clown, perhaps, but an inspiring clown.
There is a monotonous babbling in our dreams
That makes them our dependent heirs, the heirs
Of dreamers buried in our sleep, and not
The oncoming fantasies of better birth.
The apprentice knew these dreamers. If he dreamed
Their dreams, he did it in a gingerly way.
All dreams are vexing. Let them be expunged.
But let the rabbit run, the cock declaim.

Trinket pasticcio, flaunting skyey sheets,
With Crispin as the tiptoe cozener?
No, no: veracious page on page, exact.

V

A Nice Shady Home

Crispin as hermit, pure and capable,
Dwelt in the land. Perhaps if discontent
Had kept him still the pricking realist,

Choosing his element from droll confect
Of was and is and shall or ought to be,
Beyond Bordeaux, beyond Havana, far
Beyond carked Yucatan, he might have come
To colonize his polar planterdom
And jig his chits upon a cloudy knee.
But his emprize to that idea soon sped.
Crispin dwelt in the land and dwelling there
Slid from his continent by slow recess
To things within his actual eye, alert
To the difficulty of rebellious thought
When the sky is blue. The blue infected will.
It may be that the yarrow in his fields
Sealed pensive purple under its concern.
But day by day, now this thing and now that
Confined him, while it cosseted, condoned,
Little by little, as if the suzerain soil
Abashed him by carouse to humble yet
Attach. It seemed haphazard denouement.
He first, as realist, admitted that
Whoever hunts a matinal continent
May, after all, stop short before a plum
And be content and still be realist.
The words of things entangle and confuse.
The plum survives its poems. It may hang
In the sunshine placidly, colored by ground
Obliquities of those who pass beneath,
Harlequined and mazily dewed and mauved
In bloom. Yet it survives in its own form,
Beyond these changes, good, fat, guzzly fruit.
So Crispin hasped on the surviving form,
For him, of shall or ought to be in is.

Was he to bray this in profoundest brass
Arointing his dreams with fugal requiems?
Was he to company vastest things defunct
With a blubber of tom-toms harrowing the sky?
Scrawl a tragedian's testament? Prolong
His active force in an inactive dirge,

Which, let the tall musicians call and call,
Should merely call him dead? Pronounce amen
Through choirs infolded to the outmost clouds?
Because he built a cabin who once planned
Loquacious columns by the ructive sea?
Because he turned to salad-beds again?
Jovial Crispin, in calamitous crape?

Should he lay by the personal and make
Of his own fate an instance of all fate?
What is one man among so many men?
What are so many men in such a world?
Can one man think one thing and think it long?
Can one man be one thing and be it long?
The very man despising honest quilts
Lies quilted to his poll in his despite.
For realists, what is is what should be.

And so it came, his cabin shuffled up,
His trees were planted, his duenna brought
Her prismy blonde and clapped her in his hands,
The curtains flittered and the door was closed.
Crispin, magister of a single room,
Latched up the night. So deep a sound fell down
It was as if the solitude concealed
And covered him and his congenial sleep.
So deep a sound fell down it grew to be
A long soothsaying silence down and down.
The crickets beat their tambours in the wind,
Marching a motionless march, custodians.

In the presto of the morning, Crispin trod,
Each day, still curious, but in a round
Less prickly and much more condign than that
He once thought necessary. Like Candide,
Yeoman and grub, but with a fig in sight,
And cream for the fig and silver for the cream,
A blonde to tip the silver and to taste
The rapey gouts. Good star, how that to be

Annealed them in their cabin ribaldries!
Yet the quotidian saps philosophers
And men like Crispin like them in intent,
If not in will, to track the knaves of thought.
But the quotidian composed as his,
Of breakfast ribands, fruits laid in their leaves,
The tomtit and the cassia and the rose,
Although the rose was not the noble thorn
Of crinoline spread, but of a pining sweet,
Composed of evenings like cracked shutters flung
Upon the rumpling bottomness, and nights
In which those frail custodians watched,
Indifferent to the tepid summer cold,
While he poured out upon the lips of her
That lay beside him, the quotidian
Like this, saps like the sun, true fortuner.
For all it takes it gives a humped return
Exchequering from piebald fiscs unkeyed.

VI

And Daughters with Curls

Portentous enunciation, syllable
To blessed syllable affined, and sound
Bubbling felicity in cantilene,
Prolific and tormenting tenderness
Of music, as it comes to unison,
Forgather and bell boldly Crispin's last
Deduction. Thrum with a proud douceur
His grand pronunciamento and devise.
The chits came for his jigging, bluet-eyed,
Hands without touch yet touching poignantly,
Leaving no room upon his cloudy knee,
Prophetic joint, for its diviner young.
The return to social nature, once begun,
Anabasis or slump, ascent or chute,
Involved him in midwifery so dense

His cabin counted as phylactery,
Then place of vexing palankeens, then haunt
Of children nibbling at the sugared void,
Infants yet eminently old, then dome
And halidom for the unbraided femes,
Green crammers of the green fruits of the world,
Bidders and biders for its ecstasies,
True daughters both of Crispin and his clay.
All this with many mulctings of the man,
Effective colonizer sharply stopped
In the door-yard by his own capacious bloom.
But that this bloom grown riper, showing nibs
Of its eventual roundness, puerile tints
Of spiced and weathery rouges, should complex
The stopper to indulgent fatalist
Was unforeseen. First Crispin smiled upon
His goldenest demoiselle, inhabitant,
She seemed, of a country of the capuchins,
So delicately blushed, so humbly eyed,
Attentive to a coronal of things
Secret and singular. Second, upon
A second similar counterpart, a maid
Most sisterly to the first, not yet awake
Excepting to the motherly footstep, but
Marvelling sometimes at the shaken sleep.
Then third, a thing still flaxen in the light,
A creeper under jaunty leaves. And fourth,
Mere blusteriness that gewgaws jollified,
All din and gobble, blasphemously pink.
A few years more and the vermeil capuchin
Gave to the cabin, lordlier than it was,
The dulcet omen fit for such a house.
The second sister dallying was shy
To fetch the one full-pinioned one himself
Out of her botches, hot embosomer.
The third one gaping at the orioles
Lettered herself demurely as became
A pearly poetess, peaked for rhapsody.
The fourth, pent now, a digit curious.

Four daughters in a world too intricate
In the beginning, four blithe instruments
Of differing struts, four voices several
In couch, four more personæ, intimate
As buffo, yet divers, four mirrors blue
That should be silver, four accustomed seeds
Hinting incredible hues, four selfsame lights
That spread chromatics in hilarious dark,
Four questioners and four sure answerers.

Crispin concocted doctrine from the rout.
The world, a turnip once so readily plucked,
Sacked up and carried overseas, daubed out
Of its ancient purple, pruned to the fertile main.
And sown again by the stiffest realist,
Came reproduced in purple, family font,
The same insoluble lump. The fatalist
Stepped in and dropped the chuckling down his craw,
Without grace or grumble. Score this anecdote
Invented for its pith, not doctrinal
In form though in design, as Crispin willed,
Disguised pronunciamento, summary,
Autumn's compendium, strident in itself
But muted, mused, and perfectly revolved
In those portentous accents, syllables,
And sounds of music coming to accord
Upon his law, like their inherent sphere,
Seraphic proclamations of the pure
Delivered with a deluging onwardness.
Or if the music sticks, if the anecdote
Is false, if Crispin is a profitless
Philosopher, beginning with green brag,
Concluding fadedly, if as a man
Prone to distemper he abates in taste,
Fickle and fumbling, variable, obscure,
Glozing his life with after-shining flicks,
Illuminating, from a fancy gorged
By apparition, plain and common things,
Sequestering the fluster from the year,

Making gulped potions from obstreperous drops,
And so distorting, proving what he proves
Is nothing, what can all this matter since
The relation comes, benignly, to its end?

So may the relation of each man be clipped.

Peter Quince at the Clavier

I

Just as my fingers on these keys
Make music, so the selfsame sounds
On my spirit make a music, too.

Music is feeling, then, not sound;
And thus it is that when I feel,
Here in this room, desiring you,

Thinking of your blue-shadowed silk,
Is music. It is like the strain
Waked in the elders by Susanna.

Of a green evening, clear and warm,
She bathed in her still garden, while
The red-eyed elders watching, felt

The basses of their beings throb
In witching chords, and their thin blood
Pulse pizzicati of Hosanna.

II

In the green water, clear and warm,
Susanna lay.
She searched
The touch of springs,
And found

Concealed imaginings.
She sighed,
For so much melody.

Upon the bank, she stood
In the cool
Of spent emotions.
She felt, among the leaves,
The dew
Of old devotions.

She walked upon the grass,
Still quavering.
The winds were like her maids,
On timid feet,
Fetching her woven scarves,
Yet wavering.

A breath upon her hand
Muted the night.
She turned—
A cymbal crashed,
And roaring horns.

III

Soon, with a noise like tambourines,
Came her attendant Byzantines.

They wondered why Susanna cried
Against the elders by her side;

And as they whispered, the refrain
Was like a willow swept by rain.

Anon, their lamps' uplifted flame
Revealed Susanna and her shame.

And then, the simpering Byzantines
Fled, with a noise like tambourines.

IV

Beauty is momentary in the mind—
The fitful tracing of a portal;
But in the flesh it is immortal.

The body dies; the body's beauty lives.
So evenings die, in their green going,
A wave, interminably flowing.
So gardens die, their meek breath scenting
The cowl of winter, done repenting.
So maidens die, to the auroral
Celebration of a maiden's choral.

Susanna's music touched the bawdy strings
Of those white elders; but, escaping,
Left only Death's ironic scraping.
Now, in its immortality, it plays
On the clear viol of her memory,
And makes a constant sacrament of praise.

Sunday Morning

I

Complacencies of the peignoir, and late
Coffee and oranges in a sunny chair,
And the green freedom of a cockatoo
Upon a rug mingle to dissipate
The holy hush of ancient sacrifice.
She dreams a little, and she feels the dark
Encroachment of that old catastrophe,
As a calm darkens among water-lights.
The pungent oranges and bright, green wings
Seem things in some procession of the dead,

Winding across wide water, without sound.
The day is like wide water, without sound,
Stilled for the passing of her dreaming feet
Over the seas, to silent Palestine,
Dominion of the blood and sepulchre.

II

Why should she give her bounty to the dead?
What is divinity if it can come
Only in silent shadows and in dreams?
Shall she not find in comforts of the sun,
In pungent fruit and bright, green wings, or else
In any balm or beauty of the earth,
Things to be cherished like the thought of heaven?
Divinity must live within herself:
Passions of rain, or moods in falling snow;
Grievings in loneliness, or unsubdued
Elations when the forest blooms; gusty
Emotions on wet roads on autumn nights;
All pleasures and all pains, remembering
The bough of summer and the winter branch.
These are the measures destined for her soul.

III

Jove in the clouds had his inhuman birth.
No mother suckled him, no sweet land gave
Large-mannered motions to his mythy mind.
He moved among us, as a muttering king,
Magnificent, would move among his hinds,
Until our blood, commingling, virginal,
With heaven, brought such requital to desire
The very hinds discerned it, in a star.
Shall our blood fail? Or shall it come to be
The blood of paradise? And shall the earth
Seem all of paradise that we shall know?
The sky will be much friendlier then than now,
A part of labor and a part of pain,

And next in glory to enduring love,
Not this dividing and indifferent blue.

IV

She says, "I am content when wakened birds,
Before they fly, test the reality
Of misty fields, by their sweet questionings;
But when the birds are gone, and their warm fields
Return no more, where, then, is paradise?"
There is not any haunt of prophecy,
Nor any old chimera of the grave,
Neither the golden underground, nor isle
Melodious, where spirits gat them home,
Nor visionary south, nor cloudy palm
Remote on heaven's hill, that has endured
As April's green endures; or will endure
Like her remembrance of awakened birds,
Or her desire for June and evening, tipped
By the consummation of the swallow's wings.

V

She says, "But in contentment I still feel
The need of some imperishable bliss."
Death is the mother of beauty; hence from her,
Alone, shall come fulfillment to our dreams
And our desires. Although she strews the leaves
Of sure obliteration on our paths,
The path sick sorrow took, the many paths
Where triumph rang its brassy phrase, or love
Whispered a little out of tenderness,
She makes the willow shiver in the sun
For maidens who were wont to sit and gaze
Upon the grass, relinquished to their feet.
She causes boys to pile new plums and pears
On disregarded plate. The maidens taste
And stray impassioned in the littering leaves.

VI

Is there no change of death in paradise?
Does ripe fruit never fall? Or do the boughs
Hang always heavy in that perfect sky,
Unchanging, yet so like our perishing earth,
With rivers like our own that seek for seas
They never find, the same receding shores
That never touch with inarticulate pang?
Why set the pear upon those river-banks
Or spice the shores with odors of the plum?
Alas, that they should wear our colours there,
The silken weavings of our afternoons,
And pick the strings of our insipid lutes!
Death is the mother of beauty, mystical,
Within whose burning bosom we devise
Our earthly mothers waiting, sleeplessly.

VII

Supple and turbulent, a ring of men
Shall chant in orgy on a summer morn
Their boisterous devotion to the sun,
Not as a god, but as a god might be,
Naked among them, like a savage source.
Their chant shall be a chant of paradise,
Out of their blood, returning to the sky;
And in their chant shall enter, voice by voice,
The windy lake wherein their lord delights,
The trees, like serafim, and echoing hills,
That choir among themselves long afterward.
They shall know well the heavenly fellowship
Of men that perish and of summer morn.
And whence they came and whither they shall go
The dew upon their feet shall manifest.

VIII

She hears, upon that water without sound,
A voice that cries, "The tomb in Palestine
Is not the porch of spirits lingering.
It is the grave of Jesus, where he lay."
We live in an old chaos of the sun,
Or old dependency of day and night,
Or island solitude, unsponsored, free,
Of that wide water, inescapable.
Deer walk upon our mountains, and the quail
Whistle about us their spontaneous cries;
Sweet berries ripen in the wilderness;
And, in the isolation of the sky,
At evening, casual flocks of pigeons make
Ambiguous undulations as they sink,
Downward to darkness, on extended wings.

Le Monocle de Mon Oncle

I

"Mother of heaven, regina of the clouds,
O sceptre of the sun, crown of the moon,
There is not nothing, no, no, never nothing,
Like the clashed edges of two words that kill."
And so I mocked her in magnificent measure.
Or was it that I mocked myself alone?
I wish that I might be a thinking stone.
The sea of spuming thought foists up again
The radiant bubble that she was. And then
A deep up-pouring from some saltier well
Within me, bursts its water syllable.

II

A red bird flies across the golden floor.
It is a red bird that seeks out his choir

Among the choirs of wind and wet and wing.
A torrent will fall from him when he finds.
Shall I uncrumple this much-crumpled thing?
I am a man of fortune greeting heirs;
For it has come that thus I greet the spring.
These choirs of welcome choir for me farewell.
No spring can follow past meridian.
Yet you persist with anecdotal bliss
To make believe a starry *connaissance*.

III

Is it for nothing, then, that old Chinese
Sat titivating by their mountain pools
Or in the Yangtse studied out their beards?
I shall not play the flat historic scale.
You know how Utamaro's beauties sought
The end of love in their all-speaking braids.
You know the mountainous coiffures of Bath.
Alas! Have all the barbers lived in vain
That not one curl in nature has survived?
Why, without pity on these studious ghosts,
Do you come dripping in your hair from sleep?

IV

This luscious and impeccable fruit of life
Falls, it appears, of its own weight to earth.
When you were Eve, its acrid juice was sweet,
Untasted, in its heavenly, orchard air.
An apple serves as well as any skull
To be the book in which to read a round,
And is as excellent, in that it is composed
Of what, like skulls, comes rotting back to ground.
But it excels in this, that as the fruit
Of love, it is a book too mad to read
Before one merely reads to pass the time.

V

In the high west there burns a furious star.
It is for fiery boys that star was set
And for sweet-smelling virgins close to them.
The measure of the intensity of love
Is measure, also, of the verve of earth.
For me, the firefly's quick, electric stroke
Ticks tediously the time of one more year.
And you? Remember how the crickets came
Out of their mother grass, like little kin,
In the pale nights, when your first imagery
Found inklings of your bond to all that dust.

VI

If men at forty will be painting lakes
The ephemeral blues must merge for them in one,
The basic slate, the universal hue.
There is a substance in us that prevails.
But in our amours amorists discern
Such fluctuations that their scrivening
Is breathless to attend each quirky turn.
When amorists grow bald, then amours shrink
Into the compass and curriculum
Of introspective exiles, lecturing.
It is a theme for Hyacinth alone.

VII

The mules that angels ride come slowly down
The blazing passes, from beyond the sun.
Descensions of their tinkling bells arrive.
These muleteers are dainty of their way.
Meantime, centurions guffaw and beat
Their shrilling tankards on the table-boards.
This parable, in sense, amounts to this:
The honey of heaven may or may not come,
But that of earth both comes and goes at once.

Suppose these couriers brought amid their train
A damsel heightened by eternal bloom.

VIII

Like a dull scholar, I behold, in love,
An ancient aspect touching a new mind.
It comes, it blooms, it bears its fruit and dies.
This trivial trope reveals a way of truth.
Our bloom is gone. We are the fruit thereof.
Two golden gourds distended on our vines,
Into the autumn weather, splashed with frost,
Distorted by hale fatness, turned grotesque.
We hang like warty squashes, streaked and rayed,
The laughing sky will see the two of us
Washed into rinds by rotting winter rains.

IX

In verses wild with motion, full of din,
Loudened by cries, by clashes, quick and sure
As the deadly thought of men accomplishing
Their curious fates in war, come, celebrate
The faith of forty, ward of Cupido.
Most venerable heart, the lustiest conceit
Is not too lusty for your broadening.
I quiz all sounds, all thoughts, all everything
For the music and manner of the paladins
To make oblation fit. Where shall I find
Bravura adequate to this great hymn?

X

The fops of fancy in their poems leave
Memorabilia of the mystic spouts,
Spontaneously watering their gritty soils.
I am a yeoman, as such fellows go.
I know no magic trees, no balmy boughs,
No silver-ruddy, gold-vermilion fruits.

But, after all, I know a tree that bears
A semblance to the thing I have in mind.
It stands gigantic, with a certain tip
To which all birds come sometime in their time.
But when they go that tip still tips the tree.

XI

If sex were all, then every trembling hand
Could make us squeak, like dolls, the wished-for words.
But note the unconscionable treachery of fate,
That makes us weep, laugh, grunt and groan, and shout
Doleful heroics, pinching gestures forth
From madness or delight, without regard
To that first, foremost law. Anguishing hour!
Last night, we sat beside a pool of pink,
Clippered with lilies scudding the bright chromes,
Keen to the point of starlight, while a frog
Boomed from his very belly odious chords.

XII

A blue pigeon it is, that circles the blue sky,
On sidelong wing, around and round and round.
A white pigeon it is, that flutters to the ground,
Grown tired of flight. Like a dark rabbi, I
Observed, when young, the nature of mankind,
In lordly study. Every day, I found
Man proved a gobbet in my mincing world.
Like a rose rabbi, later, I pursued,
And still pursue, the origin and course
Of love, but until now I never knew
That fluttering things have so distinct a shade.

Thirteen Ways of Looking at a Blackbird

I

Among twenty snowy mountains,
The only moving thing
Was the eye of the blackbird.

II

I was of three minds,
Like a tree
In which there are three blackbirds.

III

The blackbird whirled in the autumn winds.
It was a small part of the pantomime.

IV

A man and a woman
Are one.
A man and a woman and a blackbird
Are one.

V

I do not know which to prefer,
The beauty of inflections
Or the beauty of innuendoes,
The blackbird whistling
Or just after.

VI

Icicles filled the long window
With barbaric glass.
The shadow of the blackbird
Crossed it, to and fro.
The mood
Traced in the shadow
An indecipherable cause.

VII

O thin men of Haddam,
Why do you imagine golden birds?
Do you not see how the blackbird
Walks around the feet
Of the women about you?

VIII

I know noble accents
And lucid, inescapable rhythms;
But I know, too,
That the blackbird is involved
In what I know.

IX

When the blackbird flew out of sight,
It marked the edge
Of one of many circles.

X

At the sight of blackbirds
Flying in a green light,
Even the bawds of euphony
Would cry out sharply.

XI

He rode over Connecticut
In a glass coach.
Once, a fear pierced him,
In that he mistook
The shadow of his equipage
For blackbirds.

XII

The river is moving.
The blackbird must be flying.

XIII

It was evening all afternoon.
It was snowing
And it was going to snow.
The blackbird sat
In the cedar-limbs.

Domination of Black

At night, by the fire,
The colors of the bushes
And of the fallen leaves,
Repeating themselves,
Turned in the room,
Like the leaves themselves
Turning in the wind.
Yes: but the color of the heavy hemlocks
Came striding.
And I remembered the cry of the peacocks.

The colors of their tails
Were like the leaves themselves
Turning in the wind,

In the twilight wind.
They swept over the room,
Just as they flew from the boughs of the hemlocks
Down to the ground.
I heard them cry—the peacocks.
Was it a cry against the twilight
Or against the leaves themselves
Turning in the wind,
Turning as the flames
Turned in the fire,
Turning as the tails of the peacocks
Turned in the loud fire,
Loud as the hemlocks
Full of the cry of the peacocks?
Or was it a cry against the hemlocks?

Out of the window,
I saw how the planets gathered
Like the leaves themselves
Turning in the wind.
I saw how the night came,
Came striding like the color of the heavy hemlocks.
I felt afraid.
And I remembered the cry of the peacocks.

Sea Surface Full of Clouds

I

In that November off Tehuantepec,
The slopping of the sea grew still one night
And in the morning summer hued the deck

And made one think of rosy chocolate
And gilt umbrellas. Paradisal green
Gave suavity to the perplexed machine

Of ocean, which like limpid water lay.
Who, then, in that ambrosial latitude
Out of the light evolved the moving blooms,

Who, then, evolved the sea-blooms from the clouds
Diffusing balm in that Pacific calm?
C'était mon enfant, mon bijou, mon âme.

The sea-clouds whitened far below the calm
And moved, as blooms move, in the swimming green
And in its watery radiance, while the hue

Of heaven in an antique reflection rolled
Round those flotillas. And sometimes the sea
Poured brilliant iris on the glistening blue.

II

In that November off Tehuantepec
The slopping of the sea grew still one night.
At breakfast jelly yellow streaked the deck

And made one think of chop-house chocolate
And sham umbrellas. And a sham-like green
Capped summer-seeming on the tense machine

Of ocean, which in sinister flatness lay.
Who, then, beheld the rising of the clouds
That strode submerged in that malevolent sheen,

Who saw the mortal massives of the blooms
Of water moving on the water-floor?
C'était mon frère du ciel, ma vie, mon or.

The gongs rang loudly as the windy booms
Hoo-hooed it in the darkened ocean-blooms.
The gongs grew still. And then blue heaven spread

Its crystalline pendentives on the sea
And the macabre of the water-glooms
In an enormous undulation fled.

III

In that November off Tehuantepec,
The slopping of the sea grew still one night
And a pale silver patterned on the deck

And made one think of porcelain chocolate
And pied umbrellas. An uncertain green,
Piano-polished, held the tranced machine

Of ocean, as a prelude holds and holds.
Who, seeing silver petals of white blooms
Unfolding in the water, feeling sure

Of the milk within the saltiest spurge, heard, then,
The sea unfolding in the sunken clouds?
Oh! C'était mon extase et mon amour.

So deeply sunken were they that the shrouds,
The shrouding shadows, made the petals black
Until the rolling heaven made them blue,

A blue beyond the rainy hyacinth,
And smiting the crevasses of the leaves
Deluged the ocean with a sapphire blue.

IV

In that November off Tehuantepec
The night-long slopping of the sea grew still.
A mallow morning dozed upon the deck

And made one think of musky chocolate
And frail umbrellas. A too-fluent green
Suggested malice in the dry machine

Of ocean, pondering dank stratagem.
Who then beheld the figures of the clouds
Like blooms secluded in the thick marine?

Like blooms? Like damasks that were shaken off
From the loosed girdles in the spangling must.
C'était ma foi, la nonchalance divine.

The nakedness would rise and suddenly turn
Salt masks of beard and mouths of bellowing,
Would—But more suddenly the heaven rolled

Its bluest sea-clouds in the thinking green,
And the nakedness became the broadest blooms,
Mile-mallows that a mallow sun cajoled.

V

In that November off Tehuantepec
Night stilled the slopping of the sea. The day
Came, bowing and voluble, upon the deck,

Good clown. . . . One thought of Chinese chocolate
And large umbrellas. And a motley green
Followed the drift of the obese machine

Of ocean, perfected in indolence.
What pistache one, ingenious and droll,
Beheld the sovereign clouds as jugglery

And the sea as turquoise-turbaned Sambo, neat
At tossing saucers—cloudy-conjuring sea?
C'était mon esprit bâtard, l'ignominie.

The sovereign clouds came clustering. The conch
Of loyal conjuration trumped. The wind
Of green blooms turning crisped the motley hue

To clearing opalescence. Then the sea
And heaven rolled as one and from the two
Came fresh transfigurings of freshest blue.

To the One of Fictive Music

Sister and mother and diviner love,
And of the sisterhood of the living dead
Most near, most clear, and of the clearest bloom,
And of the fragrant mothers the most dear
And queen, and of diviner love the day
And flame and summer and sweet fire, no thread
Of cloudy silver sprinkles in your gown
Its venom of renown, and on your head
No crown is simpler than the simple hair.

Now, of the music summoned by the birth
That separates us from the wind and sea,
Yet leaves us in them, until earth becomes,
By being so much of the things we are,
Gross effigy and simulacrum, none
Gives motion to perfection more serene
Than yours, out of our imperfections wrought,
Most rare, or ever of more kindred air
In the laborious weaving that you wear.

For so retentive of themselves are men
That music is intensest which proclaims
The near, the clear, and vaunts the clearest bloom,
And of all vigils musing the obscure,
That apprehends the most which sees and names,
As in your name, an image that is sure,
Among the arrant spices of the sun,
O bough and bush and scented vine, in whom
We give ourselves our likest issuance.

Yet not too like, yet not so like to be
Too near, too clear, saving a little to endow

Our feigning with the strange unlike, whence springs
The difference that heavenly pity brings.
For this, musician, in your girdle fixed
Bear other perfumes. On your pale head wear
A band entwining, set with fatal stones.
Unreal, give back to us what once you gave:
The imagination that we spurned and crave.

Cortège for Rosenbloom

Now, the wry Rosenbloom is dead
And his finical carriers tread,
On a hundred legs, the tread
Of the dead.
Rosenbloom is dead.

They carry the wizened one
Of the color of horn
To the sullen hill,
Treading a tread
In unison for the dead.

Rosenbloom is dead.
The tread of the carriers does not halt
On the hill, but turns
Up the sky.
They are bearing his body into the sky.

It is the infants of misanthropes
And the infants of nothingness
That tread
The wooden ascents
Of the ascending of the dead.

It is turbans they wear
And boots of fur
As they tread the boards

In a region of frost,
Viewing the frost;

To a chirr of gongs
And a chitter of cries
And the heavy thrum
Of the endless tread
That they tread;

To a jangle of doom
And a jumble of words
Of the intense poem
Of the strictest prose
Of Rosenbloom.

And they bury him there,
Body and soul,
In a place in the sky.
The lamentable tread!
Rosenbloom is dead.

WILLIAM CARLOS WILLIAMS

The Wanderer

A Rococo Study

ADVENT

Even in the time when as yet
I had no certain knowledge of her
She sprang from the nest, a young crow,
Whose first flight circled the forest.
I know now how then she showed me

Her mind, reaching out to the horizon,
She close above the tree tops.
I saw her eyes straining at new distance
And as the woods fell from her flying
Likewise they fell from me as I followed—
So that I strongly guessed all that I must put from me
To come through ready for the high courses.

But one day, crossing the ferry
With the great towers of Manhattan before me,
Out at the prow with the sea wind blowing,
I had been wearying many questions
Which she had put on to try me:
How shall I be a mirror to this modernity?
When lo! in a rush, dragging
A blunt boat on the yielding river—
Suddenly I saw her! And she waved me
From the white wet in midst of her playing!
She cried me, "Haia! Here I am, son!
See how strong my little finger is!
Can I not swim well?
I can fly too!" And with that a great sea-gull
Went to the left, vanishing with a wild cry—
But in my mind all the persons of the godhead
Followed after.

CLARITY

"Come!" cried my mind and by her might
That was upon us we flew above the river
Seeking her, grey gulls among the white—
In the air speaking as she had willed it:
"I am given," cried I, "now I know it!
I know now all my time is forespent!
For me one face is all the world!
For I have seen her at last, this day,
In whom age in age is united—
Indifferent, out of sequence, marvellously!

Saving alone that one sequence
Which is the beauty of all the world, for surely
Either there in the rolling smoke spheres below us
Or here with us in the air intercircling,
Certainly somewhere here about us
I know she is revealing these things!"

And as gulls we flew and with soft cries
We seemed to speak, flying, "It is she
The mighty, recreating the whole world,
This the first day of wonders!
She is attiring herself before me—
Taking shape before me for worship,
A red leaf that falls upon a stone!
It is she of whom I told you, old
Forgiveless, unreconcilable;
That high wanderer of by-ways
Walking imperious in beggary!
At her throat is loose gold, a single chain
From among many, on her bent fingers
Are rings from which the stones are fallen,
Her wrists wear a diminished state, her ankles
Are bare! Toward the river! Is it she there?"
And we swerved clamorously downward—
"I will take my peace in her henceforth!"

BROADWAY

It was then she struck—from behind,
In mid air, as with the edge of a great wing!
And instantly down the mists of my eyes
There came crowds walking—men as visions
With expressionless, animate faces;
Empty men with shell-thin bodies
Jostling close above the gutter,
Hasting—nowhere! And then for the first time
I really saw her, really scented the sweat
Of her presence and—fell back sickened!

Ominous, old, painted—
With bright lips, and lewd Jew's eyes
Her might strapped in by a corset
To give her age youth, perfect
In her will to be young she had covered
The godhead to go beside me.
Silent, her voice entered at my eyes
And my astonished thought followed her easily:
"Well, do their eyes shine, do their clothes fit?
These *live* I tell you! Old men with red cheeks,
Young men in gay suits! See them!
Dogged, quivering, impassive—
Well—are these the ones you envied?"
At which I answered her, "Marvellous old queen,
Grant me power to catch something of this day's
Air and sun into your service!
That these toilers after peace and after pleasure
May turn to you, worshippers at all hours!"
But she sniffed upon the words warily—
Yet I persisted, watching for an answer:
"To you, horrible old woman,
Who know all fires out of the bodies
Of all men that walk with lust at heart!
To you, O mighty, crafty prowler
After the youth of all cities, drunk
With the sight of thy archness! All the youth
That come to you, you having the knowledge
Rather than to those uninitiate—
To you, marvellous old queen, give me always
A new marriage—"
But she laughed loudly—
"A new grip upon those garments that brushed me
In days gone by on beach, lawn, and in forest!
May I be lifted still, up and out of terror,
Up from before the death living around me—
Torn up continually and carried
Whatever way the head of your whim is,
A burr upon those streaming tatters—"

But the night had fallen, she stilled me
And led me away.

PATERSON—THE STRIKE

At the first peep of dawn she roused me!
I rose trembling at the change which the night saw!
For there, wretchedly brooding in a corner
From which her old eyes glittered fiercely—
"Go!" she said, and I hurried shivering
Out into the deserted streets of Paterson.

That night she came again hovering
In rags within the filmy ceiling—
"Great Queen, bless me with thy tatters!"
"You are blest, go on!"
"Hot for savagery,
Sucking the air! I went into the city,
Out again, baffled onto the mountain!
Back into the city!
Nowhere
The subtle! Everywhere the electric!

"A short bread-line before a hitherto empty tea shop:
No questions—all stood patiently,
Dominated by one idea: something
That carried them as they are always wanting to be carried,
'But what is it,' I asked those nearest me,
'This thing heretofore unobtainable
That they seem so clever to have put on now!'

"Why since I have failed them can it be anything but their own
brood?
Can it be anything but brutality?
On that at least they're united! That at least
Is their bean soup, their calm bread and a few luxuries!

"But in me, more sensitive, marvellous old queen,
It sank deep into the blood that I rose upon
The tense air enjoying the dusty fight!
Heavy drink were the low, sloping foreheads,
The flat skulls with the unkempt black or blonde hair,
The ugly legs of the young girls, pistons
Too powerful for delicacy!
The women's wrists, the men's arms, red
Used to heat and cold, to toss quartered beeves
And barrels, and milk-cans, and crates of fruit!

"Faces all knotted up like burls on oaks,
Grasping, fox-snouted, thick-lipped,
Sagging breasts and protruding stomachs,
Rasping voices, filthy habits with the hands.
Nowhere you! Everywhere the electric!

"Ugly, venomous, gigantic!
Tossing me as a great father his helpless
Infant till it shriek with ecstasy
And its eyes roll and its tongue hangs out!—

"I am at peace again, old queen, I listen clearer now."

ABROAD

Never, even in a dream,
Have I winged so high nor so well
As with her, she leading me by the hand,
That first day on the Jersey mountains!
And never shall I forget
The trembling interest with which I heard
Her voice in a low thunder:
"You are safe here. Look, child, look open-mouth!
The patch of road between the steep bramble banks;
The tree in the wind, the white house there, the sky!
Speak to men of these, concerning me!
For never while you permit them to ignore me

In these shall the full of my freed voice
Come grappling the ear with intent!
Never while the air's clear coolness
Is seized to be a coat for pettiness;
Never while richness of greenery
Stands a shield for prurient minds;
Never, permitting these things unchallenged
Shall my voice of leaves and vari-coloured bark come free through!"
At which, knowing her solitude,
I shouted over the country below me:
"Waken! my people to the boughs green
With ripening fruit within you!
Waken to the myriad cinquefoil
In the waving grass of your minds!
Waken to the silent phoebe nest
Under the eaves of your spirit!"

But she, stooping nearer the shifting hills
Spoke again. "Look there! See them!
There in the oat field with the horses,
See them there! bowed by their passions
Crushed down, that had been raised as a roof beam!
The weight of the sky is upon them
Under which all roof beams crumble.
There is none but the single roof beam:
There is no love bears against the great firefly!"
At this I looked up at the sun
Then shouted again with all the might I had.
But my voice was a seed in the wind.
Then she, the old one, laughing
Seized me and whirling about bore back
To the city, upward, still laughing
Until the great towers stood above the marshland
Wheeling beneath: the little creeks, the mallows
That I picked as a boy, the Hackensack
So quiet that seemed so broad formerly:
The crawling trains, the cedar swamp on the one side—
All so old, so familiar—so new now

To my marvelling eyes as we passed
Invisible.

SOOTHSAY

Eight days went by, eight days
Comforted by no nights, until finally:
"Would you behold yourself old, beloved?"
I was pierced, yet I consented gladly
For I knew it could not be otherwise.
And she—"Behold yourself old!
Sustained in strength, wielding might in gript surges!
Not bodying the sun in weak leaps
But holding way over rockish men
With fern tree fingers on their little crags,
Their hollows, the new Atlas, to bear them
For pride and for mockery! Behold
Yourself old! winding with slow might—
A vine among oaks—to the thin tops:
Leaving the leafless leaved,
Bearing purple clusters! Behold
Yourself old! birds are behind you.
You are the wind coming that stills birds,
Shakes the leaves in booming polyphony—
Slow, winning high way amid the knocking
Of boughs, evenly crescendo,
The din and bellow of the male wind!
Leap then from forest into foam!
Lash about from low into high flames
Tipping sound, the female chorus—
Linking all lions, all twitterings
To make them nothing! Behold yourself old!"
As I made to answer she continued,
A little wistfully yet in a voice clear cut:
"Good is my overlip and evil
My underlip to you henceforth:
For I have taken your soul between my two hands
And this shall be as it is spoken."

ST. JAMES' GROVE

And so it came to that last day
When, she leading by the hand, we went out
Early in the morning, I heavy of heart
For I knew the novitiate was ended
The ecstasy was over, the life begun.

In my woollen shirt and the pale blue necktie
My grandmother gave me, there I went
With the old queen right past the houses
Of my friends down the hill to the river
As on any usual day, any errand.
Alone, walking under trees,
I went with her, she with me in her wild hair,
By Santiago Grove and presently
She bent forward and knelt by the river,
The Passaic, that filthy river.
And there dabbling her mad hands,
She called me close beside her.
Raising the water then in the cupped palm
She bathed our brows wailing and laughing:
"River, we are old, you and I,
We are old and by bad luck, beggars.
Lo, the filth in our hair, our bodies stink!
Old friend, here I have brought you
The young soul you long asked of me.
Stand forth, river, and give me
The old friend of my revels!
Give me the well-worn spirit
For here I have made a room for it,
And I will return to you forthwith
The youth you have long asked of me:
Stand forth, river, and give me
The old friend of my revels!"

And the filthy Passaic consented!

Then she, leaping up with a fierce cry:
"Enter, youth, into this bulk!
Enter, river, into this young man!"
Then the river began to enter my heart,
Eddying back cool and limpid
Into the crystal beginning of its days.
But with the rebound it leaped forward:
Muddy, then black and shrunken
Till I felt the utter depth of its rottenness
The vile breadth of its degradation
And dropped down knowing this was me now.
But she lifted me and the water took a new tide
Again into the older experiences,
And so, backward and forward,
It tortured itself within me
Until time had been washed finally under,
And the river had found its level
And its last motion had ceased
And I knew all—it became me.
And I knew this for double certain
For there, whitely, I saw myself
Being borne off under the water!
I could have shouted out in my agony
At the sight of myself departing
Forever—but I bit back my despair
For she had averted her eyes
By which I knew well what she was thinking—
And so the last of me was taken.

Then she, "Be mostly silent!"
And turning to the river, spoke again:
"For him and for me, river, the wandering,
But by you I leave for happiness
Deep foliage, the thickest beeches—
Though elsewhere they are all dying—
Tallest oaks and yellow birches
That dip their leaves in you, mourning,
As now I dip my hair, immemorial

Of me, immemorial of him,
Immemorial of these our promises!
Here shall be a bird's paradise,
They sing to you remembering my voice:
Here the most secluded spaces
For miles around, hallowed by a stench
To be our joint solitude and temple;
In memory of this clear marriage
And the child I have brought you in the late years,
Live, river, live in luxuriance
Remembering this our son,
In remembrance of me and my sorrow
And of the new wandering!"

Tract

I will teach you my townspeople
how to perform a funeral—
for you have it over a troupe
of artists—
unless one should scour the world—
you have the ground sense necessary.

See! the hearse leads.
I begin with a design for a hearse.
For Christ's sake not black—
nor white either—and not polished!
Let it be weathered—like a farm wagon—
with gilt wheels (this could be
applied fresh at small expense)
or no wheels at all:
a rough dray to drag over the ground.

Knock the glass out!
My God—glass, my townspeople!
For what purpose? Is it for the dead
to look out or for us to see

how well he is housed or to see
the flowers or the lack of them—
or what?
To keep the rain and snow from him?
He will have a heavier rain soon:
pebbles and dirt and what not.
Let there be no glass—
and no upholstery! phew!
and no little brass rollers
and small easy wheels on the bottom—
my townspeople what are you thinking of!
A rough plain hearse then
with gilt wheels and no top at all.
On this the coffin lies
by its own weight.

No wreaths please—
especially no hot-house flowers.
Some common memento is better,
something he prized and is known by:
his old clothes—a few books perhaps—
God knows what! You realize
how we are about these things,
my townspeople—
something will be found—anything—
even flowers if he had come to that.
So much for the hearse.

For heaven's sake though see to the driver!
Take off the silk hat! In fact
that's no place at all for him
up there unceremoniously
dragging our friend out to his own dignity!
Bring him down—bring him down!
Low and inconspicuous! I'd not have him ride
on the wagon at all—damn him—
the undertaker's understrapper!
Let him hold the reins

and walk at the side
and inconspicuously too!

Then briefly as to yourselves:
Walk behind—as they do in France,
seventh class, or if you ride
Hell take curtains! Go with some show
of inconvenience; sit openly—
to the weather as to grief.
Or do you think you can shut grief in?
What—from us? We who have perhaps
nothing to lose? Share with us
share with us—it will be money
in your pockets.
Go now
I think you are ready.

The Yachts

contend in a sea which the land partly encloses
shielding them from the too heavy blows
of an ungoverned ocean which when it chooses

tortures the biggest hulls, the best man knows
to pit against its beatings, and sinks them pitilessly.
Mothlike in mists, scintillant in the minute

brilliance of cloudless days, with broad bellying sails
they glide to the wind tossing green water
from their sharp prows while over them the crew crawls

ant like, solicitously grooming them, releasing,
making fast as they turn, lean far over and having
caught the wind again, side by side, head for the mark.

In a well guarded arena of open water surrounded by
lesser and greater craft which, sycophant, lumbering
and flittering follow them, they appear youthful, rare

as the light of a happy eye, live with the grace
of all that in the mind is feckless, free and
naturally to be desired. Now the sea which holds them

is moody, lapping their glossy sides, as if feeling
for some slightest flaw but fails completely.
Today no race. Then the wind comes again. The yachts

move, jockeying for a start, the signal is set and they
are off. Now the waves strike at them but they are too
well made, they slip through, though they take in canvas.

Arms with hands grasping seek to clutch at the prows.
Bodies thrown recklessly in the way are cut aside.
It is a sea of faces about them in agony, in despair

until the horror of the race dawns staggering the mind,
the whole sea become an entanglement of watery bodies
lost to the world bearing what they cannot hold. Broken,

beaten, desolate, reaching from the dead to be taken up
they cry out, failing, failing! their cries rising
in waves still as the skillful yachts pass over.

Burning the Christmas Greens

Their time past, pulled down
cracked and flung to the fire
—go up in a roar

All recognition lost, burnt clean
clean in the flame, the green
dispersed, a living red,
flame red, red as blood wakes
on the ash—

and ebbs to a steady burning
the rekindled bed become
a landscape of flame

At the winter's midnight
we went to the trees, the coarse
holly, the balsam and
the hemlock for their green

At the thick of the dark
the moment of the cold's
deepest plunge we brought branches
cut from the green trees

to fill our need, and over
doorways, about paper Christmas
bells covered with tinfoil
and fastened by red ribbons

we stuck the green prongs
in the windows hung
woven wreaths and above pictures
the living green. On the

mantle we built a green forest
and among those hemlock
sprays put a herd of small
white deer as if they

were walking there. All this!
and it seemed gentle and good
to us. Their time past,
relief! The room bare. We

stuffed the dead grate
with them upon the half burntout
log's smouldering eye, opening
red and closing under them

and we stood there looking down.
Green is a solace
a promise of peace, a fort
against the cold (though we

did not say so) a challenge
above the snow's
hard shell. Green (we might
have said) that, where

small birds hide and dodge
and lift their plaintiff
rallying cries, blocks for them
and knocks down

the unseeing bullets of
the storm. Green spruce boughs
pulled down by a weight of
snow—Transformed!

Violence leaped and appeared.
Recreant! roared to life
as the flame rose through and
our eyes recoiled from it.

In the jagged flames green
to red, instant and alive. Green!
those sure abutments. Gone!
lost to mind

and quick in the contracting
tunnel of the grate
appeared a world! Black
mountains, black and red—as

yet uncolored—and ash white,
an infant landscape shimmering
ash and flame and we, in
that instant, lost,

breathless to be witnesses,
as if we stood
ourselves refreshed among
the shining fauna of that fire.

Gulls

My townspeople, beyond in the great world,
are many with whom it were far more
profitable for me to live than here with you.
These whirr about me calling, calling!
and for my own part I answer them, loud as I can,
but they, being free, pass!
I remain! Therefore, listen!
For you will not soon have another singer.

First I say this: You have seen
the strange birds, have you not, that sometimes
rest upon our river in winter?
Let them cause you to think well then of the storms
that drive many to shelter. These things
do not happen without reason.

And the next thing I say is this:
I saw an eagle once circling against the clouds
over one of our principal churches—
Easter, it was—a beautiful day!—:
three gulls came from above the river
and crossed slowly seaward!
Oh, I know you have your own hymns, I have heard them—
and because I knew they invoked some great protector
I could not be angry with you, no matter
how much they outraged true music—

You see, it is not necessary for us to leap at each other,
and, as I told you, in the end
the gulls moved seaward very quietly.

Portrait of a Lady

Your thighs are appletrees
whose blossoms touch the sky.

Which sky? The sky
where Watteau hung a lady's
slipper. Your knees
are a southern breeze—or
a gust of snow. Agh! what
sort of man was Fragonard?
—as if that answered
anything. Ah, yes—below
the knees, since the tune
drops that way, it is
one of those white summer days,
the tall grass of your ankles
flickers upon the shore—
Which shore?—
the sand clings to my lips—
Which shore?
Agh, petals maybe. How
should I know?
Which shore? Which shore?
I said petals from an appletree.

EZRA POUND

Canto II

Hang it all, Robert Browning,
there can be but the one 'Sordello.'
But Sordello, and my Sordello?
Lo Sordels si fo di Mantovana.
So-shu churned in the sea.
Seal sports in the spray-whited circles of cliff-wash,
Sleek head, daughter of Lir,
eyes of Picasso

Under black fur-hood, lithe daughter of Ocean;
And the wave runs in the beach-groove:
'Eleanor, ἑλέναυς and ἑλέπτολις!'
        And poor old Homer blind, blind, as a bat,
Ear, ear for the sea-surge, murmur of old men's voices:
'Let her go back to the ships,
Back among Grecian faces, lest evil come on our own,
Evil and further evil, and a curse cursed on our children,
Moves, yes she moves like a goddess
And has the face of a god
        and the voice of Schoeney's daughters,
And doom goes with her in walking,
Let her go back to the ships,
        back among the Grecian voices.'
And by the beach-run, Tyro,
        Twisted arms of the sea-god,
Lithe sinews of water, gripping her, cross-hold,
And the blue-gray glass of the wave tents them,
Glare azure of water, cold-welter, close cover.
Quiet sun-tawny sand-stretch,
The gulls broad out their wings,
        nipping between the splay feathers;
Snipe come for their bath,
        bend out their wing-joints,
Spread wet wings to the sun-film,
And by Scios,
        to left of the Naxos passage,
Naviform rock overgrown,
        algæ cling to its edge,
There is a wine-red glow in the shallows,
        a tin flash in the sun-dazzle.

The ship landed in Scios,
        men wanting spring-water,
And by the rock-pool a young boy loggy with vine-must,
        'To Naxos? Yes, we'll take you to Naxos,
Cum' along, lad.' 'Not that way!'
'Aye, that way is Naxos.'
        And I said: 'It's a straight ship.'

And an ex-convict out of Italy
knocked me into the fore-stays,
(He was wanted for manslaughter in Tuscany)
And the whole twenty against me,
Mad for a little slave money.
And they took her out of Scios
And off her course . . .
And the boy came to, again, with the racket,
And looked out over the bows,
and to eastward, and to the Naxos passage.
God-sleight then, god-sleight:
Ship stock fast in sea-swirl,
Ivy upon the oars, King Pentheus,
grapes with no seed but sea-foam,
Ivy in scupper-hole.
Aye, I, Acœtes, stood there,
and the god stood by me,
Water cutting under the keel,
Sea-break from stern forrards,
wake running off from the bow,
And where was gunwale, there now was vine-trunk,
And tenthril where cordage had been,
grape-leaves on the rowlocks,
Heavy vine on the oarshafts,
And, out of nothing, a breathing,
hot breath on my ankles,
Beasts like shadows in glass,
a furred tail upon nothingness.
Lynx-purr, and heathery smell of beasts,
where tar smell had been,
Sniff and pad-foot of beasts,
eye-glitter out of black air.
The sky overshot, dry, with no tempest,
Sniff and pad-foot of beasts,
fur brushing my knee-skin,
Rustle of airy sheaths,
dry forms in the *æther*.
And the ship like a keel in ship-yard,
slung like an ox in smith's sling,

Ribs stuck fast in the ways,
        grape-cluster over pin-rack,
        void air taking pelt.
Lifeless air become sinewed,
        feline leisure of panthers,
Leopards sniffing the grape shoots by scupper-hole,
Crouched panthers by fore-hatch,
And the sea blue-deep about us,
        green-ruddy in shadows,
And Lyæus: 'From now, Acœtes, my altars,
Fearing no bondage,
        fearing no cat of the wood,
Safe with my lynxes,
        feeding grapes to my leopards,
Olibanum is my incense,
        the vines grow in my homage.'

The back-swell now smooth in the rudder-chains,
Black snout of a porpoise
        where Lycabs had been,
Fish-scales on the oarsmen.
        And I worship.
I have seen what I have seen.
        When they brought the boy I said:
'He has a god in him,
        though I do not know which god.'
And they kicked me into the fore-stays.
I have seen what I have seen:
        Medon's face like the face of a dory,
Arms shrunk into fins. And you, Pentheus,
Had as well listen to Tiresias, and to Cadmus,
        or your luck will go out of you.
Fish-scales over groin muscles,
        lynx-purr amid sea . . .
And of a later year,
        pale in the wine-red algæ,
If you will lean over the rock,
        the coral face under wave-tinge,

Rose-paleness under water-shift,
        Ileuthyeria, fair Dafne of sea-bords,
The swimmer's arms turned to branches,
Who will say in what year,
        fleeing what band of tritons,
The smooth brows, seen, and half seen,
        now ivory stillness.

And So-shu churned in the sea, So-shu also,
        using the long moon for a churn-stick . . .
Lithe turning of water,
        sinews of Poseidon,
Black azure and hyaline,
        glass wave over Tyro,
Close cover, unstillness,
        bright welter of wave-cords,
Then quiet water,
        quiet in the buff sands,
Sea-fowl stretching wing-joints,
        splashing in rock-hollows and sand-hollows
In the wave-runs by the half-dune;
Glass-glint of wave in the tide-rips against sunlight,
        pallor of Hesperus,
Grey peak of the wave,
        wave, colour of grape's pulp,
Olive grey in the near,
        far, smoke grey of the rock-slide,
Salmon-pink wings of the fish-hawk
        cast grey shadows in water,
The tower like a one-eyed great goose
        cranes up out of the olive-grove,
And we have heard the fauns chiding Proteus
        in the smell of hay under the olive-trees,
And the frogs singing against the fauns
        in the half-light.
And . . .

The Alchemist

Chant for the Transmutation of Metals

Saîl of Claustra, Aelis, Azalais,
As you move among the bright trees;
As your voices, under the larches of Paradise
Make a clear sound,
Saîl of Claustra, Aelis, Azalais,
Raimona, Tibors, Berangèrë,
'Neath the dark gleam of the sky;
Under night, the peacock-throated,
Bring the saffron-coloured shell,
Bring the red gold of the maple,
Bring the light of the birch tree in autumn
Mirals, Cembelins, Audiarda,
Remember this fire.
Elain, Tireis, Alcmena
'Mid the silver rustling of wheat,
Agradiva, Anhes, Ardenca,
From the plum-coloured lake, in stillness,
From the molten dyes of the water
Bring the burnished nature of fire;
Briseis, Lianor, Loica,
From the wide earth and the olive,
From the poplars weeping their amber,
By the bright flame of the fishing torch
Remember this fire.
Midonz, with the gold of the sun, the leaf of the poplar, by the light of the amber,
Midonz, daughter of the sun, shaft of the tree, silver of the leaf, light of the yellow of the amber,
Midonz, gift of the God, gift of the light, gift of the amber of the sun,
Give light to the metal.
Anhes of Rocacoart, Ardenca, Aemelis,
From the power of grass,

From the white, alive in the seed,
From the heat of the bud,
From the copper of the leaf in autumn,
From the bronze of the maple, from the sap in the bough;
Lianor, Ioanna, Loica,
By the stir of the fin,
By the trout asleep in the gray-green of water;
Vanna, Mandetta, Viera, Alodetta, Picarda, Manuela
From the red gleam of copper,
Ysaut, Ydone, slight rustling of leaves,
Vierna, Jocelynn, daring of spirits,
By the mirror of burnished copper,
O Queen of Cypress,
Out of Erebus, the flat-lying breadth,
Breath that is stretched out beneath the world:
Out of Erebus, out of the flat waste of air, lying beneath the world;
Out of the brown leaf-brown colourless
Bring the imperceptible cool.
Elain, Tireis, Alcmena,
Quiet this metal!
Let the manes put off their terror, let them put off their aqueous bodies with fire.
Let them assume the milk-white bodies of agate.
Let them draw together the bones of the metal.

Selvaggia, Guiscarda, Mandetta,
Rain flakes of gold on the water
Azure and flaking silver of water,
Alcyon, Phætona, Alcmena,
Pallor of silver, pale lustre of Latona,
By these, from the malevolence of the dew
Guard this alembic.
Elain, Tireis, Alodetta
Quiet this metal.

The Tree

I stood still and was a tree amid the wood,
Knowing the truth of things unseen before,
Of Daphne and the laurel bough
And that god-feasting couple old
That grew elm-oak amid the wold.
'Twas not until the gods had been
Kindly entreated, and been brought within
Unto the hearth of their heart's home
That they might do this wonder thing;
Nathless I have been a tree amid the wood
And many a new thing understood
That was rank folly to my head before.

The Tomb of Akr Çaar

"I am thy soul, Nikoptis. I have watched
These five millennia, and thy dead eyes
Moved not, nor ever answer my desire,
And thy light limbs, wherethrough I leapt aflame,
Burn not with me nor any saffron thing.

See, the light grass sprang up to pillow thee,
And kissed thee with a myriad grassy tongues;
But not thou me.
I have read out the gold upon the wall,
And wearied out my thought upon the signs.
And there is no new thing in all this place.

I have been kind. See, I have left the jars sealed,
Lest thou shouldst wake and whimper for thy wine.
And all thy robes I have kept smooth on thee.
O thou unmindful! How should I forget!
—Even the river many days ago,
The river? thou wast over young.

And three souls came upon Thee—
And I came.
And I flowed in upon thee, beat them off;
I have been intimate with thee, known thy ways.
Have I not touched thy palms and finger-tips,
Flowed in, and through thee and about thy heels?
How 'came I in'? Was I not thee and Thee?

And no sun comes to rest me in this place,
And I am torn against the jagged dark,
And no light beats upon me, and you say
No word, day after day.

Oh! I could get me out, despite the marks
And all their crafty work upon the door,
Out through the glass-green fields. . . .

. . . . . .

Yet it is quiet here:

I do not go."

Portrait d'une Femme

Your mind and you are our Sargasso Sea,
London has swept about you this score years
And bright ships left you this or that in fee:
Ideas, old gossip, oddments of all things,
Strange spars of knowledge and dimmed wares of price.
Great minds have sought you—lacking someone else.
You have been second always. Tragical?
No. You preferred it to the usual thing:
One dull man, dulling and uxorious,
One average mind—with one thought less, each year.
Oh, you are patient, I have seen you sit
Hours, where something might have floated up.
And now you pay one. Yes, you richly pay.

You are a person of some interest, one comes to you
And takes strange gain away:
Trophies fished up; some curious suggestion;
Fact that leads nowhere; and a tale or two,
Pregnant with mandrakes, or with something else
That might prove useful and yet never proves,
That never fits a corner or shows use,
Or finds its hour upon the loom of days:
The tarnished, gaudy, wonderful old work;
Idols and ambergris and rare inlays,
These are your riches, your great store; and yet
For all this sea-hoard of deciduous things,
Strange woods half sodden, and new brighter stuff:
In the slow float of differing light and deep,
No! there is nothing! In the whole and all,
Nothing that's quite your own.
Yet this is you.

Apparuit

Golden rose the house, in the portal I saw
thee, a marvel, carven in subtle stuff, a
portent. Life died down in the lamp and flickered,
caught at the wonder.

Crimson, frosty with dew, the roses bend where
thou afar, moving in the glamorous sun,
drinkst in life of earth, of the air, the tissue
golden about thee.

Green the ways, the breath of the fields is thine there,
open lies the land, yet the steely going
darkly hast thou dared and the dreaded æther
parted before thee.

Swift at courage thou in the shell of gold, cast-
ing a-loose the cloak of the body, camest

straight, then shone thine oriel and the stunned light
    faded about thee.

Half the graven shoulder, the throat aflash with
strands of light inwoven about it, loveli-
est of all things, frail alabaster, ah me!
    swift in departing.

Clothed in goldish weft, delicately perfect,
gone as wind! The cloth of the magical hands:
Thou a slight thing, thou in access of cunning
    dar'dst to assume this?

A Virginal

"No, no! Go from me. I have left her lately.
I will not spoil my sheath with lesser brightness.
For my surrounding air hath a new lightness;
Slight are her arms, yet they have bound me straitly
And left me cloaked as with a gauze of æther;
As with sweet leaves; as with subtle clearness.
Oh, I have picked up magic in her nearness
To sheathe me half in half the things that sheathe her.
No, no! Go from me. I have still the flavour,
Soft as spring wind that's come from birchen bowers.
Green come the shoots, aye April in the branches,
As winter's wound with her sleight hand she staunches,
Hath of the trees a likeness of the savour:
As white their bark, so white this lady's hours."

The Return

See, they return; ah, see the tentative
Movements, and the slow feet,
The trouble in the pace and the uncertain
Wavering!

See, they return, one, and by one,
With fear, as half-awakened;
As if the snow should hesitate
And murmur in the wind,
        and half turned back;
These were the "Wing'd-with-Awe,"
        Inviolable.

Gods of the wingèd shoe!
With them the silver hounds,
        sniffing the trace of air!

Haie! Haie!
    These were the swift to harry;
These the keen-scented;
These were the souls of blood.

Slow on the leash,
        pallid the leash-men!

The River-Merchant's Wife: A Letter

While my hair was still cut straight across my forehead
I played about the front gate, pulling flowers.
You came by on bamboo stilts, playing horse,
You walked about my seat, playing with blue plums.
And we went on living in the village of Chokan:
Two small people, without dislike or suspicion.
At fourteen I married My Lord you.
I never laughed, being bashful.
Lowering my head, I looked at the wall.
Called to, a thousand times, I never looked back.

At fifteen I stopped scowling,
I desired my dust to be mingled with yours
For ever and for ever and for ever.
Why should I climb the look out?

At sixteen you departed,
You went into far Ku-to-yen, by the river of swirling eddies,
And you have been gone five months.
The monkeys make sorrowful noise overhead.

You dragged your feet when you went out.
By the gate now, the moss is grown, the different mosses,
Too deep to clear them away!
The leaves fall early this autumn, in wind.
The paired butterflies are already yellow with August
Over the grass in the West garden;
They hurt me. I grow older.
If you are coming down through the narrows of the river Kiang
Please let me know beforehand,
And I will come out to meet you
As far as Cho-fu-Sa.

By Rihaku

Dance Figure

For the Marriage in Cana of Galilee

Dark eyed,
O woman of my dreams,
Ivory sandalled,
There is none like thee among the dancers,
None with swift feet.

I have not found thee in the tents,
In the broken darkness.
I have not found thee at the well-head
Among the women with pitchers.

Thine arms are as a young sapling under the bark;
Thy face as a river with lights.

White as an almond are thy shoulders;
As new almonds stripped from the husk.

They guard thee not with eunuchs;
Not with bars of copper.

Gilt turquoise and silver are in the place of thy rest.
A brown robe, with threads of gold woven in patterns, hast thou
gathered about thee,
O Nathat-Ikanaie, 'Tree-at-the-river.'

As a rillet among the sedge are thy hands upon me;
Thy fingers a frosted stream.

Thy maidens are white like pebbles;
Their music about thee!

There is none like thee among the dancers;
None with swift feet.

Ité

Go, my songs, seek your praise from the young and from the
intolerant,
Move among the lovers of perfection alone.
Seek ever to stand in the hard Sophoclean light
And take your wounds from it gladly.

Lament of the Frontier Guard

By the North Gate, the wind blows full of sand,
Lonely from the beginning of time until now!
Trees fall, the grass goes yellow with autumn.
I climb the towers and towers
to watch out the barbarous land:
Desolate castle, the sky, the wide desert.
There is no wall left to this village.
Bones white with a thousand frosts,
High heaps, covered with trees and grass;

Who brought this to pass?
Who has brought the flaming imperial anger?
Who has brought the army with drums and with kettle-drums?
Barbarous kings.
A gracious spring, turned to blood-ravenous autumn,
A turmoil of wars-men, spread over the middle kingdom,
Three hundred and sixty thousand,
And sorrow sorrow like rain.
Sorrow to go, and sorrow, sorrow returning.
Desolate, desolate fields,
And no children of warfare upon them,
        No longer the men for offence and defence.
Ah, how shall you know the dreary sorrow at the North Gate,
With Rihaku's name forgotten,
And we guardsmen fed to the tigers.

By Rihaku

Taking Leave of a Friend

Blue mountains to the north of the walls,
White river winding about them;
Here we must make separation
And go out through a thousand miles of dead grass.

Mind like a floating wide cloud,
Sunset like the parting of old acquaintances
Who bow over their clasped hands at a distance.
Our horses neigh to each other
        as we are departing.

By Rihaku

ALFRED KREYMBORG

Arabs

Melancholy lieth dolorously ill,
One heel full fatally smitten:
Melancholy twitcheth and sigheth:
"Must such as I, because of an itch,
Move from the cheery sloth of a couch,
From watching my valorous nomad musings
Coming and passing like pilgrims en route
From mooning philosophy on to the sun—
Must such as I, almost ready to follow them,
Legs follow musings as sheep follow bells—
Must such as I, because of a scratch
Imprinted by small ignominious teeth
Of a small, black, common, effeminate witch,
Surely not one of my bidding—*move?*
What way is this, God, to make a man move?"
And his bed-fellow,
Happiness, petrified, groaneth:
"What way is this, God, to make a man stone?"

Nun Snow

A Pantomime of Beads

Earth Voice

Is she
Thoughtless of life,
A lover of imminent death,
Nun Snow
Touching her strings of white beads?

Is it her unseen hands
Which urge the beads to tremble?
Does Nun Snow,
Aware of the death she must die alone,
Away from the nuns
Of the green beads,
Of the ochre and brown,
Of the purple and black—
Does she improvise
Along those soundless strings
In the worldly hope
That the answering, friendly tune,
The faithful, folk-like miracle,
Will shine in a moment or two?

Moon Voice

Or peradventure,
Are the beads merely wayward,
On an evening so soft,
And One Wind
Is so gentle a mesmerist
As he draws them and her with his hand?

Earth Voice

Was it Full Moon,
Who contrives tales of this order,
And himself loves the heroine,
Nun Snow—

Wind Voice

Do you see his beads courting hers?—
Lascivious monk!—

Earth Voice

Was it Full Moon,
Slyly innocent of guile,
Propounder of sorrowless whimseys,
Who breathed that suspicion?
Is it One Wind,

The wily, scholarly pedant—
Is it he who retorts—

Wind Voice

Like olden allegros
In olden sonatas,
All tales have two themes,
She is beautiful,
He is beautiful,
With the traditional movement,
Their beads court each other,
Revealing a cadence as fatally true
As the sum which follows a one-plus-one—
So, why inquire further?
Nay, inquire further,
Deduce it your fashion!
Nun Snow,
As you say,
Touches her strings of white beads.
Full Moon,
Let you add,
His lute of yellow strings;
And, our Night
Is square, nay,
Our Night
Is round, nay
Our Night
Is a blue balcony—
And therewith close your inquisition!

Earth Voice

Who urged the beads to tremble?
They're still now!
Fallen, or cast over me!
Nun, Moon, and Wind are gone!
Are they betraying her?—

Moon Voice

Ask our Night—

Earth Voice

Did the miracle appear?—

Moon Voice

Ask our Night,
Merely a child on a balcony,
Letting down her hair and
Black beads, a glissando—
Ask her what she means,
Dropping the curtain so soon!

JOHN GOULD FLETCHER

Irradiations

I

The spattering of the rain upon pale terraces
Of afternoon is like the passing of a dream
Amid the roses shuddering 'gainst the wet green stalks
Of the streaming trees—the passing of the wind
Upon the pale lower terraces of my dream
Is like the crinkling of the wet grey robes
Of the hours that come to turn over the urn
Of the day and spill its rainy dream.
Vague movement over the puddled terraces:
Heavy gold pennons—a pomp of solemn gardens
Half hidden under the liquid veil of spring:
Far trumpets like a vague rout of faded roses
Burst 'gainst the wet green silence of distant forests:
A clash of cymbals—then the swift swaying footsteps
Of the wind that undulates along the languid terraces.
Pools of rain—the vacant terraces

Wet, chill and glistening
Towards the sunset beyond the broken doors of to-day.

II

The iridescent vibrations of midsummer light
Dancing, dancing, suddenly flickering and quivering
Like little feet or the movement of quick hands clapping,
Or the rustle of furbelows or the clash of polished gems.
The palpitant mosaic of the midday light
Colliding, sliding, leaping and lingering:
O, I could lie on my back all day,
And mark the mad ballet of the midsummer sky.

III

Over the roof-tops race the shadows of clouds;
Like horses the shadows of clouds charge down the street.

Whirlpools of purple and gold,
Winds from the mountains of cinnabar,
Lacquered mandarin moments, palanquins swaying and balanc-
    ing
Amid the vermilion pavilions, against the jade balustrades.
Glint of the glittering wings of dragon-flies in the light:
Silver filaments, golden flakes settling downwards,
Rippling, quivering flutters, repulse and surrender,
The sun broidered upon the rain,
The rain rustling with the sun.

Over the roof-tops race the shadows of clouds;
Like horses the shadows of clouds charge down the street.

IV

The balancing of gaudy broad pavilions
Of summer against the insolent breeze:
The bellying of the sides of striped tents,

Swelling taut, shuddering in quick collapse,
Silent under the silence of the sky.

Earth is streaked and spotted
With great splashes and dapples of sunlight:
The sun throws an immense circle of hot light upon the world,
Rolling slowly in ponderous rhythm
Darkly, musically forward.
All is silent under the steep cone of afternoon:
The sky is imperturbably profound.
The ultimate divine union seems about to be accomplished,
All is troubled at the attainment
Of the inexhaustible infinite.
The rolling and the tossing of the sides of immense pavilions
Under the whirling wind that screams up the cloudless sky.

V

Flickering of incessant rain
On flashing pavements:
Sudden scurry of umbrellas:
Bending, recurved blossoms of the storm.

The winds came clanging and clattering
From long white highroads whipping in ribbons up summits:
They strew upon the city gusty wafts of apple-blossom,
And the rustling of innumerable translucent leaves.
Uneven tinkling, the lazy rain
Dripping from the eaves.

VI

The fountain blows its breathless spray
From me to you and back to me.

Whipped, tossed, curdled,
Crashing, quivering:
I hurl kisses like blows upon your lips.
The dance of a bee drunken with sunlight:

Irradiant ecstasies, white and gold,
Sigh and relapse.

The fountain tosses pallid spray
Far in the sorrowful, silent sky.

VII

The trees, like great jade elephants,
Chained, stamp and shake 'neath the gadflies of the breeze;
The trees lunge and plunge, unruly elephants:
The clouds are their crimson howdah-canopies,
The sunlight glints like the golden robe of a Shah.
Would I were tossed on the wrinkled backs of those trees.

VIII

Brown bed of earth, still fresh and warm with love,
Now hold me tight:
Broad field of sky, where the clouds laughing move,
Fill up my pores with light:
You trees, now talk to me, chatter and scold or weep,
Or drowsing stand:
You winds, now play with me, you wild things creep,
You boulders, bruise my hand!
I now am yours and you are mine: it matters not
What gods herein I see:
You grow in me, I am rooted to this spot,
We drink and pass the cup, immortally.

IX

O seeded grass, you army of little men
Crawling up the long slope with quivering, quick blades of steel:
You who storm millions of graves, tiny green tentacles of earth,
Interlace yourselves tightly over my heart,
And do not let me go:
For I would lie here forever and watch with one eye
The pilgrimaging ants in your dull, savage jungles,

The while with the other I see the stiff lines of the slope
Break in mid-air, a wave surprisingly arrested,
And above them, wavering, dancing, bodiless, colourless, unreal,
The long thin lazy fingers of the heat.

X

To-day you shall have but little song from me,
For I belong to the sunlight.
This I would not barter for any kingdom.
I am a wheeling swallow,
Blue all over is my delight.
I am a drowsy grass-blade
In the greenest shadow.

Blue Symphony

I

The darkness rolls upward.
The thick darkness carries with it
Rain and a ravel of cloud.
The sun comes forth upon earth.

Palely the dawn
Leaves me facing timidly
Old gardens sunken:
And in the walks is water.

Sombre wreck—autumnal leaves;
Shadowy roofs
In the blue mist,
And a willow-branch that is broken.

Oh, old pagodas of my soul, how you glittered across green trees!
Blue and cool:
Blue, tremulously,
Blow faint puffs of smoke

Across sombre pools.
The damp green smell of rotted wood;
And a heron that cries from out the water.

II

Through the upland meadows
I go alone.
For I dreamed of someone last night
Who is waiting for me.

Flower and blossom, tell me, do you know of her?

Have the rocks hidden her voice?
They are very blue and still.

Long upward road that is leading me,
Light hearted I quit you,
For the long loose ripples of the meadow-grass
Invite me to dance upon them.

Quivering grass
Daintily poised
For her foot's tripping.
Oh, blown clouds, could I only race up like you,
Oh, the last slopes that are sun-drenched and steep!

Look, the sky!
Across black valleys
Rise blue-white aloft
Jagged unwrinkled mountains, ranges of death.

Solitude. Silence.

III

One chuckles by the brook for me:
One rages under the stone.

One makes a spout of his mouth.
One whispers—one is gone.

One over there on the water
Spreads cold ripples
For me
Enticingly.
The vast dark trees
Flow like blue veils
Of tears
Into the water.
Sour sprites,
Moaning and chuckling,
What have you hidden from me?

"In the palace of the blue stone she lies forever
Bound hand and foot."

Was it the wind
That rattled the reeds together?
Dry reeds,
A faint shiver in the grasses.

IV

On the left hand there is a temple:
And a palace on the right-hand side.
Foot passengers in scarlet
Pass over the glittering tide.

Under the bridge
The old river flows
Low and monotonous
Day after day.

I have heard and have seen
All the news that has been:
Autumn's gold and Spring's green!

Now in my place
I see foot passengers
Crossing the river:
Pilgrims of autumn
In the afternoons.
Lotus pools:
Petals in the water.
These are my dreams.

For me silks are outspread.
I take my ease, unthinking.

V

And now the lowest pine-branch
Is drawn across the disc of the sun.
Old friends who will forget me soon,
I must go on,
Towards those blue death-mountains
I have forgot so long.

In the marsh grasses
There lies forever
My last treasure,
With the hopes of my heart.
The ice is glazing over,
Torn lanterns flutter,
On the leaves is snow.
In the frosty evening
Toll the old bell for me
Once, in the sleepy temple.

Perhaps my soul will hear.

Afterglow:
Before the stars peep
I shall creep out into darkness.

H. D.

At Baia

I should have thought
In a dream you would have brought
Some lovely perilous thing,
Orchids piled in a great sheath,
As who would say (in a dream)
I send you this,
Who left the blue veins
Of your throat unkissed.

Why was it that your hands
(That never took mine)
Your hands that I could see
Drift over the orchid heads
So carefully,
Your hands, so fragile, sure to lift
So gently, the fragile flower stuff—
Ah, ah, how was it

You never sent (in a dream)
The very form, the very scent,
Not heavy, not sensuous,
But perilous—perilous—
Of orchids, piled in a great sheath,
And folded underneath on a bright scroll
Some word:

Flower sent to flower;
For white hands, the lesser white,
Less lovely of flower leaf,

Or

Lover to lover, no kiss,
No touch, but forever and ever this.

Not Honey

Not honey,
Not the plunder of the bee
From meadow or sand-flower
Or mountain bush;
From winter-flower or shoot
Born of the later heat:
Not honey, not the sweet
Stain on the lips and teeth:
Not honey, not the deep
Plunge of soft belly
And the clinging of the gold-edged
Pollen-dusted feet.

Not so—
Though rapture blind my eyes,
And hunger crisp
Dark and inert my mouth,
Not honey, not the south,
Not the tall stalk
Of red twin-lilies,
Nor light branch of fruit tree
Caught in flexible light branch.

Not honey, not the south;
Ah, flower of purple iris,
Flower of white,
Or of the iris, withering the grass—
For fleck of the sun's fire,
Gathers such heat and power,
That shadow-print is light,

Cast through the petals
Of the yellow iris flower.

Not iris—old desire—old passion—
Old forgetfulness—old pain—
Not this, nor any flower,
But if you turn again,
Seek strength of arm and throat,
Touch as the god:
Neglect the lyre-note;
Knowing that you shall feel,
About the frame,
No trembling of the string
But heat more passionate
Of bone and the white shell
And fiery tempered steel.

Song

You are as gold
As the half-ripe grain
That merges to gold again,
As white as the white rain
That beats through
The half-opened flowers
Of the great flower tufts
Thick on the black limbs
Of an Illyrian apple bough.

Can honey distil such fragrance
As your bright hair—
For your face is as fair as rain,
Yet as rain that lies clear
On white honey-comb,
Lends radiance to the white wax,
So your hair on your brow
Casts light for a shadow.

The Garden

I

You are clear,
O rose, cut in rock.

I could scrape the colour
From the petals,
Like spilt dye from a rock.
If I could break you
I could break a tree.

If I could stir
I could break a tree,
I could break you.

II

O wind, rend open the heat,
Cut apart the heat,
Slit it to tatters.

Fruit cannot drop
Through this thick air;
Fruit cannot fall into heat
That presses up and blunts
The points of pears,
And rounds grapes.

Cut the heat;
Plough through it,
Turning it on either side
Of your path.

MARIANNE MOORE

England

With its baby rivers and little towns, each with its abbey or its cathedral;
with voices—one voice perhaps, echoing through the transept—the
criterion of suitability and convenience: and Italy with its equal
shores—contriving an epicureanism from which the grossness has been

extracted: and Greece with its goats and its gourds, the nest of modified illusions:
and France, the "chrysalis of the nocturnal butterfly" in
whose products, mystery of construction diverts one from what was originally one's
object—substance at the core: and the East with its snails, its emotional

shorthand and jade cockroaches, its rock crystal and its imperturbability,
all of museum quality: and America where there
is the little old ramshackle victoria in the south, where cigars are smoked on the
street in the north; where there are no proof readers, no silkworms, no digressions;

the wild man's land; grass-less, links-less, language-less country —in which letters are written
not in Spanish, not in Greek, not in Latin, not in shorthand,
but in plain American which cats and dogs can read! The letter "a" in psalm and calm when

pronounced with the sound of "a" in candle, is very noticeable but

why should continents of misapprehension have to be accounted for by the
fact? Does it follow that because there are poisonous toadstools
which resemble mushrooms, both are dangerous? In the case of mettlesomeness which may be
mistaken for appetite, of heat which may appear to be haste, no con-

clusions may be drawn. To have misapprehended the matter, is to have confessed
that one has not looked far enough. The sublimated wisdom
of China, Egyptian discernment, the cataclysmic torrent of emotion compressed
in the verbs of the Hebrew language, the books of the man who is able

to say, "I envy nobody but him and him only, who catches more fish than
I do,"—the flower and fruit of all that noted superi-
ority—should one not have stumbled upon it in America, must one imagine
that it is not there? It has never been confined to one locality.

The Mind Is an Enchanting Thing

is an enchanted thing
like the glaze on a
katydid-wing
subdivided by sun
till the nettings are legion.
Like Gieseking playing Scarlatti;
like the apteryx-awl
as a beak, or the
kiwi's rain-shawl

of haired feathers, the mind
feeling its way as though blind,
walks along with its eyes on the ground.

It has memory's ear
that can hear without
having to hear.
Like the gyroscope's fall,
truly unequivocal
because trued by regnant certainty,

it is a power of
strong enchantment. It
is like the dove-
neck animated by
sun; it is memory's eye;
it's conscientious inconsistency.

It tears off the veil; tears
the temptation, the
mist the heart wears,
from its eyes,—if the heart
has a face; it takes apart
dejection. It's fire in the dove-neck's

iridescence; in the
inconsistencies
of Scarlatti.
Unconfusion submits
its confusion to proof; it's
not a Herod's oath that cannot change.

Part of a Novel, Part of a Poem, Part of a Play

THE STEEPLE-JACK

Dürer would have seen a reason for living
in a town like this, with eight stranded whales
to look at; with the sweet sea air coming into your house
on a fine day, from water etched
with waves as formal as the scales
on a fish.

One by one, in two's, in three's, the seagulls keep
flying back and forth over the town clock,
or sailing around the lighthouse without moving the wings—
rising steadily with a slight
quiver of the body—or flock
mewing where

a sea the purple of the peacock's neck is
paled to greenish azure as Dürer changed
the pine green of the Tyrol to peacock blue and guinea
grey. You can see a twenty-five-
pound lobster; and fishnets arranged
to dry. The

whirlwind fife-and-drum of the storm bends the salt
marsh grass, disturbs stars in the sky and the
star on the steeple; it is a privilege to see so
much confusion. Disguised by what
might seem austerity, the sea-
side flowers and

trees are favoured by the fog so that you have
the tropics at first hand: the trumpet-vine,
fox-glove, giant snap-dragon, a salpiglossis that has

spots and stripes; morning-glories, gourds,
    or moon-vines trained on fishing-twine
at the back

door. There are no banyans, frangipani, nor
    jack-fruit trees; nor an exotic serpent
life. Ring lizard and snake-skin for the foot, or crocodile;
but here they've cats, not cobras, to
    keep down the rats. The diffident
little newt

with white pin-dots on black horizontal spaced
    out bands lives here; yet there is nothing that
ambition can buy or take away. The college student
named Ambrose sits on the hill-side
    with his not-native books and hat
and sees boats

at sea progress white and rigid as if in
    a groove. Liking an elegance of which
the source is not bravado, he knows by heart the antique
sugar-bowl-shaped summer-house of
    interlacing slats, and the pitch
of the church

spire, not true, from which a man in scarlet lets
    down a rope as a spider spins a thread;
he might be part of a novel, but on the sidewalk a
sign says C. J. Poole, Steeple Jack,
    in black and white; and one in red
and white says

Danger. The church portico has four fluted
    columns, each a single piece of stone, made
modester by white-wash. This would be a fit haven for
waifs, children, animals, prisoners,
    and presidents who have repaid
sin-driven

senators by not thinking about them. There
are a school-house, a post-office in a
store, fish-houses, hen-houses, a three-masted schooner on
the stocks. The hero, the student,
the steeple-jack, each in his way,
is at home.

It could not be dangerous to be living
in a town like this, of simple people,
who have a steeple-jack placing danger signs by the church
while he is gilding the solid-
pointed star, which on a steeple
stands for hope.

THE HERO

Where there is personal liking we go.
Where the ground is sour; where there are
weeds of beanstalk height,
snakes' hypodermic teeth, or
the wind brings the 'scarebabe voice'
from the neglected yew set with
the semi-precious cat's eyes of the owl—
awake, asleep, 'raised ears extended to fine points', and so
on—love won't grow.

We do not like some things, and the hero
doesn't; deviating head-stones
and uncertainty;
going where one does not wish
to go; suffering and not
saying so; standing and listening where something
is hiding. The hero shrinks
as what it is flies out on muffled wings, with twin yellow
eyes—to and fro—

with quavering water-whistle note, low,
high, in basso-falsetto chirps
until the skin creeps.

Jacob when a-dying, asked
Joseph: Who are these? and blessed
both sons, the younger most, vexing Joseph. And
Joseph was vexing to some.
Cincinnatus was; Regulus; and some of our fellow
men have been, though

devout, like Pilgrim having to go slow
to find his roll; tired but hopeful—
hope not being hope
until all ground for hope has
vanished; and lenient, looking
upon a fellow creature's error with the
feelings of a mother—a
woman or a cat. The decorous frock-coated Negro
by the grotto

answers the fearless sightseeing hobo
who asks the man she's with, what's this,
what's that, where's Martha
buried, 'Gen-ral Washington
there; his lady, here'; speaking
as if in a play—not seeing her; with a
sense of human dignity
and reverence for mystery, standing like the shadow
of the willow.

Moses would not be grandson to Pharaoh.
It is not what I eat that is
my natural meat,
the hero says. He's not out
seeing a sight but the rock
crystal thing to see—the startling El Greco
brimming with inner light—that
covets nothing that it has let go. This then you may know
as the hero.

The Monkeys

Winked too much and were afraid of snakes. The zebras, supreme in
their abnormality; the elephants with their fog-coloured skin
and strictly practical appendages
were there, the small cats; and the parakeet—
trivial and humdrum on examination, destroying
bark and portions of the food it could not eat.

I recall their magnificence, now not more magnificent
that it is dim. It is difficult to recall the ornament,
speech, and precise manner of what one might
call the minor acquaintances twenty
years back; but I shall not forget him—that Gilgamesh among
the hairy carnivora—that cat with the

wedge-shaped, slate-gray marks on its forelegs and the resolute tail,
astringently remarking, 'They have imposed on us with their pale
half-fledged protestations, trembling about
in inarticulate frenzy, saying
it is not for us to understand art; finding it
all so difficult, examining the thing

as if it were inconceivably arcanic, as symmet-
rically frigid as if it has been carved out of chrysoprase
or marble—strict with tension, malignant
in its power over us and deeper
than the sea when it proffers flattery in exchange for hemp,
rye, flax, horses, platinum, timber, and fur.'

The Fish

Wade
  through black jade.
Of the crow-blue mussell-shells, one keeps
adjusting the ash-heaps:
  opening and shutting itself like

an
injured fan.
  The barnacles which encrust the side
  of the wave, cannot hide
    there for the submerged shafts of the

sun,
split like spun
  glass, move themselves with spotlight swiftness
  into the crevices—
    in and out, illuminating

the
turquoise sea
  of bodies. The water drives a wedge
  of iron through the iron edge
    of the cliff; whereupon the stars,

pink
rice-grains, ink
  bespattered jelly-fish, crabs like green
  lilies, and submarine
    toadstools, slide each on the other.

All
external
  marks of abuse are present on this
  defiant edifice—
    all the physical features of

ac-
cident—lack
of cornice, dynamite grooves, burns, and
hatchet strokes, these things stand
out on it; the chasm-side is

dead.
Repeated
evidence has proved that it can live
on what cannot revive
its youth. The sea grows old in it.

Poetry

I, too, dislike it: there are things that are important beyond all this fiddle.
Reading it, however, with a perfect contempt for it, one discovers in
it after all, a place for the genuine.
Hands that can grasp, eyes
that can dilate, hair that can rise
if it must, these things are important not because a

high-sounding interpretation can be put upon them but because they are
useful. When they become so derivative as to become unintelligible,
the same thing may be said for all of us, that we
do not admire what
we cannot understand: the bat
holding on upside down or in quest of something to

eat, elephants pushing, a wild horse taking a roll, a tireless wolf under
a tree, the immovable critic twitching his skin like a horse that feels a flea, the base-
ball fan, the statistician—

nor is it valid
to discriminate against 'business documents and

school-books'; all these phenomena are important. One must make a distinction
however: when dragged into prominence by half poets, the result is not poetry,
nor till the poets among us can be
'literalists of
the imagination'—above
insolence and triviality and can present

for inspection, imaginary gardens with real toads in them, shall we have
it. In the meantime, if you demand on the one hand,
the raw material of poetry in
all its rawness and
that which is on the other hand
genuine, then you are interested in poetry.

His Shield

The pin-swin or spine-swine
(the edgehog miscalled hedgehog) with
all his edges out,
echidna and echinoderm in distressed-
pincushion thorn-fur coats,
the spiny pig or porcupine,
the rhino with horned snout,—
everything is battle-dressed.

Pig-fur won't do, I'll wrap
myself in salamander-skin
like Presbyter John.
A lizard in the midst of flames, a firebrand
that is life, asbestos-

eyed asbestos-eared with tattooed nap
and permanent pig on
the instep; he can withstand

fire and won't drown. In his
unconquerable country of
unpompous gusto,
gold was so common none considered it; greed
and flattery were
unknown. Though rubies large as tennis-
balls conjoined in streams so
that the mountain seemed to bleed,

the inextinguishable
salamander styled himself but
presbyter. His shield
was his humility. In Carpasian
linen coat, flanked by his
household lion-cubs and sable
retinue, he revealed
a formula safer than

an armorer's: the power of relinquishing
what one would keep; that is freedom.
Become dinosaur-
skulled, quilled or salamander-wooled, more ironshod
and javelin-dressed than
a hedgehog battalion of steel; but be
dull. Don't be envied or
armed with a measuring-rod.

ROBINSON JEFFERS

Continent's End

At the equinox when the earth was veiled in a late rain,
 wreathed with wet poppies, waiting spring,
The ocean swelled for a far storm and beat its boundary, the
 ground-swell shook the beds of granite.

I gazing at the boundaries of granite and spray, the established
 sea-marks, felt behind me
Mountain and plain, the immense breadth of the continent, be-
 fore me the mass and doubled stretch of water.

I said: You yoke the Aleutian seal-rocks with the lava and coral
 sowings that flower the south,
Over your flood the life that sought the sunrise faces ours that
 has followed the evening star.

The long migrations meet across you and it is nothing to you,
 you have forgotten us, mother.
You were much younger when we crawled out of the womb and
 lay in the sun's eye on the tideline.

It was long and long ago; we have grown proud since then and
 you have grown bitter; life retains
Your mobile soft unquiet strength; and envies hardness, the
 insolent quietness of stone.

The tides are in our veins, we still mirror the stars, life is your
 child, but there is in me
Older and harder than life and more impartial, the eye that
 watched before there was an ocean.

That watched you fill your beds out of the condensation of thin vapor and watched you change them,
That saw you soft and violent wear your boundaries down, eat rock, shift places with the continents.

Mother, though my song's measure is like your surf-beat's ancient rhythm I never learned it of you.
Before there was any water there were tides of fire, both our tones flow from the older fountain.

Birds

The fierce musical cries of a couple of sparrow hawks hunting on the headland,
Hovering and darting, their heads northwestward,
Prick like silver arrows shot through a curtain the noise of the ocean
Trampling its granite; their red backs gleam
Under my window around the stone corners; nothing gracefuller, nothing
Nimbler in the wind. Westward the wave-gleaners,
The old gray sea-going gulls are gathered together, the northwest wind wakening
Their wings to the wild spirals of the wind-dance.
Fresh as the air, salt as the foam, play birds in the bright wind, fly falcons
Forgetting the oak and the pinewood, come gulls
From the Carmel sands and the sands at the river-mouth, from Lobos and out of the limitless
Power of the mass of the sea, for a poem
Needs multitude, multitudes of thoughts, all fierce, all flesh-eaters, musically clamorous
Bright hawks that hover and dart headlong, and ungainly
Gray hungers fledged with desire of transgression, salt slimed beaks, from the sharp
Rock-shores of the world and the secret waters.

Love the Wild Swan

"I hate my verses, every line, every word.
Oh pale and brittle pencils ever to try
One grass-blade's curve, or the throat of one bird
That clings to twig, ruffled against white sky.
Oh cracked and twilight mirrors ever to catch
One color, one glinting flash, of the splendor of things.
Unlucky hunter, Oh bullets of wax,
The lion beauty, the wild-swan wings, the storm of the wings."
—This wild swan of a world is no hunter's game.
Better bullets than yours would miss the white breast,
Better mirrors than yours would crack in the flame.
Does it matter whether you hate your . . . self? At least
Love your eyes that can see, your mind that can
Hear the music, the thunder of the wings. Love the wild swan.

Apology for Bad Dreams

I

In the purple light, heavy with redwood, the slopes drop seaward,
Headlong convexities of forest, drawn in together to the steep ravine. Below, on the sea-cliff,
A lonely clearing; a little field of corn by the streamside; a roof under spared trees. Then the ocean
Like a great stone someone has cut to a sharp edge and polished to shining. Beyond it, the fountain
And furnace of incredible light flowing up from the sunk sun.
In the little clearing a woman
Is punishing a horse; she had tied the halter to a sapling at the edge of the wood, but when the great whip
Clung to the flanks the creature kicked so hard she feared he would snap the halter; she called from the house
The young man her son; who fetched a chain tie-rope, they working together

Noosed the small rusty links round the horse's tongue
And tied him by the swollen tongue to the tree.
Seen from this height they are shrunk to insect size.
Out of all human relation. You cannot distinguish
The blood dripping from where the chain is fastened,
The beast shuddering; but the thrust neck and the legs
Far apart. You can see the whip fall on the flanks . . .
The gesture of the arm. You cannot see the face of the woman.
The enormous light beats up out of the west across the cloud-bars of the trade-wind. The ocean
Darkens, the high clouds brighten, the hills darken together. Unbridled and unbelievable beauty
Covers the evening world . . . not covers, grows apparent out of it, as Venus down there grows out
From the lit sky. What said the prophet? "I create good: and I create evil: I am the Lord."

II

This coast crying out for tragedy like all beautiful places,
(The quiet ones ask for quieter suffering: but here the granite cliff the gaunt cypresses crown
Demands what victim? The dykes of red lava and black what Titan? The hills like pointed flames
Beyond Soberanes, the terrible peaks of the bare hills under the sun, what immolation?)
This coast crying out for tragedy like all beautiful places: and like the passionate spirit of humanity
Pain for its bread: God's, many victims', the painful deaths, the horrible transfigurements: I said in my heart,
"Better invent than suffer: imagine victims
Lest your own flesh be chosen the agonist, or you
Martyr some creature to the beauty of the place." And I said,
"Burn sacrifices once a year to magic
Horror away from the house, this little house here
You have built over the ocean with your own hands
Beside the standing boulders: for what are we,
The beast that walks upright, with speaking lips
And little hair, to think we should always be fed,

Sheltered, intact, and self-controlled? We sooner more liable
Than the other animals. Pain and terror, the insanities of desire; not accidents but essential,
And crowd up from the core:" I imagined victims for those wolves, I made them phantoms to follow,
They have hunted the phantoms and missed the house. It is not good to forget over what gulfs the spirit
Of the beauty of humanity, the petal of a lost flower blown seaward by the night-wind, floats to its quietness.

III

Boulders blunted like an old bear's teeth break up from the headland; below them
All the soil is thick with shells, the tide-rock feasts of a dead people.
Here the granite flanks are scarred with ancient fire, the ghosts of the tribe
Crouch in the nights beside the ghost of a fire, they try to remember the sunlight,
Light has died out of their skies. These have paid something for the future
Luck of the country, while we living keep old griefs in memory, though God's
Envy is not a likely fountain of ruin, to forget evils calls down
Sudden reminders from the cloud: remembered deaths be our redeemers;
Imagined victims our salvation: white as the half moon at midnight
Someone flamelike passed me, saying, "I am Tamar Cauldwell, I have my desire,"
Then the voice of the sea returned, when she had gone by, the stars to their towers.
. . . Beautiful country burn again, Point Pinos down to the Sur Rivers
Burn as before with bitter wonders, land and ocean and the Carmel water.

IV

He brays humanity in a mortar to bring the savor
From the bruised root: a man having bad dreams, who invents victims, is only the ape of that God.
He washes it out with tears and many waters, calcines it with fire in the red crucible,
Deforms it, makes it horrible to itself: the spirit flies out and stands naked, he sees the spirit,
He takes it in the naked ecstasy; it breaks in his hand, the atom is broken, the power that massed it
Cries to the power that moves the stars, "I have come home to myself, behold me.
I bruised myself in the flint mortar and burnt me
In the red shell, I tortured myself, I flew forth,
Stood naked of myself and broke me in fragments,
And here am I moving the stars that are me."
I have seen these ways of God: I know of no reason
For fire and change and torture and the old returnings.
He being sufficient might be still. I think they admit no reason; they are the ways of my love.
Unmeasured power, incredible passion, enormous craft: no thought apparent but burns darkly
Smothered with its own smoke in the human brain-vault: no thought outside: a certain measure in phenomena:
The fountains of the boiling stars, the flowers on the foreland, the ever-returning roses of dawn.

T. S. ELIOT

The Love Song of J. Alfred Prufrock

S'io credesse che mia risposta fosse
A persona che mai tornasse al mondo,

Questa fiamma staria senza piu scosse.
Ma perciocche giammai di questo fondo
Non torno vivo alcun, s'i'odo il vero,
Senza tema d'infamia ti rispondo.

Let us go then, you and I,
When the evening is spread out against the sky
Like a patient etherized upon a table;
Let us go, through certain half-deserted streets,
The muttering retreats
Of restless nights in one-night cheap hotels
And sawdust restaurants with oyster-shells:
Streets that follow like a tedious argument
Of insidious intent
To lead you to an overwhelming question. . . .
Oh, do not ask, "What is it?"
Let us go and make our visit.
In the room the women come and go
Talking of Michelangelo.
The yellow fog that rubs its back upon the window-panes,
The yellow smoke that rubs its muzzle on the window-panes,
Licked its tongue into the corners of the evening,
Lingered upon the pools that stand in drains,
Let fall upon its back the soot that falls from chimneys,
Slipped by the terrace, made a sudden leap,
And seeing that it was a soft October night,
Curled once about the house, and fell asleep.

And indeed there will be time
For the yellow smoke that slides along the street,
Rubbing its back upon the window-panes;
There will be time, there will be time
To prepare a face to meet the faces that you meet;
There will be time to murder and create,
And time for all the works and days of hands
That lift and drop a question on your plate;
Time for you and time for me,
And time yet for a hundred indecisions,

And for a hundred visions and revisions,
Before the taking of a toast and tea.
In the room the women come and go
Talking of Michelangelo.
And indeed there will be time
To wonder, "Do I dare?" and, "Do I dare?"
Time to turn back and descend the stair,
With a bald spot in the middle of my hair—
(They will say: "How his hair is growing thin!")
My morning coat, my collar mounting firmly to the chin,
My necktie rich and modest, but asserted by a simple pin—
(They will say: "But how his arms and legs are thin!")
Do I dare
Disturb the universe?
In a minute there is time
For decisions and revisions which a minute will reverse.

For I have known them all already, known them all:
Have known the evenings, mornings, afternoons,
I have measured out my life with coffee spoons;
I know the voices dying with a dying fall
Beneath the music from a farther room.
    So how should I presume?

And I have known the eyes already, known them all—
The eyes that fix you in a formulated phrase,
And when I am formulated, sprawling on a pin,
When I am pinned and wriggling on the wall,
Then how should I begin
To spit out all the butt-ends of my days and ways?
    And how should I presume?

And I have known the arms already, known them all—
Arms that are braceleted and white and bare
(But in the lamplight, downed with light brown hair!)
Is it perfume from a dress
That makes me so digress?

Arms that lie along a table, or wrap about a shawl.
  And should I then presume?
  And how should I begin?

. . . . .

Shall I say, I have gone at dusk through narrow streets
And watched the smoke that rises from the pipes
Of lonely men in shirt-sleeves, leaning out of windows? . . .
I should have been a pair of ragged claws
Scuttling across the floors of silent seas.

. . . . .

And the afternoon, the evening, sleeps so peacefully!
Smoothed by long fingers,
Asleep . . . tired . . . or it malingers,
Stretched on the floor, here beside you and me.
Should I, after tea and cakes and ices,
Have the strength to force the moment to its crisis?
But though I have wept and fasted, wept and prayed,
Though I have seen my head (grown slightly bald) brought in upon a platter,
I am no prophet—and here's no great matter;
I have seen the moment of my greatness flicker,
And I have seen the eternal Footman hold my coat, and snicker,
And in short, I was afraid.

And would it have been worth it, after all,
After the cups, the marmalade, the tea,
Among the porcelain, among some talk of you and me,
Would it have been worth while,
To have bitten off the matter with a smile,
To have squeezed the universe into a ball
To roll it toward some overwhelming question,
To say: "I am Lazarus, come from the dead,
Come back to tell you all, I shall tell you all"—
If one, settling a pillow by her head,
  Should say: "That was not what I meant at all;
  That is not it, at all."

And would it have been worth it, after all,
Would it have been worth while,
After the sunsets and the dooryards and the sprinkled streets,
After the novels, after the teacups, after the skirts that trail along
  the floor—
And this, and so much more?—
It is impossible to say just what I mean!
But as if a magic lantern threw the nerves in patterns on a screen:
Would it have been worth while
If one, settling a pillow or throwing off a shawl,
And turning toward the window, should say:
  "That is not it at all,
  That is not what I meant at all."

. . . . .

No! I am not Prince Hamlet, nor was meant to be;
Am an attendant lord, one that will do
To swell a progress, start a scene or two,
Advise the prince; no doubt, an easy tool,
Deferential, glad to be of use,
Politic, cautious, and meticulous;
Full of high sentence, but a bit obtuse;
At times, indeed, almost ridiculous—
Almost, at times, the Fool.

I grow old . . . I grow old . . .
I shall wear the bottoms of my trousers rolled.

Shall I part my hair behind? Do I dare to eat a peach?
I shall wear white flannel trousers, and walk upon the beach.
I have heard the mermaids singing, each to each.
I do not think that they will sing to me.

I have seen them riding seaward on the waves
Combing the white hair of the waves blown back
When the wind blows the water white and black.
We have lingered in the chambers of the sea
By sea-girls wreathed with seaweed red and brown
Till human voices wake us, and we drown.

Portrait of a Lady

Thou hast committed—
Fornication: but that was in another country,
And besides, the wench is dead.
"The Jew of Malta."

I

Among the smoke and fog of a December afternoon
You have the scene arrange itself—as it will seem to do—
With "I have saved this afternoon for you";
And four wax candles in the darkened room,
Four rings of light upon the ceiling overhead,
An atmosphere of Juliet's tomb
Prepared for all the things to be said, or left unsaid.
We have been, let us say, to hear the latest Pole
Transmit the Preludes, through his hair and finger-tips.
"So intimate, this Chopin, that I think his soul
Should be resurrected only among friends
Some two or three, who will not touch the bloom
That is rubbed and questioned in the concert room."
—And so the conversation slips
Among velleities and carefully caught regrets
Mingled with remote cornets
And begins.

"You do not know how much they mean to me, my friends,
And how, how rare and strange it is, to find
In a life composed so much, so much of odds and ends,
(For indeed I do not love it . . . you knew? you are not blind.
How keen you are!)
To find a friend who has these qualities,
Who has, and gives
Those qualities upon which friendship lives.
How much it means that I say this to you—
Without these friendships—life, what *cauchemar!*"

Among the windings of the violins
And the ariettes
Of cracked cornets
Inside my brain a dull tom-tom begins
Absurdly hammering a prelude of its own,
Capricious monotone
That is at least one definite "false note."
—Let us take the air, in a tobacco trance,
Admire the monuments,
Discuss the late events,
Correct our watches by the public clocks,
Then sit for half an hour and drink our bocks.

II

Now that lilacs are in bloom
She has a bowl of lilacs in her room
And twists one in her fingers while she talks.
"Ah, my friend, you do not know, you do not know
What life is, you who hold it in your hands";
(Slowly twisting the lilac stalks)
"You let it flow from you, you let it flow,
And youth is cruel, and has no remorse
And smiles at situations which it cannot see."
I smile, of course,
And go on drinking tea.
"Yet with these April sunsets, that somehow recall
My buried life, and Paris in the Spring,
I feel immeasurably at peace, and find the world
To be wonderful and youthful, after all."

The voice returns like the insistent out-of-tune
Of a broken violin on an August afternoon:
"I am always sure that you understand
My feelings, always sure that you feel,
Sure that across the gulf you reach your hand.
You are invulnerable, you have no Achilles' heel.
You will go on, and when you have prevailed
You can say: at this point many a one has failed.

But what have I, but what have I, my friend,
To give you, what can you receive from me?
Only the friendship and the sympathy
Of one about to reach her journey's end.
I shall sit here, serving tea to friends . . ."

I take my hat: how can I make a cowardly amends
For what she has said to me?

You will see me any morning in the park
Reading the comics and the sporting page.
Particularly I remark
An English countess goes upon the stage.
A Greek was murdered at a Polish dance,
Another bank defaulter has confessed.
I keep my countenance,
I remain self-possessed
Except when a street piano, mechanical and tired
Reiterates some worn-out common song
With the smell of hyacinths across the garden
Recalling things that other people have desired.
Are these ideas right or wrong?

III

The October night comes down; returning as before,
Except for a slight sensation of being ill at ease,
I mount the stairs and turn the handle of the door
And feel as if I had mounted on my hands and knees.

"And so you are going abroad; and when do you return?
But that's a useless question.
You hardly know when you are coming back,
You will find so much to learn."
My smile falls heavily among the bric-à-brac.
"Perhaps you can write to me."
My self-possession flares up for a second;
This is as I had reckoned.
"I have been wondering frequently of late

(But our beginnings never know our ends)
Why we have not developed into friends."
I feel like one who smiles, and turning shall remark
Suddenly, his expression in a glass.
My self-possession gutters; we are really in the dark.

"For everybody said so, all our friends,
They were all sure our feelings would relate
So closely! I myself can hardly understand.
We must leave it now to fate.
You will write at any rate.
Perhaps it is not too late.
I shall sit here, serving tea to friends."

And I must borrow every changing shape
To find expression . . . dance, dance
Like a dancing bear,
Cry like a parrot, chatter like an ape.
Let us take the air, in a tobacco trance—

Well! and what if she should die some afternoon,
Afternoon grey and smoky, evening yellow and rose;
Should die and leave me sitting pen in hand
With the smoke coming down above the housetops;
Doubtful, for quite a while
Not knowing what to feel or if I understand
Or whether wise or foolish, tardy or too soon . . .
Would she not have the advantage, after all?
This music is successful, with a "dying fall"
Now that we talk of dying—
And should I have the right to smile?

Sweeney Among the Nightingales

ὤμοι πέπληγμαι καιρίαν πληγὴν ἔσω.

Why should I speak of the nightingale? The nightingale sings of adulterous wrong.

Apeneck Sweeney spreads his knees
Letting his arms hang down to laugh,
The zebra stripes along his jaw
Swelling to maculate giraffe.

The circles of the stormy moon
Slide westward to the River Plate,
Death and the Raven drift above
And Sweeney guards the hornèd gate.

Gloomy Orion and the Dog
Are veiled; and hushed the shrunken seas;
The person in the Spanish cape
Tries to sit on Sweeney's knees

Slips and pulls the table cloth
Overturns a coffee cup,
Reorganized upon the floor
She yawns and draws a stocking up;

The silent man in mocha brown
Sprawls at the window-sill and gapes;
The waiter brings in oranges
Bananas, figs and hot-house grapes;

The silent vertebrate exhales,
Contracts and concentrates, withdraws;
Rachel *née* Rabinovitch
Tears at the grapes with murderous paws;

She and the lady in the cape
Are suspect, thought to be in league;
Therefore the man with heavy eyes
Declines the gambit, shows fatigue,

Leaves the room and reappears
Outside the window, leaning in,
Branches of wistaria
Circumscribe a golden grin;

The host with someone indistinct
Converses at the door apart,
The nightingales are singing near
The Convent of the Sacred Heart,

And sang within the bloody wood
When Agamemnon cried aloud,
And let their liquid siftings fall
To stain the stiff dishonoured shroud.

Whispers of Immortality

Webster was much possessed by death
And saw the skull beneath the skin;
And breastless creatures underground
Leaned backward with a lipless grin.

Daffodil bulbs instead of balls
Stared from the sockets of the eyes!
He knew that thought clings round dead limbs
Tightening its lusts and luxuries.

Donne, I suppose, was such another
Who found no substitute for sense
To seize and clutch and penetrate,
Expert beyond experience.

He knew the anguish of the marrow
The ague of the skeleton;

No contact possible to flesh
Allayed the fever of the bone.

. . . .

Grishkin is nice; her Russian eye
Is underlined for emphasis;
Uncorseted, her friendly bust
Gives promise of pneumatic bliss.

The couched Brazilian jaguar
Compels the scampering marmoset
With subtle effluence of cat;
Grishkin has a maisonette:

The sleek and sinuous jaguar
Does not in his arboreal gloom
Distil so rank a feline smell
As Grishkin in a drawing-room

And even abstracter entities
Circumambulate her charm;
But our lot crawls between dry ribs
To keep its metaphysics warm.

Gerontion

Thou hast nor youth nor age
But as it were an after dinner sleep
Dreaming of both.

Here I am, an old man in a dry month,
Being read to by a boy, waiting for rain.
I was neither at the hot gates
Nor fought in the warm rain
Nor knee deep in the salt marsh, heaving a cutlass,
Bitten by flies, fought.
My house is a decayed house,

And the Jew squats on the window sill, the owner,
Spawned in some estaminet of Antwerp,
Blistered in Brussels, patched and peeled in London.
The goat coughs at night in the field overhead;
Rocks, moss, stonecrop, iron, merds.
The woman keeps the kitchen, makes tea,
Sneezes at evening, poking the peevish gutter.

I an old man,
A dull head among windy spaces.
Signs are taken for wonders. "We would see a sign!"
The word within a word, unable to speak a word,
Swaddled with darkness. In the juvescence of the year
Came Christ the tiger.

In depraved May, dogwood and chestnut, flowering judas,
To be eaten, to be divided, to be drunk
Among whispers; by Mr. Silvero
With caressing hands, at Limoges
Who walked all night in the next room;

By Hakagawa, bowing among the Titians;
By Madame de Tornquist, in the dark room
Shifting the candles; Fraulein von Kulp
Who turned in the hall, one hand on the door. Vacant shuttles
Weave the wind. I have no ghosts,
An old man in a draughty house
Under a windy knob.

After such knowledge, what forgiveness? Think now
History has many cunning passages, contrived corridors
And issues, deceives with whispering ambitions,
Guides us by vanities. Think now
She gives when our attention is distracted
And what she gives, gives with such supple confusions
That the giving famishes the craving. Gives too late
What's not believed in, or if still believed,
In memory only, reconsidered passion. Gives too soon
Into weak hands, what's thought can be dispensed with

Till the refusal propagates a fear. Think
Neither fear nor courage saves us. Unnatural vices
Are fathered by our heroism. Virtues
Are forced upon us by our impudent crimes.
These tears are shaken from the wrath-bearing tree.

The tiger springs in the new year. Us he devours. Think at last
We have not reached conclusion, when I
Stiffen in a rented house. Think at last
I have not made this show purposelessly
And it is not by any concitation
Of the backward devils.
I would meet you upon this honestly.
I that was near your heart was removed therefrom
To lose beauty in terror, terror in inquisition.
I have lost my passion: why should I need to keep it
Since what is kept must be adulterated?
I have lost my sight, smell, hearing, taste and touch:
How should I use it for your closer contact?

These with a thousand small deliberations
Protract the profit, of their chilled delirium,
Excite the membrane, when the sense has cooled,
With pungent sauces, multiply variety
In a wilderness of mirrors. What will the spider do,
Suspend its operations, will the weevil
Delay? De Bailhache, Fresca, Mrs. Cammell, whirled
Beyond the circuit of the shuddering Bear
In fractured atoms. Gull against the wind, in the windy straits
Of Belle Isle, or running on the Horn,
White feathers in the snow, the Gulf claims,
And an old man driven by the Trades
To a sleepy corner.

Tenants of the house,
Thoughts of a dry brain in a dry season.

The Hollow Men

A penny for the Old Guy.

I

We are the hollow men
We are the stuffed men
Leaning together
Headpiece filled with straw. Alas!
Our dried voices, when
We whisper together
Are quiet and meaningless
As wind and dry grass
Or rats' feet over broken glass
In our dry cellar

Shape without form, shade without colour,
Paralysed force, gesture without motion;

Those who have crossed
With direct eyes, to death's other Kingdom
Remember us—if at all—not as lost
Violent souls, but only
As the hollow men
The stuffed men.

II

Eyes I dare not meet in dreams
In death's dream kingdom
These do not appear:
There, the eyes are
Sunlight on a broken column
There, is a tree swinging
And voices are
In the wind's singing

More distant and more solemn
Than a fading star.

Let me be no nearer
In death's dream kingdom
Let me also wear
Such deliberate disguises
Rat's coat, crowskin, crossed staves
In a field
Behaving as the wind behaves
No nearer—
Not that final meeting
In the twilight kingdom

III

This is the dead land
This is cactus land
Here the stone images
Are raised, here they receive
The supplication of a dead man's hand
Under the twinkle of a fading star.

Is it like this
In death's other kingdom
Waking alone
At the hour when we are
Trembling with tenderness
Lips that would kiss
Form prayers to broken stone.

IV

The eyes are not here
There are no eyes here
In this valley of dying stars
In this hollow valley
This broken jaw of our lost kingdoms

In this last of meeting places
We grope together
And avoid speech
Gathered on this beach of the tumid river

Sightless, unless
The eyes reappear
As the perpetual star
Multifoliate rose
Of death's twilight kingdom
The hope only
Of empty men.

V

Here we go round the prickly pear
Prickly pear, prickly pear
Here we go round the prickly pear
At five o'clock in the morning.

Between the idea
And the reality
Between the motion
And the act
Falls the Shadow
        For Thine is the Kingdom.

Between the conception
And the creation
Between the emotion
And the response
Falls the Shadow
        Life is very long.

Between the desire
And the spasm
Between the potency
And the existence
Between the essence

And the descent
Falls the Shadow.
For Thine is the Kingdom.

For Thine is
Life is
For Thine is the

This is the way the world ends
This is the way the world ends
This is the way the world ends
Not with a bang but a whimper.

Animula

'Issues from the hand of God, the simple soul'
To a flat world of changing lights and noise,
To light, dark, dry or damp, chilly or warm;
Moving between the legs of tables and of chairs,
Rising or falling, grasping at kisses and toys,
Advancing boldly, sudden to take alarm,
Retreating to the corner of arm and knee,
Eager to be reassured, taking pleasure
In the fragrant brilliance of the Christmas tree,
Pleasure in the wind, the sunlight and the sea;
Studies the sunlit pattern on the floor
And running stags around a silver tray;
Confounds the actual and the fanciful,
Content with playing-cards and kings and queens,
What the fairies do and what the servants say.
The heavy burden of the growing soul
Perplexes and offends more, day by day;
Week by week, offends and perplexes more
With the imperatives of 'is and seems'
And may and may not, desire and control.
The pain of living and the drug of dreams
Curl up the small soul in the window seat
Behind the *Encyclopædia Britannica.*

Issues from the hand of time the simple soul
Irresolute and selfish, misshapen, lame,
Unable to fare forward or retreat,
Fearing the warm reality, the offered good,
Denying the importunity of the blood,
Shadow of its own shadows, spectre in its own gloom,
Leaving disordered papers in a dusty room;
Living first in the silence after the viaticum.

Pray for Guiterriez, avid of speed and power,
For Boudin, blown to pieces,
For this one who made a great fortune,
And that one who went his own way.
Pray for Floret, by the boarhound slain between the yew trees,
Pray for us now and at the hour of our birth.

Marina

Quis hic locus, quae regio, quae mundi plaga?

What seas what shores what grey rocks and what islands
What water lapping the bow
And scent of pine and the woodthrush singing through the fog
What images return
O my daughter.
Those who sharpen the tooth of the dog, meaning
Death
Those who glitter with the glory of the hummingbird, meaning
Death
Those who sit in the stye of contentment, meaning
Death
Those who suffer the ecstasy of the animals, meaning
Death

Are become unsubstantial, reduced by a wind,
A breath of pine, and the woodsong fog
By this grace dissolved in place

What is this face, less clear and clearer
The pulse in the arm, less strong and stronger—
Given or lent? more distant than stars and nearer than the eye

Whispers and small laughter between leaves and hurrying feet
Under sleep, where all the waters meet.

Bowsprit cracked with ice and paint cracked with heat.
I made this, I have forgotten
And remember.
The rigging weak and the canvas rotten
Between one June and another September.
Made this unknowing, half conscious, unknown, my own.
The garboard strake leaks, the seams need caulking.
This form, this face, this life
Living to live in a world of time beyond me; let me
Resign my life for this life, my speech for that unspoken,
The awakened, lips parted, the hope, the new ships.

What seas what shores what granite islands towards my timbers
And woodthrush calling through the fog
My daughter.

Ash-Wednesday

I

Because I do not hope to turn again
Because I do not hope
Because I do not hope to turn
Desiring this man's gift and that man's scope
I no longer strive to strive towards such things
(Why should the agèd eagle stretch its wings?)
Why should I mourn
The vanished power of the usual reign?

Because I do not hope to know again
The infirm glory of the positive hour

Because I do not think
Because I know I shall not know
The one veritable transitory power
Because I cannot drink
There, where trees flower, and springs flow, for there is nothing again

Because I know that time is always time
And place is always and only place
And what is actual is actual only for one time
And only for one place
I rejoice that things are as they are and
I renounce the blessèd face
And renounce the voice
Because I cannot hope to turn again
Consequently I rejoice, having to construct something
Upon which to rejoice

And pray to God to have mercy upon us
And I pray that I may forget
These matters that with myself I too much discuss
Too much explain
Because I do not hope to turn again
Let these words answer
For what is done, not to be done again
May the judgment not be too heavy upon us

Because these wings are no longer wings to fly
But merely vans to beat the air
The air which is now thoroughly small and dry
Smaller and dryer than the will
Teach us to care and not to care
Teach us to sit still.

Pray for us sinners now and at the hour of our death
Pray for us now and at the hour of our death.

II

Lady, three white leopards sat under a juniper-tree
In the cool of the day, having fed to satiety
On my legs my heart my liver and that which had been contained
In the hollow round of my skull. And God said
Shall these bones live? shall these
Bones live? And that which had been contained
In the bones (which were already dry) said chirping:
Because of the goodness of this Lady
And because of her loveliness, and because
She honours the Virgin in meditation,
We shine with brightness. And I who am here dissembled
Proffer my deeds to oblivion, and my love
To the posterity of the desert and the fruit of the gourd.
It is this which recovers
My guts the strings of my eyes and the indigestible portions
Which the leopards reject. The Lady is withdrawn
In a white gown, to contemplation, in a white gown.
Let the whiteness of bones atone to forgetfulness.
There is no life in them. As I am forgotten
And would be forgotten, so I would forget
Thus devoted, concentrated in purpose. And God said
Prophesy to the wind, to the wind only for only
The wind will listen. And the bones sang chirping
With the burden of the grasshopper, saying

Lady of silences
Calm and distressed
Torn and most whole
Rose of memory
Rose of forgetfulness
Exhausted and life-giving
Worried reposeful
The single Rose
Is now the Garden
Where all loves end
Terminate torment
Of love unsatisfied
The greater torment

Of love satisfied
End of the endless
Journey to no end
Conclusion of all that
Is inconclusible
Speech without word and
Word of no speech
Grace to the Mother
For the Garden
Where all love ends.

Under a juniper-tree the bones sang, scattered and shining
We are glad to be scattered, we did little good to each other,
Under a tree in the cool of the day, with the blessing of sand,
Forgetting themselves and each other, united
In the quiet of the desert. This is the land which ye
Shall divide by lot. And neither division nor unity
Matters. This is the land. We have our inheritance.

III

At the first turning of the second stair
I turned and saw below
The same shape twisted on the banister
Under the vapour in the fetid air
Struggling with the devil of the stairs who wears
The deceitful face of hope and of despair.

At the second turning of the second stair
I left them twisting, turning below;
There were no more faces and the stair was dark,
Damp, jaggèd, like an old man's mouth drivelling, beyond repair,
Or the toothed gullet of an agèd shark.

At the first turning of the third stair
Was a slotted window bellied like the fig's fruit
And beyond the hawthorn blossom and a pasture scene
The broadbacked figure drest in blue and green
Enchanted the maytime with an antique flute.

Blown hair is sweet, brown hair over the mouth blown,
Lilac and brown hair;
Distraction, music of the flute, stops and steps of the mind over
 the third stair,
Fading, fading; strength beyond hope and despair
Climbing the third stair.

Lord, I am not worthy
Lord, I am not worthy

 but speak the word only.

IV

Who walked between the violet and the violet
Who walked between
The various ranks of varied green
Going in white and blue, in Mary's colour,
Talking of trivial things
In ignorance and in knowledge of eternal dolour
Who moved among the others as they walked,
Who then made strong the fountains and made fresh the springs

Made cool the dry rock and made firm the sand
In blue of larkspur, blue of Mary's colour,
Sovegna vos
Here are the years that walk between, bearing
Away the fiddles and the flutes, restoring
One who moves in the time between sleep and waking, wearing

White light folded, sheathed about her, folded.
The new years walk, restoring
Through a bright cloud of tears, the years, restoring
With a new verse the ancient rhyme. Redeem
The time. Redeem
The unread vision in the higher dream
While jewelled unicorns draw by the gilded hearse.
The silent sister veiled in white and blue
Between the yews, behind the garden god,

Whose flute is breathless, bent her head and signed but spoke no
word

But the fountain sprang up and the bird sang down
Redeem the time, redeem the dream
The token of the word unheard, unspoken

Till the wind shake a thousand whispers from the yew

And after this our exile

V

If the lost word is lost, if the spent word is spent
If the unheard, unspoken
Word is unspoken, unheard;
Still is the unspoken word, the Word unheard,
The Word without a word, the Word within
The world and for the world;
And the light shone in darkness and
Against the Word the unstilled world still whirled
About the centre of the silent Word.

O my people, what have I done unto thee.

Where shall the word be found, where will the word
Resound? Not here, there is not enough silence
Not on the sea or on the islands, not
On the mainland, in the desert or the rain land,
For those who walk in darkness
Both in the day time and in the night time
The right time and the right place are not here
No place of grace for those who avoid the face
No time to rejoice for those who walk among noise and deny the
voice

Will the veiled sister pray for
Those who walk in darkness, who chose thee and oppose thee,
Those who are torn on the horn between season and season, time
and time, between

Hour and hour, word and word, power and power, those who
wait
In darkness? Will the veiled sister pray
For children at the gate
Who will not go away and cannot pray:
Pray for those who chose and oppose

O my people, what have I done unto thee.

Will the veiled sister between the slender
Yew trees pray for those who offend her
And are terrified and cannot surrender
And affirm before the world and deny between the rocks
In the last desert between the last blue rocks
The desert in the garden the garden in the desert
Of drouth, spitting from the mouth the withered apple-seed.

O my people.

VI

Although I do not hope to turn again
Although I do not hope
Although I do not hope to turn

Wavering between the profit and the loss
In this brief transit where the dreams cross
The dreamcrossed twilight between birth and dying
(Bless me father) though I do not wish to wish these things
From the wide window towards the granite shore
The white sails still fly seaward, seaward flying
Unbroken wings

And the lost heart stiffens and rejoices
In the lost lilac and the lost sea voices
And the weak spirit quickens to rebel
For the bent golden-rod and the lost sea smell
Quickens to recover
The cry of quail and the whirling plover
And the blind eye creates

The empty forms between the ivory gates
And smell renews the salt savour of the sandy earth

This is the time of tension between dying and birth
The place of solitude where three dreams cross
Between blue rocks
But when the voices shaken from the yew-tree drift away
Let the other yew be shaken and reply.

Blessèd sister, holy mother, spirit of the fountain, spirit of the garden,
Suffer us not to mock ourselves with falsehood
Teach us to care and not to care
Teach us to sit still
Even among these rocks,
Our peace in His will
And even among these rocks
Sister, mother
And spirit of the river, spirit of the sea,
Suffer me not to be separated

And let my cry come unto Thee.

Burnt Norton

τοῦ λόγου δ'ἐόντος ξυνοῦ ζώουσιν οἱ πολλοί ὡς ἰδίαν ἔχοντες φρόνησιν.

I. p. 77. Fr. 2.

ὁδὸς ἄνω κάτω μία καὶ ὡυτή.

I. p. 89. Fr. 60.

Diels: *Die Fragmente der Vorsokratiker* (Herakleitos).

I

Time present and time past
Are both perhaps present in time future,

And time future contained in time past.
If all time is eternally present
All time is unredeemable.
What might have been is an abstraction
Remaining a perpetual possibility
Only in a world of speculation.
What might have been and what has been
Point to one end, which is always present.
Footfalls echo in the memory
Down the passage which we did not take
Towards the door we never opened
Into the rose-garden. My words echo
Thus, in your mind.
                                        But to what purpose
Disturbing the dust on a bowl of rose-leaves
I do not know.
                                Other echoes
Inhabit the garden. Shall we follow?
Quick, said the bird, find them, find them,
Round the corner. Through the first gate,
Into our first world, shall we follow
The deception of the thrush? Into our first world.
There they were, dignified, invisible,
Moving without pressure, over the dead leaves,
In the autumn heat, through the vibrant air,
And the bird called, in response to
The unheard music hidden in the shrubbery,
And the unseen eyebeam crossed, for the roses
Had the look of flowers that are looked at.
There they were as our guests, accepted and accepting.
So we moved, and they, in a formal pattern,
Along the empty alley, into the box circle,
To look down into the drained pool.
Dry the pool, dry concrete, brown edged,
And the pool was filled with water out of sunlight,
And the lotos rose, quietly, quietly,
The surface glittered out of heart of light,
And they were behind us, reflected in the pool.
Then a cloud passed, and the pool was empty.

Go, said the bird, for the leaves were full of children,
Hidden excitedly, containing laughter.
Go, go, go, said the bird: human kind
Cannot bear very much reality.
Time past and time future
What might have been and what has been
Point to one end, which is always present.

II

Garlic and sapphires in the mud
Clot the bedded axle-tree.
The trilling wire in the blood
Sings below inveterate scars
And reconciles forgotten wars.
The dance along the artery
The circulation of the lymph
Are figured in the drift of stars
Ascend to summer in the tree
We move above the moving tree
In light upon the figured leaf
And hear upon the sodden floor
Below, the boarhound and the boar
Pursue their pattern as before
But reconciled among the stars.

At the still point of the turning world. Neither flesh nor fleshless;
Neither from nor towards; at the still point, there the dance is,
But neither arrest nor movement. And do not call it fixity.
Where past and future are gathered. Neither movement from nor towards,
Neither ascent nor decline. Except for the point, the still point,
There would be no dance, and there is only the dance.
I can only say, *there* we have been: but I cannot say where.
And I cannot say, how long, for that is to place it in time.

The inner freedom from the practical desire,
The release from action and suffering, release from the inner
And the outer compulsion, yet surrounded

By a grace of sense, a white light still and moving,
Erhebung without motion, concentration
Without elimination, both a new world
And the old made explicit, understood
In the completion of its partial ecstasy,
The resolution of its partial horror.
Yet the enchainment of past and future
Woven in the weakness of the changing body,
Protects mankind from heaven and damnation
Which flesh cannot endure.
Time past and time future
Allow but a little consciousness.
To be conscious is not to be in time
But only in time can the moment in the rose-garden,
The moment in the arbour where the rain beat,
The moment in the draughty church at smoke-fall
Be remembered; involved with past and future.
Only through time time is conquered.

III

Here is a place of disaffection
Time before and time after
In a dim light: neither daylight
Investing form with lucid stillness
Turning shadow into transient beauty
With slow rotation suggesting permanence
Nor darkness to purify the soul
Emptying the sensual with deprivation
Cleansing the affection from the temporal.
Neither plenitude nor vacancy. Only a flicker
Over the strained time-ridden faces
Distracted from distraction by distraction
Filled with fancies and empty of meaning
Tumid apathy with no concentration
Men and bits of paper, whirled by the cold wind
That blows before and after time,
Wind in and out of unwholesome lungs
Time before and time after.

Eructation of unhealthy souls
Into the faded air, the torpid
Driven on the wind that sweeps the gloomy hills of London,
Hampstead and Clerkenwell, Campden and Putney,
Highgate, Primrose and Ludgate. Not here
Not here the darkness, in this twittering world.

Descend lower, descend only
Into the world of perpetual solitude,
World not world, but that which is not world,
Internal darkness, deprivation
And destitution of all property,
Desiccation of the world of sense,
Evacuation of the world of fancy,
Inoperancy of the world of spirit;
This is the one way, and the other
Is the same, not in movement
But abstention from movement; while the world moves
In appetency, on its metalled ways
Of time past and time future.

IV

Time and the bell have buried the day,
The black cloud carries the sun away.
Will the sunflower turn to us, will the clematis
Stray down, bend to us; tendril and spray
Clutch and cling?
Chill
Fingers of yew be curled
Down on us? After the kingfisher's wing
Has answered light to light, and is silent, the light is still
At the still point of the turning world.

V

Words move, music moves
Only in time; but that which is only living
Can only die. Words, after speech, reach

Into the silence. Only by the form, the pattern,
Can words or music reach
The stillness, as a Chinese jar still
Moves perpetually in its stillness.
Not the stillness of the violin, while the note lasts,
Not that only, but the co-existence,
Or say that the end precedes the beginning,
And the end and the beginning were always there
Before the beginning and after the end.
And all is always now. Words strain,
Crack and sometimes break, under the burden,
Under the tension, slip, slide, perish,
Decay with imprecision, will not stay in place,
Will not stay still. Shrieking voices
Scolding, mocking, or merely chattering.
Always assail them. The Word in the desert
Is most attacked by voices of temptation,
The crying shadow in the funeral dance,
The loud lament of the disconsolate chimera.
The detail of the pattern is movement,
As in the figure of the ten stairs.
Desire itself is movement
Not in itself desirable;
Love is itself unmoving,
Only the cause and end of movement,
Timeless, and undesiring
Except in the aspect of time
Caught in the form of limitation
Between un-being and being.
Sudden in a shaft of sunlight
Even while the dust moves
There rises the hidden laughter
Of children in the foliage
Quick now, here, now, always—
Ridiculous the waste sad time
Stretching before and after.

JOHN CROWE RANSOM

Bells for John Whiteside's Daughter

There was such speed in her little body,
And such lightness in her footfall,
It is no wonder that her brown study
Astonishes us all.

Her wars were bruited in our high window.
We looked among orchard trees and beyond,
Where she took arms against her shadow,
Or harried unto the pond

The lazy geese, like a snow cloud
Dripping their snow on the green grass,
Tricking and stopping, sleepy and proud,
Who cried in goose, Alas,

For the tireless heart within the little
Lady with rod that made them rise
From their noon apple-dreams, and scuttle
Goose-fashion under the skies!

But now go the bells, and we are ready;
In one house we are sternly stopped
To say we are vexed at her brown study,
Lying so primly propped.

Lady Lost

This morning, there flew up the lane
A timid lady-bird to our bird-bath

And eyed her image dolefully as death;
This afternoon, knocked on our windowpane
To be let in from the rain.

And when I caught her eye
She looked aside, but at the clapping thunder
And sight of the whole earth blazing up like tinder
Looked in on us again most miserably,
Indeed as if she would cry.

So I will go out into the park and say,
"Who has lost a delicate brown-eyed lady
In the West End Section? Or has anybody
Injured some fine woman in some dark way,
Last night or yesterday?

"Let the owner come and claim possession,
No questions will be asked. But stroke her gently
With loving words, and she will evidently
Resume her full soft-haired white-breasted fashion,
And her right home and her right passion."

Blue Girls

Twirling your blue skirts, traveling the sward
Under the towers of your seminary,
Go listen to your teachers old and contrary
Without believing a word.

Tie the white fillets then about your lustrous hair
And think no more of what will come to pass
Than bluebirds that go walking on the grass
And chattering on the air.

Practice your beauty, blue girls, before it fail;
And I will cry with my loud lips and publish
Beauty which all our power shall never establish,
It is so frail.

For I could tell you a story which is true:
I know a lady with a terrible tongue,
Blear eyes fallen from blue,
All her perfections tarnished—and yet it is not long
Since she was lovelier than any of you.

Here Lies a Lady

Here lies a lady of beauty and high degree.
Of chills and fever she died, of fever and chills,
The delight of her husband, her aunts, an infant of three,
And of medicos marveling sweetly on her ills.

For either she burned, and her confident eyes would blaze,
And her fingers fly in a manner to puzzle their heads—
What was she making? Why, nothing; she sat in a maze
Of old scraps of laces, snipped into curious shreds—

Or this would pass, and the light of her fire decline
Till she lay discouraged and cold as a thin stalk white and blown,
And would not open her eyes, to kisses, to wine.
The sixth of these states was her last; the cold settled down.

Sweet ladies, long may ye bloom, and toughly I hope ye may thole,
But was she not lucky? In flowers and lace and mourning,
In love and great honor we bade God rest her soul
After six little spaces of chill, and six of burning.

Captain Carpenter

Captain Carpenter rose up in his prime
Put on his pistols and went riding out
But had got well nigh nowhere at that time
Till he fell in with ladies in a rout.

It was a pretty lady and all her train
That played with him so sweetly but before

An hour she'd taken a sword with all her main
And twined him of his nose for evermore.

Captain Carpenter mounted up one day
And rode straight way into a stranger rogue
That looked unchristian but be that as it may
The Captain did not wait upon prologue.

But drew upon him out of his great heart
The other swung against him with a club
And cracked his two legs at the shinny part
And let him roll and stick like any tub.

Captain Carpenter rode many a time
From male and female took he sundry harms
He met the wife of Satan crying "I'm
The she-wolf bids you shall bear no more arms."

Their strokes and counters whistled in the wind
I wish he had delivered half his blows
But where she should have made off like a hind
The bitch bit off his arms at the elbows.

And Captain Carpenter parted with his ears
To a black devil that used him in this wise
O jesus ere his threescore and ten years
Another had plucked out his sweet blue eyes.

Captain Carpenter got up on his roan
And sallied from the gate in hell's despite
I heard him asking in the grimmest tone
If any enemy yet there was to fight?

"To any adversary it is fame
If he risk to be wounded by my tongue
Or burnt in two beneath my red heart's flame
Such are the perils he is cast among.

"But if he can he has a pretty choice
From an anatomy with little to lose

Whether he cut my tongue and take my voice
Or whether it be my round red heart he choose."

It was the neatest knave that ever was seen
Stepping in perfume from his lady's bower
Who at this word put in his merry mien
And fell on Captain Carpenter like a tower.

I would not knock old fellows in the dust
But there lay Captain Carpenter on his back
His weapons were the old heart in his bust
And a blade shook between rotten teeth alack.

The rogue in scarlet and gray soon knew his mind
He wished to get his trophy and depart;
With gentle apology and touch refined
He pierced him and produced the Captain's heart.

God's mercy rest on Captain Carpenter now
I thought him Sirs an honest gentleman
Citizen husband soldier and scholar enow
Let jangling kites eat of him if they can.

But God's deep curses follow after those
That shore him of his goodly nose and ears
His legs and strong arms at the two elbows
And eyes that had not watered seventy years.

The curse of hell upon the sleek upstart
Who got the Captain finally on his back
And took the red vitals of his heart
And made the kites to whet their beaks clack clack.

Husband Betrayed

And so he called her Pigeon,
Saying to himself, "She flutters walking

And in sweet monotone she twitters talking."
Nothing was said of her religion.

There was wood-wildness in her,—say a dove,
For doves are pigeons not domesticated
And whoso catches one is soon frustrated,
Expecting quick return of love.

At all events she had a snowy bosom
And trod so mincingly that you would say
She only wanted wings to fly away,
Easy and light and lissome.

She pecked her food with ravished cries,
She sunned her bosom by the wall in the morning,
Preening prettily in the sun and turning
In her birdwise.

But there was heavy dudgeon
When he that should have married him a woman
To sit and drudge and serve him as was common
Discovered he had wived a pigeon.

Little Boy Blue

He rubbed his eyes and wound the silver horn.
Then the continuum was cracked and torn
With tumbling imps of music being born.

The blowzy sheep lethargic on the ground
Suddenly burned where no fire could be found
And straight up stood their fleeces every pound.

The old bellwether rose and rang his bell,
The seven-days' lambs went skipping and skipped well,
And Baa Baa Baa, the flock careered pellmell.

The yellow cows that milked the savoury cud
Propped on the green grass or the yellow mud
Felt such a tingle in their lady blood,

They ran and tossed their hooves and horns of blue
And jumped the fence and gambolled kangaroo,
Divinely singing as they wandered Moo.

A plague on such a shepherd of the sheep
That careless boy with pretty cows to keep!
With such a burden I should never sleep.

But when his notes had run around the sky,
When they proceeded to grow faint and die,
He stuffed his horn with straw and put it by.

And when the legs were tired beneath the sheep
And there were spent and sleepy cows to keep,
He rubbed his eyes again and went to sleep.

CONRAD AIKEN

Preludes to Attitude

I

Two coffees in the Español, the last
Bright drops of golden Barsac in a goblet,
Fig paste and candied nuts. . . . Hardy is dead,
And James and Conrad dead, and Shakspere dead,
And old Moore ripens for an obscene grave,
And Yeats for an arid one; and I, and you—
What winding sheet for us, what boards and bricks,
What mummeries, candles, prayers, and pious frauds?

You shall be lapped in Syrian scarlet, woman,
And wear your pearls, and your bright bracelets, too,
Your agate ring, and round your neck shall hang
Your dark blue lapis with its specks of gold.
And I, beside you—ah! but will that be?
For there are dark streams in this dark world, lady,
Gulf Streams and Arctic currents of the soul;
And I may be, before our consummation
Beds us together, cheek by jowl, in earth,
Swept to another shore, where my white bones
Will lie unhonored, or defiled by gulls.

What dignity can death bestow on us,
Who kiss beneath a streetlamp, or hold hands
Half hidden in a taxi or replete
With coffee, figs and Barsac make our way
To a dark bedroom in a wormworn house?
The aspidistra guards the door; we enter,
Per aspidistra—then ad astra—is it?—
And lock ourselves securely in our gloom
And loose ourselves from terror. . . . Here's my hand,
The white scar on my thumb, and here's my mouth
To stop your murmur; speechless let us lie,
And think of Hardy, Shakspere, Yeats and James;
Comfort our panic hearts with magic names;
Stare at the ceiling, where the taxi lamps
Make ghosts of light; and see, beyond this bed,
That other bed in which we will not move;
And, whether joined or separate, will not love.

II

Sleep: and between the closed eyelids of sleep,
From the dark spirit's still unresting grief,
The one tear burns its way. O God, O God,
What monstrous world is this, whence no escape
Even in sleep? Between the fast-shut lids
This one tear comes, hangs on the lashes, falls:
Symbol of some gigantic dream, that shakes

The secret-sleeping soul. . . . And I descend
By a green cliff that fronts the worldlong sea;
Disastrous shore; where bones of ships and rocks
Are mixed; and beating waves bring in the sails
Of unskilled mariners, ill-starred. The gulls
Fall in a cloud upon foul flotsam there;
The air resounds with cries of scavengers.

Dream: and between the close-locked lids of dream
The terrible infinite intrudes its blue:
Ice: silence: death: the abyss of Nothing.
O God, O God, let the sore soul have peace.
Deliver it from this bondage of harsh dreams.
Release this shadow from its object, this object
From its shadow. Let the fleet soul go nimbly,—
Down,—down,—from step to step of dark,—
From dark to deeper dark, from dark to rest.
And let no Theseus-thread of memory
Shine in that labyrinth, or on those stairs,
To guide her back; nor bring her, where she lies,
Remembrance of a torn world well forgot.

III

—You went to the verge, you say, and came back safely?
Some have not been so fortunate,—some have fallen.
Children go lightly there, from crag to crag,
And coign to coign,—where even the goat is wary,—
And make sport of it. . . . They fling down pebbles,
Following, with eyes undizzied, the long curve,
The long slow outward curve, into the abyss,
As far as eye can follow; and they themselves
Turn back, unworried, to the here and now. . . .
But you have been there, too?—

—I saw at length
The space-defying pine, that on the last
Outjutting rock has cramped its powerful roots.
There stood I too: under that tree I stood:

My hand against its resinous bark: my face
Turned out and downward to the fourfold kingdom.
The wind roared from all quarters. The waterfall
Came down, it seemed, from Heaven. The mighty sound
Of pouring elements,—earth, air, and water,—
The cry of eagles, chatter of falling stones,—
These were the frightful language of that place.
I understood it ill, but understood.—

—You understood it? Tell me, then, its meaning.
It was an all, a nothing, or a something?
Chaos, or divine love, or emptiness?
Water and earth and air and the sun's fire?
Or else, a question simply?—

—Water and fire were there,
And air and earth; there too was emptiness;
All, and nothing, and something too, and love.
But these poor words, these squeaks of ours, in which
We strive to mimic, with strained throats and tongues,
The spawning and outrageous elements—
Alas, how paltry are they! For I saw—
—What did you see?

—I saw myself and God.
I saw the ruin in which godhead lives:
Shapeless and vast: the strewn wreck of the world:
Sadness unplumbed: misery without bound.
Wailing I heard, but also I heard joy.
Wreckage I saw, but also I saw flowers.
Hatred I saw, but also I saw love. . . .
And thus, I saw myself.

—And this alone?

—And this alone awaits you, when you dare
To that sheer verge where horror hangs, and tremble
Against the falling rock; and, looking down,
Search the dark kingdom. It is to self you come,—

And that is God. It is the seed of seeds:
Seed for disastrous and immortal worlds.

It is the answer that no question asked.

IV

Winter for a moment takes the mind; the snow
Falls past the arclight; icicles guard a wall;
The wind moans through a crack in the window;
A keen sparkle of frost is on the sill.
Only for a moment; as spring too might engage it,
With a single crocus in the loam, or a pair of birds;
Or summer with hot grass; or autumn with a yellow leaf.
Winter is there, outside, is here in me:
Drapes the planets with snow, deepens the ice on the moon,
Darkens the darkness that was already darkness.
The mind too has its snows, its slippery paths,
Walls bayonetted with ice, leaves ice-encased,
Here is the in-drawn room, to which you return
When the wind blows from Arcturus: here is the fire
At which you warm your hands and glaze your eyes;
The piano, on which you touch the cold treble;
Five notes like breaking icicles; and then silence.

The alarm-clock ticks, the pulse keeps time with it,
Night and the mind are full of sounds. I walk
From the fire-place, with its imaginary fire,
To the window, with its imaginary view.
Darkness, and snow ticking the window: silence,
And the knocking of chains on a motor-car, the tolling
Of a bronze bell, dedicated to Christ.
And then the uprush of angelic wings, the beating
Of wings demonic, from the abyss of the mind:
The darkness filled with a feathery whistling, wings
Numberless as the flakes of angelic snow,
The deep void swarming with wings and sound of wings,
The winnowing of chaos, the aliveness
Of depth and depth and depth dedicated to death.

Here are the bickerings of the inconsequential,
The chatterings of the ridiculous, the iterations
Of the meaningless. Memory, like a juggler,
Tosses its colored balls into the light, and again
Receives them into darkness. Here is the absurd,
Grinning like an idiot, and the omnivorous quotidian,
Which will have its day. A handful of coins,
Tickets, items from the news, a soiled handkerchief,
A letter to be answered, notice of a telephone call,
The petal of a flower in a volume of Shakspere,
The program of a concert. The photograph, too,
Propped on the mantel, and beneath it a dry rosebud;
The laundry bill, matches, an ash-tray, Utamaro's
Pearl-fishers. And the rug, on which are still the crumbs
Of yesterday's feast. These are the void, the night,
And the angelic wings that make it sound.

What is the flower? It is not a sigh of color,
Suspiration of purple, sibilation of saffron,
Nor aureate exhalation from the tomb.
Yet it is these because you think of these,
An emanation of emanations, fragile
As light, or glisten, or gleam, or coruscation,
Creature of brightness, and as brightness brief.
What is the frost? It is not the sparkle of death,
The flash of time's wing, seeds of eternity;
Yet it is these because you think of these.
And you, because you think of these, are both
Frost and flower, the bright ambiguous syllable
Of which the meaning is both no and yes.

Here is the tragic, the distorting mirror
In which your gesture becomes grandiose;
Tears form and fall from your magnificent eyes,
The brow is noble, and the mouth is God's.
Here is the God who seeks his mother, Chaos,—
Confusion seeking solution, and life seeking death.
Here is the rose that woos the icicle; the icicle
That woos the rose. Here is the silence of silences

Which dreams of becoming a sound, and the sound
Which will perfect itself in silence. And all
These things are only the uprush from the void,
The wings angelic and demonic, the sound of the abyss
Dedicated to death. And this is you.

V

Rimbaud and Verlaine, precious pair of poets,
Genius in both (but what is genius?) playing
Chess on a marble table at an inn
With chestnut blossom falling in blond beer
And on their hair and between knight and bishop—
Sunlight squared between them on the chess-board,
Cirrus in heaven, and a squeal of music
Blown from the leathern door of St. Sulpice—

Discussing, between moves, iamb and spondee
Anacoluthon and the open vowel
God the great peacock with his angel peacocks
And his dependent peacocks the bright stars:
Disputing too of fate as Plato loved it,
Or Sophocles, who hated and admired,
Or Socrates, who loved and was amused:

Verlaine puts down his pawn upon a leaf
And closes his long eyes, which are dishonest,
And says "Rimbaud, there is one thing to do:
We must take rhetoric, and wring its neck! . . ."
Rimbaud considers gravely, moves his Queen;
And then removes himself to Timbuctoo.

And Verlaine dead,—with all his jades and mauves;
And Rimbaud dead in Marseilles with a vision,
His leg cut off, as once before his heart;
And all reported by a later lackey,
Whose virtue is his tardiness in time.

Let us describe the evening as it is:—
The stars disposed in heaven as they are:

Verlaine and Shakspere rotting, where they rot,
Rimbaud remembered, and too soon forgot;

Order in all things, logic in the dark;
Arrangement in the atom and the spark;
Time in the heart and sequence in the brain—

Such as destroyed Rimbaud and fooled Verlaine.
And let us then take godhead by the neck—

And strangle it, and with it, rhetoric.

VI

So, in the evening, to the simple cloister:
This place of boughs, where sounds of water, softly,
Lap on the stones. And this is what you are:
Here, in this dusty room, to which you climb
By four steep flights of stairs. The door is closed:
The furies of the city howl behind you:
The last bell plunges rock-like to the sea:
The horns of taxis wail in vain. You come
Once more, at evening, to this simple cloister;
Hushed by the quiet walls, you stand at peace.

What ferns of thought are these, the cool and green,
Dripping with moisture, that festoon these walls?
What water-lights are these, whose pallid rings
Dance with the leaves, or speckle the pale stones?
What spring is this, that bubbles the cold sand,
Urging the sluggish grains of white and gold? . . .
Peace. The delicious silence throngs with ghosts
Of wingèd sound and shadow. These are you.

Now in the evening, in the simple cloister,
You stand and wait; you stand and listen, waiting
For wingèd sounds and wingèd silences,
And long-remembered shadows. Here the rock
Lets down its vine of many colored flowers:

Waiting for you, or waiting for the lizard
To move his lifted claw, or shift his eye
Quick as a jewel. Here the lizard waits
For the slow snake to slide among cold leaves.
And, on the bough that arches the deep pool,
Lapped in a sound of water, the brown thrush
Waits, too, and listens, till his silence makes
Silence as deep as song. And time becomes
A timeless crystal, an eternity,
In which the gone and coming are at peace.

What bird is this, whose silence fills the trees
With rich delight? What leaves and boughs are these,
What lizard, and what snake? . . . The bird is gone:
And while you wait, another comes and goes,—
Another and another; yet your eye,
Although it has not moved, can scarcely say
If birds have come and gone,—so quick, so brief,—
Or if the thrush who waits there is the same . . .
The snake and lizard change, yet are the same:
The flowers, many-colored, on the vine,
Open and close their multitude of stars,—
Yet are the same. . . . And all these things are you.

Thus in the evening, in the simple cloister,
Eternity adds ring to ring, the darker
Beyond the brighter; and your silence fills
With such a world of worlds,—so still, so deep,—
As never voice could speak, whether it were
The ocean's or the bird's. The night comes on:
You wait and listen, in the darkened room,
To all these ghosts of change. And they are you.

VII

Then came I to the shoreless shore of silence,
Where never summer was nor shade of tree,
Nor sound of water, nor sweet light of sun,

But only nothing and the shore of nothing,
Above, below, around, and in my heart:

Where day was not, nor night, nor space, nor time,
Where no bird sang, save him of memory,
Nor footstep marked upon the marl, to guide
My halting footstep; and I turned for terror,
Seeking in vain the Pole Star of my thought;

Where it was blown among the shapeless clouds,
And gone as soon as seen, and scarce recalled,
Its image lost and I directionless;
Alone upon the brown sad edge of chaos,
In the wan evening that was evening always;

Then closed my eyes upon the sea of nothing
While memory brought back a sea more bright,
With long, long waves of light, and the swift sun,
And the good trees that bowed upon the wind;
And stood until grown dizzy with that dream;

Seeking in all that joy of things remembered
One image, one the dearest, one most bright,
One face, one star, one daisy, one delight,
One hour with wings most heavenly and swift,
One hand the tenderest upon the heart;

But still no image came, save of that sea,
No tenderer thing than thought of tenderness,
No heart or daisy brighter than the rest;
And only sadness at the bright sea lost,
And mournfulness that all had not been praised.

O lords of chaos, atoms of desire,
Whirlwind of fruitfulness, destruction's seed,
Hear now upon the void my late delight,
The quick brief cry of memory, that knows
At the dark's edge how great the darkness is.

VIII

Beloved, let us once more praise the rain.
Let us discover some new alphabet,
For this, the often-praised; and be ourselves,
The rain, the chickweed, and the burdock leaf,
The green-white privet flower, the spotted stone,
And all that welcomes rain; the sparrow, too,—
Who watches with a hard eye, from seclusion,
Beneath the elm-tree bough, till rain is done.

There is an oriole who, upside down,
Hangs at his nest, and flicks an orange wing,—
Under a tree as dead and still as lead;
There is a single leaf, in all this heaven
Of leaves, which rain has loosened from its twig:
The stem breaks, and it falls, but it is caught
Upon a sister leaf, and thus she hangs;
There is an acorn cup, beside a mushroom,
Which catches three drops from the stooping cloud.

The timid bee goes back to hive; the fly
Under the broad leaf of the hollyhock
Perpends stupid with cold; the raindark snail
Surveys the wet world from a watery stone . . .
And still the syllables of water whisper:
The wheel of cloud whirs slowly: while we wait
In the dark room; and in your heart I find
One silver raindrop,—on a hawthorn leaf,—
Orion in a cobweb, and the World.

IX

Nothing to say, you say? Then we'll say nothing:
But step from rug to rug and hold our breaths,
Count the green ivy-strings against the window,
The pictures on the wall. Let us exchange
Pennies of gossip, news from nowhere, names
Held in despite or honor; we have seen

The weather-vanes veer westward, and the clouds
Obedient to the wind; have walked in snow;
Forgotten and remembered—

But we are strangers;
Came here by paths which never crossed; and stare
At the blind mystery of each to each.
You've seen the sea and mountains? taken ether?
And slept in hospitals from Rome to Cairo?
Why so have I; and lost my tonsils, too;
And drunk the waters of the absolute.
But is it this we meet for, of an evening,
Is it this—

O come, like Shelley,
For god's sake let us sit on honest ground
And tell harsh stories of the deaths of kings!
Have out our hearts, confess our blood,
Our foulness and our virtue! I have known
Such sunsets of despair as god himself
Might weep for of a Sunday; and then slept
As dreamlessly as Jesus in his tomb.
I have had time in one hand, space in the other,
And mixed them to no purpose. I have seen
More in a woman's eye than can be liked,
And less than can be known. And as for you—

O creature of the frost and sunlight, worm
Uplifted by the atom's joy, receiver
Of stolen goods, unconscious thief of god—
Tell me upon this sofa how you came
From darkness to this darkness, from what terror
You found this restless pause in terror, learned
The bitter light you follow. We will talk—

But it is time to go, and I must go;
And what we thought, and silenced, none shall know.

X

The first note, simple; the second note, distinct;
The third note, harsh; the fourth, an innuendo;
The fifth, a humble triad; and the sixth—
Suddenly—is the chord of chords, that breaks
The evening; and from evening calls the angel,
One voice divinely singing.

Thus, at random,
This coil of worlds in which we grope; and thus
Our comings and our goings. So the twilight
Deepens the hour from rose to purple; so
One bell-note is the death-note, and completes
The half-remembered with the soon-forgotten.
The threes and fives compute our day; we move
To doom with all things moving.

You and I
Are things compounded of time's heart-beats, stretching
The vascular instant from the vascular past;
You, with forgotten worlds, and I with worlds
Forgotten and remembered. Yet the leaf,
With all its bleeding veins, is not more torn
Than you are torn, this moment, from the last.
Can you rejoin it? Is it here, or there?
Where is that drop of blood you knew last year?
Where is that image which you loved, that frame
Of ghostly apparitions in your thought,
Alchemic mystery of your childhood, lost
With all its dizzy colors? . . . It is gone.
Only the echo's echo can be heard.
Thrice-mirrored, the ghost pales.

You plunge, poor soul,
From time's colossal brink into that chasm
Of change and limbo and immortal flux;
And bring up only, in your blood-stained hands,
One grain of sand that sparkles. Plunge again,

Poor diver, among weeds and death! and bring
The pearl of brightness up. It is this instant
When all is well with us: when hell and heaven
Arch in a chord of glory over madness;
When Pole Star sings to Sirius; and the wave
Of ultimate Ether breaks on ultimate Nothing.
The world's a rose which comes this night to flower:
This evening is its light. And it is we,
Who, with our harmonies and discords, woven
Of myriad things forgotten and remembered,
Urge the vast twilight to immortal bloom.

Preludes to Definition

I

And there I saw the seed upon the mountain
but it was not a seed it was a star
but it was not a star it was a world
but it was not a world it was a god
but it was not a god it was a laughter

blood red within and lightning for its rind
the root came out like gold and it was anger
the root came out like fire and it was fury
the root came out like horn and it was purpose
but it was not a root it was a hand

destructive strong and eager full of blood
and broke the rocks and set them on each other
and broke the waters into shafts of light
and set them end to end and made them seas
and out of laughter wrung a grief of water

and thus beneath the web of mind I saw
under the west and east of web I saw
under the bloodshot spawn of stars I saw
under the water and the inarticulate laughter
the coiling down the coiling in the coiling

mean and intense and furious and secret
profound and evil and despatched in darkness
shot homeward foully in a filth of effort
clotted and quick and thick and without aim
spasm of concentration of the sea

and there I saw the seed upon the shore
but it was not a seed it was a man
but it was not a man it was a god
magnificent and humble in the morning
with angels poised upon his either hand.

II

On that wild verge in the late light he stood,
the last one, who was alone, the naked one,
wingless unhappy one who had climbed there,
bruised foot and bruised hand,
first beholder of the indecipherable land,

the nameless land, the selfless land,
stood and beheld it from the granite cliff
the far beneath, the far beyond, the far above,
water and wind, the cry of the alone
his own the valley, his own the unthinking stone

and said—as I with labor have shaped this,
out of a cloud this world of rock and water,
as I have wrought with thought, or unthinking wrought,
so that a dream is brought
in agony and joy to such a realm as this

let now some god take also me and mould me
some vast and dreadful or divine dream hold me
and shape me suddenly beyond my purpose
beyond my power
to a new wilderness of hour

that I may be to him as this to me,
out of a cloud made shore and sea,

instant agony and then the splendid shape
in which is his escape,
myself at last only a well-made dream to be—

and as he spoke, his own divine dream took
sudden kingdom of the wide world, and broke
the orders into rainbows, the numbers down,
all things to nothing; and he himself became
a cloud, in which the lightning dreamed a name.

III

Still the same function, still the same habit come,
the endless algebra that marks the mind.
A leads to b and b to c; we wait
in vain for change. No sudden Clytemnestra
walks from the scene and with her takes the world—

or so the sentry said. And watched the moon
pull half the desert downward as she went,
involved in silvered trees and dunes and towers
shadows of spears and whatnot. Moons and moons—
all gone in one, and all the tides gone too,
salt blood, salt water. What's left but dark. What's left
but night, night which is function of the day;
or so the sentry said.

And saw his feet,
sandalled, and semi-prehensile, on the sand,
gripping the moonchilled sand and then releasing,
forward and back along the wall's foot, turning
under the fig-tree. Lately it had a shadow,
but now had none. And "a-prime" leads to "b-prime,"
build how you will. Nuisance, that there should be
no wildness left in nature—no chance of dicethrow
to change the world, or changed then change it back—
the two plus two makes eight—!

Clytemnestra
walked on the terrace when the moon had sunk,

and licked her little finger. Tasted blood.
Addressed herself: Woman, you've changed the world,
you should have been a man. And henceforth men—
use them, use them! Smiled, and walked in the dark,
and heard, below the wall, the sentry's cough.

IV

What without speech we knew and could not say
what without thought we did and could not change
violence of the hand which the mind thought strange
let us take these things into another world,
another dream

what without love we touched pronouncing good
what without touch we loved and gave no sign
violence of spirit which only spirit knew divine
let us take these things into another world,
another sleep

walk with me heliotrope fly with me sparrow
come beating of my heart and learn how life is narrow
how little, and ill, will be remembered by tomorrow
let us give our lives into another world
another hand

where like old rocks we shall be heaped forgetful;
or waste away like stars in fiery stillness;
no clock with mortal cry to speak our illness;
let us take our deaths into another time
another god

come girl, come golden-breasted girl, and walk
on the so silent and sun-sandalled path
between the foremath and the aftermath
let us hurl our joy into another chaos, another wrath
and make it love

what without speech we know we then shall say
and all our violence will there be gay

what without thought we do will be but play
and our unspoken love as bright as day
and we shall live.

EDNA ST. VINCENT MILLAY

On Hearing a Symphony of Beethoven

Sweet sounds, oh, beautiful music, do not cease!
Reject me not into the world again.
With you alone is excellence and peace,
Mankind made plausible, his purpose plain.
Enchanted in your air benign and shrewd,
With limbs a-sprawl and empty faces pale,
The spiteful and the stingy and the rude
Sleep like the scullions in the fairy-tale.
This moment is the best the world can give:
The tranquil blossom on the tortured stem.
Reject me not, sweet sounds; oh, let me live,
Till Doom espy my towers and scatter them,
A city spell-bound under the aging sun.
Music my rampart, and my only one.

What Lips My Lips Have Kissed

What lips my lips have kissed, and where, and why
I have forgotten, and what arms have lain
Under my head till morning; but the rain
Is full of ghosts tonight, that tap and sigh
Upon the glass and listen for reply;
And in my heart there stirs a quiet pain
For unremembered lads that not again
Will turn to me at midnight with a cry.

Thus in the winter stands the lonely tree,
Nor knows what birds have vanished one by one,
Yet knows its boughs more silent than before:
I cannot say what loves have come and gone;
I only know that summer sang in me
A little while, that in me sings no more.

Renascence

All I could see from where I stood
Was three long mountains and a wood;
I turned and looked another way,
And saw three islands in a bay.
So with my eyes I traced the line
Of the horizon, thin and fine,
Straight around till I was come
Back to where I started from;
And all I saw from where I stood
Was three long mountains and a wood.
Over these things I could not see;
These were the things that bounded me;
And I could touch them with my hand,—
Almost, I thought, from where I stand.
And all at once things seemed so small
My breath came short, and scarce at all.
But, sure, the sky is big, I said;
Miles and miles above my head;
So here upon my back I'll lie
And look my fill into the sky.
And so I looked, and, after all,
The sky was not so very tall.
The sky, I said, must somewhere stop,
And—sure enough!—I see the top.
The sky, I thought, is not so grand;
I 'most could touch it with my hand!
And, reaching up my hand to try,
I screamed to feel it touch the sky.
I screamed, and—lo!—Infinity

Came down and settled over me;
And, pressing of the Undefined
The definition on my mind,
Held up before my eyes a glass
Through which my shrinking sight did pass
Until it seemed I must behold
Immensity made manifold;
Whispered to me a word whose sound
Deafened the air for worlds around,
And brought unmuffled to my ears
The gossiping of friendly spheres,
The creaking of the tented sky,
The ticking of Eternity.

I saw and heard, and knew at last
The How and Why of all things, past,
And present, and forevermore.
The universe, cleft to the core,
Lay open to my probing sense
That, sick'ning, I would fain pluck thence
But could not—nay! But needs must suck
At the great wound, and could not pluck
My lips away till I had drawn
All venom out—Ah, fearful pawn!
For my omniscience paid I toll
In infinite remorse of soul.
All sin was of my sinning, all
Atoning mine, and mine the gall
Of all regret. Mine was the weight
Of every brooded wrong, the hate
That stood behind each envious thrust,
Mine every greed, mine every lust.
And all the while for every grief,
Each suffering, I craved relief
With individual desire—
Craved all in vain! And felt fierce fire
About a thousand people crawl;
Perished with each—then mourned for all!
A man was starving in Capri;

He moved his eyes and looked at me;
I felt his gaze, I heard his moan,
And knew his hunger as my own.
I saw at sea a great fog-bank
Between two ships that struck and sank;
A thousand screams the heavens smote;
And every scream tore through my throat.
No hurt I did not feel, no death
That was not mine; mine each last breath
That, crying, met an answering cry
From the compassion that was I.
All suffering mine, and mine its rod;
Mine, pity like the pity of God.
Ah, awful weight! Infinity
Pressed down upon the finite me!
My anguished spirit, like a bird,
Beating against my lips I heard;
Yet lay the weight so close about
There was no room for it without.
And so beneath the weight lay I
And suffered death, but could not die.

Deep in the earth I rested now;
Cool is its hand upon the brow
And soft its breast beneath the head
Of one who is so gladly dead.
And all at once, and over all,
The pitying rain began to fall;
I lay and heard each pattering hoof
Upon my lowly, thatchèd roof,
And seemed to love the sound far more
Than ever I had done before.
For rain it hath a friendly sound
To one who's six feet underground;
And scarce the friendly voice or face:
A grave is such a quiet place.

The rain, I said, is kind to come
And speak to me in my new home.

I would I were alive again
To kiss the fingers of the rain,
To drink into my eyes the shine
Of every slanting silver line,
To catch the freshened, fragrant breeze
From drenched and dripping apple-trees.
For soon the shower will be done,
And then the broad face of the sun
Will laugh above the rain-soaked earth
Until the world with answering mirth
Shakes joyously, and each round drop
Rolls, twinkling, from its grass-blade top,
How can I bear it; buried here,
While overhead the sky grows clear
And blue again after the storm?
O, multi-coloured, multiform,
Beloved beauty over me,
That I shall never, never see
Again! Spring-silver, autumn-gold
That I shall never more behold!
Sleeping your myriad magics through,
Close-sepulchred away from you!
O God, I cried, give me new birth,
And put me back upon the earth!
Upset each cloud's gigantic gourd
And let the heavy rain, down-poured
In one big torrent, set me free,
Washing my grave away from me!
I ceased; and, through the breathless hush
That answered me, the far-off rush
Of herald wings came whispering
Like music down the vibrant string
Of my ascending prayer, and—crash!
Before the wild wind's whistling lash
The startled storm-clouds reared on high
And plunged in terror down the sky,
And the big rain in one black wave
Fell from the sky and struck my grave.

I know not how such things can be
I only know there came to me
A fragrance such as never clings
To aught save happy living things;
A sound as of some joyous elf
Singing sweet songs to please himself,
And, through and over everything,
A sense of glad awakening.
The grass, a tip-toe at my ear,
Whispering to me I could hear;
I felt the rain's cool finger-tips
Brushed tenderly across my lips,
Laid gently on my sealèd sight,
And all at once the heavy night
Fell from my eyes and I could see—
A drenched and dripping apple-tree.
A last long line of silver rain,
A sky grown clear and blue again.
And as I looked a quickening gust
Of wind blew up to me and thrust
Into my face a miracle
Of orchard-breath, and with the smell—
I know not how such things can be!—
I breathed my soul back into me.
Ah! Up then from the ground sprang I
And hailed the earth with such a cry
As is not heard save from a man
Who has been dead, and lives again.
About the trees my arms I wound;
Like one gone mad I hugged the ground;
I raised my quivering arms on high;
I laughed and laughed into the sky,
Till at my throat a strangling sob
Caught fiercely, and a great heart-throb
Sent instant tears into my eyes;
O God, I cried, no dark disguise
Can e'er hereafter hide from me
Thy radiant identity!

Thou canst not move across the grass
But my quick eyes will see Thee pass,
Nor speak, however silently,
But my hushed voice will answer Thee.
I know the path that tells Thy way
Through the cool eve of every day;
God, I can push the grass apart
And lay my fingers on Thy heart!
The world stands out on either side
No wider than the heart is wide;
Above the world is stretched the sky—
No higher than the soul is high.
The heart can push the sea and land
Farther away on either hand;
The soul can split the sky in two,
And let the face of God shine through.
But East and West will pinch the heart
That cannot keep them pushed apart;
And he whose soul is flat—the sky
Will cave in on him by and by.

ARCHIBALD MACLEISH

Ars Poetica

A poem should be palpable and mute
As a globed fruit

Dumb
As old medallions to the thumb

Silent as the sleeve-worn stone
Of casement ledges where the moss has grown—

A poem should be wordless
As the flight of birds

A poem should be motionless in time
As the moon climbs

Leaving, as the moon releases
Twig by twig the night-entangled trees,

Leaving, as the moon behind the winter leaves,
Memory by memory the mind—

A poem should be motionless in time
As the moon climbs

A poem should be equal to:
Not true

For all the history of grief
An empty doorway and a maple leaf

For love
The leaning grasses and two lights above the sea—

A poem should not mean
But be.

L'An Trentiesme de Mon Eage

And I have come upon this place
By lost ways, by a nod, by words,
By faces, by an old man's face
At Morlaix lifted to the birds,

By hands upon the tablecloth
At Aldebori's, by the thin
Child's hands that opened to the moth
And let the flutter of the moonlight in,

By hands, by voices, by the voice
Of Mrs. Husman on the stair,
By Margaret's "If we had the choice
To choose or not"—through her thick hair,

By voices, by the creak and fall
Of footsteps on the upper floor,
By silence waiting in the hall
Between the doorbell and the door,

By words, by voices, a lost way—
And here above the chimney stack
The unknown constellations sway—
And by what way shall I go back?

The Too-Late Born

We too, we too, descending once again
The hills of our own land, we too have heard
Far off—Ah, que ce cor a longue haleine—
The horn of Roland in the passages of Spain,
The first, the second blast, the failing third,
And with the third turned back and climbed once more
The steep road southward, and heard faint the sound
Of swords, of horses, the disastrous war,
And crossed the dark defile at last, and found
At Ronçevaux upon the darkening plain
The dead against the dead and on the silent ground
The silent slain—

Einstein

Standing between the sun and moon preserves
A certain secrecy. Or seems to keep
Something inviolate if only that
His father was an ape.
Sweet music makes
All of his walls sound hollow and he heard
Sighs in the panelling and underfoot

Melancholy voices. So there is a door
Behind the seamless arras and within
A living something:—but no door that will
Admit the sunlight nor no windows where
The mirror moon can penetrate his bones
With cold deflection. He is small and tight
And solidly contracted into space
Opaque and perpendicular which blots
Earth with its shadow. And he terminates
In shoes which bearing up against the sphere
Attract his concentration,
                                        for he ends
If there why then no farther, as, beyond
Extensively the universe itself,
Or chronologically the two dates
Original and ultimate of time,

Einstein upon a public bench Wednesday the ninth contemplates finity

Nor could Jehovah and the million stars
Staring within their solitudes of light,
Nor all night's constellations be contained
Between his boundaries,
                                        nor could the sun
Receive him nor his groping roots run down
Into the loam and steaming sink of time
Where coils the middle serpent and the ooze
Breeds maggots.
                              But it seems assured he ends
Precisely at his shoes in proof whereof
He can revolve in orbits opposite
The orbit of the earth and so refuse
All planetary converse. And he wears
Clothes that distinguish him from what is not
His own circumference, as first a coat
Shaped to his back or modelled in reverse
Of the surrounding cosmos and below
Trousers preserving his detachment from
The revolutions of the stars.
                                        His hands

Einstein descends the Hartmannsweilerstrasse

And face go naked and alone converse
With what encloses him, as rough and smooth
And sound and silence and the intervals
Of rippling ether and the swarming motes
Clouding a privy: move to them and make
Shadows that mirror them within his skull
In perpendiculars and curves and planes
And bodiless significances blurred
As figures undersea and images
Patterned from eddies of the air.
                    Which are
Perhaps not shadows but the thing itself
And may be understood.

Einstein ultimately before a mirror accepts the hypothesis of exterior reality

                    Decorticate
The petals of the enfolding world and leave
A world in reason which is in himself
And has his own dimensions. Here do trees
Adorn the hillsides and hillsides enrich
The hazy marches of the sky and skies
Kindle and char to ashes in the wind,
And winds blow toward him from the verge, and
  suns
Rise on his dawn and on his dusk go down
And moons prolong his shadow. And he moves
Here as within a garden in a close
And where he moves the bubble of the world
Takes centre and there circle round his head
Like golden flies in summer the gold stars.

Disintegrates.

                    For suddenly he feels
The planet plunge beneath him, and a flare
Falls from the upper darkness to the dark
And awful shadows loom across the sky

That have no life from him and suns go out
And livid as a drowned man's face the moon
Floats to the lapsing surface of the night
And sinks discolored under.
So he knows
Less than a world and must communicate
Beyond his knowledge.

Einstein unsuccessfully after lunch attempts to enter, essaying synthesis with what's not he, the Bernese Oberland

Outstretched on the earth
He plunges both his arms into the swirl
Of what surrounds him but the yielding grass
Excludes his finger tips and the soft soil
Will not endure confusion with his hands,
Nor will the air receive him nor the light
Dissolve their difference but recoiling turns
Back from his touch. By which denial he can
Crawl on the earth and sense the opposing sun
But not make answer to them.
Put out leaves
And let the old remembering wind think through
A green intelligence, or under sea
Float out long filaments of amber in
The numb and wordless revery of tides.

In autumn the black branches dripping rain
Bruise his uncovered bones and in the spring
His swollen tips are gorged with aching blood
That bursts the laurel.
But although they seize
His sense he has no name for them, no word
To give them meaning and no utterance
For what they say. Feel the new summer's sun
Crawl up the warmed relaxing hide of earth
And weep for his lost youth, his childhood home
And a wide water on an inland shore!
Or to the night's mute asking in the blood
Give back a girl's name and three notes together!

He cannot think the smell of after rain
Nor close his thought around the long smooth lag
And falter of a wind, nor bring to mind
Dusk and the whippoorwill.

Einstein dissolved in violins invades the molecular structure of F. P. Paepke's Sommergarten. Is repulsed

But violins
Split out of trees and strung to tone can sing
Strange nameless words that image to the ear
What has no waiting image in the brain.
She plays in darkness and the droning wood
Dissolves to reverberations of a world
Beating in waves against him, till his sense
Trembles to rhythm and his naked brain
Feels without utterance in form the flesh
Of dumb and incommunicable earth,
And knows at once, and without knowledge how,
The stroke of the blunt rain, and blind receives
The sun.
When he a moment occupies
The hollow of himself and like an air
Pervades all other.
But the violin
Presses its dry insistence through the dream
That swims above it, shivering its speech
Back to a rhythm that becomes again
Music and vaguely ravels into sound.

To Einstein asking at the gate of stone none opens

So then there is no speech that can resolve
Their texture to clear thought and enter them.

The Virgin of Chartres whose bleaching bones still
wear
The sapphires of her glory knew a word—
That now is three round letters like the three
Round empty staring punctures in a skull.
And there were words in Rome once and one time
Words at Eleusis.
Now there are no words

Nor names to name them and they will not speak
But grope against his groping touch and throw
The long unmeaning shadows of themselves
Across his shadow and resist his sense.

Einstein hearing behind the wall of the Grand Hôtel du Nord the stars discovers the Back Stair

Why then if they resist destroy them. Dumb
Yet speak them in their elements. Whole,
Break them to reason.
He lies upon his bed
Exerting on Arcturus and the moon
Forces proportional inversely to
The squares of their remoteness, and conceives
The universe.
Atomic.
He can count
Ocean in atoms and weigh out the air
In multiples of one and subdivide
Light to its numbers.
If they will not speak
Let them be silent in their particles.
Let them be dead and he will lie among
Their dust and cipher them,—undo the signs
Of their unreal identities and free
The pure and single factor of all sums,—
Solve them to unity.
Democritus
Scooped handfuls out of stones and like the sea
Let earth run through his fingers. Well, he too,
He can achieve obliquity and learn
The cold distortion of the winter's sun
That breaks the surfaces of summer.

Einstein on the terrasse of The Acacias forces the secret door

Stands
Facing the world upon a windy slope
And with his mind relaxes the stiff forms
Of all he sees so that the heavy hills
Impend like rushing water and the earth
Hangs on the steep and momentary crest
Of overflowing ruin.

Overflow!
Sweep over into movement and dissolve
All differences in the indifferent flux!
Crumble to eddyings of dust and drown
In change the thing that changes!
There begins
A vague unquiet in the fallow ground,
A seething in the grass, a bubbling swirl
Over the surface of the fields that spreads
Around him gathering until the green
Boils and beneath the frothy loam the rocks
Ferment and simmer and like thinning smoke
The trees melt into nothing.
Still he stands
Watching the vortex widen and involve
In swirling dissolution the whole earth
And circle through the skies till swaying time
Collapses crumpling into dark the stars
And motion ceases and the sifting world
Opens beneath.
When he shall feel infuse
His flesh with the rent body of all else
And spin within his opening brain the motes
Of suns and worlds and spaces. *Einstein enters*

Like a foam
His flesh is withered and his shrivelling
And ashy bones are scattered on the dark.
But still the dark denies him. Still withstands
The dust his penetration and flings back
Himself to answer him.
Which seems to keep
Something inviolate. A living something.

You, Andrew Marvell

And here face down beneath the sun,
And here upon earth's noonward height,

To feel the always coming on,
The always rising of the night.

To feel creep up the curving east
The earthly chill of dusk and slow
Upon those under lands the vast
And ever-climbing shadow grow,

And strange at Ecbatan the trees
Take leaf by leaf the evening, strange,
The flooding dark about their knees,
The mountains over Persia change,

And now at Kermanshah the gate,
Dark, empty, and the withered grass,
And through the twilight now the late
Few travellers in the westward pass.

And Baghdad darken and the bridge
Across the silent river gone,
And through Arabia the edge
Of evening widen and steal on,

And deepen on Palmyra's street
The wheel rut in the ruined stone,
And Lebanon fade out and Crete
High through the clouds and overblown,

And over Sicily the air
Still flashing with the landward gulls,
And loom and slowly disappear
The sails above the shadowy hulls,

And Spain go under and the shore
Of Africa, the gilded sand,
And evening vanish and no more
The low pale light across that land,

Nor now the long light on the sea—
And here face downward in the sun

To feel how swift, how secretly,
The shadow of the night comes on. . . .

Memorial Rain

Ambassador Puser the ambassador
Reminds himself in French, felicitous tongue,
What these (young men no longer) lie here for
In rows that once, and somewhere else, were young—

All night in Brussels the wind had tugged at my door:
I had heard the wind at my door and the trees strung
Taut, and to me who had never been before
In that country it was a strange wind blowing
Steadily, stiffening the walls, the floor,
The roof of my room. I had not slept for knowing
He too, dead, was a stranger in that land
And felt beneath the earth in the wind's flowing
A tightening of roots and would not understand,
Remembering lake winds in Illinois,
That strange wind. I had felt his bones in the sand
Listening.

—Reflects that these enjoy
Their country's gratitude, that deep repose,
That peace no pain can break, no hurt destroy,
That rest, that sleep—

At Ghent the wind rose.
There was a smell of rain and a heavy drag
Of wind in the hedges but not as the wind blows
Over fresh water when the waves lag
Foaming and the willows huddle and it will rain:
I felt him waiting.

—Indicates the flag
Which (may he say) enisles in Flanders' plain
This little field these happy, happy dead
Have made America—

In the ripe grain
The wind coiled glistening, darted, fled,
Dragging its heavy body: at Waereghem
The wind coiled in the grass above his head:
Waiting—listening—

—Dedicates to them
This earth their bones have hallowed, this last gift
A grateful country—

Under the dry grass stem
The words are blurred, are thickened, the words sift
Confused by the rasp of the wind, by the thin grating
Of ants under the grass, the minute shift
And tumble of dusty sand separating
From dusty sand. The roots of the grass strain,
Tighten, the earth is rigid, waits—he is waiting—

And suddenly, and all at once, the rain!

The people scatter, they run into houses, the wind
Is trampled under the rain, shakes free, is again
Trampled. The rain gathers, running in thinned
Spurts of water that ravel in the dry sand
Seeping into the sand under the grass roots, seeping
Between cracked boards to the bones of a clenched hand:
The earth relaxes, loosens; he is sleeping,
He rests, he is quiet, he sleeps in a strange land.

MARK VAN DOREN

Morning Worship

I wake and hear it raining.
Were I dead, what would I give

Lazily to lie here,
Like this, and live?

Or better yet: birdsong,
Brightening and spreading—
How far would I come then
To be at the world's wedding?

Now that I lie, though,
Listening, living,
(Oh, but not forever,
Oh, end arriving)

How shall I praise them:
All the sweet beings
Eternally that outlive
Me and my dying?

Mountains, I mean; wind, water, air;
Grass, and huge trees; clouds, flowers,
And thunder, and night.

Turtles, I mean, and toads; hawks, herons, owls;
Graveyards, and towns, and trout; roads, gardens,
Red berries, and deer.

Lightning, I mean, and eagles; fences; snow;
Sunrise, and ferns; waterfalls, serpents,
Green islands, and sleep.

Horses, I mean; butterflies, whales;
Mosses, and stars; and gravelly
Rivers, and fruit.

Oceans, I mean; black valleys; corn;
Brambles, and cliffs; rock, dirt, dust, ice;
And warnings of flood.

How shall I name them?
And in what order?

Each would be first.
Omission is murder.

Maidens, I mean, and apples; needles; leaves;
Worms, and planets, and clover; whirlwinds; dew;
Bulls; geese—

Stop. Lie still.
You will never be done.
Leave them all there,
Old lover. Live on.

Once the Wind

They left him hanging for the deed
His black-eyed brother did.
And still beneath that basswood tree
No wildflower goes to bed.

No daisy but is darker there
For staring all night long
At something once the wind turned round,
Careless of right, of wrong.

They came next day and cut him down,
And the false brother groaned.
But still the black-eyed Susans gaze
At what the wind turned round.

And would, if any man could read,
Tell what was done amiss.
But no man now remembers it,
So long ago it is.

Nap

I lay me down, but down is deep
Past dark, past death, past deep's idea;

Is the soft seas themselves, that drain
Away as my own mind does, my own
Bones that will not be, not be
Again; not be my bones; not my
Own bones, that settle separately,
Softly, down and down—oh, sweet
Non-being, not my own, wherein
I sink like light in water, dimming
Slowly, oh, so slowly, deep
By deep, beyond the dark of death's idea.

E. E. CUMMINGS

My Father Moved Through Dooms of Love

My father moved through dooms of love
through sames of am through haves of give,
singing each morning out of each night
my father moved through depths of height

this motionless forgetful where
turned at his glance to shining here;
that if (so timid air is firm)
under his eyes would stir and squirm

newly as from unburied which
floats the first who, his april touch
drove sleeping selves to swarm their fates
woke dreamers to their ghostly roots

and should some why completely weep
my father's fingers brought her sleep:
vainly no smallest voice might cry
for he could feel the mountains grow.

Lifting the valleys of the sea
my father moved through griefs of joy;
praising a forehead called the moon
singing desire into begin

joy was his song and joy so pure
a heart of star by him could steer
and pure so now and now so yes
the wrists of twilight would rejoice

keen as midsummer's keen beyond
conceiving mind of sun will stand,
so strictly (over utmost him
so hugely) stood my father's dream

his flesh was flesh his blood was blood:
no hungry man but wished him food;
no cripple wouldn't creep one mile
uphill to only see him smile.

Scorning the pomp of must and shall
my father moved through dooms of feel;
his anger was as right as rain
his pity was as green as grain

septembering arms of year extend
less humbly wealth to foe and friend
than he to foolish and to wise
offered immeasurable is

proudly and (by octobering flame
beckoned) as earth will downward climb,
so naked for immortal work
his shoulders marched against the dark

his sorrow was as true as bread:
no liar looked him in the head;
if every friend became his foe
he'd laugh and build a world with snow.

My father moved through theys of we,
singing each new leaf out of each tree
(and every child was sure that spring
danced when she heard my father sing)

then let men kill which cannot share,
let blood and flesh be mud and mire,
scheming imagine, passion willed,
freedom a drug that's bought and sold

giving to steal and cruel kind,
a heart to fear, to doubt a mind,
to differ a disease of same,
conform the pinnacle of am

though dull were all we taste as bright,
bitter all utterly things sweet,
maggoty minus and dumb death
all we inherit, all bequeath

and nothing quite so least as truth
—i say though hate were why men breathe—
because my father lived his soul
love is the whole and more than all

Anyone Lived in a Pretty How Town

Anyone lived in a pretty how town
(with up so floating many bells down)
spring summer autumn winter
he sang his didn't he danced his did.

Women and men (both little and small)
cared for anyone not at all
they sowed their isn't they reaped their same
sun moon stars rain

children guessed (but only a few
and down they forgot as up they grew

autumn winter spring summer)
that noone loved him more by more

when by now and tree by leaf
she laughed his joy she cried his grief
bird by snow and stir by still
anyone's any was all to her

someones married their everyones
laughed their cryings and did their dance
(sleep wake hope and then) they
said their nevers they slept their dream

stars rain sun moon
(and only the snow can begin to explain
how children are apt to forget to remember
with up so floating many bells down)

one day anyone died i guess
(and noone stooped to kiss his face)
busy folk buried them side by side
little by little and was by was

all by all and deep by deep
and more by more they dream their sleep
noone and anyone earth by april
wish by spirit and if by yes.

Women and men (both dong and ding)
summer autumn winter spring
reaped their sowing and went their came
sun moon stars rain

As Freedom Is a Breakfastfood

As freedom is a breakfastfood
or truth can live with right and wrong
or molehills are from mountains made

—long enough and just so long
will being pay the rent of seem
and genius please the talentgang
and water most encourage flame

as hatracks into peachtrees grow
or hopes dance best on bald men's hair
and every finger is a toe
and any courage is a fear
—long enough and just so long
will the impure think all things pure
and hornets wail by children stung

or as the seeing are the blind
and robins never welcome spring
nor flatfolk prove their world is round
nor dingsters die at break of dong
and common's rare and millstones float
—long enough and just so long
tomorrow will not be too late

worms are the words but joy's the voice
down shall go which and up come who
breasts will be breasts thighs will be thighs
deeds cannot dream what dreams can do
—time is a tree (this life one leaf)
but love is the sky and i am for you
just so long and long enough

Always Before Your Voice My Soul

Always before your voice my soul
half-beautiful and wholly droll
is as some smooth and awkward foal,
whereof young moons begin
the newness of his skin,

so of my stupid sincere youth
the exquisite failure uncouth

discovers a trembling and smooth
Unstrength, against the strong
silences of your song;

or as a single lamb whose sheen
of full unsheared fleece is mean
beside its lovelier friends, between
your thoughts more white than wool
My thought is sorrowful:

but my heart smote in trembling thirds
of anguish quivers to your words,
As to a flight of thirty birds
shakes with a thickening fright
the sudden fooled light.

it is the autumn of a year:
When through the thin air stooped with fear,
across the harvest whitely peer
empty of surprise
death's faultless eyes

(whose hand my folded soul shall know
while on faint hills do frailly go
The peaceful terrors of the snow,
and before your dead face
which sleeps, a dream shall pass)

and these my days their sounds and flowers
Fall in a pride of petaled hours,
like flowers at the feet of mowers
whose bodies strong with love
through meadows hugely move.

yet what am i that such and such
mysteries very simply touch
me, whose heart-wholeness overmuch
Expects of your hair pale,
a terror musical?

while in an earthless hour my fond
soul seriously yearns beyond
this fern of sunset frond on frond
opening in a rare
slowness of glories air . . .

The flute of morning stilled in noon—
noon the implacable bassoon—
now Twilight seeks the thrill of moon,
washed with a wild and thin
despair of violin

Somewhere I Have Never Travelled, Gladly Beyond

Somewhere i have never travelled, gladly beyond
any experience, your eyes have their silence:
in your most frail gesture are things which enclose me,
or which i cannot touch because they are too near

your slightest look easily will unclose me
though i have closed myself as fingers,
you open always petal by petal myself as Spring opens
(touching skilfully, mysteriously) her first rose

or if your wish be to close me, i and
my life will shut very beautifully, suddenly,
as when the heart of this flower imagines
the snow carefully everywhere descending;

nothing which we are to perceive in this world equals
the power of your intense fragility: whose texture
compels me with the colour of its countries,
rendering death and forever with each breathing

(i do not know what it is about you that closes
and opens; only something in me understands
the voice of your eyes is deeper than all roses)
nobody, not even the rain, has such small hands

H. PHELPS PUTNAM

Hasbrouck and the Rose

Hasbrouck was there and so were Bill
And Smollet Smith the poet, and Ames was there.
After his thirteenth drink, the burning Smith,
Raising his fourteenth trembling in the air,
Said, "Drink with me, Bill, drink up to the Rose."
But Hasbrouck laughed like old men in a myth,
Inquiring, "Smollet, are you drunk? What rose?"
And Smollet said, "I drunk? It may be so;
Which comes from brooding on the flower, the flower
I mean toward which mad hour by hour
I travel brokenly; and I shall know,
With Hermes and the alchemists—but, hell,
What use is it talking that way to you?
Hard-boiled, unbroken egg, what can you care
For the enfolded passion of the Rose?"
Then Hasbrouck's voice rang like an icy bell:

"Arcane romantic flower, meaning what?
Do you know what it meant? Do I?
We do not know.
Unfolding pungent rose, the glowing bath
Of ecstasy and clear forgetfulness;
Closing and secret bud one might achieve
By long debauchery—
Except that I have eaten it, and so
There is no call for further lunacy.
In Springfield, Massachusetts, I devoured
The mystic, the improbable, the Rose.
For two nights and a day, rose and rosette,
And petal after petal and the heart,

I had my banquet by the beams
Of four electric stars which shone
Weakly into my room, for there,
Drowning their light and gleaming at my side,
Was the incarnate star
Whose body bore the stigma of the Rose.
And that is all I know about the flower;
I have eaten it—it has disappeared.
There is no Rose."

Young Smollet Smith let fall his glass; he said
"Oh Jesus, Hasbrouck, am I drunk or dead?"

Hymn to Chance

How shall we summon you?
The tiny names of gods will not serve us now,
Nor the magic names of the various sons of gods,
Nor the names of their mothers murmured tenderly,
Nor the masks of creatures which you have assumed.
Gray hands enfolding all our lives,
Gray hands, caress the stumbling of our tongues.

Lord Gardener, you have made our lives arise,
Thin shoots of green articulated bone,
Growing and bending and falling under your breath.
You have grafted on these stems our nervy flesh
Enriched with blood and our slow-blooming brains;
You have made our fingers wise with restlessness.
You have laid the earth out and the sea and the lower skies,
You have set us on loose feet beside the earth
That your many colored garden may run wild.
And now from these garnished jaws your garden sings,
Lord Chance,
And your flowers coruscate with blossoming.

Ye are munificent, how shall we count your gifts?
We enumerate like groping babyhood,

For our thoughts are bound and packaged in your hands,
The world is formed and furled in your ceaseless hands,
The hours and days drip from your fingertips,
The ages and our lives fall clustering
And the seasons fall unjustly from your hands.

Lord Prince of Hell, you have given us thought, the worm
Which coils insistently through our too sensate dust.
It is this disease, Lord Death, which corrupts us all,
For we lie to animate our meagreness,
To make us to ourselves less mean
And our companions less like mangled fools.

Lord Costumer, the cabinets of our blood
Have been hung with robes to clothe our nakedness;
You have given us the burning skin of joy,
You have turned our feet from circling slavery
With the brilliance of a dollar thrown in the air.
You have given the close bitter gown of grief,
The acid lining of our joyousness.
You have given us spirit, Lord, we are not abashed,
And we have known quietude when our muscles moved
Smoothly in laboring or in love
And our nerves made harmony of their clamoring.
We have raised ourselves immense memorials,
And our laughter, like your own, has lapped the world.

You have given us the variable one, the infinite and the small,
Which we have repaid with stiff ingratitude.
We have insulted you as Lady Luck;
We have made our lives a foolishness
Because your eyes were neither cool nor kind.
We are the victims of unfounded lust,
We have discovered laws, forgive us, Lord;
Forgive us, Lord, we are neither fine nor swift,
We have not known our proper elegance.
We have said tomorrow comes and the twinkling sun
Will not refuse to flatter us with heat;
We have hid ourselves in minuscules of time.

We have made ourselves low beds in an empty room;
But our beds drift in the dark and our lies dissolve
And there is your face shimmering and your hands
Weaving the chaos where we come and go.

Grand Anarch, there is disrepute for us,
But our words are not disreputable nor mean;
We have spoken for ourselves and our dignity,
Tearing our cheapness from us for a while.
At this moment now, conceive us once again
More suitable to the curving of your hands;
Make us tough and mystical,
Give us such eyes as will penetrate your eyes
And lungs to draw the breath you give to us.
Hear us for we do not beg;
We only pray you heal our idiot ways
And the kind of lonely madness which we have
Of bleeding one another on the road.
We travel in the belly of the wind;
It is you, Lord, who will make us lame or swift.

About Women

Fair golden thoughts and lovely words—
Away, away from her they call,
For women are the silly birds,
And perching on a sunny wall
They chirp the answer and the all;
They hold for true all futile things—
Life, death, and even love—they fall
To dreaming over jeweled rings.

Their bodies are uncouthly made,
And heavy swollen like a pear,
And yet their conquered, undismayed
And childish lovers call them fair.
Their honor fills them full of care,

Their honor that is nothingness,
The mystery of empty air,
The veil of vain delightfulness.

Their subtleties are thin and pale,
Their hearts betray them in their eyes:
They are a simple flute, and frail,
With triple stops for playing lies.
These poor machines of life are wise
To scorn the metaphysic glow,
The careless game that laughs and dies,
The heady grace they cannot know.

Well, give them kisses, scatter flowers,
And whisper that you cannot stay;
We shall have clarity and hours
Which women shall not take away.

LOUISE BOGAN

Old Countryside

Beyond the hour we counted rain that fell
On the slant shutter, all has come to proof.
The summer thunder, like a wooden bell,
Rang in the storm above the mansard roof,

And mirrors cast the cloudy day along
The attic floor; wind made the clapboards creak.
You braced against the wall to make it strong,
A shell against your cheek.

Long since, we pulled brown oak-leaves to the ground
In a winter of dry trees; we heard the cock

Shout its unplaceable cry, the axe's sound
Delay a moment after the axe's stroke.

Far back, we saw, in the stillest of the year,
The scrawled vine shudder, and the rose-branch show
Red to the thorns, and, sharp as sight can bear,
The thin hound's body arched against the snow.

Summer Wish

That cry's from the first cuckoo of the year.
I wished before it ceased.

FIRST VOICE

We call up the green to hide us
This hardened month, by no means the beginning
Of the natural year, but of the shortened span
Of leaves upon the earth. We call upon
The weed as well as the flower: groundsel, stellaria.
It is the month to make the summer wish;
It is time to ask
The wish from summer as always: *It will be,*
It will be.
That tool we have used
So that its haft is smooth; it knows the hand.
Again we lift the wish to its expert uses,
Tired of the bird that calls one long note downward,
And the forest in cast-iron. No longer, no longer,
The season of the lying equinox
Wherein false cock-crow sounds!

SECOND VOICE

In March the shadow
Already falls with a look of summer, fuller
Upon the snow, because the sun at last
Is almost centered. Later, the sprung moss
Is the tree's shadow; under the black spruces

It lies where lately snow lay, bred green from the cold
Cast down from melting branches.

FIRST VOICE

A wish like a hundred others.
You cannot, as once, yearn forward. The blood now never
Stirs hot to memory, or to the fantasy
Of love, with which, both early and late, one lies
As with a lover.
Now do you suddenly envy
Poor praise you told long since to keep its tongue,
Of pride's acquired accent,—pomposity, arrogance,
That trip in their latinity? With these at heart
You could make a wish, crammed with the nobility
Of error. It would be no use. You cannot
Take yourself in.

SECOND VOICE

Count over what these days have: lilies
Returned in little to an earth unready,
To the sun not accountable;
The hillside mazed and leafless, but through the ground
The leaf from the bulb, the unencouraged green
Heaving the metal earth, presage of thousand
Shapes of young leaves—lanceolate, trefoil,
Peach, willow, plum, the lilac like a heart.

FIRST VOICE

Memory long since put by,—to what end the dream
That drags back lived-out life with the wrong words,
The substitute meaning?
Those that you once knew there play out false time,
Elaborate yesterday's words, that they were deaf to
Being dead ten years.—Call back in anguish
The anger in childhood that defiled the house
In walls and timber with its violence?
Now must you listen again
To your own tears, shed as a child, hold the bruise
With your hand, and weep, fallen against the wall,

And beg, *Don't, don't,* while the pitiful rage goes on
That cannot stem itself?
Or, having come into woman's full estate,
Enter the rich field, walk between the bitter
Bowed grain, being compelled to serve,
To heed unchecked in the heart the reckless fury
That tears fresh day from day, destroys its traces,—
Now bear the blow too young?

SECOND VOICE

In early April
At six o'clock the sun has not set; on the walls
It shines with scant light, pale, dilute, misplaced,
Light there's no use for. At overcast noon
The sun comes out in a flash, and is taken
Slowly back to the cloud.

FIRST VOICE

Not memory, and not the renewed conjecture
Of passion that opens the breast, the unguarded look
Flaying clean the raped defence of the body,
Breast, bowels, throat, now pulled to the use of the eyes
That see and are taken. The body that works and sleeps,
Made vulnerable, night and day, to delight that changes
Upon the lips that taste it, to the lash of jealousy
Struck on the face, so the betraying bed
Is gashed clear, cold on the mind, together with
Every embrace that agony dreads but sees
Open as the love of dogs.

SECOND VOICE

The cloud shadow flies up the bank, but does not
Blow off like smoke. It stops at the bank's edge.
In the field by trees two shadows come together.
The trees and the cloud throw down their shadow upon
The man who walks there. Dark flows up from his feet
To his shoulders and throat, then has his face in its mask,
Then lifts.

FIRST VOICE

Will you turn to yourself, proud breast,
Sink to yourself, to an ingrained, pitiless
Rejection of voice and touch not your own, press sight
Into a myth no eye can take the gist of;
Clot up the bone of phrase with the black conflict
That claws it back from sense?
                                        Go into the breast . . .
You have traced that lie, before this, out to its end,
Heard bright wit headstrong in the beautiful voice
Changed to a word mumbled across the shoulder
To one not there; the gentle self split up
Into a yelling fiend and a soft child.
You have seen the ingrown look
Come at last upon a vision too strong
Ever to turn away.

The breast's six madnesses repeat their dumb-show.

SECOND VOICE

In the bright twilight children call out in the fields.
The evening takes their cry. How late it is!
Around old weeds worn thin and bleached to their pith
The field has leaped to stalk and strawberry blossom.
The orchard by the road
Has the pear-tree full at once of flowers and leaves,
The cherry with flowers only.

FIRST VOICE

The mind for refuge, the grain of reason, the will,
Pulled by a wind it thinks to point and name?
Malicious symbol, key for rusty wards,
The crafty knight in the game, with its mixed move,
Prey to an end not evident to craft. . . .

SECOND VOICE

Fields are ploughed inward
From edge to center; furrows squaring off

Make dark lines far out in irregular fields,
On hills that are builded like great clouds that over them
Rise, to depart.
Furrow within furrow, square within a square,
Draw to the center where the team turns last.
Horses in half-ploughed fields
Make earth they walk upon a changing color.

FIRST VOICE

The year's begun; the share's again in the earth.

Speak out the wish like music, that has within it
The horn, the string, the drum pitched deep as grief.
Speak it like laughter, outward. O brave, O generous
Laughter that pours from the well of the body and draws
The bane that cheats the heart: aconite, nightshade,
Hellebore, hyssop, rue,—symbols and poisons
We drink, in fervor, thinking to gain thereby
Some difference, some distinction.
Speak it, as that man said, *as though the earth spoke,*
By the body of rock, shafts of heaved strata, separate,
Together.
Though it be but for sleep at night,
Speak out the wish.
The vine we pitied is in leaf; the wild
Honeysuckle blows by the granite.

SECOND VOICE

See now
Open above the field, stilled in wing-stiffened flight,
The stretched hawk fly.

HORACE GREGORY

Fortune for Mirabel

Tell, tell our fortune, Mirabel,
Shuffle the pack and cut
Cards spread face upward on the carpet
Over the faded green sweet and violet pastures.
The hour-glass, time, the blonde girl and brunette.
Give us good cards tonight: the faces
Beautiful and new—and love, Mirabel,
The pink heart pierced and the great round yellow sun;
We shall be rich tonight: laurels for fame,
The gold-mine falling from your right hand,
And O the lute and ribbons and the harp!

—Not the unopened letter nor the blind eye
Nor the fire card bright as war flowing through Spain
Nor the lightning card, troopship in storm
Nor the quick arrow pointing nowhere to the sky.
Not now tonight and not the spotted devil,
The faithless dancing psychiatric patient,
Who wept, always the lover, not the man,
Sold the pawn ticket—not tonight, Mirabel,
Not the deep cypress vista and the urn,
The kidnapped ten-year-old, the head
In pear tree branches and one delicate frosted hand
On the back stair
—Nor the green island card that means go home
To the dark house with the gas shut off
Where morning papers drop to the floor,
The milkman passes and the landlord waits—not these tonight.

But the bridal card in white, pale blossoms in yellow air,
New homes unlocked, unwept,

And the great good fortune sun card shining down.
Is it love, Mirabel, behind the pearly gates?
This last card? Or the black faceless end
Behind each card, even the laurels hidden, the dancer dead,
Tonight over and gray light glancing
On tired, powerless sleeping breasts and arms,
Mirabel: Good morning.

The Passion of M'Phail

IV

The lunchroom bus boy who looked like Orson Welles,
Romeo, Brutus, and a man from Mars in his two eyes,
the bellhop who was Joe Louis to the life,
the Greek fruit peddler who in church on Sundays
was a lightning-struck dead image of J. P. Morgan,
the Italian barber who in a mirror was more like
John Barrymore than Barrymore himself,
the Woolworth demonstration cold-cream girl
who was Garbo at a glance, only more real,
the shoe clerk who in midnight rain outside of Lindy's
should have been Clark Gable,
the Second Avenue ex-Baptist minister
who was born to have a face like Cordell Hull's—
why do they look at me like that,
why do they stare,
sleepwalking through my dreams?
What was the big mistake?
They looked like power and fame,
like love, like everything you need;
and you would think their looks would put them where
they could dictate a letter or run a bank
or kiss a microphone or float a yacht or sleep in
a genuine imitation Marie Antoinette bed
or get somewhere before they die
instead of dropping into dreams too deep
to tell themselves who, what, or where they are

until a fire turns them out into the street
or a shot is heard and the police are at the door.

Chorus for Survival

XIV

Ask no return for love that's given
embracing mistress, wife or friend,
ask no return:
on this deep earth or in pale heaven,
awake and spend
hands, lips, and eyes in love,
in darkness burn,
the limbs entwined until the soul ascend.

Ask no return of seasons gone:
the fire of autumn and the first hour of spring,
the short bough blossoming
through city windows when night's done,
when fears adjourn
backward in memory where all loves end

in self again, again the inward tree
growing against the heart
and no heart free.
From love that sleeps behind each eye
in double symmetry
ask no return,
even in enmity, look! I shall take your hand;
nor can our limbs disjoin in separate ways again,
walking, even at night on foreign land
through houses open to the wind, through cold and rain,
waking alive, meet, kiss and understand.

MALCOLM COWLEY

Stone Horse Shoals

"To wade the sea-mist, then to wade the sea
at dawn, let drift your garments one by one,
follow the clean stroke of a sea-gull's wing
breast-high against the sun;
follow a sail to sunward, slowly nearing
the lazy lobster boats at Stone Horse Shoals,
and pass them silent, on a strong ebb-tide
into an ocean empty to the poles."

The tall man clenched his eyes against the world;
his face was gray and shook like a torn sail.
"I have lived," he said, "a life that moved in spirals
turned inward like the shell of a sea-snail.
I have been the shadow at the heart of shadows,
I have stared too many years at my own face;
on Stone Horse Shoals, among the lobster boats,
I will shed my carapace.

"Something will die there, something move and watch
its shadow fathoms downward on the sand,
summer and winter. In another season
another man comes wading to the land,
where other blossoms fade among the dunes
and other children. . . . I am tired," he said,
"But I can see a naked body climbing
a naked seacoast, naked of the dead,

"naked of language. There are signs inscribed
on stones and trees, familiar vocables;
I hope to rise out of the sea as white,

as empty and chalk-smooth as cockleshells.
And children digging naked in the sand
will find my shell and on it scratch new words
that soon will blossom out," he said, "and bear
new fruit, strange to the tongue of men and birds."

The Long Voyage

Not that the pines were darker there,
nor mid-May dogwood brighter there,
nor swifts more swift in summer air;
it was my own country,

having its thunderclap of spring,
its long midsummer ripening,
its corn hoar-stiff at harvesting,
almost like any country,

yet being mine; its face, its speech,
its hills bent low within my reach,
its river birch and upland beech
were mine, of my own country.

Now the dark waters at the bow
fold back, like earth against the plow;
foam brightens like the dogwood now
at home, in my own country.

Eight Melons

August and on the vine eight melons sleeping,
drinking the sunlight, sleeping, while below
their roots obscurely work in the dark loam;

motionless center of the living garden,
eight belly-shaped, eight woman-colored melons
swelling and feeding the seeds within them. Guns

west of the mountain at the Frenchman's Bridge;
they are fighting now at the cold river, they
are dying for tomorrow. While the melons

sleep, smile in sleeping, in their bellies hoard
September sweetness, life to outlast the snow.

THEODORE SPENCER

Song

I who love you bring
Against our cherishing
These faults I daren't deny
Lest love should prove a lie.
But Oh, if you love me forgive me,
And none of this is true.

A too resilient mind
That seeking fact, must find
Reasons on every side
Why fact should be denied.
But Oh, if you love me forgive me,
And none of this is true.

A body that has wooed
More pleasure than it should,
And for that pleasure sought
What it had thrived without.
But Oh, if you love me forgive me,
And none of this is true.

And until now, a soul
That could find no goal

Beyond body and mind;
And so turned blind.
But Oh, if you love me forgive me,
And none of this is true.

A Reason for Writing

No word that is not flesh, he said,
Can hold my wavering ear; but when
That golden physical flesh is clear,
I dance in a glory like your glory
With force to stir the dead.

No word that is not thought, he said,
Can hook my slippery mind; but when
That silver accurate thought I find,
I dance in a glory like your glory
With force to stir the dead.

Words both flesh and thought, he said,
Hold and hook my heart; and when
The gold, the silver, shudder apart,
Still in a glory like your glory
I'll dance to stir the dead.

Spring Song

I have come again, gentlemen and ladies,
Whatever you call me, ladies, gentlemen;
Dancing, dancing down, sweet ladies,
And up with a dance I come, kind gentlemen;
I am here; we are dancing again.

Brown leaf on a dust-hill, ladies, ladies;
A running ant from the dust-hill, gentlemen;
Look out of the window; here I am;

Look back to the bedroom; here I am.
Sleep; and we'll fall together, gentlemen—
Falling towers and crumpled gowns
To a dust, a most sleepy dust, ladies,
From towers and golden gowns. But sleep,
Oh sleep again, and I'll promise you green,
A green, shattering sun-blade green,
With a daffodil prance like forever, gentlemen,
Forever a tower of gold like a daffodil.

I have come again, gentlemen and ladies,
Whatever you call me, a leaf and a dust-hill;
Dancing up, gentlemen, sweet ladies;
And dancing down, ladies, kind gentlemen.
I am here; we are dancing again.

R. P. BLACKMUR

All Things Are a Flowing

Flowers do better here than peas and beans,
Here nothing men may save can save its mark;
Reason a glitter flowing blues to greens
Beyond the offshore shoals gains ocean dark.
  The poor within us climb the cliff and stare
  Through second eyes and are sea-beggared there.

Sun warms the flesh, but in the marrow, wind;
The seagulls over head and neater tern
Scream woodthrush in the birches out of mind.
How warm a marrow cold enough to burn!
  There is no shelter here, no self-warm lair,
  When every lung eddies the ocean air.

All's weather here and sure, visible change;
It is the permutation of the stone,
The inner crumbling of the mountain range,
Breathes in our ears sea râle and moan.
  And this the steadied heart, our own, must bear:
  Suncalm and stormcalm, both in breathless air.

Here men wear natural colours, mostly blue,
Colour of fusion, shade of unison,
Colour of nothingness seen twice, come true,
Colour the gods must be that come undone:
  Colour of succour and mirage, O snare
  And reservoir, death ravens in arrear.

Half-Tide Ledge

Sunday the sea made morning worship, sang
Venite, Kyrie, and a long Amen,
over a flowing cassock did put on
glittering blindness, surplice of the sun.
Towards high noon her eldest, high-run tide
rebelled at formal song and in the Sanctus
made heavy heavy mockery of God,
and I, almost before I knew it, saw
the altar ledges of the Lord awash.
These are the obsequies I think on most.

Scarabs for the Living

I

O sailor sailor tell me why
though in the seawine of your eye
I see nothing dead and nothing die
I know from the stillness seething there
my heart's hope is my soul's despair.

II

To meditate upon the tiger, turn
your human eyes from his past-human stare;
beyond his cage a pigeon tops an urn,
beyond the pigeon falls the twilight air,
and there, steadfast, he sees a viewless lair.

III

Lay down one hand before you like a tool
and let the other, in your mind, grow strange;
then let the strangers meet. Who but a fool
or a passionate man, thinks loss is blood-exchange,
if the cold hand should warm and the hot cool!

IV

Within this windless covert silence drops
leaf by leaf and birches make bare bones;
a startled woodcock's whistling flight new-stops
the wind beyond the woods, and I, alone,
feel my still flight trembling into stone.

V

There is, besides the warmth, in this new love—
besides the radiance, the spring—the chill
that in the old had seemed the slow, the still
amounting up of that indifferent will
in which we die. I keep last winter's glove.

VI

Oh, I was honest in the womb
where I had neither time nor room
nor any secret hope to hide.
Now there are love and work this side
of honesty, two hopes that lied.

VII

The chickadee-dee-dee is not a bird
like stilted heron fishing minnie pools

that in their fleeing shriek the sky like fools;
the chickadee (dee-dee) is most a word
to keep the thicket warm when summer cools.

VIII

It is the slow encroachment, word by word,
of sleep upon the wakened mind, the slow
manoeuvre of unseemly vertigo,
whereby disease in order is inferred;
and in the sleep a blotting fall of snow.

IX

Quiet the self, and silence brims like spring:
the soaking in of light, the gathering
of shadow up, after each passing cloud,
the green life eating into death aloud,
the hum of seasons; all on beating wing.

JOHN PEALE BISHOP

Speaking of Poetry

The ceremony must be found
That will wed Desdemona to the huge Moor.

It is not enough—
To win the approval of the Senator
Or to outwit his disapproval; honest Iago
Can manage that: it is not enough. For then,
Though she may pant again in his black arms
(His weight resilient as a Barbary stallion's)
She will be found
When the ambassadors of the Venetian state arrive
Again smothered. These things have not been changed,
Not in three hundred years

(Tupping is still tupping
Though that particular word is obsolete.
Naturally, the ritual would not be in Latin.)

For though Othello had his blood from kings
His ancestry was barbarous, his ways African,
His speech uncouth. It must be remembered
That though he valued an embroidery—
Three mulberries proper on a silk like silver—
It was not for the subtlety of the stitches,
But for the magic in it. Whereas, Desdemona
Once contrived to imitate in needlework
Her father's shield, and plucked it out
Three times, to begin again, each time
With diminished colors. This is a small point
But indicative.

Desdemona was small and fair,
Delicate as a grasshopper
At the tag-end of summer: a Venetian
To her noble finger-tips.

O, it is not enough
That they should meet, naked, at dead of night
In a small inn on a dark canal. Procurers
Less expert than Iago can arrange as much.

The ceremony must be found

Traditional, with all its symbols
Ancient as the metaphors in dreams;
Strange, with never before heard music; continuous
Until the torches deaden at the bedroom door.

Ode

Why will they never sleep
Those great women who sit

Peering at me with parrot eyes?
They sit with grave knees; they keep
Perpetual stare; and their hands move
As though hands could be aware—
Forward and back, to begin again—
As though on tumultuous shuttles of wind they wove
Shrouds out of air.

The three are sisters. There is one
Who sits divine in weeping stone
On a small chair of skeleton
And is most inescapable.
I have walked through many mirrors
But always accompanied.
I have been as many men, as many ghosts,
As there were days. The boy was seen
Always at rainfall, mistily, not lost.
I have tried changing shapes
But always, alone, I have heard
Her shadow coming nearer, and known
The awful grasp of striding hands
Goddess! upon
The screaming metamorphosis.

One has a face burned hard
As the red Cretan clay,
Who wears a white torso scarred
With figures like a calendar.
She sits among broken shafts
Of stone; she is and still will be
Who feeds on cities, gods and men,
Weapons of bronze and curious ornaments,
Reckoning the evens as the odds.
Her least movement recalls the sea.

The last has idiot teeth
And a brow not made
For any thought but suffering.
Tired, she repeats

In idiot singing
A song shaped like a ring:
"Now is now and never Then
Dead Virgins will bear no men
And now that we speak of love, of love,
The woman's beneath
That's burdened with love
And the man's above
While the thing is done and done.

A Recollection

Famously she descended, her red hair
Unbound and bronzed by sea-reflections, caught
Crinkled with sea-pearls. The fine slender taut
Knees that let down her feet upon the air,

Young breasts, slim flanks and golden quarries were
Odder than when the young distraught
Unknown Venetian, painting her portrait, thought
He'd not imagined what he painted there.

And I too commerced with that golden cloud:
Lipped her delicious hands and had my ease
Faring fantastically, perversely proud.

All loveliness demands our courtesies.
Since she was dead I praised her as I could
Silently, among the Barberini bees.

Fiametta

Fiametta walks under the quincebuds
  In a gown the color of flowers;
Her small breasts shine through the silken stuff
  Like raindrops after showers.
The green hem of her dress is silk, but duller
Than her eye's green color.

Her shadow restores the grass's green—
    Where the sun had gilded it;
The air has given her copper hair
    The sanguine that was requisite.
Whatever her flaws, my lady
Has no fault in her young body.

She leans with her long slender arms
    To pull down morning upon her—
Fragrance of quince, white light and falling cloud.
    The day shall have lacked due honor
Until I shall have rightly praised
Her standing thus with slight arms upraised.

Admonition

Lock your bedroom doors with terror.
Comb your hair between two lights.
In the gold Venetian chamber
But for them let all be sombre.
Sit, and see reflected lights
Color time within your mirror.

Comb, comb, your bright hair. Rain
Fiery threads upon a shadow.
Stare until you see dilated
Eyes stare out as once the excited
Young men coming out of shadow,
Stared into a burning pain.

Find the loveliest shroud you own.
Stilt a ceremonious
Height on gilded heels. Then summon
To a rarity grown common
Starved arachnid, the dead-louse
And whatever feeds on bone.

The Return

Night and we heard heavy cadenced hoofbeats
Of troops departing; the last cohorts left
By the North Gate. That night some listened late
Leaning their eyelids toward Septentrion.

Morning blared and the young tore down the trophies
And warring ornaments: arches were strong
And in the sun but stone; no longer conquest
Circled our columns; all our state was down

In fragments. In the dust, old men with tufted
Eyebrows whiter than sunbaked faces gulped
As it fell. But they no more than we remembered
The old sea-fights, the soldiers' names and sculptors'.

We did not know the end was coming: nor why
It came; only that long before the end
Were many wanted to die. Then vultures starved
And sailed more slowly in the sky.

We still had taxes. Salt was high. The soldiers
Gone. Now there was much drinking and lewd
Houses all night loud with riot. But only
For a time. Soon the taverns had no roofs.

Strangely it was the young, the almost boys,
Who first abandoned hope; the old still lived
A little, at last a little lived in eyes.
It was the young whose child did not survive.

Some slept beneath the simulacra, until
The gods' faces froze. Then was fear.
Some had response in dreams, but morning restored
Interrogation. Then O then, O ruins!

Temples of Neptune invaded by the sea
And dolphins streaked like streams sportive
As sunlight rode and over the rushing floors
The sea unfurled and what was blue raced silver.

YVOR WINTERS

Heracles

Note: Heracles is treated as a sungod, the treatment being based on the discussion in Anthon's Classical Dictionary.

Eurystheus, trembling, called me to the throne,
Alcmena's son, heavy with thews and still.
He drove me on my fatal road alone:
I went, subservient to Hera's will.

For, when I had resisted, she had struck
Out of the sky and spun my wit: I slew
My children, quicker than a stroke of luck,
With motion lighter than my sinew knew.

Compelled down ways obscure with analogue
To force the Symbols of the Zodiac—
Bright Lion, Boundless Hydra, Fiery Dog—
I spread them on my arms as on a rack:

Spread them and broke them in the groaning wood,
And yet the Centaur stung me from afar,
His blood envenomed with the Hydra's blood:
Thence was I outcast from the earthy war.

Nessus the Centaur, with his wineskin full,
His branch and thyrsus, and his fleshy grip—

Her whom he could not force he yet could gull,
And she drank poison from his bearded lip.

Older than man, evil with age, is life:
Injustice, direst perfidy, my bane
Drove me to win my lover and my wife;
By love and justice I at last was slain.

The numbered Beings of the wheeling track
I carried singly to the empty throne,
And yet, when I had come exhausted back,
Was forced to wait without the gate, alone.

Commanded thus to pause before the gate,
I felt from my hot breast the tremors pass,
White flame dissecting the corrupted State,
Eurystheus vibrant in his den of brass:

Vibrant with horror, though a jewelled king,
Lest, the heat mounting, madness turn my brain
For one dry moment, and the palace ring
With crystal terror ere I turn again.

This stayed me, too: my life was not my own,
But I my life's; a god I was, not man.
Grown Absolute, I slew my flesh and bone;
Timeless, I knew the Zodiac my span.

This was my grief, that out of grief I grew—
Translated as I was from earth at last,
From the sad pain that Deïanira knew.
Transmuted slowly in a fiery blast,

Perfect, and moving perfectly, I raid
Eternal silence to eternal ends:
And Deïanira, an imperfect shade,
Retreats in silence as my arc descends.

Sonnet to the Moon

Now every leaf, though colorless, burns bright
With disembodied and celestial light,
And drops without a movement or a sound
A pillar of darkness to the shifting ground.

The lucent, thin, and alcoholic flame
Runs in the stubble with a nervous aim,
But, when the eye pursues, will point with fire
Each single stubble-tip and strain no higher.

O triple goddess! Contemplate my plight!
Opacity, my fate! Change, my delight!
The yellow tom-cat, sunk in shifting fur,
Changes and dreams, a phosphorescent blur.

Sullen I wait, but still the vision shun.
Bodiless thoughts and thoughtless bodies run.

Sir Gawaine and the Green Knight

Reptilian green the wrinkled throat,
Green as a bough of yew the beard;
He bent his head, and so I smote;
Then for a thought my vision cleared.

The head dropped clean; he rose and walked;
He fixed his fingers in the hair;
The head was unabashed and talked;
I understood what I must dare.

His flesh, cut down, arose and grew.
He bade me wait the season's round,
And then, when he had strength anew,
To meet him on his native ground.

The year declined; and in his keep
I passed in joy a thriving yule;
And whether waking or in sleep,
I lived in riot like a fool.

He beat the woods to bring me meat.
His lady, like a forest vine,
Grew in my arms; the growth was sweet;
And yet what thoughtless force was mine!

By practice and conviction formed,
With ancient stubbornness ingrained,
Although her body clung and swarmed,
My own identity remained.

Her beauty, lithe, unholy, pure
Took shapes that I had never known;
And had I once been insecure,
Had grafted laurel in my bone.

And then, since I had kept the trust,
Had loved the lady, yet was true,
The knight withheld his giant thrust
And let me go with what I knew.

I left the green bark and the shade,
Where growth was rapid, thick, and still;
I found a road that men had made
And rested on a dying hill.

JOHN WHEELWRIGHT

Train Ride

After rain, through afterglow, the unfolding fan
of railway landscape sidled on the pivot

of a larger arc into the green of evening;
I remembered that noon I saw a gradual bud
still white; though dead in its warm bloom;
always the enemy is the foe at home.
  And I wondered what surgery could recover
our lost, long stride of indolence and leisure
which is labor in reverse; what physic recalls the smile
not of lips, but of eyes as of the sea bemused.
  We, when we disperse from common sleep to several
tasks, we gather to despair; we, who assembled
once for hopes from common toil to dreams
or sickish and hurting or triumphal rapture;
always the enemy is our foe at home.
  We, deafened with far scattered city rattles
to the hubbub of forest birds (never having
"had time" to grieve or to hear through vivid sleep
the sea knock on its cracked and hollow stones)
so that the stars, almost, and birds comply,
and the garden-wet; the trees retire; We are
a scared patrol, fearing the guns behind;
always the enemy is the foe at home.
  What wonder that we fear our own eyes' look
and fidget to be at home alone, and pitifully
put off age by some change in brushing the hair
and stumble to our ends like smothered runners at their tape;
  Then (as while the stars herd to the great trough
the blind, in the always-only-outward of their dismantled
archways, awake at the smell of warmed stone
or to the sound of reeds, lifting from the dim
into their segment of green dawn) *always*
our enemy is our foe at home, more
certainly than through spoken words or from grief-
twisted writing on paper, unblotted by tears
the thought came:
                    There is no physic
for the world's ill, nor surgery; it must
(hot smell of tar on wet salt air)
burn in a fever forever, an incense pierced
with arrows, whose name is Love and another name

Rebellion (the twinge, the gulf, split seconds,
the very raindrop, render, and instancy
of Love).
  All Poetry to this not-to-be-looked-upon sun
of Passion is the moon's cupped light; all
Politics to this moon, a moon's reflected
cupped light, like the moon of Rome, after
the deep wells of Grecian light sank low;
always the enemy is the foe at home.
  But these three are friends whose arms twine
without words; as, in a still air,
the great grove leans to wind, past and to come.

Fish Food

As you drank deep as Thor, did you think of milk or wine?
Did you drink blood, while you drank the salt deep?
Or see through the film of light, that sharpened your rage with
  its stare,
a shark, dolphin, turtle? Did you not see the Cat
who, when Thor lifted her, unbased the cubic ground?
You would drain fathomless flagons to be slaked with vacuum—
The sea's teats have suckled you, and you are sunk far
in bubble-dreams, under swaying translucent vines
of thundering interior wonder. Eagles can never now
carry parts of your body, over cupped mountains
as emblems of their anger, embers to fire self-hate
to other wonders, unfolding white flaming vistas.
Fishes now look upon you, with eyes which do not gossip.
Fishes are never shocked. Fishes will kiss you, each
fish tweak you; every kiss takes bits of you away,
till your bones alone will roll, with the Gulf Stream's swell.
So has it been already, so have the carpers and puffers
nibbled your carcass of fame, each to his liking. Now
in tides of noon, the bones of your thought-suspended structures
gleam as you intended. Noon pulled your eyes with small
magnetic headaches; the will seeped from your blood. Seeds

of meaning popped from the pods of thought. And you fall. And
the unseen
churn of Time changes the pearl-hued ocean;
like a pearl-shaped drop, in a huge water-clock
falling; from *came* to *go,* from *come* to *went.* And you fell.
Waters received you. Waters of our Birth in Death dissolve you.
Now you have willed it, may the Great Wash take you.
As the Mother-Lover takes your woe away, and cleansing
grief and you away, you sleep, you do not snore.
Lie still. Your rage is gone on a bright flood
away; as, when a bad friend held out his hand
you said, "Do not talk any more. I know you meant no harm."
What was the soil whence your anger sprang, who are deaf
as the stones to the whispering flight of the Mississippi's rivers?
What did you see as you fell? What did you hear as you sank?
Did it make you drunken with hearing?
I will not ask any more. You saw or heard no evil.

ALLEN TATE

Idiot

The idiot greens the meadows with his eyes,
The meadow creeps implacable and still;
A dog barks, the hammock swings, he lies.
One two three the cows bulge on the hill.

Motion that is not time erects snowdrifts
While sister's hand sieves waterfalls of lace.
With a palm fan closer than death he lifts
The Ozarks and tilted seas across his face.

In the long sunset where impatient sound
Strips niggers to a multiple of backs

Flies yield their heat, magnolias drench the ground
With Appomattox! The shadows lie in stacks.

The julep glass weaves echoes in Jim's kinks
While ashy Jim puts murmurs in the day:
Now in the idiot's heart a chamber stinks
Of dead asters, as the potter's field of May.

All evening the marsh is a slick pool
Where dream wild hares, witch hazel, pretty girls.
"Up from the important picnic of a fool
Those rotted asters!" Eddy on eddy swirls

The innocent mansion of a panther's heart!
It crumbles, tick-tick time drags it in
Till now his arteries lag and now they start
Reverence with the frigid gusts of sin:

The stillness pelts the eye, assaults the hair;
A beech sticks out a branch to warn the stars,
A lightning-bug jerks angles in the air,
Diving. "I am the captain of new wars!"

The dusk runs down the lane driven like hail;
Far off a precise whistle is escheat
To the dark; and then the towering weak and pale
Covers his eyes with memory like a sheet.

Last Days of Alice

Alice grown lazy, mammoth but not fat,
Declines upon her lost and twilight age;
Above in the dozing leaves the grinning cat
Quivers forever with his abstract rage:

Whatever light swayed on the perilous gate
Forever sways, nor will the arching grass,

Caught when the world clattered, undulate
In the deep suspension of the looking-glass.

Bright Alice! always pondering to gloze
The spoiled cruelty she had meant to say
Gazes learnedly down her airy nose
At nothing, nothing thinking all the day.

Turned absent-minded by infinity
She cannot move unless her double move,
The All-Alice of the world's entity
Smashed in the anger of her hopeless love,

Love for herself who, as an earthly twain,
Pouted to join her two in a sweet one;
No more the second lips to kiss in vain
The first she broke, plunged through the glass alone—

Alone to the weight of impassivity,
Incest of spirit, theorem of desire,
Without will as chalky cliffs by the sea,
Empty as the bodiless flesh of fire:

All space, that heaven is a dayless night,
A nightless day driven by perfect lust
For vacancy, in which her bored eyesight
Stares at the drowsy cubes of human dust.

—We too back to the world shall never pass
Through the shattered door, a dumb shade-harried crowd
Being all infinite, function depth and mass
Without figure, a mathematical shroud

Hurled at the air—blessèd without sin!
O God of our flesh, return us to Your wrath,
Let us be evil could we enter in
Your grace, and falter on the stony path!

The Robber Bridegroom

TALK BETWEEN BIRD AND GIRL

Turn back. Turn, young lady dear
A murderer's house you enter here

I was wooed and won little bird

(I have watched them come bright girls
Out of the rising sun, with curls)
The stair is tall the cellar deep
The wind coughs in the halls

I never wish to sleep

From the ceiling the sky falls
It will press you and press you dear

It is my desire to fear

(What a child! she desires her fear)
The house is whirling night, the guests
Grains of dust from the northwest

I do not come for rest

There is no rest for the dead

Ready for the couch of my groom

In a long room beneath the dew
Where the walls embrace and cling

I wear my wedding ring

He will cut off your finger
And the blood will linger

Little bird!

The Mediterranean

Quem das finem, rex magne, dolorum?

Where we went in the boat was a long bay
A slingshot wide, walled in by towering stone—
Peaked margin of antiquity's delay,
And we went there out of time's monotone:

Where we went in the black hull no light moved
But a gull white-winged along the feckless wave,
The breeze, unseen but fierce as a body loved,
That boat drove onward like a willing slave:

Where we went in the small ship the seaweed
Parted and gave to us the murmuring shore
And we made feast and in our secret need
Devoured the very plates Aeneas bore:

Where derelict you see through the low twilight
The green coast that you, thunder-tossed, would win,
Drop sail, and hastening to drink all night
Eat dish and bowl—to take that sweet land in!

Where we feasted and caroused on the sandless
Pebbles, affecting our day of piracy,
What prophecy of eaten plates could landless
Wanderers fulfil by the ancient sea?

We for that time might taste the famous age
Eternal here yet hidden from our eyes
When lust of power undid its stuffless rage;
They, in a wineskin, bore earth's paradise.

Let us lie down once more by the breathing side
Of Ocean, where our live forefathers sleep
As if the Known Sea still were a month wide—
Atlantis howls but is no longer steep!

What country shall we conquer, what fair land
Unman our conquest and locate our blood?
We've cracked the hemispheres with careless hand!
Now, from the Gates of Hercules we flood

Westward, westward till the barbarous brine
Whelms us to the tired world where tasseling corn,
Fat beans, grapes sweeter than muscadine
Rot on the vine: in that land were we born.

Shadow and Shade

The shadow streamed into the wall—
The wall, break-shadow in the blast;
We lingered wordless while a tall
Shade enclouded the shadow's cast.

The torrent of the reaching shade
Broke shadow into all its parts,
What then had been of shadow made
Found exigence in fits and starts

Where nothing properly had name
Save that still element the air,
Burnt sea of universal frame
In which impounded now we were:

I took her hand, I shut her eyes
And all her shadow cleft with shade,
Shadow was crushed beyond disguise
But, being fear, was unafraid.

I asked fair shadow at my side:
What more shall fiery shade require?

We lay long in the immense tide
Of shade and shadowy desire

And saw the dusk assail the wall,
The black surge, mounting, crash the stone!
Companion of this lust, we fall,
I said, lest we should die alone.

Ode to the Confederate Dead

Row after row with strict impunity
The headstones yield their names to the element.
The wind whirrs without recollection;
In the riven troughs the splayed leaves
Pile up, of nature the casual sacrament
To the seasonal eternity of death;
Then driven by the fierce scrutiny
Of heaven to their election in the vast breath,
They sough the rumor of mortality.

Autumn is desolation in the plot
Of a thousand acres where these memories grow
From the inexhaustible bodies that are not
Dead, but feed the grass row after rich row.
Think of the autumns that have come and gone!—
Ambitious November with the humors of the year,
With a particular zeal for every slab,
Staining the uncomfortable angels that rot
On the slabs, a wing chipped here, an arm there:
The brute curiosity of an angel's stare
Turns you, like them, to stone,
Transforms the heaving air
Till plunged to a heavier world below
You shift your sea-space blindly
Heaving, turning like the blind crab.

Dazed by the wind, only the wind
The leaves flying, plunge

You know who have waited by the wall
The twilight certainty of an animal,
Those midnight restitutions of the blood
You know—the immitigable pines, the smoky frieze
Of the sky, the sudden call: you know the rage,
The cold pool left by the mounting flood,
Of muted Zeno and Parmenides.
You who have waited for the angry resolution
Of those desires that should be yours tomorrow,
You know the unimportant shrift of death
And praise the vision
And praise the arrogant circumstance
Of those who fall
Rank upon rank, hurried beyond decision—
Here by the sagging gate, stopped by the wall.

Seeing, seeing only the leaves
Flying, plunge and expire

Turn your eyes to the immoderate past,
Turn to the inscrutable infantry rising
Demons out of the earth—they will not last.
Stonewall, Stonewall, and the sunken fields of hemp,
Shiloh, Antietam, Malvern Hill, Bull Run.
Lost in that orient of the thick and fast
You will curse the setting sun.

Cursing only the leaves crying
Like an old man in a storm

You hear the shout, the crazy hemlocks point
With troubled fingers to the silence which
Smothers you, a mummy, in time.

The hound bitch
Toothless and dying, in a musty cellar
Hears the wind only.

Now that the salt of their blood
Stiffens the saltier oblivion of the sea,

Seals the malignant purity of the flood,
What shall we who count our days and bow
Our heads with a commemorial woe
In the ribboned coats of grim felicity,
What shall we say of the bones, unclean,
Whose verdurous anonymity will grow?
The ragged arms, the ragged heads and eyes
Lost in these acres of the insane green?
The gray lean spiders come, they come and go;
In a tangle of willows without light
The singular screech-owl's tight
Invisible lyric seeds the mind
With the furious murmur of their chivalry.

We shall say only the leaves
Flying, plunge and expire

We shall say only the leaves whispering
In the improbable mist of nightfall
That flies on multiple wing:
Night is the beginning and the end
And in between the ends of distraction
Waits mute speculation, the patient curse
That stones the eyes, or like the jaguar leaps
For his own image in a jungle pool, his victim.

What shall we say who have knowledge
Carried to the heart? Shall we take the act
To the grave? Shall we, more hopeful, set up the grave
In the house? The ravenous grave?
Leave now
The shut gate and the decomposing wall:
The gentle serpent, green in the mulberry bush,
Riots with his tongue through the hush—
Sentinel of the grave who counts us all!

HART CRANE

Voyages

(II)

And yet this great wink of eternity,
Of rimless floods, unfettered leewardings,
Samite sheeted and processioned where
Her undinal vast belly moonward bends,
Laughing the wrapt inflections of our love;

Take this Sea, whose diapason knells
On scrolls of silver snowy sentences,
The sceptred terror of whose sessions rends
As her demeanors motion well or ill,
All but the pieties of lovers' hands.

And onward, as bells off San Salvador
Salute the crocus lustres of the stars,
In these poinsettia meadows of her tides,—
Adagios of islands, O my Prodigal,
Complete the dark confessions her veins spell.

Mark how her turning shoulders wind the hours,
And hasten while her penniless rich palms
Pass superscription of bent foam and wave,—
Hasten, while they are true,—sleep, death, desire,
Close round one instant in one floating flower.

Bind us in time, O Seasons clear, and awe.
O minstrel galleons of Carib fire,
Bequeath us to no earthly shore until
Is answered in the vortex of our grave
The seal's wide spindrift gaze toward paradise.

The River

(from *The Bridge*)

. . . and past the din and slogans of the year—

Stick your patent name on a signboard
brother—all over—going west—young man
Tintex—Japalac—Certain-teed Overalls ads
and land sakes! under the new playbill ripped
in the guaranteed corner—see Bert Williams what?
Minstrels when you steal a chicken just
save me the wing for if it isn't
Erie it ain't for miles around a
Mazda—and the telegraphic night coming on
    Thomas

a Ediford—and whistling down the tracks
a headlight rushing with the sound—can you
imagine—while an EXPRESS makes time like
SCIENCE—COMMERCE and the HOLYGHOST
RADIO ROARS IN EVERY HOME WE HAVE THE NORTHPOLE
WALLSTREET AND VIRGINBIRTH WITHOUT STONES OR
WIRES OR EVEN RUNning brooks connecting ears
and no more sermons windows flashing roar
Breathtaking—as you like it . . . eh?

So the 20th Century—so
whizzed the Limited—roared by and left
three men, still hungry on the tracks, ploddingly
watching the tail lights wizen and converge, slipping gimleted and neatly out of sight.

*

to those whose addresses are never near

The last bear, shot drinking in the Dakotas
Loped under wires that span the mountain stream.
Keen instruments, strung to a vast precision
Bind town to town and dream to ticking dream.
But some men take their liquor slow—and count
—Though they'll confess no rosary nor clue—
The river's minute by the far brook's year.

Under a world of whistles, wires and steam
Caboose-like they go ruminating through
Ohio, Indiana—blind baggage—
To Cheyenne tagging . . . Maybe Kalamazoo.

Time's rendings, time's blendings they construe
As final reckonings of fire and snow;
Strange bird-wit, like the elemental gist
Of unwalled winds they offer, singing low
My Old Kentucky Home and *Casey Jones,*
Some Sunny Day. I heard a road-gang chanting so.
And afterwards, who had a colt's eyes—one said,
"Jesus! Oh I remember watermelon days!" And sped
High in a cloud of merriment, recalled
"—And when my Aunt Sally Simpson smiled," he drawled—
"It was almost Louisiana, long ago."

"There's no place like Booneville though, Buddy,"
One said, excising a last burr from his vest,
"—For early trouting." Then peering in the can,
"—But I kept on the tracks." Possessed, resigned,
He trod the fire down pensively and grinned,
Spreading dry shingles of a beard. . . .

Behind
My father's cannery works I used to see
Rail-squatters ranged in nomad raillery,
The ancient men—wifeless or runaway
Hobo-trekkers that forever search
An empire wilderness of freight and rails.
Each seemed a child, like me, on a loose perch,
Holding to childhood like some termless play.
John, Jake or Charley, hopping the slow freight
—Memphis to Tallahassee—riding the rods,
Blind fists of nothing, humpty-dumpty clods.

Yet they touch something like a key perhaps.
From pole to pole across the hills, the states

—They know a body under the wide rain;
Youngsters with eyes like fjords, old reprobates
With racetrack jargon,—dotting immensity
They lurk across her, knowing her yonder breast
Snow-silvered, sumac-stained or smoky blue—
Is past the valley-sleepers, south or west.
—As I have trod the rumorous midnights, too,

but who have touched her, knowing her without name

And past the circuit of the lamp's thin flame
(O Nights that brought me to her body bare!)
Have dreamed beyond the print that bound her
name.
Trains sounding the long blizzards out—I heard
Wail into distances I knew were hers.
Papooses crying on the wind's long mane
Screamed redskin dynasties that fled the brain,
—Dead echoes! But I knew her body there,
Time like a serpent down her shoulder, dark,
And space, an eaglet's wing, laid on her hair.

Under the Ozarks, domed by Iron Mountain,
The old gods of the rain lie wrapped in pools
Where eyeless fish curvet a sunken fountain
And re-descend with corn from querulous crows.
Such pilferings make up their timeless eatage,
Propitiate them for their timber torn
By iron, iron—always the iron dealt cleavage!
They doze now, below axe and powder horn.

nor the myths of her fathers . . .

And Pullman breakfasters glide glistening steel
From tunnel into field—iron strides the dew—
Straddles the hill, a dance of wheel on wheel.
You have a half-hour's wait at Siskiyou,
Or stay the night and take the next train through.
Southward, near Cairo passing, you can see
The Ohio merging,—borne down Tennessee;
And if it's summer and the sun's in dusk
Maybe the breeze will lift the River's musk

—As though the waters breathed that you might
 know
Memphis Johnny, Steamboat Bill, Missouri Joe.
Oh, lean from the window, if the train slows down,
As though you touched hands with some ancient
 clown,
—A little while gaze absently below
And hum *Deep River* with them while they go.

Yes, turn again and sniff once more—look see,
O Sheriff, Brakeman and Authority—
Hitch up your pants and crunch another quid,
For you too, feed the River timelessly.
And few evade full measure of their fate;
Always they smile out eerily what they seem.
I could believe hc joked at heaven's gate—
Dan Midland—jolted from the cold brake-beam.

Down, down—born pioneers in time's despite,
Grimed tributaries to an ancient flow—
They win no frontier by their wayward plight,
But drift in stillness, as from Jordan's brow.

You will not hear it as the sea; even stone
Is not more hushed by gravity . . . But slow,
As loth to take more tribute—sliding prone
Like one whose eyes were buried long ago

The River, spreading, flows—and spends your
 dream.
What are you, lost within this tideless spell?
You are your father's father, and the stream—
A liquid theme that floating niggers swell.

Damp tonnage and alluvial march of days—
Nights turbid, vascular with silted shale
And roots surrendered down of moraine clays:
The Mississippi drinks the farthest dale.

O quarrying passion, undertowed sunlight!
The basalt surface drags a jungle grace
Ochreous and lynx-barred in lengthening might;
Patience! and you shall reach the biding place!

Over De Soto's bones the freighted floors
Throb past the City storied of three thrones.
Down two more turns the Mississippi pours
(Anon tall ironsides up from salt lagoons)

And flows within itself, heaps itself free.
All fades but one thin skyline 'round . . . Ahead
No embrace opens but the stinging sea;
The River lifts itself from its long bed,

Poised wholly on its dream, a mustard glow
Tortured with history, its one will—flow!
—The Passion spreads in wide tongues, choked and slow,
Meeting the Gulf, hosannas silently below.

The Dance

(from *The Bridge*)

The swift red flesh, a winter king—
Who squired the glacier woman down the sky
She ran the neighing canyons all the spring;
She spouted arms; she rose with maize—to die.

And in the autumn drouth, whose burnished hands
With mineral wariness found out the stone
Where prayers, forgotten, streamed the mesa sands?
He holds the twilight's dim, perpetual throne.

Mythical brows we saw retiring—loth,
Disturbed and destined, into denser green.
Greeting they sped us, on the arrow's oath:
Now lie incorrigibly what years between . . .

Then you shall see her truly—your blood remembering its first invasion of her secrecy, its first encounters with her kin, her chieftain lover . . . his shade that haunts the lakes and hills

There was a bed of leaves, and broken play;
There was a veil upon you, Pocahontas, bride—
O Princess whose brown lap was virgin May;
And bridal flanks and eyes hid tawny pride.

I left the village for dogwood. By the canoe
Tugging below the mill-race, I could see
Your hair's keen crescent running, and the blue
First moth of evening take wing stealthily.

What laughing chains the water wove and threw!
I learned to catch the trout's moon whisper; I
Drifted how many hours I never knew,
But, watching, saw that fleet young crescent die,—

And one star, swinging, take its place, alone,
Cupped in the larches of the mountain pass—
Until, immortally, it bled into the dawn.
I left my sleek boat nibbling margin grass . . .

I took the portage climb, then chose
A further valley-shed; I could not stop.
Feet nozzled wat'ry webs of upper flows;
One white veil gusted from the very top.

O Appalachian Spring! I gained the ledge;
Steep, inaccessible smile that eastward bends
And northward reaches in that violet wedge
Of Adirondacks!—wisped of azure wands,

Over how many bluffs, tarns, streams I sped!
—And knew myself within some boding shade:—
Grey tepees tufting the blue knolls ahead,
Smoke swirling through the yellow chestnut
glade . . .

A distant cloud, a thunder-bud—it grew,
That blanket of the skies: the padded foot
Within,—I heard it; 'til its rhythm drew,
—Siphoned the black pool from the heart's hot root!

A cyclone threshes in the turbine crest,
Swooping in eagle feathers down your back;
Know, Maquokeeta, greeting; know death's best;
—Fall, Sachem, strictly as the tamarack!

A birch kneels. All her whistling fingers fly.
The oak grove circles in a crash of leaves;
The long moan of a dance is in the sky.
Dance, Maquokeeta: Pocahontas grieves . . .

And every tendon scurries toward the twangs
Of lightning deltaed down your saber hair.
Now snaps the flint in every tooth; red fangs
And splay tongues thinly busy the blue air . . .

Dance, Maquokeeta! snake that lives before,
That casts his pelt, and lives beyond! Sprout, horn!
Spark, tooth! Medicine-man, relent, restore—
Lie to us,—dance us back the tribal morn!

Spears and assemblies: black drums thrusting on—
O yelling battlements,—I, too, was liege
To rainbows currying each pulsant bone:
Surpassed the circumstance, danced out the siege!

And buzzard-circleted, screamed from the stake;
I could not pick the arrows from my side.
Wrapped in that fire, I saw more escorts wake—
Flickering, sprint up the hill groins like a tide.

I heard the hush of lava wrestling your arms,
And stag teeth foam about the raven throat;
Flame cataracts of heaven in seething swarms
Fed down your anklets to the sunset's moat.

O, like the lizard in the furious noon,
That drops his legs and colors in the sun,
—And laughs, pure serpent, Time itself, and moon
Of his own fate, I saw thy change begun!

And saw thee dive to kiss that destiny
Like one white meteor, sacrosanct and blent
At last with all that's consummate and free
There, where the first and last gods keep thy tent.

*

Thewed of the levin, thunder-shod and lean,
Lo, through what infinite seasons dost thou gaze—
Across what bivouacs of thin angered slain,
And see'st thy bride immortal in the maize!

Totem and fire-gall, slumbering pyramid—
Though other calendars now stack the sky,
Thy freedom is her largesse, Prince, and hid
On paths thou knewest best to claim her by.

High unto Labrador the sun strikes free
Her speechless dream of snow, and stirred again,
She is the torrent and the singing tree;
And she is virgin to the last of men . . .

West, west and south! winds over Cumberland
And winds across the llano grass resume
Her hair's warm sibilance. Her breasts are fanned
O stream by slope and vineyard—into bloom!

And when the caribou slant down for salt
Do arrows thirst and leap? Do antlers shine
Alert, star-triggered in the listening vault
Of dusk?—And are her perfect brows to thine?

We danced, O Brave, we danced beyond their farms,
In cobalt desert closures made our vows . . .
Now is the strong prayer folded in thine arms,
The serpent with the eagle in the boughs.

Indiana

(from *The Bridge*)

. . . and read her in a mother's farewell gaze.

The morning-glory, climbing the morning long
  Over the lintel on its wiry vine,
Closes before the dusk, furls in its song
      As I close mine . . .

And bison thunder rends my dreams no more
  As once my womb was torn, my boy, when you
Yielded your first cry at the prairie's door . . .
      Your father knew

Then, though we'd buried him behind us, far
  Back on the gold trail—then his lost bones stirred . . .
But you who drop the scythe to grasp the oar
      Knew not, nor heard.

How we, too, Prodigal, once rode off, too—
  Waved Seminary Hill a gay good-bye . . .
We found God lavish there in Colorado
      But passing sly.

The pebbles sang, the firecat slunk away
  And glistening through the sluggard freshets came
In golden syllables loosed from the clay
      His gleaming name.

A dream called Eldorado was his town,
  It rose up shambling in the nuggets' wake,
It had no charter but a promised crown
      Of claims to stake.

But we,—too late, too early, howsoever—
  Won nothing out of fifty-nine—those years—

But gilded promise, yielded to us never,
        And barren tears . . .

The long trail back! I huddled in the shade
Of wagon-tenting looked out once and saw
Bent westward, passing on a stumbling jade
        A homeless squaw—

Perhaps a halfbreed. On her slender back
  She cradled a babe's body, riding without rein.
Her eyes, strange for an Indian's, were not black
        But sharp with pain

And like twin stars. They seemed to shun the gaze
  Of all our silent men—the long team line—
Until she saw me—when their violet haze
        Lit with love shine . . .

I held you up—I suddenly the bolder,
  Knew that mere words could not have brought us
    nearer.
She nodded—and that smile across her shoulder
        Will still endear her

As long as Jim, your father's memory, is warm.
  Yes, Larry, now you're going to sea, remember
You were the first—before Ned and this farm,—
        First-born, remember—

And since then—all that's left to me of Jim
  Whose folks, like mine, came out of Arrowhead.
And you're the only one with eyes like him—
        Kentucky bred!

I'm standing still, I'm old, I'm half of stone!
  Oh, hold me in those eyes' engaging blue;
There's where the stubborn years gleam and atone,—
        Where gold is true!

Down the dim turnpike to the river's edge—
  Perhaps I'll hear the mare's hoofs to the ford . . .
Write me from Rio . . . and you'll keep your
    pledge;
      I know your word!

Come back to Indiana—not too late!
  (Or will you be a ranger to the end?)
Good-bye . . . Good-bye . . . oh, I shall always
    wait
  You, Larry, traveller—
                stranger,
                      son,
                          —my friend—

Atlantis

(from *The Bridge*)

Music is then the knowledge of that which relates to love in harmony and system.
—Plato

Through the bound cable strands, the arching path
Upward, veering with light, the flight of strings,—
Taut miles of shuttling moonlight syncopate
The whispered rush, telepathy of wires.
Up the index of night, granite and steel—
Transparent meshes—fleckless the gleaming staves—
Sibylline voices flicker, waveringly stream
As though a god were issue of the strings. . . .

And through that cordage, threading with its call
One arc synoptic of all tides below—
Their labyrinthine mouths of history
Pouring reply as though all ships at sea
Complighted in one vibrant breath made cry,—
"Make thy love sure—to weave whose song we ply!"

—From black embankments, moveless soundings hailed,
So seven oceans answer from their dream.

And on, obliquely up bright carrier bars
New octaves trestle the twin monoliths
Beyond whose frosted capes the moon bequeaths
Two worlds of sleep (O arching strands of song!)—
Onward and up the crystal-flooded aisle
White tempest nets file upward, upward ring
With silver terraces the humming spars,
The loft of vision, palladium helm of stars.

Sheerly the eyes, like seagulls stung with rime—
Slit and propelled by glistening fins of light—
Pick biting way up towering looms that press
Sidelong with flight of blade on tendon blade
—Tomorrows into yesteryear—and link
What cipher-script of time no traveller reads
But who, through smoking pyres of love and death,
Searches the timeless laugh of mythic spears.

Like hails, farewells—up planet-sequined heights
Some trillion whispering hammers glimmer Tyre:
Serenely, sharply up the long anvil cry
Of inchling æons silence rivets Troy.
And you, aloft there—Jason! hesting Shout!
Still wrapping harness to the swarming air!
Silvery the rushing wake, surpassing call,
Beams yelling Æolus! splintered in the straits!

From gulfs unfolding, terrible of drums,
Tall Vision-of-the-Voyage, tensely spare—
Bridge, lifting night to cycloramic crest
Of deepest day—O Choir, translating time
Into what multitudinous Verb the suns
And synergy of waters ever fuse, recast
In myriad syllables,—Psalm of Cathay!
O Love, thy white, pervasive Paradigm . . . !

We left the haven hanging in the night—
Sheened harbor lanterns backward fled the keel.
Pacific here at time's end, bearing corn,—
Eyes stammer through the pangs of dust and steel.
And still the circular, indubitable frieze
Of heaven's meditation, yoking wave
To kneeling wave, one song devoutly binds—
The vernal strophe chimes from deathless strings!

O Thou steeled Cognizance whose leap commits
The agile precincts of the lark's return;
Within whose lariat sweep encinctured sing
In single chrysalis the many twain,—
Of stars Thou art the stitch and stallion glow
And like an organ, Thou, with sound of doom—
Sight, sound and flesh Thou leadest from time's realm
As love strikes clear direction for the helm.

Swift peal of secular light, intrinsic Myth
Whose fell unshadow is death's utter wound,—
O River-throated—iridescently upborne
Through the bright drench and fabric of our veins;
With white escarpments swinging into light,
Sustained in tears the cities are endowed
And justified conclamant with ripe fields
Revolving through their harvests in sweet torment.

Forever Deity's glittering Pledge, O Thou
Whose canticle fresh chemistry assigns
To rapt inception and beatitude,—
Always through blinding cables, to our joy,
Of thy white seizure springs the prophecy:
Always through spiring cordage, pyramids
Of silver sequel, Deity's young name
Kinetic of white choiring wings . . . ascends.

Migrations that must needs void memory,
Inventions that cobblestone the heart,—
Unspeakable Thou Bridge to Thee, O Love.

Thy pardon for this history, whitest Flower,
O Answerer of all,—Anemone,—
Now while thy petals spend the suns about us, hold—
(O Thou whose radiance doth inherit me)
Atlantis,—hold thy floating singer late!

So to thine Everpresence, beyond time,
Like spears ensanguined of one tolling star
That bleeds infinity—the orphic strings,
Sidereal phalanxes, leap and converge:
—One Song, one Bridge of Fire! Is it Cathay,
Now pity steeps the grass and rainbows ring
The serpent with the eagle in the leaves . . . ?
Whispers antiphonal in azure swing.

Paraphrase

Of a steady winking beat between
Systole, diastole spokes-of-a-wheel
One rushing from the bed at night
May find the record wedged in his soul.

Above the feet the clever sheets
Lie guard upon the integers of life:
For what skims in between uncurls the toe,
Involves the hands in purposeless repose.

But from its bracket how can the tongue tell
When systematic morn shall sometime flood
The pillow—how desperate is the light
That shall not rouse, how faint the crow's cavil

As, when stunned in that antarctic blaze,
Your head, unrocking to a pulse, already
Hallowed by air, posts a white paraphrase
Among bruised roses on the papered wall.

In Shadow

Out in the late amber afternoon,
Confused among chrysanthemums,
Her parasol, a pale balloon,
Like a waiting moon, in shadow swims.

Her furtive lace and misty hair
Over the garden dial distill
The sunlight,—then withdrawing, wear
Again the shadows at her will.

Gently yet suddenly, the sheen
Of stars inwraps her parasol.
She hears my step behind the green
Twilight, stiller than shadows, fall.

"Come, it is too late,—too late
To risk alone the light's decline:
Nor has the evening long to wait,"—
But her own words are night's and mine.

Legend

As silent as a mirror is believed
Realities plunge in silence by . . .

I am not ready for repentance;
Nor to match regrets. For the moth
Bends no more than the still
Imploring flame. And tremorous
In the white falling flakes
Kisses are,—
The only worth all granting.

It is to be learned—
This cleaving and this burning,

But only by the one who
Spends out himself again.

Twice and twice.
(Again the smoking souvenir,
Bleeding eidolon!) and yet again.
Until the bright logic is won
Unwhispering as a mirror
Is believed.

Then, drop by caustic drop, a perfect cry
Shall string some constant harmony,—
Relentless caper for all those who step
The legend of their youth into the noon.

Voyages

(VI)

Where icy and bright dungeons lift
Of swimmers their lost morning eyes,
And ocean rivers, churning, shift
Green borders under stranger skies,

Steadily as a shell secretes
Its beating leagues of monotone,
Or as many waters trough the sun's
Red kelson past the cape's wet stone;

O rivers mingling toward the sky
And harbor of the phœnix' breast—
My eyes pressed black against the prow,
—Thy derelict and blinded guest

Waiting, afire, what name, unspoke,
I cannot claim: let thy waves rear
More savage than the death of kings,
Some splintered garland for the seer.

Beyond siroccos harvesting
The solstice thunders, crept away,
Like a cliff swinging or a sail
Flung into April's inmost day—

Creation's blithe and petalled word
To the lounged goddess when she rose
Conceding dialogue with eyes
That smile unsearchable repose—

Still fervid covenant, Belle Isle,
—Unfolded floating dais before
Which rainbows twine continual hair—
Belle Isle, white echo of the oar!

The imaged Word, it is, that holds
Hushed willows anchored in its glow.
It is the unbetrayable reply
Whose accent no farewell can know.

LEONIE ADAMS

Country Summer

Now the rich cherry whose sleek wood
And top with silver petals traced,
Like a strict box its gems encased,
Has spilt from out that cunning lid,
All in an innocent green round,
Those melting rubies which it hid;
With moss ripe-strawberry-encrusted,
So birds get half, and minds lapse merry
To taste that deep-red lark's-bite berry,
And blackcap-bloom is yellow-dusted.

The wren that thieved it in the eaves
A trailer of the rose could catch
To her poor droopy sloven thatch,
And side by side with the wren's brood,—
A lovely time of beggars' luck—
Opens the quaint and hairy bud.
And full and golden is the yield
Of cows that never have to house,
But all night nibble under boughs,
Or cool their sides in the moist field.

Into the rooms flow meadow airs,
The warm farm-baking smell blows round;
Inside and out and sky and ground
Are much the same; the wishing star,
Hesperus, kind and early-born,
Is risen only finger-far.
All stars stand close in summer air,
And tremble, and look mild as amber;
When wicks are lighted in the chamber
You might say stars were settling there.

Now straightening from the flowery hay,
Down the still light the mowers look;
Or turn, because their dreaming shook,
And they waked half to other days,
When left alone in yellow-stubble,
The rusty-coated mare would graze.
Yet thick the lazy dreams are born;
Another thought can come to mind,
But like the shivering of the wind,
Morning and evening in the corn.

Sundown

This is the time lean woods shall spend
A steeped-up twilight, and the pale evening drink,

And the perilous roe, the leaper to the west brink,
Trembling and bright, to the caverned cloud descend.

Now shall you see pent oak gone gusty and frantic,
Stooped with dry weeping, ruinously unloosing
The sparse disheveled leaf, or reared and tossing
A dreary scarecrow bough in funeral antic.

Aye, tatter you and rend,
Oak heart, to your profession mourning, not obscure
The outcome, not crepuscular, on the deep floor,
Sable and gold match lusters and contend.

And rags of shrouding will not muffle the slain.
This is the immortal extinction, the priceless wound
Not to be staunched; the live gold leaks beyond,
And matter's sanctified, dipped in a gold stain.

OSCAR WILLIAMS

The Leg in the Subway

When I saw the woman's leg on the floor of the subway train,
Protrude beyond the panel (while her body overflowed my
  mind's eye),
When I saw the pink stocking, black shoe, curve bulging with
  warmth,
The delicate etching of the hair behind the flesh-colored gauze,
When I saw the ankle of Mrs. Nobody going nowhere for a
  nickel,
When I saw this foot motionless on the moving motionless floor,
My mind caught on a nail of a distant star, I was wrenched out
Of the reality of the subway ride, I hung in a socket of distance:
And this is what I saw:

The long tongue of the earth's speed was licking the leg,
Upward and under and around went the long tongue of speed:
It was made of a flesh invisible, it dripped the saliva of miles:
It drank moment, lit shivers of insecurity in niches between bones:
It was full of eyes, it stopped licking to look at the passengers:
It was as alive as a worm, and busier than anybody in the train:

It spoke saying: To whom does this leg belong? Is it a bonus leg
For the rush hour? Is it a forgotten leg? Among the many
Myriads of legs did an extra leg fall in from the Out There?
O Woman, sliced off bodily by the line of the panel, shall I roll
Your leg into the abdominal nothing, among the digestive teeth?
Or shall I fit it in with the pillars that hold up the headlines?
But nobody spoke, though all the faces were talking silently,
As the train zoomed, a zipper closing up swiftly the seam of time.

Alas, said the long tongue of the speed of the earth quite faintly,
What is one to do with an incorrigible leg that will not melt—
But everybody stopped to listen to the train vomiting cauldrons
Of silence, while somebody's jolted-out afterthought trickled down
The blazing shirt-front solid with light bulbs, and just then
The planetary approach of the next station exploded atoms of light,
And when the train stopped, the leg had grown a surprising mate,
And the long tongue had slipped hurriedly out through a window:

I perceived through the hole left by the nail of the star in my mind
How civilization was as dark as a wood and dimensional with things
And how birds dipped in chromium sang in the crevices of our deeds.

Dinner Guest

Evening, and the slender sugar tongs of a bird's small voice
Pick up the flawless square of our mood from the rim of
thought:
We see the down on the big blond face of the Everywhere,
And the sudden flashing of the carnivorous smile of nature.

We are having dinner with the formal ogre of allness
At the Arts Club among the mirrors and paintings of mirrors:
It is a breakwater moment and against a wall of grinning face
We perceive a radio, the last tooth posted within that mirth.

The cuckoo of light hops out, calling intimate time of the heart
Across the immaculate landscape of the tablecloth and the wine
Of realization, while the hands like gaunt animals are prowling
At the fable's edge, pecking at the crumbs of recrimination.

Dinner time, and the nervous system stretches its starved legs
Into the future, like a driven nail stretching out its length
Into a sea of wood; we are held by a hunger that is good for life;
And Tom Thumb is the guest of the ogre with the gracious
mouth.

The famous paintings around us know how to stay adroitly dead
Giving off the soft lustre of the past and without blinking:
The dinner in the Arts Club flows on, a river of abstraction,
We are miles from the insane beggar who mumbled for a nickel.

Whatever we die of, we shall never die of compassion
In a world lined to the browline with the bins of injustice;
Our fears leaven the bank balance to a frightening sum,
But the genial dinner ransoms the moment fallen among bandits.

We need no death's-head like the Egyptians had at their feasts,
The murdered circumstance stands with wet paws on the marble
Escaped from a movie of the future in the corner arcade;
Dining rooms grow dangerous in an age of guess and garble.

Though we soak our walls in music, patch the eye's blindspots
With murals of morals and dash about in a mess of mass,
We go through a lot of nature with our stupendous digestion
To reach the certainty of one noble sensation at the heart.

Ours is a last supper, without disciples; it is the atom supping
With the boulder, the bead of sweat with the cold great lake,
The eyeball's gloss with a planet on fire, the dot entertained
By encyclopedias of nonsense; man is the guest of the ogre mind.

The Man Coming Toward You

The man coming toward you is falling forward on all fronts:
He has just come in from the summer hot box of circumstance,
His obedient arm pulls a ticket from the ticket machine,
A bell announces to the long tables his presence on the scene;
The room is crowded with Last Suppers and the air is angry;
The halleluiahs lift listless heads; the man is hungry.

He looks at the people, the rings of lights, the aisles, the chairs,
They mass and attack his eyes and they take him unawares,
But in a moment it is over and the immense hippopotamus cries
And swims away to safety in the vast past of his eyes;
The weeks recoil before the days, the years before the months;
The man is hungry and keeps moving forward on all fronts.

His hair is loosening, his teeth are at bay, he breathes fear,
His nails send futile tendrils into the belly of the atmosphere;
Every drop of his blood is hanging loose in the universe;
His children's faces everywhere bring down the college doors;
He is growing old on all fronts; his foes and his friends
Are bleeding behind invisible walls bedecked with dividends;

His wife is aging, and his skin puts on its anonymous gloves;
The man is helpless, surrounded by two billion hates and loves;
Look at him squirm inside his clothes, the harpies around his
ears,

In just one minute his brother will have aged four thousand
years.
Who records his stupendous step on the delicate eardrum of
Chance?
The man coming toward you is marching forward on all fronts.

The Last Supper

I

Apostles of the hidden sun
Are come unto the room of breath
Hung with the banging blinds of death,
The body twelve, the spirit one,
Far as the eye, in earth arrayed,
The night shining, the supper laid.

II

The wine shone on the table that evening of history
Like an enormous ruby in the bauble and mystery.

In the glowing walls of the flickering decanter
There moved His face as at the world's center.

The hands of Judas showed up red and hurried
And the light hit them so, like a cross carried.

The faces of the others were there and moving
In the crystal of the dome, swiftly hovering.

The saints, under a lens, shrunken to pigmies,
Gesticulated in birds or in colored enigmas.

Outside there was a storm, the sound of temblors,
The blood bubbled and sprang into the tumblers.

When the morning came like a white wall of stone,
The day lay in the glass and the blood was gone.

MARYA ZATURENSKA

The White Dress

Imperceptively the world became haunted by her white dress.
Walking in forest or garden, he would start to see,
Her flying form; sudden, swift, brief as a caress
The flash of her white dress against a darkening tree.

And with forced unconcern, withheld desire, and pain
He beheld her at night; and when sleepless in his bed,
Her light footfalls seemed loud as cymbals; deep as his disdain,
Her whiteness entered his heart, flowed through from feet to head.

Or it was her face at a window, her swift knock at the door,
Then she appeared in her white dress, her face as white as her gown;
Like snow in midsummer she came and left the rich day poor;
And the sun chilled and grew higher, remote, and the moon slipped down.

So the years passed; more fierce in pursuit her image grew;
She became the dream abjured, the ill uncured, the deed undone,
The life one never lived, the answer one never knew
Till the white shadow swayed the moon, stayed the expiring sun.

Until at his life's end, the shadow of the white face, the white dress
Became his inmost thought, his private wound, the word unspoken,
All that he cherished in failure, all that had failed his success;
She became the crystal orb, half-seen, untouched, unbroken.

There on his death bed, kneeling at the bed's foot, he trembling
saw,
The image of the Mother-Goddess, enormous, archaic, cruel,
Overpowering the universe, creating her own inexorable law,
Molded of stone, but her fire and ice flooded the room like a pool.

And she was the shadow in the white dress, no longer slight and
flying,
But solid as death. Her cold, firm, downward look,
Brought close to the dissolving mind the marvellous act of dying,
And on her lap, the clasped, closed, iron book.

Lightning for Atmosphere

The warriors, tigers, flowers of Delacroix
Painted upon the walls ablaze with light
Pure light, cloud blanched, that unstained white,
Queen of the colors, whom all other tints destroy,
Color of the dwindling moon.

Or white lightning, seascapes of Chateaubriand
Shores the dramatic ocean beats upon,
Where the lone hero, gloomy on the wild strand
Sees friends and lovers and companions gone,
Hawk, gull, and heron flying.

White-capped mountains, peaks of dazzling snow
Cloud-pointed Alps, sharp unclimbable heights
Burning effulgence of the northern lights
Toward whose clear radiance, our desire grows,
White heat of the infinite.

The intense young lady seen in a dream long gone
Ringleted, lonely in her villa by the sea
Peers through a misted window, sees the floating swan,
Wild geese whiten the sky, lighten the fir tree
Shrill, sound-shattering solitude.

White-gowned in the thin, nocturnal air
She throws her book aside and her fine ear
Hears flying catches of joy, the ecstatic fear,
Whiteness of the abyss; through her soul's precipice
Dark flows the midnight of her hanging hair.

She through a deep hallucination seeing
Strong waves from sheer, salt oceans, drowned lovers
Pallid and proud. The white blank mind discovers
Figures rising from waterfalls, appearing, fleeing
Into damp creeks, into the steep ravines.

All hearts have their precipices, Alps, white peaks
Moments when the white bird with the deep wound must come
To sing and swoon upon enchanted willows,
The heart disguises its symbols, peers through the hid ravines
Steep-gaping between wars.

HOWARD BAKER

A Letter from the Country

To a Young Editor

If you are bound to till a soil where farms
Long sown to whirlwinds lavishly crop storms,
  Then I suggest your program be
  One of informed tenacity.

You'll find the manners of our rural folk
Too mild, where smoking tractors stain the oak,
  Where lakebeds heave up to the sun
  And deserts with deep rivers run:

A fetid land, for there plain fruits are spurned,
Raised to be gazed at, fingered, and be burned;
    Years pass, where almanacs are mad,
    Harvestless save to reap a fad.

These things, I mean, are merely outward signs.
For there are inward wolves who trace our vines
    And mark, in name of sensuous truth,
    Each grape with orgiastic tooth:

Magicians of the senses, necromancers,
And arty exhibitionistic dancers—
    These you must steadily defy
    Lest they give you their evil eye.

Defiance, bent like a familiar cloak;
Hate, choicest heirloom from your buried folk;
    And frugal narrow-mindedness—
    Cut from these cloths your usual dress.

Be much hedged in. Rehearse the ancient ways
Till to your strong windbreak on wholesome days,
    Timid, to fright still uninured,
    Comes Amaryllis, reassured;

Comes softly, briar-scratched, with tangled hair,
Leading those others who wait and shyly stare—
    Masters who fled the savage wave,
    Returned unkempt from their high cave.

Then lean your head to their slow syllables:
Whispering deep seas beneath the fleeting gulls:
    The torch of Hecuba, the birth,
    Ruined Ilium fading into earth:

Of sin, and change, which never changes sin,
Speak these, the seashells; their voice is the thin
    Threaded impalpable high cry,
    The constant in humanity.

Pity alone one who in learned tone
Drops wistful notes on youths and seasons flown;
  The rest, come back from Death's black lands,
  Once held Death off with naked hands.

Visitors from impending quiet, they!
They patiently await a better day.
  Meanwhile a tale, though poor of laurel,
  Is worth retelling for its moral.

Hold to your cottage, yet be swift to sting
The pedlar who displays a ciphered ring
  And nostrums made of standard parts,
  Who lisps of shortcuts to the arts;

Lest unobserved he spell his runic schemes,
Rest in a bed of cold ill-natured dreams;
  Leave with your napkin your cheer at table.
  That is the lesson; this the fable:

A bee who made a pasture her domain
Taught cows that it was healthful to abstain
  Till she herself was through with clover;
  And many picnics chased to cover.

She reigned a vixen till one day, too kind,
She let a cow, low bowing, come behind,
  Catch up and wrap her in its tongue.
  Mussed and enraged, she would have stung,

Except that vengeance seemed a richer feast
If taken in the inwards of the beast.
  So down a warm canal she moved—
  Lethe for her, it almost proved.

She slept; dreamt regal dreams of one cow's fate;
Awoke with verdict sealed, but rather late;
  With stinger poised, the sheath withdrawn,
  She noticed that the cow was gone.

ROBERT PENN WARREN

Ballad of a Sweet Dream of Peace

1. And Don't Forget Your Corset Cover, Either

And why, in God's name, is that elegant bureau
Standing out here in the woods and dark?
Because, in God's name, it would create a furor
If such a Victorian piece were left in the middle of Central Park,
To corrupt the morals of young and old
With its marble top and drawer pulls gilt gold
And rosewood elaborately scrolled,
And would you, in truth, want your own young sister to see it in the Park?
But she knows all about it, her mother has told her,
And besides, these days, she is getting much older,
And why, in God's name, is that bureau left in the woods?
All right, I'll tell you why.
It has as much right there as you or I,
For the woods are God's temple, and even a bureau has moods.
But why, in God's name, is that elegant bureau left all alone in the woods?

It is left in the woods for the old lady's sake,
For there's privacy here for a household chore,
And Lord, I can't tell you the time it can take
To apply her own mixture of beeswax and newt-oil to bring out the gloss once more.
For the poor old hands move slower each night,
And can't manage to hold the cloth very tight,
And it's hard without proper light.

But why, in God's name, all this privacy for a simple household chore?
In God's name, sir! would you simply let
Folks see how naked old ladies can get?
Then let the old bitch buy some clothes like other folks do.
She once had some clothes, I am told,
But they're long since ruined by the damp and mold,
And the problem is deeper when bones let the wind blow through.
Besides it's not civil to call her a bitch, and her your own grandma, too.

2. *Keepsakes*

Oh, what brings her out in the dark and night?
She has mislaid something, just what she can't say,
But something to do with the bureau, all right.
Then why, in God's name, does she polish so much, and not look in a drawer right away?
Every night, in God's name, she does look there,
But finds only a Book of Common Prayer,
A ribbon-tied lock of gold hair,
A bundle of letters, some contraceptives, and an orris-root sachet.
Well, what is the old fool hunting for?
Oh, nothing, oh, nothing that's in the top drawer,
For that's left by late owners who had their own grief to withstand,
And she tries to squinch and frown
As she peers at the Prayer Book upside down,
And the contraceptives are something she can't understand,
And oh, how bitter the tears she sheds, with some stranger's old letters in hand!

You're lying, you're lying, she can't shed a tear!
Not with eyeballs gone, and the tear ducts, too.
You are trapped in a vulgar error, I fear,
For asleep in the bottom drawer is a thing that may prove instructive to you:
Just an old-fashioned doll with a china head,
And a cloth body naked and violated

By a hole through which sawdust once bled,
But drop now by drop, on a summer night, from her heart it is
treacle bleeds through.
In God's name, what!—Do I see her eyes move?
Of course, and she whispers, "I died for love,"
And your grandmother whines like a dog in the dark and shade,
For she's hunting somebody to give
Her the life they had promised her she would live,
And I shudder to think what a stink and stir will be made
When some summer night she opens the drawer and finds that
poor self she'd mislaid.

3. Go It, Granny—Go It, Hog!

Out there in the dark, what's that horrible chomping?
Oh, nothing, just hogs that forage for mast,
And if you call, "Hoo-pig!" they'll squeal and come romping,
For they'll know from your voice you're the boy who slopped
them in dear, dead days long past.
Any hogs that I slopped are long years dead,
And eaten by somebody and evacuated,
So it's simply absurd, what you said.
You fool, poor fool, all Time is a dream, and we're all one Flesh,
at last,
And the hogs know that, and that's why they wait,
Though tonight the old thing is a little bit late,
But they're mannered, these hogs, as they wait for her creaky
old tread.
Polite, they will sit in a ring,
Till she finishes work, the poor old thing:
Then old bones get knocked down with a clatter to wake up the
dead,
And it's simply absurd how loud she can scream with no shred
of a tongue in her head.

4. Friends of the Family, or Bowling a Sticky Cricket

Who else, in God's name, comes out in these woods?
Old friends of the family, whom you never saw,

Like yon cranky old coot, who mumbles and broods,
With yachting cap, rusty frock coat, and a placard proclaiming,
"I am the Law!"
What makes him go barefoot at night in God's dew?
In God's name, you idiot, so would you
If you'd suffered as he had to
When expelled from his club for the horrible hobby that taught him the nature of law.
They learned that he drowned his crickets in claret.
The club used cologne, and so couldn't bear it.
But they drown them in claret in Buckingham Palace!
Fool, law is inscrutable, so
Barefoot in dusk and dew he must go,
And at last each cries out in a dark stone-glimmering place,
"I have heard the voice in the dark, seeing not who utters. Show me Thy face!"

5. *You Never Knew Her Either, Though You Thought You Did, Inside Out*

Why now, in God's name, is her robe de nuit
So torn and bedraggled, and what is that stain?
It's only dried blood, in God's name, that you see.
But why does she carry that leaf in her hand? Will you try, in God's name, to explain?
It's a burdock leaf under which she once found
Two toads in coitu on the bare black ground,
So now she is nightly bound
To come forth to the woods to embrace a thorn tree, to try to understand pain,
And then wipes the blood on her silken hair,
And cries aloud, "Oh, we need not despair,
For I bleed, oh, I bleed, and God lives!" And the heart may stir
Like water beneath wind's tread
That wanders whither it is not said.
Oh, I almost forgot—will you please identify her?
She's the afternoon one who to your bed came, lip damp, the breath like myrrh.

6. *I Guess You Ought to Know Who You Are*

Could that be a babe crawling there in night's black?
Why, of course, in God's name, and birth-blind, but you'll see
How to that dead chestnut he'll crawl a straight track,
Then give the astonishing tongue of a hound with a coon treed up in a tree.
Well, who is the brat, and what's he up to?
He's the earlier one that they thought would be you,
And perhaps, after all, it was true,
For it's hard in these matters to tell sometimes. *But look, in God's name, I am me!*
If you are, there's the letter a hog has in charge,
With a gold coronet and your own name writ large,
And in French, most politely, "Répondez s'il vous plaît."
Now don't be alarmed we are late.
What's time to a hog? We'll just let them wait.
But for when you are ready, our clients usually say
That to shut the eyes tight and get down on the knees is the quickest and easiest way.

7. *Rumor Unverified Stop Can You Confirm Stop*

Yes, clients report it the tidiest way,
For the first time at least, when all is so strange
And helpers get awkward sometimes with delay.
But later, of course, you can try other methods that fancy suggests you arrange.
There are clients, in fact, who, when ennui gets great,
Will struggle, or ingeniously irritate
The helpers to acts I won't state:
For Reality's all, and to seek it, some welcome, at whatever cost, any change.
But speaking of change, there's a rumor astir
That the woods are sold, and the purchaser
Soon comes, and if credulity's not now abused,
Will, on this property, set
White foot-arch familiar to violet,
And heel that, smiting the stone, is not what is bruised,

And subdues to sweetness the pathside garbage, or thing body had refused.

End of Season

Leave now the beach, and even that perfect friendship
—Hair frosting, careful teeth—that came, oh! late,
Late, late, almost too late: that thought like a landslip;
Or only the swimmer's shape for which you would wait,
Bemused and pure among the bright umbrellas, while
Blue mountains breathed and the dark boys cried their bird-throated syllable.

Leave beach, *spiaggia, playa, plage, or spa,*
Where beginnings are always easy; or leave, even,
The Springs where your grandpa went in Arkansas
To purge the rheumatic guilt of beef and bourbon,
And slept like a child, nor called out with the accustomed nightmare,
But lolled his old hams, stained hands, in that Lethe, as others, others, before.

For waters wash our guilt and dance in the sun:
And the prophet, hairy and grim in the leonine landscape,
Came down to Jordan; toward moon-set de Leon
Woke, while squat Time clucked like the darkling ape;
And Dante's *duca,* smiling in the blessèd clime,
With rushes, sea-wet, wiped from that sad brow the infernal grime.

You'll come, you'll come! and with the tongue gone wintry
You'll greet in town the essential face, which now wears
The mask of travel, smudge of history;
And wordless, each one clasps, and stammering, stares:
You will have to learn a new language to say what is to say,
But it will never be useful in schoolroom, customs, or café.

For purity was wordless, and perfection
But the bridegroom's sleep or the athlete's marble dream,

And the annual sacrament of sea and sun,
Which browns the face and heals the heart, will seem
Silence, expectant to the answer, which is Time:
For all our conversation is index to our common crime.

On the last day swim far out, should the doctor permit
—Crawl, trudgeon, breast—or deep and wide-eyed, dive
Down the glaucous glimmer where no voice can visit;
But the mail lurks in the box at the house where you live:
Summer's wishes, winter's wisdom—you must think
On the true nature of Hope, whose eye is round and does not
wink.

Revelation

Because he had spoken harshly to his mother,
The day became astonishingly bright,
The enormity of distance crept to him like a dog now,
And earth's own luminescence seemed to repel the night.

Roof was rent like the loud paper tearing to admit
Sun-sulphurous splendor where had been before
But the submarine glimmer by kindly countenances lit,
As slow, phosphorescent dignities light the ocean floor.

By walls, by walks, chrysanthemum and aster,
All hairy, fat-petalled species, lean, confer,
And his ears, and heart, should burn at that insidious whisper
Which concerns him so, he knows; but he cannot make out the
words.

The peacock screamed, and his feathered fury made
Legend shake, all day, while the sky ran pale as milk;
That night, all night, the buck rabbit stamped in the moonlit
glade,
And the owl's brain glowed like a coal in the grove's combustible
dark.

When Sulla smote and Rome was rent, Augustine
Recalled how Nature, shuddering, tore her gown,
And kind changed kind, and the blunt herbivorous tooth dripped blood;
At Duncan's death, at Dunsinane, chimneys blew down.

But, oh! his mother was kinder than ever Rome,
Dearer than Duncan—no wonder, then, Nature's frame
Thrilled in voluptuous hemispheres far off from his home;
But not in terror: only as the bride, as the bride.

In separateness only does love learn definition,
Though Brahma smiles beneath the dappled shade,
Though tears, that night, wet the pillow where the boy's head was laid
Dreamless of splendid antipodal agitation;

And though across what tide and tooth Time is,
He was to lean back toward that recalcitrant face,
He would think, than Sulla more fortunate, how once he had learned
Something important about love, and about love's grace.

Pursuit

The hunchback on the corner, with gum and shoelaces,
Has his own wisdom and pleasures, and may not be lured
To divulge them to you, for he has merely endured
Your appeal for his sympathy and your kind purchases;
And wears infirmity but as the general who turns
Apart, in his famous old greatcoat there on the hill
At dusk when the rapture and cannonade are still,
To muse withdrawn from the dead, from his gorgeous sub alterns;
Or stares from the thicket of his familiar pain, like a fawn
That meets you a moment, wheels, in imperious innocence is gone.

Go to the clinic. Wait in the outer room,
Where like an old possum the snag-nailed hand will hump
On its knee in murderous patience, and the pomp
Of pain swells like the Indies, or a plum.
And there you will stand, as on the Roman hill,
Stunned by each withdrawn gaze and severe shape,
The first barbarian victor stood to gape
At the sacrificial fathers, white-robed, still;
And even the feverish old Jew regards you with authority
Till you feel like one who has come too late, or improperly
clothed, to a party.

The doctor will take you now. He is burly and clean;
Listening, like lover or worshiper, bends at your heart;
But cannot make out just what it tries to impart;
So smiles; says you simply need a change of scene.
Of scene, of solace: therefore Florida,
Where Ponce de Leon clanked among the lilies,
Where white sails skit on blue and cavort like fillies,
And the shoulder gleams in the moonlit corridor.
A change of love: if love is a groping Godward, though blind,
No matter what crevice, cranny, chink, bright in dark, the pale
tentacle find.

In Florida consider the flamingo,
Its color passion but its neck a question;
Consider even that girl the other guests shun
On beach, at bar, in bed, for she may know
The secret you are seeking, after all;
Or the child you humbly sit by, excited and curly,
That screams on the shore at the sea's sunlit hurlyburly,
Till the mother calls its name, toward nightfall.
Till you sit alone: in the dire meridians, off Ireland, in fury
Of spume-tooth and dawnless sea-heave, salt rimes the lookout's
devout eye.

Till you sit alone—which is the beginning of error—
Behind you the music and lights of the great hotel:
Solution, perhaps, is public, despair personal,

But history held to your breath clouds like a mirror.
There are many states, and towns in them, and faces,
But meanwhile, the little old lady in black, by the wall,
Who admires all the dancers, and tells you how just last fall
Her husband died in Ohio, and damp mists her glasses;
She blinks and croaks, like a toad or a Norn, in the horrible
light,
And rattles her crutch, which may put forth a small bloom, perhaps white.

DELMORE SCHWARTZ

Starlight Like Intuition Pierced the Twelve

The starlight's intuitions pierced the twelve,
The brittle night sky sparkled like a tune
Tinkled and tapped out on the xylophone.
Empty and vain, a glittering dune, the moon
Arose too big, and, in the mood which ruled,
Seemed like a useless beauty in a pit;
And then one said, after he carefully spat:
'No matter what we do, he looks at it!

'I cannot see a child or find a girl
Beyond his smile which glows like that spring moon.'
'—Nothing no more the same,' the second said,
'Though all may be forgiven, never quite healed
The wound I bear as witness, standing by;
No ceremony surely appropriate,
Nor secret love, escape or sleep because
No matter what I do, he looks at it—'

'Now,' said the third, 'no thing will be the same:
I am as one who never shuts his eyes,

The sea and sky no more are marvellous,
I know no more true freshness or surprise!'
'Now,' said the fourth, 'nothing will be enough,
—I heard his voice accomplishing all wit:
No word can be unsaid, no deed withdrawn,
—No matter what is said, he measures it!'

'Vision, imagination, hope or dream
Believed, denied, the scene we wished to see?
It does not matter in the least: for what
Is altered if it is not true? That we
Saw goodness, as it is—*this* is the awe
And the abyss which we will not forget,
His story now the skull which holds all thought:
No matter what I think, I think of it!'

'And I will never be what once I was,'
Said one for long as single as a knife,
'And we will never be as once we were;
We have died once, this is a second life.'
'My mind is spilled in moral chaos,' one
Righteous as Job exclaimed, 'now infinite
Suspicion of my heart stems what I will,
—No matter what I choose, he stares at it!'

'I am as one native in summer places,
—Ten weeks' excitement paid for by the rich;
Debauched by that, and then all winter bored,'
The sixth declared, 'his peak left us a ditch.'
'He came to make this life more difficult,'
The seventh said, 'No one will ever fit
His measures' heights, all is inadequate:
No matter what we have, what good is it?'

'He gave forgiveness to us: what a gift!'
The eighth chimed in. 'But now we know *how much*
Must be forgiven. But if forgiven, what?
The crime which was will be; and the least touch
Revives the memory: what is forgiveness worth?'

The ninth spoke thus: 'Who now will ever sit
At ease in Zion at the Easter feast?
No matter what the place, he touches it!'

'And I will always stammer, since he spoke,'
One, who had been most eloquent, said, stammering,
'I looked too long at the sun; like too much light,
Too much of goodness is a boomerang,'
Laughed the eleventh of the troop, 'I must
Try what he tried: I saw the infinite
Who walked the lake and raised the hopeless dead:
No matter what the feat, he first accomplished it!'

So spoke the twelfth; and then the twelve in chorus:
'Unspeakable unnatural goodness is
Risen and shines, and never will ignore us;
He glows forever in all consciousness;
Forgiveness, love, and hope possess the pit,
And bring our endless guilt, like shadow's bars:
No matter what we do, he stares at it!
What pity can each deny? what debt defer?
We know he looks at us like all the stars,
And we shall never be as once we were,
This life will never be what once it was!'

The Conclusion

How slow time moves when torment stops the clock!
How dormant and delinquent, under the dawn,
The uproarious roaring of the bursting cock:
Now pain ticks on, now all and nothing must be borne,
And I remember: pain is the cost of being born.

2

For when the flowers of infatuation fade
The furs which love in all its warmth discloses

Become the fires of pride and are betrayed
By those whom love has terrified and pride has made afraid.

No matter what time prepares, no matter how time amazes
The images and hopes by which we love or die,
Pride is not love, and pride is merely pride,
Until it becomes a living death which denies
How it is treacherous, and faithless: how it betrays
Everyone, one by one, and every vow,
Seeking praise absolute, hides with other whores
Whom pride and time seduces and love ignores.

3

This will be true long after heart and heart
Have recognized and forgotten all that was ripening, ripe, rotten-ripe and rotten:
Have known too soon, too soon by far how much of love has been forgotten:
Have known the little deaths before death do us part:
Nothing will ever pass at last to nothingness beyond decay
Until the night is all, and night is known all day.

At a Solemn Musick

Let the musicians begin,
Let every instrument awaken and instruct us
In love's willing river and love's dear discipline:
We wait, silent, in consent and in the penance
Of patience, awaiting the serene exaltation
Which is the liberation and conclusion of expiation.

Now may the chief musician say:
"Lust and emulation have dwelt among us
Like barbarous kings: have conquered us:
Have inhabited our hearts: devoured and ravished
—With the savage greed and avarice of fire—
The substance of pity and compassion."

Now may all the players play:
"The river of the morning, the morning of the river
Flow out of the splendor of the tenderness of surrender."

Now may the chief musician say:
"Nothing is more important than summer."

And now the entire choir shall chant:
"How often the astonished heart,
Beholding the laurel,
Remembers the dead,
And the enchanted absolute,
Snow's kingdom, sleep's dominion."

Then shall the chief musician declare:
"The phoenix is the meaning of the fruit,
Until the dream is knowledge and knowledge is a dream."

And then, once again, the entire choir shall cry, in passionate unity,
Singing and celebrating love and love's victory,
Ascending and descending the heights of assent, climbing and chanting triumphantly:
Before the morning was, you were:
Before the snow shone,
And the light sang, and the stone,
Abiding, rode the fullness or endured the emptiness,
You were: you were alone.

In the Naked Bed, in Plato's Cave

In the naked bed, in Plato's cave,
Reflected headlights slowly slid the wall,
Carpenters hammered under the shaded window,
Wind troubled the window curtains all night long,
A fleet of trucks strained uphill, grinding,
Their freights covered, as usual.

The ceiling lightened again, the slanting diagram
Slid slowly forth.
Hearing the milkman's chop,
His striving up the stair, the bottle's chink,
I rose from bed, lit a cigarette,
And walked to the window. The stony street
Displayed the stillness in which buildings stand,
The street-lamp's vigil and the horse's patience.
The winter sky's pure capital
Turned me back to bed with exhausted eyes.

Strangeness grew in the motionless air. The loose
Film grayed. Shaking wagons, hooves' waterfalls,
Sounded far off, increasing, louder and nearer.
A car coughed, starting. Morning, softly
Melting the air, lifted the half-covered chair
From underseas, kindled the looking-glass,
Distinguished the dresser and the white wall.
The bird called tentatively, whistled, called,
Bubbled and whistled, so! Perplexed, still wet
With sleep, affectionate, hungry and cold. So, so,
O son of man, the ignorant night, the travail
Of early morning, the mystery of beginning
Again and again,
while History is unforgiven.

At This Moment of Time

Some who are uncertain compel me. They fear
The Ace of Spades. They fear
Love offered suddenly, turning from the mantelpiece,
Sweet with decision. And they distrust
The fireworks by the lakeside, first the spuft,
Then the colored lights, rising.
Tentative, hesitant, doubtful, they consume
Greedily Caesar at the prow returning,
Locked in the stone of his act and office.
While the brass band brightly bursts over the water

They stand in the crowd lining the shore
Aware of the water beneath Him. They know it. Their eyes
Are haunted by water.

Disturb me, compel me. It is not true
That "no man is happy," but that is not
The sense which guides you. If we are
Unfinished (we are, unless hope is a bad dream),
You are exact. You tug my sleeve
Before I speak, with a shadow's friendship,
And I remember that we who move
Are moved by clouds that darken midnight.

Socrates' Ghost Must Haunt Me Now

Socrates' ghost must haunt me now,
Notorious death has let him go,
He comes to me with a clumsy bow,
Saying in his disuséd voice,
That I do not know I do not know,
The mechanical whims of appetite
Are all that I have of conscious choice,
The butterfly caged in electric light
Is my only day in the world's great night,
Love is not love, it is a child
Sucking his thumb and biting his lip,
But grasp it all, there may be more!
From the topless sky to the bottomless floor
With the heavy head and the finger tip:
All is not blind, obscene, and poor.
Socrates stands by me stockstill,
Teaching hope to my flickering will,
Pointing to the sky's inexorable blue
—Old Noumenon, come true, come true!

"Mentrechè il Vento, Come Fa, Si Tace"

Will you perhaps consent to be
Now that a little while is still
(Ruth of sweet wind) now that a little while
My mind's continuing and unreleasing wind
Touches this single of your flowers, this one only,
Will you perhaps consent to be
My many-branchéd, small and dearest tree?

My mind's continuing and unreleasing wind
—The wind which is wild and restless, tired and asleep,
The wind which is tired, wild and still continuing,
The wind which is chill, and warm, wet, soft, in every influence,
Lusts for Paris, Crete and Pergamus,
Is suddenly off for Paris and Chicago,
Judaea, San Francisco, the Midi,
—May I perhaps return to you
Wet with an Attic dust and chill from Norway
My dear, so-many-branchéd smallest tree?

Would you perhaps consent to be
The very rack and crucifix of winter, winter's wild
Knife-edged, continuing and unreleasing,
Intent and stripping, ice-caressing wind?
My dear, most dear, so-many-branchéd smallest tree
My mind's continuing and unreleasing wind
Touches this single of your flowers, faith in me,
Wide as the—sky!—accepting as the (air)!
—Consent, consent, consent to be
My many-branchéd, small and dearest tree.

RICHARD EBERHART

The Groundhog

In June, amid the golden fields,
I saw a groundhog lying dead.
Dead lay he; my senses shook,
And mind outshot our naked frailty.
There lowly in the vigorous summer
His form began its senseless change,
And made my senses waver dim
Seeing nature ferocious in him.
Inspecting close his maggots' might
And seething cauldron of his being,
Half with loathing, half with a strange love,
I poked him with an angry stick.
The fever arose, became a flame
And Vigour circumscribed the skies,
Immense energy in the sun,
And through my frame of sunless trembling.
My stick had done nor good nor harm.
Then stood I silent in the day
Watching the object, as before;
And kept my reverence for knowledge
Trying for control, to be still,
To quell the passion of the blood;
Until I had bent down on my knees
Praying for joy in the sight of decay.
And so I left; and I returned
In Autumn strict of eye, to see
The sap gone out of the groundhog,
But the bony sodden hulk remained.
But the year had lost its meaning,
And in intellectual chains
I lost both love and loathing,

Mured up in the wall of wisdom.
Another summer took the fields again
Massive and burning, full of life,
But when I chanced upon the spot
There was only a little hair left,
And bones bleaching in the sunlight
Beautiful as architecture;
I watched them like a geometer,
And cut a walking stick from a birch.
It has been three years, now.
There is no sign of the groundhog.
I stood there in the whirling summer,
My hand capped a withered heart,
And thought of China and of Greece,
Of Alexander in his tent;
Of Montaigne in his tower,
Of Saint Theresa in her wild lament.

1934

Caught upon a thousand thorns, I sing,
Like a rag in the wind,
Caught in the blares of the automobile horns
And on the falling airplane's wing.
Caught napping in my study
Among a thousand books of poetry.

Doing the same thing over and over again
Brings about an obliteration of pain.
Each day dies in a paper litter
As the heart becomes less like a rapier.
In complexity, feeling myself absurd
Dictating an arbitrary word,

My self my own worst enemy,
Hunting the past through all its fears,
That on the brain that glory burst
Bombing a ragged future's story,

Caught in iron individuality
As in the backwash of a sea

Knowing not whether to fight out,
Or keep silent; to talk about the weather,
Or rage again through wrong and right,
Knowing knowledge is a norm of nothing,
And I have been to the Eastern seas
And walked on all the Hebrides.

Ashamed of loving a long-practised selfhood,
Lost in a luxury of speculation,
At the straight grain of a pipe I stare
And spit upon all worlds of Spain;
Time like a certain sedative
Quelling the growth of the purpose tree.

Aware of the futility of action,
Of the futility of prayer aware,
Trying to pry from the vest of poetry
The golden heart of mankind's deep despair,
Unworthy of a simple love
In august, elected worlds to move

Stern, pliant in the modern world, I sing,
Afraid of nothing and afraid of everything,
Curtailing joy, withholding irony,
Pleased to condemn contemporaneity
Seeking the reality, skirting
The dangerous absolutes of fear and hope,

And I have eased reality and fiction
Into a kind of intellectual fruition
Strength in solitude, life in death,
Compassion by suffering, love in strife,
And ever and still the weight of mystery
Arrows a way between my words and me.

MURIEL RUKEYSER

Ajanta

NOTE: *In India, between the second century B.C. and the sixth century A.D., a school of Buddhist painter-monks worked on the walls of the Ajanta caves, keeping a tradition in painting that was lost in the East after them and never known in the West. Based on the religious analogy between the space of the body and the space of the universe, the treatment of bodies in these scenes of the life of the gods is such that the deepest background is the wall on which the paintings are done—the figures in the round but shadowless, start forward, seeming to fill the cave. Reality is fully accepted, then, the function of such an art is to fill with creation an accepted real world.*

Came in my full youth to the midnight cave
nerves ringing; and this thing I did alone.
Wanting my fulness and not a field of war,
for the world considered annihilation, a star
called Wormwood rose and flickered, shattering
bent light over the dead boiling up in the ground,
the biting yellow of their corrupted lives
streaming to war, denying all our words.
Nothing was left among the tainted weather
but world-walking and the shadowless Ajanta.
Hallucination and the metal laugh
in clouds, and the mountain-spectre riding storm.
Nothing was certain but a moment of peace,
a hollow behind the unbreakable waterfall.
All the way to the cave, the teeming forms of death,
and death, the price of the body, cheap as air.
I blessed my heart on the expiation journey
for it had never been unable to suffer:
when I met the man whose face looked like the future,
when I met the whore with the dying red hair,
the child myself who is my murderer.
So came I between heaven and my grave

past the serene smile of the *voyeur,* to
this cave where the myth enters the heart again.

II. THE CAVE

Space to the mind, the painted cave of dream.
This is not a womb, nothing but good emerges:
this is a stage, neither unreal nor real
where the walls are the world, the rocks and palaces
stand on a borderland of blossoming ground.
If you stretch your hand, you touch the slope of the world
reaching in interlaced gods, animals, and men.
There is no background. The figures hold their peace
in a web of movement. There is no frustration,
every gesture is taken, everything yields connections.
The heavy sensual shoulders, the thighs, the blood-born flesh
and earth turning into color, rocks into their crystals,
water to sound, fire to form; life flickers
uncounted into the supple arms of love.
The space of these walls is the body's living space;
tear open your ribs and breathe the color of time
where nothing leads away, the world comes forward
in flaming sequences. Pillars and prisms. Riders
and horses and the figures of consciousness,
red cow grows long, goes running through the world.
Flung into movement in carnal purity,
these bodies are sealed—warm lip and crystal hand
in a jungle of light. Color-sheeted, seductive
foreboding eyelid lowered on the long eye,
fluid and vulnerable. The spaces of the body
are suddenly limitless, and riding flesh
shapes constellations over the golden breast,
confusion of scents and illuminated touch—
monster touch, the throat printed with brightness,
wide outlined gesture where the bodies ride.
Bells, and the spirit flashing. The religious bells,
bronze under the sunlight like breasts ringing,
bronze in the closed air, the memory of walls,
great sensual shoulders in the web of time.

III. LES TENDRESSES BESTIALES

A procession of caresses alters the ancient sky
until new constellations are the body shining:
There's the Hand to steer by, there the horizon Breast,
and the Great Stars kindling the fluid hill.
All the rooms open into magical boxes,
nothing is tilted, everything flickers
sexual and exquisite.
The panther with its throat along my arm
turns black and flows away.
Deep in all streets passes a faceless whore
and the checkered men are whispering one word.
The face I know becomes the night-black rose.
The sharp face is now an electric fan
and says one word to me.
The dice and the alcohol and the destruction
have drunk themselves and cast.
Broken bottle of loss, and the glass
turned bloody into the face.
Now the scene comes forward, very clear.
Dream-singing, airborne, surrenders the recalled,
the gesture arrives riding over the breast,
singing, singing, tender atrocity,
the silver derelict wearing fur and claws.
Oh love, I stood under the apple branch,
I saw the whipped bay and the small dark islands,
and night sailing the river and the foghorn's word.
My life said to you: I want to love you well.
The wheel goes back and I shall live again,
but the wave turns, my birth arrives and spills
over my breast the world bearing my grave,
and your eyes open in earth. You touched my life.
My life reaches the skin, moves under your smile,
and your shoulders and your throat and your face and your thighs
flash.

I am haunted by interrupted acts,

introspective as a leper, enchanted
by a repulsive clew,
a gross and fugitive movement of the limbs.
Is this the love that shook the lights to flame?
Sheeted avenues thrash in the wind,
torn streets, the savage parks.
I am plunged deep. Must find the midnight cave.

IV. BLACK BLOOD

A habit leading to murder, smoky laughter
hated at first, but necessary later.
Alteration of motives. To stamp in terror
around the deserted harbor, down the hill
until the woman laced into a harp
screams and screams and the great clock strikes,
swinging its giant figures past the face.
The Floating Man rides on the ragged sunset
asking and asking. Do not say, Which loved?
Which was beloved? Only, Who most enjoyed?
Armored ghost of rage, screaming and powerless.
Only find me and touch my blood again.
Find me. A girl runs down the street
singing Take me, yelling Take me Take
Hang me from the clapper of a bell
and you as hangman ring it sweet tonight,
for nothing clean in me is more than cloud
unless you call it.—As I ran I heard
a black voice beating among all that blood:
"Try to live as if there were a God."

V. THE BROKEN WORLD

Came to Ajanta cave, the painted space of the breast,
the real world where everything is complete,
there are no shadows, the forms of incompleteness.
The great cloak blows in the light, rider and horse arrive,
the shoulders turn and every gift is made.
No shadows fall. There is no source of distortion.

In our world, a tree casts the shadow of a woman,
a man the shadow of a phallus, a hand raised
the shadow of the whip.
Here everything is itself,
here all may stand
on summer earth.
Brightness has overtaken every light,
and every myth netted itself in flesh.
New origins, and peace given entire
and the spirit alive.
In the shadowless cave
the naked arm is raised.
Animals arrive,
interlaced, and gods
interlaced, and men
flame-woven.
I stand and am complete.

Crawls from the door,
black at my two feet
the shadow of the world.
World, not yet one,
enters the heart again.
The naked world, and the old noise of tears,
the fear, the expiation and the love,
a world of the shadowed and alone.
The journey, and the struggles of the moon.

Boy with His Hair Cut Short

Sunday shuts down on this twentieth-century evening.
The L passes. Twilight and bulb define
the brown room, the overstuffed plum sofa,
the boy, and the girl's thin hands above his head.
A neighbor radio sings stocks, news, serenade.

He sits at the table, head down, the young clear neck exposed,
watching the drugstore sign from the tail of his eye;

tattoo, neon, until the eye blears, while his
solicitous tall sister, simple in blue, bending
behind him, cuts his hair with her cheap shears.

The arrow's electric red always reaches its mark,
successful neon! He coughs, impressed by that precision.
His child's forehead, forever protected by his cap,
is bleached against the lamplight as he turns head
and steadies to let the snippets drop.

Erasing the failure of weeks with level fingers,
she sleeks the fine hair, combing: "You'll look fine tomorrow!
You'll surely find something, they can't keep turning you down;
the finest gentleman's not so trim as you!" Smiling, he raises
the adolescent forehead wrinkling ironic now.

He sees his decent suit laid out, new-pressed,
his carfare on the shelf. He lets his head fall, meeting
her earnest hopeless look, seeing the sharp blades splitting,
the darkened room, the impersonal sign, her motion,
the blue vein, bright on her temple, pitifully beating.

KARL SHAPIRO

Nostalgia

My soul stands at the window of my room,
  And I ten thousand miles away;
My days are filled with Ocean's sound of doom,
  Salt and cloud and the bitter spray.
Let the wind blow, for many a man shall die.

My selfish youth, my books with gilded edge,
  Knowledge and all gaze down the street;

The potted plants upon the window ledge
  Gaze down with selfish lives and sweet.
Let the wind blow, for many a man shall die.

My night is now her day, my day her night,
  So I lie down, and so I rise;
The sun burns close, the star is losing height,
  The clock is hunted down the skies.
Let the wind blow, for many a man shall die.

Truly a pin can make the memory bleed,
  A world explode the inward mind
And turn the skulls and flowers never freed
  Into the air, no longer blind.
Let the wind blow, for many a man shall die.

Laughter and grief join hands. Always the heart
  Clumps in the breast with heavy stride;
The face grows lined and wrinkled like a chart.
  The eyes bloodshot with tears and tide.
Let the wind blow, for many a man shall die.

The Fly

O hideous little bat, the size of snot,
With polyhedral eye and shabby clothes,
To populate the stinking cat you walk
The promontory of the dead man's nose,
Climb with the fine leg of a Duncan-Phyfe
    The smoking mountains of my food
        And in a comic mood
    In mid-air take to bed a wife.

Riding and riding with your filth of hair
On gluey foot or wing, forever coy,
Hot from the compost and green sweet decay,
Sounding your buzzer like an urchin toy—
You dot all whiteness with diminutive stool,

In the tight belly of the dead
 Burrow with hungry head
And inlay maggots like a jewel.

At your approach the great horse stomps and paws
Bringing the hurricane of his heavy tail;
Shod in disease you dare to kiss my hand
Which sweeps against you like an angry flail;
Still you return, return, trusting your wing
 To draw you from the hunter's reach
 That learns to kill to teach
 Disorder to the tinier thing.

My peace is your disaster. For your death
Children like spiders cup their pretty hands
And wives resort to chemistry of war.
In fens of sticky paper and quicksands
You glue yourself to death. Where you are stuck
 You struggle hideously and beg
 You amputate your leg
 Imbedded in the amber muck.

But I, a man, must swat you with my hate,
Slap you across the air and crush your flight,
Must mangle with my shoe and smear your blood,
Expose your little guts pasty and white,
Knock your head sidewise like a drunkard's hat,
 Pin your wings under like a crow's,
 Tear off your flimsy clothes
 And beat you as one beats a rat.

Then like Gargantua I stride among
The corpses strewn like raisins in the dust,
The broken bodies of the narrow dead
That catch the throat with fingers of disgust
I sweep. One gyrates like a top and falls
 And stunned, stone blind, and deaf
 Buzzes its frightful F
 And dies between three cannibals.

Epitaph for John and Richard

There goes the clock; there goes the sun;
Greenwich is right with Arlington;
The signal's minutes are signifying
That somebody old has finished dying,
That somebody young has just begun.

What do you think you earned today
Except the waste, except the pay,
Except the power to be spending?
And now your year is striking, ending,
What do you think you have put away?

Only a promise, only a life
Squandered in secret with a wife
In bedtime feigning and unfeigning;
The blood has long since ceased complaining;
The clock has satisfied the strife.

They will not cast your honored head
Or say from lecterns what you said,
But only keep you with them all
Committed in the City Hall;
Once born, once married, and once dead.

Travelogue for Exiles

Look and remember. Look upon this sky;
Look deep and deep into the sea-clean air,
The unconfined, the terminus of prayer.
Speak now and speak into the hallowed dome.
What do you hear? What does the sky reply?
The heavens are taken: this is not your home.

Look and remember. Look upon this sea;
Look down and down into the tireless tide.

What of a life below, a life inside,
A tomb, a cradle in the curly foam?
The waves arise; sea-wind and sea agree
The waters are taken: this is not your home.

Look and remember. Look upon this land,
Far, far across the factories and the grass.
Surely, there, surely, they will let you pass.
Speak then and ask the forest and the loam.
What do you hear? What does the land command?
The earth is taken: this is not your home.

The Twins

Likeness has made them animal and shy.
See how they turn their full gaze left and right.
Seeking the other, yet not moving close;
Nothing in their relationship is gross,
But soft, conspicuous, like giraffes. And why
Do they not speak except by sudden sight?

Sisters kiss freely and unsubtle friends
Wrestle like lovers; brothers loudly laugh:
These in a dreamier bondage dare not touch.
Each is the other's soul and hears too much
The heartbeat of the other; each apprehends
The sad duality and the imperfect half.

The one lay sick, the other wandered free,
But like a child to a small plot confined
Walked a short way and dumbly reappeared.
Is it not all-in-all of what they feared,
The single death, the obvious destiny
That maims the miracle their will designed?

For they go emptily from face to face,
Keeping the instinctive partnership of birth
A ponderous marriage and a sacred name;

Theirs is the pride of shouldering each the same
The old indignity of Esau's race
And Dromio's denouement of tragic mirth.

Poet

Il arrive que l'esprit demande la poésie

Left leg flung out, head cocked to the right,
Tweed coat or army uniform, with book,
Beautiful eyes, who is this walking down?
Who, glancing at the pane of glass looks sharp
And thinks it is not he—as when a poet
Comes swiftly on some half-forgotten poem
And loosely holds the page, steady of mind,
Thinking it is not his?

And when will *you* exist?—Oh, it is I,
Incredibly skinny, stooped, and neat as pie,
Ignorant as dirt, erotic as an ape,
Dreamy as puberty—with dirty hair!
Into the room like kangaroo he bounds,
Ears flopping like the most primitive hound's;
His chin received all questions as he bows
Mouthing a green bon-bon.

Has no more memory than rubber. Stands
Waist-deep in heavy mud of thought and broods
At his own wetness. When he would get out,
To his surprise he lifts in air a phrase
As whole and clean and silvery as a fish.
Which jumps and dangles on his damned hooked grin,
But like a name-card on a man's lapel
Calls him a conscious fool.

And childlike he remembers all his life
And cannily constructs it, fact by fact,
As boys paste postage stamps in careful books,

Denoting pence and legends and profiles,
Nothing more valuable.—And like a thief,
His eyes glassed over and concealed with guilt,
Fondles his secrets like a case of tools,
And waits in empty doors.

By men despised for knowing what he is,
And by himself. But he exists for women.
As dolls to girls, as perfect wives to men,
So he to women. And to himself a thing,
All ages, epicene, without a trade.
To girls and wives always alive and fated;
To men and scholars always dead like Greek
And always mistranslated.

Towards exile and towards shame he lures himself,
Tongue winding on his arm, and thinks like Eve
By biting apple will become most wise.
Sentio ergo sum: he feels his way
And words themselves stand up for him like Braille
And punch and perforate his parchment ear.
All language falls like Chinese on his soul,
Image of song unsounded.

This is the coward's coward that in his dreams
Sees shapes of pain grow tall. Awake at night
He peers at sounds and stumbles at a breeze.
And none holds life less dear. For as a youth
Who by some accident observes his love
Naked and in some natural ugly act,
He turns with loathing and with flaming hands,
Seared and betrayed by sight.

He is the business man, on beauty trades,
Dealer in arts and thoughts who, like the Jew,
Shall rise from slums and hated dialects
A tower of bitterness. Shall be always strange,
Hunted and then sought after. Shall be sat
Like an ambassador from another race

At tables rich with music. He shall eat flowers,
Chew honey and spit out gall. They shall all smile
And love and pity him.

His death shall be by drowning. In that hour
When the last bubble of pure heaven's air
Hovers within his throat, safe on his bed,
A small eternal figurehead in terror,
He shall cry out and clutch his days of straw
Before the blackest wave. Lastly, his tomb
Shall list and founder in the troughs of grass.
And none shall speak his name.

Waitress

Whoever with the compasses of his eyes
Is plotting the voyage of your steady shape
As you come laden through the room and back
And rounding your even bottom like a Cape
Crooks his first finger, whistles through his lip
Till you arrive, all motion, like a ship,

He is my friend—consider his dark pangs
And love of Niger, naked indigence,
Dance him the menu of a poem and squirm
Deep in the juke-box jungle, green and dense.
Surely he files his teeth, punctures his nose,
Carves out the god and takes off all his clothes.

For once, the token on the table's edge
Sufficing, proudly and with hair unpinned
You mounted the blueplate, stretched out and grinned
Like Christmas fish and turkey pink and skinned,
Eyes on the half-shell, loin with parsley stuck,
Thigh bones and ribs and little toes to suck.

I speak to you, ports of the northern myth,
This dame is carved and eaten. One by one

God knows what hour, her different parts go home,
Lastly her pants and day or night is done;
But on the restaurant the sign of fear
Reddens and blazes—"English spoken here."

JOSÉ GARCIA VILLA

There Came You Wishing Me

There came you wishing me * * *
And so I said * * *
And then you turned your head
With the greatest beauty

Smiting me mercilessly!
And then you said * * *
So that my heart was made
Into the strangest country . . .

* * * you said, so beauteously,
So that an angel came
To hear that name,
And we caught him tremulously!

Be Beautiful, Noble, Like the Antique Ant

Be beautiful, noble, like the antique ant,
Who bore the storms as he bore the sun,
Wearing neither gown nor helmet,
Though he was archbishop and soldier:
Wore only his own flesh.

Salute characters with gracious dignity:
Though what these are is left to

Your own terms. Exact: the universe is
Not so small but these will be found
Somewhere. Exact: they will be found.

Speak with great moderation: but think
With great fierceness, burning passion:
Though what the ant thought
No annals reveal, nor his descendants
Break the seal.

Trace the tracelessness of the ant,
Every ant has reached this perfection.
As he comes, so he goes,
Flowing as water flows,
Essential but secret like a rose.

God Said, "I Made a Man"

God said, "I made a man
Out of clay—
   But so bright he, he spun
Himself to brightest Day

Till he was all shining gold,
And oh,
   He was lovely to behold!
But in his hands held he a bow

Aimed at me who created
Him. And I said,
   'Wouldst murder me
Who am thy Fountainhead!'

Then spoke he the man of gold:
'I will not
   Murder thee! I do but
Measure thee. Hold

Thy peace! And this I did.
But I was curious
  Of this so regal head.
'Give thy name!'—'Sir! Genius'."

Now, If You Will Look in My Brain

Now, if you will look in my brain
You will see not Because
But Cause—
The strict Rose whose clean
Light utters all my pain.
Dwelleth there my God
With a strict Rod
And a most luminous mien.

And He whippeth! lo how
He whippeth! O see
The rod's velocity
In utterest unmercy
Carve, inflict upon his brow
The majesty of its doomèd Now.

My Mouth Is Very Quiet

My mouth is very quiet
Reverencing the luminance of my brain:
If words must find an outlet
They must work with jewelled pain.

They must cut a way immaculate
To leave the brain incorrupt:
They must repay their Debt
Like archangels undropt.

The miracle of a word is to my mouth
The miracle of God in my brain:

Archangels holding to His North and South,
His East and West by an inviolable chain.

An archangel upon my mouth
May blow his silver trumpet:
But he holds to his North or South,
Blows—and again is quiet.

The Way My Ideas Think Me

The way my ideas think me
Is the way I unthink God.
As in the name of heaven I make hell
That is the way the Lord says me.

And all is adventure and danger
And I roll Him off cliffs and mountains
But fast as I am to push Him off
Fast am I to reach Him below.

And it may be then His turn to push me off,
I wait breathless for that terrible second:
And if He push me not, I turn around in anger:
"O art thou the God I would have!"

Then He pushes me and I plunge down, down!
And when He comes to help me up
I put my arms around Him, saying, "Brother,
Brother." . . . This is the way we are.

Saw God Dead but Laughing

Saw God dead but laughing.
Uttered the laugh for Him.
Heard my skull crack with doom
Tragedian laughing!

Peered into the cracked skull—
Saw the tragic monkhood
In the shape of God's deathhead
Laughter upon its mouth a jewel.

Jewel bright, O Jewel bright,
Laughter of the Lord.
Laughter with eternity immured
O laugh bright, laugh bright.

Then did the Lord laugh louder
I laughing for Him,
I from the heart's honeycomb
Feeding braver, braver,

Till all the universe was Laughter
But the Laughter of the Lord
O the Laughter of His Word
That could laugh only—after His murder.

Mostly Are We Mostless

Mostly are we mostless
And neverness is all we become.
The tiger is tigerless
The flame is flameless.

Dig up Time like a tiger
Dig up the beautiful grave
The grave is graveless
And God is Godless.

I saw myself reflected
In the great eye of the grave.
I saw God helpless
And headless there.

Until I put my head on Him.
Then he uprose superb.

He took the body of me
And crumpled me to immortality.

JOHN HALL WHEELOCK

The Gardener

Father, whom I knew well for forty years
Yet never knew, I have come to know you now—
In age, make good at last those old arrears.

Though time, that snows the hair and lines the brow,
Has equalled us, it was not time alone
That brought me to the knowledge I here avow.

Some profound divination of your own
In all the natural effects you sought
Planted a secret that is now made known.

These woodland ways, with your heart's labor bought,
Trees that you nurtured, gardens that you planned,
Surround me here, mute symbols of your thought.

Your meaning beckons me on every hand,
Grave aisles and vistas, in their silence, speak
A language which I now can understand.

In all you did, as in yourself, unique—
Servant of beauty, whom I seek to know,
Discovering here the clue to what I seek.

When down the nave of your great elms I go
That soar their gothic arches where the sky,
Nevertheless, with all its stars will show,

Or when the moon of summer, riding high,
Spills through the leaves her light from far away,
I feel we share the secret, you and I.

All these you loved and left. We may not stay
Long with the joy our hearts are set upon:
This is a thing that here you tried to say.

The night has fallen; the day's work is done;
Your groves, your lawns, the passion of this place
Cry out your love of them—but you are gone.

O father, whom I may no more embrace
In childish fervor, but, standing far apart,
Look on your spirit rather than your face,

Time now has touched me also, and my heart
Has learned a sadness that yours earlier knew,
Who labored here, though with the greater art.

The truth is on me now that was with you:
How life is sweet, even its very pain,
The years how fleeting and the days how few.

Truly, your labors have not been in vain;
These woods, these walks, these gardens—everywhere
I look, the glories of your love remain.

Therefore, for you, now beyond praise or prayer,
Before the night falls that shall make us one,
In which neither of us will know or care,

This kiss, father, from him who was your son.

Song On Reaching Seventy

Shall not a man sing as the night comes on?
He would be braver than that bird

Which shrieks for terror and is gone
Into the gathering dark, and he has heard
Often, at evening's hush,
Upon some towering sunset bough
A belated thrush
Lift up his heart against the menacing night,
Till silence covered all. Oh, now
Before the coming of a greater night
How bitterly sweet and dear
All things have grown! How shall we bear the brunt,
The fury and joy of every sound and sight,
Now almost cruelly fierce with all delight:
The clouds of dawn that blunt
The spearhead of the sun; the clouds that stand,
Raging with light, around his burial;
The rain-pocked pool
At the wood's edge; a bat's skittering flight
Over the sunset-colored land;
Or, heard toward morning, the cock pheasant's call!
Oh, every sight and sound
Has meaning now! Now, also, love has laid
Upon us her old chains of tenderness,
So that to think of the belovèd one,
Love is so great, is to be half afraid—
It is like looking at the sun,
That blinds the eye with truth.
Yet longing remains unstilled,
Age will look into the face of youth
With longing, over a gulf not to be crossed.
Oh, joy that is almost pain, pain that is joy,
Unimaginable to the younger man or boy—
Nothing is quite fulfilled,
Nothing is lost;
But all is multiplied till the heart almost
Aches with its burden: there and here
Become as one, the present and the past;
The dead, who were content to lie
Far from us, have consented to draw near—
We are thronged with memories,

Move amid two societies,
And learn at last
The dead are the only ones who never die.

Great night, hold back
A little longer yet your mountainous, black
Waters of darkness from this shore,
This island garden, this paradisal spot,
The haunt of love and pain,
Which we must leave, whether we would or not,
And where we shall not come again.
More time—oh, but a little more,
Till, stretched to the limits of being, the taut heart break,
Bursting the bonds of breath,
Shattering the wall
Between us and our world, and we awake
Out of the dream of self into the truth of all,
The price for which is death.

HORATIO COLONY

The Gold That Fell on Danae

The gold that fell on Danae
Was some of it like molten honey
Of which the drops had motile tails;
Some of it was like grit of stars,
And sparks like those flung off in wars,
And there were stones like August hails.

It struck both tenderly and hard,
Her body was but little scarred;
Some nuggets like the heads of nails
Wounded her flesh but quickly went

Into a melted golden scent
Which gave a vapor up like veils.

And as the golden vapor rose
It whetted Danae's ears and toes;
The god of gold was in her, round her,
With clink of gold her ears rang loud,
And not one Perseus, but a crowd
Inside her made her sink and founder.

Gold, gold was in the little room,
A person armed with a soft broom
Could have swept silts of gold up high;
Gold-spilth was on the walls, the ceiling,
And still the gold went feeling, feeling,
Touching on eyebrow and on eye.

And even when it died away
Its singes, scorches stood to fray
The limping flesh of Danae,
And yet her bruises were delicious
And colorful, yet meretricious
And passionate for all to see.

Autumnal

In the woods the fox is no more timorous;
Of old men's gold I know the hard cold feel;
The wealth so glorious
Young men come here to steal.

The maple tree of flame is the bold crier;
With fire and gold the mountain side is struck;
Someone's mouth calls out Fire;—
Oberon burns with Puck.

It was as if a Greek went on the street
Of old Pompeii burning where he met

The odors sharp and sweet
Of houses in a sweat.

And in my mouth a tooth awakens keen;
I long for taste of apples, grapes and pears;
Panting I stop and lean
On fire like burning stairs.

I think of orchards burned, consumed through spite
Of someone jealous of the teeming fruit;
The heavy limbs ignite,
Stars from the branches shoot.

The flame of beeches on my back is hot,
The fire of sumacs is like burning stoves;
Leaves gathered are a clot
Of blood infused with cloves.

Summer Lightning

Etiolated flame is now abroad,
And in between the hills there is a glare
Like that from unseen bonfires; night is flawed
With lanterns swaying in the sultry air;
Flames play like moths, and hover round earth's must;
There is the apparition of bright hair
And in the woods a three-tined fork is thrust.

There are viewless wings of fire that must strike moths
In their munchings, flittings, useless copulations;
The forest fancies of the twilit Goths
Are rampant; there are obscure cerebrations
In the brains of birds; the wings of some now whir
Like wheels of prayer in China; and there runs
An aching to the tips of each beast's fur.

This is Night's culture, this is what they call
Aestheticism, with attendant pallor,

White nakedness and lights ephemeral,
With many a sharp neurosis and a fervor
And inspiration from the sexual parts,
The conic breasts, the thighs of grief and dolor,
The arid breath of desiccated hearts.

Thunder over Earth

Earth lay like one revealed
By lightning which forever forked and britched;
Earth lay as in a storm-wet lily field;
Earth's body by the dream-storm was enriched—
In her there sprouted buds
Of Asia: in her veins were eastern bloods.

There was a thunderhead
That piled up in the west like Babel pile,
By many clouds and bygone sunsets fed,
The tower seen for many a lengthened mile
With rim enwreathed with lustres
And fragments of high airs and lurid blusters.

The gallant waterbirds
Shone in the flashes on the silvered lake;
And there were gathered horses and wild herds
Under the trees; and the storm made to ache
The fields with heavy wet,
While in beleaguered towns were pitchers set.

And a great bull was struck
Beneath the bellied green of maple tree;
Again one heard the distant splashing duck;
Then thunder sounded loud in ecstasy
And shut out every sound
Save that one of himself cast all around.

The Young Prince

The young prince violent in wrath
Slays all his pets; he decimates their ranks
By thousands, and like naked lord of Gath
Beheads their bodies, binds them onto planks
To burn or drown—

And he has now beheaded
The gaudy parrot which on golden shavings
Was in a palace of his own once bedded—
The bird so splendid in his raucous ravings
Against the rain—

The bees are stamped to death,
Canary birds and carps are disembowelled,
The swan like Desdemona yields her breath,
The pony's side gapes open, deeply rowelled
With a sharp poison spur—

And the death bright
Pleasures the boy, for thus his father mows
The ranks of men in the delicious fight—
And he himself the seed of empire sows
And power over races—

JOHN L. SWEENEY

The Wind's Head

Wherever the wind's head walks
with its proud antlers bending
the weather, canting south and north

to toss a cornstalk cloud
into a corner of the torn sky, I
see the danger of talk, the swift
evaporation of will into a drift
of words, the condensation of thought
loosed like a toy balloon, soon
out of reach of all but the wind's head.

Only an artful calm
the guarded eye
the quiet ready arm
can serve. For
we have learned to fear
the livid nerve
that twitches near
the wounded tiger's heart.

Exaction

While the unturned stone
    (its earth-side alive
    as only self-love is alive)
Hides the inhabited moss
    (its brother-side dead
    as only daylight is dead)
The eyes turn back into the head
And the mind's poor insects thrive.

When the stern choice
    (its hill-side all clarity
    as only charity is clear)
Claims the whole heart's voice
    (its cave-side bright
    as only the dark night is bright)
The eyes return to simple sight
The mind unwinds from fear.

Separation

Make the most of it, mood,
Conjuror of remembrances,
The present's most feeling absentee,
Your only food and good
Is present me.

Noticing comes when the wave has rolled
Towards the unreachable stacked crest
Near another coast
Folded and pulled
And pressed into the past.

The wave and the mood
That makes the distant crest a pain
Are truest of separates.

The sight of seabirds blown
Or shells unreasonably and out of season
Stranded and strewn
Are obliterative 'Egypt'
Desperately written over the crossed-out word.

STANLEY KUNITZ

Lovers Relentlessly

Lovers relentlessly contend to be
Superior in their identity:

The compass of the ego is designed
To circumscribe intact a lesser mind

With definition; tender thought would wrest
Each clean protective secret from the breast;

Affection's eyes go deep, make morbid lesion
In pride's tissue, are ferocious with possession;

Love's active hands are desperate to own
The subtly reasoned flesh on branching bone;

Lovers regard the simple moon that spills
White magic in a garden, bend their wills

Obliquely on each other; lovers eat
The small ecstatic heart to be complete;

Engaged in complicate analysis
Of passionate destruction, lovers kiss;

In furious involvement thcy would make
A double meaning single. Some must break

Upon the wheel of love, but not the strange,
The secret lords, whom only death can change.

Deciduous Branch

Winter, that coils in the thickets now,
Will glide from the fields; the swinging rain
Be knotted with flowers; on every bough
A bird will meditate again.

Lord, in the night if I should die,
Who entertained your thrilling worm,
Corruption wastes more than the eye
Can pick from this imperfect form.

I lie awake, hearing the drip
Upon my sill; thinking, the sun

Has not been promised; we who strip
Summer to seed shall be undone.

Now, while the antler of the eaves
Liquefies, drop by drop, I brood
On a Christian thing: unless the leaves
Perish, the tree is not renewed.

If all our perishable stuff
Be nourished to its rot, we clean
Our trunk of death, and in our tough
And final growth are evergreen.

Foreign Affairs

We are two countries girded for the war,
Whisking our scouts across the pricked frontier
To ravage in each other's fields, cut lines
Along the lacework of strategic nerves,
Loot stores; while here and there,
In ambushes that trace a valley's curves,
Stark witness to the dangerous charge we bear,
A house ignites, a train's derailed, a bridge
Blows up sky-high, and water floods the mines.
Who first attacked? Who turned the other cheek?
Aggression perpetrated is as soon
Denied, and insult rubbed into the injury
By cunning agents trained in these affairs,
With whom it's touch-and-go, don't-tread-on-me,
I-dare-you-to, keep-off, and kiss-my-hand.
Tempers could sharpen knives, and do; we live
In states provocative
Where frowning headlines scare the coffee cream
And doomsday is the eighth day of the week.

Our exit through the slammed and final door
Is twenty times rehearsed, but when we face
The imminence of cataclysmic rupture,

A lesser pride goes down upon its knees.
Two countries separated by desire!—
Whose diplomats speed back and forth by plane,
Portmanteaus stuffed with fresh apologies
Outdated by events before they land.
Negotiations wear them out: they're driven mad
Between the protocols of tears and rapture.

Locked in our fated and contiguous selves,
These worlds that too much agitate each other,
Interdependencies from hip to head,
Twin principalities both slave and free,
We coexist, proclaiming Peace together.
Tell me no lies! We are divided nations
With malcontents by thousands in our streets,
These thousands torn by inbred revolutions.
A triumph is demanded, not moral victories
Deduced from small advances, small retreats.
Are the gods of our fathers not still daemonic?
On the steps of the Capitol
The outraged lion of our years roars panic,
And we suffer the guilty cowardice of the will,
Gathering its bankrupt slogans up for flight
Like gold from ruined treasuries.
And yet, and yet, although the murmur rises,
We are what we are, and only life surprises.

EDWARD DORO

To a Lad Who Would Wed Himself with Music

Set not your heart to woo that basilisk
And hope to have a kindly fate

Of love and fortune flowing, for the risk
    Is ominous and great.

Stifle your flambeaux eyes with icy water
    And wish away that mythic one
Whom I name as Beauty's eldest daughter,
    Whom Bach first looked upon.

Obdurate boy! Now is the nuptial tide,
    And minutes trip on one another
In haste to bring you Music for your bride
    And Beauty for your mother.

Before you leave, before the wedding kiss,
    The low avowal, and the ring,
Remember, lad, her troth will lead to this:
    Long, bitter questioning.

Clap both quivering hands upon your ears,
    Give heed only to what I tell!
While there is time, escape the festal cheers.
    Music belongs in hell.

Open Letter for John Doe

Unless the febrile brow be cool,
Unless the countenance take on a carven shape,
The monarch of this century will not escape
The clap of chaos in his ear.
He will go a faltering fool
Unless the moody eye grow clear,
Unless the mobile mouth do otherwise than gape.

Be mentor to the heart; and lessen
The delirious impact of its passion on the mind.
This wall of nerve and tissue providently lined
Accepts the blood that yet must stay
Humbly the inmate of its prison,

Unknowing of the riotous day,
Subjected to the sentence by its keeper signed.

Where would the nimble glance be off?
Where would the giddy masquerade of laughter fare?
Flashing, painting its frenzies on a stark-white air?
Better to bend the arrant will
Than gobble out of heaven's trough
Or chase for water deep in hell
Or think to down the dragon growling in his lair!

Be yours the sure hypothesis:
A blue hawk winging high above a burning field,
So near to flaming fury, yet by distance steeled.
To his vision there has been
Nothing at fault, nothing amiss:
A pastoral, a quiet scene;
Lechery and madness in an ice of calm congealed.

Pitiless truth! Know it for such,
The frank philippic over which I have no sway.
Against the hurried body do these words inveigh,
Against the mind beyond control,
Lusting to know oblivion's touch.
O patient one, O suffering soul,
These prodigals will cry your mercy some dark day!

KENNETH BURKE

Enigma

I love you as a stranded ship the beach
Where a dead body glistens on the shore.
And while the moonlight gives a form to each,
I hear the formless jungle's distant roar.

My thoughts of you are like the nameless clutter
Of wavelets twinkling on the ocean's tide;
Ten thousand dumb for every one I utter—
Dumb as this drowned man lying on his side.

The cliff that rises by the water's edge—
Were I there, looking down upon the sea,
I could not know, on peering from its ledge,
Whether the body was my love, or me.

The Wrens

The wrens are back!

Their liquid song, pouring across the lawn—
(Or, if the sunlight pours, the wren's song glitters)
Up from the porch,
                    Into the bedroom, where
It is the play of light across a pond,
Sounding as small waves look: new copper coins
Between the seer and the sun.

                              Herewith
Is made a contract binding the brightly waked
Sleeper and his wren, neither the wren's
Nor his, but differently owned by both.

Behind the giving-forth, wren history;
Man-history behind the taking-in.

(Mark the city as a place where no
Wrens sing, as though April were seas of sand,
With spring not the burial of lilac,
                    but heat quaking above stone.)

                              After magnetic storms
Had made all men uneasy, but those the most
That feared the loss of salary or love,

The wrens are back!

The Conspirators

Beyond earshot of others, furtively,
He whispered, "You best"; she, "You above all."
It was a deal. They did conspire together,
Using the legalities, planning for preferment.

Going into the market, they got tables,
Chairs, and other properties from the public
Stock-pile, taking absolute possession
For them alone. These things, all no one else's,
They thought, plotting further to increase
Their store. To have, to hold, to love—theirs only.

And after dark, behind drawn blinds, with doors locked,
And lights off, wordless in wedded privacy,
They went and got out the family jewels,
Put his and hers together, playing treasure.

Mercy Killing

Faithfully
We had covered the nasturtiums
Keeping them beyond
Their season

Until, farewell-minded,
Thinking of age and ailments,
And noting their lack of lustre,
I said:

"They want to die;
We should let the flowers die."

That night
With a biting clear full moon
They lay exposed.

In the morning,
Still shaded
While the sun's line
Crawled towards them from the northwest,
Under a skin of ice
They were at peace.

Stout Affirmation

Whomsoever there are—
Whether enemies, than which there is several,
Or friends, than which there is few—
Hear me of what I am speak of,
Leaving me promulge.

A great amt. of beauties emplenish the world,
Wherein I would o'erglance upon.
There are those which you go out and exclaim:
"Why! How brim-brim!"

I shall be concerning sank ships
Throughout the entire Endure-Myself,
And may my foes become stumbled.
But I want you should, my dear, transpire—
Always transpire, grace-full thanlike one.

You, most prettier sing-rabbit,
And by never,
And lessermost from beneath not—
Prith, give on't.

YES ! ! !

J. V. CUNNINGHAM

The Metaphysical Amorist

You are the problem I propose,
My dear, the text my musings glose:
I call you for convenience love.
By definition you're a cause
Inferred by necessary laws—
You are so to the saints above.
But in this shadowy lower life
I sleep with a terrestrial wife
And earthy children I beget.
Love is a fiction I must use,
A privilege I can abuse,
And sometimes something I forget.

Now, in the heavenly other place
Love is in the eternal mind
The luminous form whose shade she is,
A ghost discarnate, thought defined.
She was so to my early bliss,
She is so while I comprehend
The forms my senses apprehend,
And in the end she will be so.

Her whom my hands embrace I kiss,
Her whom my mind infers I know.
The one exists in time and space
And as she was she will not be;
The other is in her own grace
And is *She is* eternally.

Plato! you shall not plague my life.
I married a terrestrial wife.

And Hume! she is not mere sensation
In sequence of observed relation.
She has two forms—ah, thank you, Duns!—,
I know her in both ways at once.
I knew her, yes, before I knew her,
And by both means I must construe her,
And none among you shall undo her.

To a Friend, on Her Examination for the Doctorate in English

After these years of lectures heard,
Of papers read, of hopes deferred,
Of days spent in the dark stacks
In learning the impervious facts
So well you can dispense with 'em,
Now that the final day has come
When you shall answer name and date
Where fool and scholar judge your fate
What have you gained?
A learnèd grace
And lines of knowledge on the face,
A spirit weary but composed
By true perceptions well-disposed,
A soft voice and historic phrase
Sounding the speech of Tudor days,
What ignorance cannot assail
Or daily novelty amaze,
Knowledge enforced by firm detail.

What revels will these trials entail!
What gentle wine confuse your head
While gossip lingers on the dead
Till all the questions wash away,
For you have learned, not what to say,
But how the saying must be said.

Agnosco Veteris Vestigia Flammae

I have been here. Dispersed in meditation,
I sense the traces of the old surmise—
Passion dense as fatigue, faithful as pain,
As joy foreboding. O my void, my being
In the suspended sources of experience,
Massive in promise, unhistorical
Being of unbeing, of all futures full,
Unrealised in none, how love betrays you,
Turns you to process and a fluid fact
Whose future specifies its past, whose past
Precedes it, and whose history is its being.

GENE DERWOOD

Star

Star, star, shining bright,
With new spectrum in the night,
Telescope game gone earnest now,
Prophets down to '50 brought
And the method shoved to naught,
Puddentame remains my name.
Ask again, I'll say the same
And let you soon know how.

First star I've seen tonight,
When the grain admires the blight,
At the gate the farmer enters
While the shine on water feathers
These new colours will change weathers.
I'll say the name till Puddentame

Rings in your head the very same.
Spite and spike the bombish mentors.

Make your wish come out of you,
Struck in water, say it true.
Star and stars are overhead,
Now the night is purpling rich
Fertilizing our deep ditch,
First was written when my name
Answers you with Puddentame,
Star crack wings and raise dead.

Elegy on Gordon Barber

Lamentably Drowned in his Eighteenth Year

When in the mirror of a permanent tear
Over the iris of your mother's eye
I beheld the dark tremor of your face, austere
With space of death, spun too benign for youth,
Icicle of the past to pierce her living sigh—
I saw you wish the last kiss of mother's mouth,
Who took the salted waters rather in the suck
Of seas, sighing yourself to fill and drench
With water the plum-rich glory of your breast
Where beat the heart escaping from war's luck.

Gordon, I mourn your wrist, your running foot,
Your curious brows, your thigh, your unborn daughters,
Yet mourn more deep the drought-caught war dry boy
Who goes, a killer, to join you in your sleep
And envy you what made you blench
Taking your purple back to drought-less waters.
What choke of terror filled you in the wet
What fierce surprise caught you when play turned fate
And all the rains you loved became your net,
Formlessly yielding, yet stronger than your breath?
Then did you dream of mother or hopes hatched

When the cold cramp held you from nape to foot
And time dissolved, promise dissolved, in Death?
Did you cry 'cruel' to all the hands that stretched
Not near, but played afar, when you sank down
Your sponge of lungs hurt to the quick
Till you had left the quick to join the dead,
Whom, now, your mother mourns, grief-sick.
You were too young to drown.

Never will you take bride to happy bed,
Who lay awash in water yet no laving
Needed, so pure so young for sudden leaving.
Gone, gone is Gordon, tall and brilliant lad
Whose mind was science. Now hollow his skull
A noble sculpture, is but sunken bone,
His cells from water come by water laid
Grave-deep, to water gone.
Lost, lost the hope he had
Washed to a cipher his splendour and his skill.

But Gordon's gone, it's other boys who live afraid.

Two years, and lads have grown to hold a gun.
In dust must splendid lads go down and choke,
Red dry their hands and dry their one day's sun
From which they earthward fall to fiery tomb
Bomb-weighted, from bloodying children's hair.

Never a boy but takes as cross Cain's crime
And goes to death by making death, to pass
Death's gate distorted with the dried brown grime—
Better the watery death than death by air
Or death by sand
Where fall hard fish of fear
Loud in unwetted dust.

Spun on a lucky wave, O early boy!
Now ocean's fish you are
As heretofore.

Perhaps you had sweet mercy's tenderness
To win so soon largesse of choice
That you, by grace, went gayly to the wave
And all our mourning should be to rejoice.

WELDON KEES

The Conversation in the Drawing Room

—That spot of blood on the drawing room wall,
No larger than a thumbnail when I looked a moment ago,
Is spreading, Cousin Agatha, and growing brighter.

Nonsense. The oriole warbles in the sunlight.
The fountains gush luxuriantly above the pool.
The weather is ideal: on the paths a sheen
Of summer provides a constant delight.
I am thinking of affiliating with a new theosophist group.

—Once you could hide it with a nickel.
Now it strangely assumes the shape and size of a palm,
And puts out fingers, Cousin Agatha. Look, examine it!

Some aberration of the wallpaper, no doubt.
Did you have an omelette for lunch, and asparagus?
Mrs. Pisgah's husband spoke from the beyond during the séance
Last night at Madame Irani's. He seemed to have a cold.
The tamborine did not function with its usual zest.

—And a wrist, Cousin Agatha, and an arm!
Like those maps in a cinema that spread
Like wind blowing over a field of wheat, Cousin Agatha!

I have warned you, Hobart, about reading *The Turn of the Screw*

And that story of Balzac's, whatever the name of it is,
Just before retiring. They always have a decidedly bad effect
upon you.
I believe I will put another aspirin in the lily's vase.
And now I must go to take my nap in the sunroom.

—Cousin Agatha, it moves like a fish, wet,
Wet like a fish, becomes a moving thing
That spreads and reaches from the wall!

I cannot listen to you any more just now, Hobart.
Kindly speak to Marie about the place cards for this evening.
Ah, there is the oriole again; how beautiful the view
From this window!—Yet why, one wonders, must Hobart begin
Gasping and screaming in such a deplorable fashion
There in the drawing room? It is scarcely considerate.
Youthful animal spirits, one supposes, combined
With a decided taste for the macabre. Where is the barbital?
Marie can never learn to leave it here, by the incense burner.
Ah, now he has stopped and only thrashes about, rather feebly,
on the floor.
It is a beautiful afternoon; I will get up about three-fifteen.
Everything is blissfully quiet now; I am ready for sleep.

Report of the Meeting

The scientists removed their coats and hats
And climbed upon an antiseptic stage.
A toothless lion suffered in his cage,
Ignoring them. The men of science sat.

One breathed an introductory gasp,
Stood up and fastened glasses to his nose,
And told the crowd—before he grew verbose—
The Life Elixir lay within their grasp.

"We hold this meeting here today
So you may see this ancient lion fed

The Life Elixir." As an afterthought he said,
"It has a bitter taste." He told them of the way

The scientists poured liquids into vats
For years uncountable; examined sperms,
Blood, sputum, knee-jerk, heartbeat, germs;
Invented baffling mazes where white rats

Learned methods of success or went insane;
Experimented with the brains of larks;
Filled notebooks with a million puzzling marks;
And doped retarded monkeys with cocaine.

"The years went by in study without rest
In search of the Elixir that would bring
Eternal life to man and beast; and then one Spring,"
He said, "we were rewarded with success."

This ended his remarks. Applause.
The men of science went within the cage
And fed the lion, who had reached an age
Of weariness and trust. (They had, however, dulled his claws.)

The beast on whom the remedy was tried
Watched them file out with tolerant disdain,
Yawned at the crowd and shook his mane,
Grew cross, dozed fitfully, and died.

Silence; and then a thousand metronomes
Ticked violently, the air blurred, people hissed
And took their leave; some mumbled, "Fake." The scientists
Returned, annoyed and puzzled, to their homes,

Where they wrote monographs on every phase
Of the affair, constructed graphs and charts and plans,
Cut up the lion, placed its parts in pans,
And did not venture on the streets for days.

Robinson

The dog stops barking after Robinson has gone.
His act is over. The world is a gray world,
Not without violence, and he kicks under the grand piano,
The nightmare chase well under way.

The mirror from Mexico, stuck to the wall,
Reflects nothing at all. The glass is black.
Robinson alone provides the image Robinsonian.

Which is all of the room—walls, curtains,
Shelves, bed, the tinted photograph of Robinson's first wife,
Rugs, vases, panatellas in a humidor.
They would fill the room if Robinson came in.

The pages in the books are blank,
The books that Robinson has read. That is his favorite chair,
Or where the chair would be if Robinson were here.

All day the phone rings. It could be Robinson
Calling. It never rings when he is here.

Outside, white buildings yellow in the sun.
Outside, the birds circle continuously
Where trees are actual and take no holiday.

A Brief Introduction to the History of Culture

Such was the natural course of decay . . . Tasso bowed before the mutilation; indeed, professed his readiness to make every change demanded . . .

"And if the name of 'Mage' offends these gentlemen,
It shall be 'Sage' instead. I've cut that queer enchanted wand,

Those cold blue foaming waters opening,
Although no bright Jerusalem was there.
My characters instead go underground through caves.
Let odors of black art float up from other manuscripts,
Not mine.

"And I have cut the resurrection of the buried man,
The metamorphosis of warriors into creatures of the sea.
(Two Marys guide me to the Eucharist.)
The ship was marvelous, but it will have to go
As well; I multiply the orthodox. Those stanzas that conclude
A canto near the end—although examined, tolerated,
Almost, one might say, approved,
By the Inquisitor, I've doctored anyway.

"—Of course, the marvels must come out,
The kisses-stanza, and the parrot, too—
It seems a shame. Impediments at Rome,
Monsignor Silvio. I look toward Venice furtively.
Have I been over-theological?"

River Song

By the public hook for the private eye,
Near the neutral river where the children were,
I was hung for the street, to watch the sky.

When they strung me there, I waved like a flag
Near the bright blue river where the children played,
And my smile became part of the cultural lag.

I named three martyrs. My mother came
To the grayish river where the children stared:
"My son, you have honored the family name."

I was happy. Then a parade went by
Near the shadowy river where the children waved,
And the uniforms made me shiver and cry.

I tried to get down. What I had learned
Near the sunless river where the children screamed
Was only pain. My ropemarks burned.

But I couldn't move. Had I been thrown
By the darkening river where the children failed,
Or had I come there quite alone?

The bands were playing when they cut me down
By the dirty river where the children cried,
And a man made a speech in a long black gown.

He called me a hero. I didn't care.
The river ran blood and the children died.
And I wanted to die, but they left me there.

Back

Much cry and little wool:
I have come back
As empty-handed as I went.

Although the woods were full,
And past the track
The heavy boughs were bent

Down to my knees with fruit
Ripe for a still life, I had meant
My trip as a search for stones.

But the beach was bare
Except for the drying bones
Of a fish, shells, an old wool

Shirt, a rubber boot,
A strip of lemon rind.
They were not what I had in mind:

It was merely stones.
Well, the days are full.
This day at least is spent.

Much cry and little wool:
I have come back
As empty-handed as I went.

Aspects of Robinson

Robinson at cards at the Algonquin; a thin
Blue light comes down once more outside the blinds.
Gray men in overcoats are ghosts blown past the door.
The taxis streak the avenues with yellow, orange, and red.
This is Grand Central, Mr. Robinson.

Robinson on a roof above the Heights; the boats
Mourn like the lost. Water is slate, far down.
Through sounds of ice cubes dropped in glass, an osteopath,
Dressed for the links, describes an old Intourist tour.
—Here's where old Gibbons jumped from, Robinson.
Robinson walking in the Park, admiring the elephant.
Robinson buying the *Tribune,* Robinson buying the *Times.* Robinson
Saying, "Hello. Yes, this is Robinson. Sunday
At five? I'd love to. Pretty well. And you?"
Robinson alone at Longchamps, staring at the wall.

Robinson afraid, drunk, sobbing. Robinson
In bed with a Mrs. Morse. Robinson at home;
Decisions: Toynbee or luminol? Where the sun
Shines, Robinson in flowered trunks, eyes toward
The breakers. Where the night ends, Robinson in East Side bars.

Robinson in Glen plaid jacket, Scotch-grain shoes,
Black four-in-hand and oxford button-down,

The jeweled and silent watch that winds itself, the brief-
Case, covert topcoat, clothes for spring, all covering
His sad and usual heart, dry as a winter leaf.

Robinson at Home

Curtains drawn back, the door ajar.
All winter long, it seemed, a darkening
Began. But now the moonlight and the odors of the street
Conspire and combine toward one community.

These are the rooms of Robinson.
Bleached, wan, and colorless this light, as though
All the blurred daybreaks of the spring
Found an asylum here, perhaps for Robinson alone,

Who sleeps. Were there more music sifted through the floors
And moonlight of a different kind,
He might awake to hear the news at ten,
Which will be shocking, moderately.

This sleep is from exhaustion, but his old desire
To die like this has known a lessening.
Now there is only this coldness that he has to wear.
But not in sleep. —Observant scholar, traveller,

Or uncouth bearded figure squatting in a cave,
A keen-eyed sniper on the barricades,
A heretic in catacombs, a famed roué,
A beggar on the streets, the confidant of Popes—

All these are Robinson in sleep, who mumbles as he turns,
"There is something in this madhouse that I symbolize—
This city—nightmare—black—"
He wakes in sweat
To the terrible moonlight and what might be
Silence. It drones like wires far beyond the roofs,
And the long curtains blow into the room.

Relating to Robinson

Somewhere in Chelsea, early summer;
And, walking in the twilight toward the docks,
I thought I made out Robinson ahead of me.

From an uncurtained second-story room, a radio
Was playing *There's A Small Hotel;* a kite
Twisted above dark rooftops and slow drifting birds.
We were alone there, he and I,
Inhabiting the empty street.

Under a sign for Natural Bloom Cigars,
While lights clicked softly in the dusk from red to green,
He stopped and gazed into a window
Where a plaster Venus, modeling a truss,
Looked out at Eastbound traffic. (But Robinson,
I knew, was out of town: he summers at a place in Maine,
Sometimes on Fire Island, sometimes the Cape,
Leaves town in June and comes back after Labor Day.)
And yet, I almost called out, "Robinson!"

There was no chance. Just as I passed,
Turning my head to search his face,
His own head turned with mine
And fixed me with dilated, terrifying eyes
That stopped my blood. His voice
Came at me like an echo in the dark.

"I thought I saw the whirlpool opening.
Kicked all night at a bolted door.
You must have followed me from Astor Place.
An empty paper floats down at the last.
And then a day as huge as yesterday in pairs
Unrolled its horror on my face
Until it blocked—" Running in sweat
To reach the docks, I turned back
For a second glance, I had no certainty,

There in the dark, that it was Robinson
Or someone else.

The block was bare. The Venus
Bathed in blue fluorescent light,
Stared toward the river. As I hurried West,
The lights across the bay were coming on.
The boats moved silently and the low whistles blew.

ELIZABETH BISHOP

The Fish

I caught a tremendous fish
and held him beside the boat
half out of water, with my hook
fast in a corner of his mouth.
He didn't fight.
He hadn't fought at all.
He hung a grunting weight,
battered and venerable
and homely. Here and there
his brown skin hung in strips
like ancient wall-paper,
and its pattern of darker brown
was like wall-paper:
shapes like full-blown roses
stained and lost through age.
He was speckled with barnacles,
fine rosettes of lime,
and infested
with tiny white sea-lice,
and underneath two or three
rags of green weed hung down.

While his gills were breathing in
the terrible oxygen
—the frightening gills,
fresh and crisp with blood,
that can cut so badly—
I thought of the coarse white flesh
packed in like feathers,
the big bones and the little bones,
the dramatic reds and blacks
of his shiny entrails,
and the pink swim-bladder
like a big peony.
I looked into his eyes
which were far larger than mine
but shallower, and yellowed,
the irises backed and packed
with tarnished tinfoil
seen through the lenses
of old scratched isinglass.
They shifted a little, but not
to return my stare.
—It was more like the tipping
of an object toward the light.
I admired his sullen face,
the mechanism of his jaw,
and then I saw
that from his lower lip
—if you could call it a lip—
grim, wet, and weapon-like,
hung five old pieces of fish-line,
or four and a wire leader
with the swivel still attached,
with all their five big hooks
grown firmly in his mouth.
A green line, frayed at the end
where he broke it, two heavier lines,
and a fine black thread
still crimped from the strain and snap
when it broke and he got away.

Like medals with their ribbons
frayed and wavering,
a five-haired beard of wisdom
trailing from his aching jaw.
I stared and stared
and victory filled up
the little rented boat,
from the pool of bilge
where oil had spread a rainbow
around the rusted engine
to the bailer rusted orange,
the sun-cracked thwarts,
the oarlocks on their strings,
the gunnels—until everything
was rainbow, rainbow, rainbow!
And I let the fish go.

Invitation to Miss Marianne Moore

From Brooklyn, over the Brooklyn Bridge, on this fine morning,
  please come flying.
In a cloud of fiery pale chemicals,
  please come flying,
to the rapid rolling of thousands of small blue drums
descending out of the mackerel sky
over the glittering grandstand of harbor-water,
  please come flying.

Whistles, pennants and smoke are blowing. The ships
are signaling cordially with multitudes of flags
rising and falling like birds all over the harbor.
Enter: two rivers, gracefully bearing
countless little pellucid jellies
in cut-glass epergnes dragging with silver chains.
The flight is safe; the weather is all arranged.
The waves are running in verses this fine morning.
  Please come flying.

Come with the pointed toe of each black shoe
trailing a sapphire highlight,
with a black capeful of butterfly wings and bon-mots,
with heaven knows how many angels all riding
on the broad black brim of your hat,
   please come flying.

Bearing a musical inaudible abacus,
a slight censorious frown, and blue ribbons,
   please come flying.
Facts and skyscrapers glint in the tide; Manhattan
is all awash with morals this fine morning,
   so please come flying.

Mounting the sky with natural heroism,
above the accidents, above the malignant movies,
the taxicabs and injustices at large,
while horns are resounding in your beautiful ears
that simultaneously listen to
a soft uninvented music, fit for the musk deer,
   please come flying.

For whom the grim museums will behave
like courteous male bower-birds,
for whom the agreeable lions lie in wait
on the steps of the Public Library,
eager to rise and follow through the doors
up into the reading rooms,
   please come flying.
We can sit down and weep; we can go shopping,
or play at a game of constantly being wrong
with a priceless set of vocabularies,
or we can bravely deplore, but please
   please come flying.

With dynasties of negative constructions
darkening and dying around you,
with grammar that suddenly turns and shines
like flocks of sandpipers flying,
   please come flying.

Come like a light in the white mackerel sky,
come like a daytime comet
with a long unnebulous train of words,
from Brooklyn, over the Brooklyn Bridge, on this fine morning,
please come flying.

ROBERT LOWELL

The Quaker Graveyard in Nantucket

(For Warren Winslow, Dead at Sea)

Let man have dominion over the fishes of the sea and the fowls of the air and the beasts and the whole earth, and every creeping creature that moveth upon the earth.

I

A brackish reach of shoal off Madaket,—
The sea was still breaking violently and night
Had steamed into our North Atlantic Fleet,
When the drowned sailor clutched the drag-net. Light
Flashed from his matted head and marble feet,
He grappled at the net
With the coiled, hurdling muscles of his thighs:
The corpse was bloodless, a botch of reds and whites,
Its open, staring eyes
Were lustreless dead-lights
Or cabin-windows on a stranded hulk
Heavy with sand. We weight the body, close
Its eyes and heave it seaward whence it came,
Where the heel-headed dogfish barks its nose
On Ahab's void and forehead; and the name
Is blocked in yellow chalk.

Sailors, who pitch this portent at the sea
Where dreadnaughts shall confess
Its hell-bent deity,
When you are powerless
To sand-bag this Atlantic bulwark, faced
By the earth-shaker, green, unwearied, chaste
In his steel scales: ask for no Orphean lute
To pluck life back. The guns of the steeled fleet
Recoil and then repeat
The hoarse salute.

II

Whenever winds are moving and their breath
Heaves at the roped-in bulwarks of this pier,
The terns and sea-gulls tremble at your death
In these home waters. Sailor, can you hear
The Pequod's sea wings, beating landward, fall
Headlong and break on our Atlantic wall
Off 'Sconset, where the yawing S-boats splash
The bellbuoy, with ballooning spinnakers,
As the entangled, screeching mainsheet clears
The blocks: off Madaket, where lubbers lash
The heavy surf and throw their long lead squids
For blue-fish? Sea-gulls blink their heavy lids
Seaward. The winds' wings beat upon the stones,
Cousin, and scream for you and the claws rush
At the sea's throat and wring it in the slush
Of this old Quaker graveyard where the bones
Cry out in the long night for the hurt beast
Bobbing by Ahab's whaleboats in the East.

III

All you recovered from Poseidon died
With you, my cousin, and the harrowed brine
Is fruitless on the blue beard of the god,
Stretching beyond us to the castles in Spain,
Nantucket's westward haven. To Cape Cod

Guns, cradled on the tide,
Blast the eelgrass about a waterclock
Of bilge and backwash, roil the salt and sand
Lashing earth's scaffold, rock
Our warships in the hand
Of the great God, where time's contrition blues
Whatever it was these Quaker sailors lost
In the mad scramble of their lives. They died
When time was open-eyed,
Wooden and childish; only bones abide
There, in the nowhere, where their boats were tossed
Sky-high, where mariners had fabled news
Of Is, the swashing castle. What it cost
Them is their secret. In the monster's slick
I see the Quakers drown and hear their cry:
'If God himself had not been on our side,
If God himself had not been on our side,
When the Atlantic rose against us, why,
Then it had swallowed us up quick.'

IV

This is the end of the whaleroad and the whale
Who spewed Nantucket bones on the thrashed swell
And stirred the troubled waters to whirlpools
To send the Pequod packing off to hell:
This is the end of them, three-quarters fools,
Snatching at straws to sail
Seaward and seaward on the turntail whale,
Spouting out blood and water as it rolls,
Sick as a dog to these Atlantic shoals:
Clamavimus, O depths. Let the sea-gulls wail

For water, for the deep where the high tide
Mutters to its hurt self, mutters and ebbs.
Waves wallow in their wash, go out and out,
Leave only the death-rattle of the crabs,
The beach increasing, its enormous snout
Sucking the ocean's side.

This is the end of running on the waves;
We are poured out like water. Who will dance
The mast-lashed master of Leviathans
Up from this field of Quakers in their unstoned graves?

V

When the whale's viscera go and the roll
Of its corruption overruns this world
Beyond tree-swept Nantucket and Wood's Hole
And Martha's Vineyard, Sailor, will your sword
Whistle and fall and sink into the fat?
In the great ash-pit of Jehoshaphat
The bones cry for the blood of the white whale,
The fat flukes arch and whack about its ears,
The death-lance churns into the sanctuary, tears
The gun-blue swingle, heaving like a flail,
And hacks the coiling life out: it works and drags
And rips the sperm-whale's midriff into rags,
Gobbets of blubber spill to wind and weather,
Sailor, and gulls go round the stoven timbers
Where the morning stars sing out together
And thunder shakes the white surf and dismembers
The red flag hammered in the mast-head. Hide,
Our steel, Jonas Messias, in Thy side.

VI

Our Lady of Walsingham

There once the penitents took off their shoes
And then walked barefoot the remaining mile;
And the small trees, a stream and hedgerows file
Slowly along the munching English lane,
Like cows to the old shrine, until you lose
Track of your dragging pain.
The stream flows down under the druid tree,
Shiloah's whirlpools gurgle and make glad

The castle of God. Sailor, you were glad
And whistled Sion by that stream. But see:

Our Lady, too small for her canopy,
Sits near the altar. There's no comeliness
At all or charm in that expressionless
Face with its heavy eyelids. As before,
This face, for centuries a memory,
Non est species, neque decor,
Expressionless, expresses God: it goes
Past castled Sion. She knows what God knows,
Not Calvary's Cross nor crib at Bethlehem
Now, and the world shall come to Walsingham.

VII

The empty winds are creaking and the oak
Splatters and splatters on the cenotaph,
The boughs are trembling and a gaff
Bobs on the untimely stroke
Of the greased wash exploding on a shoal-bell
In the old mouth of the Atlantic. It's well;
Atlantic, you are fouled with the blue sailors,
Sea-monsters, upward angel, downward fish:
Unmarried and corroding, spare of flesh
Mart once of supercilious, wing'd clippers,
Atlantic, where your bell-trap guts its spoil
You could cut the brackish winds with a knife
Here in Nantucket, and cast up the time
When the Lord God formed man from the sea's slime
And breathed into his face the breath of life,
And blue-lung'd combers lumbered to the kill.
The Lord survives the rainbow of His will.

The Drunken Fisherman

Wallowing in this bloody sty,
I cast for fish that pleased my eye

(Truly Jehovah's bow suspends
No pots of gold to weight its ends);
Only the blood-mouthed rainbow trout
Rose to my bait. They flopped about
My canvas creel until the moth
Corrupted its unstable cloth.

A calendar to tell the day;
A handkerchief to wave away
The gnats; a couch unstuffed with storm
Pouching a bottle in one arm;
A whiskey bottle full of worms;
And bedroom slacks: are these fit terms
To mete the worm whose molten rage
Boils in the belly of old age?

Once fishing was a rabbit's foot—
O wind blow cold, O wind blow hot,
Let suns stay in or suns step out:
Life danced a jig on the sperm-whale's spout—
The fisher's fluent and obscene
Catches kept his conscience clean.
Children, the raging memory drools
Over the glory of past pools.

Now the hot river, ebbing, hauls
Its bloody waters into holes;
A grain of sand inside my shoe
Mimics the moon that might undo
Man and Creation too; remorse
Stinking, has puddled up its source;
Here tantrums thrash to a whale's rage.
This is the pot-hole of old age.

Is there no way to cast my hook
Out of this dynamited brook?
The Fisher's sons must cast about
When shallow waters peter out.
I will catch Christ with a greased worm,

And when the Prince of Darkness stalks
My bloodstream to its Stygian term . . .
On water the Man-Fisher walks.

Falling Asleep over the Aeneid

An old man in Concord forgets to go to Morning Service. He falls asleep, while reading Virgil, and dreams that he is Aeneas at the funeral of Pallas, an Italian prince.

The sun is blue and scarlet on my page,
And *yuck-a, yuck-a, yuck-a, yuck-a,* rage
The yellowhammers mating. Yellow fire
Blankets the captives dancing on their pyre,
And the scorched lictor screams and drops his rod.
Trojans are singing to their drunken God,
Ares. Their helmets catch on fire. Their files
Clank by the body of my comrade—miles
Of filings! Now the scythe-wheeled chariot rolls
Before their lances long as vaulting poles,
And I stand up and heil the thousand men,
Who carry Pallas to the bird-priest. Then
The bird-priest groans, and as his birds foretold,
I greet the body, lip to lip. I hold
The sword that Dido used. It tries to speak,
A bird with Dido's sworded breast. Its beak
Clangs and ejaculates the Punic word
I hear the bird-priest chirping like a bird.
I groan a little. 'Who am I, and why?'
It asks, a boy's face, though its arrow-eye
Is working from its socket. 'Brother, try,
O Child of Aphrodite, try to die:
To die is life.' His harlots hang his bed
With feathers of his long-tailed birds. His head
Is yawning like a person. The plumes blow;
The beard and eyebrows ruffle. Face of snow,
You are the flower that country girls have caught,
A wild bee-pillaged honeysuckle brought

To the returning bridegroom—the design
Has not yet left it, and the petals shine;
The earth, its mother, has, at last, no help:
It is itself. The broken-winded yelp
Of my Phoenician hounds, that fills the brush
With snapping twigs and flying, cannot flush
The ghost of Pallas. But I take his pall,
Stiff with its gold and purple, and recall
How Dido hugged it to her, while she toiled,
Laughing—her golden threads, a serpent coiled
In cypress. Now I lay it like a sheet;
It clinks and settles down upon his feet,
The careless golden hair that seemed to burn
Beforehand. Left foot, right foot—as they turn,
More pyres are rising: armored horses, bronze,
And gagged Italians, who must pass by ones
Across the bitter river, when my thumb
Tightens into their wind-pipes. The beaks drum;
Their headman's cow-horned death's head bites its tongue,
And stiffens, as it eyes the hero slung
Inside his feathered hammock on the crossed
Staves of the eagles that we winged. Our cost
Is nothing to the lovers, whoring Mars
And Venus, father's lover. Now the car's
Plumage is ready, and my marshals fetch
His squire, Acoetes, white with age, to hitch
Aethon, the hero's charger, and its ears
Prick, and it steps and steps, and stately tears
Lather its teeth; and then the harlots bring
The hero's charms and baton—but the King,
Vain-glorious Turnus, carried off the rest.
'I was myself, but Ares thought it best
The way it happened.' At the end of time,
He sets his spear, as my descendants climb
The knees of Father Time, his beard of scalps,
His scythe, the arc of steel that crowns the Alps.
The elephants of Carthage hold those snows,
Terms of Numidian horse unsling their bows,
The flaming turkey-feathered arrows swarm

Beyond the Alps. 'Pallas,' I raise my arm
And shout, 'Brother, eternal health. Farewell
Forever.' Church is over, and its bell
Frightens the yellowhammers, as I wake,
And watch the whitecaps wrinkle up the lake.
Mother's great aunt, who died when I was eight,
Stands by the parlor sabre. 'Boy, it's late.
Virgil must keep the Sabbath.' Forty years!
It all comes back. My Uncle Charles appears,
Blue-capped and bird-like. Phillips Brooks and Grant
Are frowning at his coffin, and my aunt,
Hearing his colored volunteers parade
Through Concord, laughs, and tells her English maid
To clip his yellow nostril hairs, and fold
His colors on him. It is I. I hold
His sword to keep from falling, for the dust
On the stuffed birds is breathless, for the bust
Of young Augustus weighs on Virgil's shelf:
It scowls into my glasses at itself.

JEAN GARRIGUE

From This There's No Returning

From this there's no returning, none,
Nor setting forth from out the centered night:
From this there's no appealing for release:
Captivity is torment that we want,
The only meaning that the wind has taught.

From this there's no returning, none
From this at night when in our arms we're caught
And irresponsibly time's worth we burn
And irretrievably are altered then:
From this there's no returning, none.

From this there's no returning though there is,
I do return, I must, though I would not.
What do I speak of then, what difference?
The touch that saw, love's better sight,
Is numb, for light is gone. And gone
The whole world of the body, gone.

The blood aches like the eye that cannot see,
The heart that heard its own at back of night
Now hears the roar of its disunity
And ever guilty of its want
The soul that heard its body lock it out.

O melancholy of analysis!
Break not your dark leaves here upon my thought.
The golden visage of the darkness came,
The wrath of morning was abated then
And, had I died in joy's perfection, I
Would I had died then.

What is this force that now sends out the day
To travel backwards to its source again?
What if I'm left and must endure alone
The cosmos that the agéd night upturned
When iron from its pole was outward drawn
And from the dark great images of sun?

Touch saw: or did you counterfeit the day?
Or you or night break through to bring what day
Or memory intensely hid? Or you
Or night that you, veined by great lights so lay
Till memory its buried elations found
And memory like radium was freed?

Yet that which wrought a world so altering me
(What if I'm left alone and must endure)
Is like an unforgiveness here:
O origin I cannot cry for, praise,

That must so temper all my days
Teaches me too: we each must be alone.

O love, deceiver and deceived, remark
How close your torment that begins
Responsibilities you cannot hold for long!
For each of us must be alone.
It's circumstance the blood's brined in:
Wrong, wrong is done when we deny this to

Imitate perfection in a void,
Animal, forgetful, cry: we're world!
Wed disparities, defeats, to find
Two halves in one, two miseries allied
Till joy outrides its naturalness to be
Madness in union, death in unity.

O love, our demon sun, you cried to us:
You need not be alone for you may die:
Let us a madness, evil, so to think
We need not be alone until we die,
So stung and harrowed, heart-piercéd, we cry:
From this there's no returning till we die.

Labor and thought, O salvage us from this
Presumptive logic, dread paralysis!
That we, upon these plural routes traverse
'Twixt dual aptitudes the real, unreal
Nor robbing not a joy beyond its bounds,
Hold real, not unreal real, within our arms.

So negatives of these excesses nulled,
Nor joy affronting not reality,
We wrestle with profundities awhile
Where boisterous nature from its eminence
Looks on, approves, excels to reconcile
The dark and day that in espousals arm.

O intellectual dream that us exceeds
As nature's energy of forms defies

The imitative purpose of our pride!
We're pitched between these norms so to perfect
The heart that must endure its fear and hope,
The heart that must perfect its lonely want.

So to perfect and take a sweetness there
And bless the source of life that in us runs
Which seeks the purity it pours forth from:
O spirit air and winds invisibly that run
To marry in one direction sped,
And star that grazes on the mountainside

And earth to animals allied:
O blessed and blesser bound in us
That teaches how we must be unified
By what great purpose and whose holy pride.

Homage to Ghosts

Always within me lies
That former form of experience
If suddenly I bare my eyes.
Always dismembering me, although
It is so altered and so changed
I know it and know it not.
O, I ponder that time set
Some things beneath its yoke
And set not it
And yet my passion and my want
Built a lasting place wherein
Obediently it lies
And still evades all consequence
Of an ordinary demise.

But I see that even mind
Alters substance between time.
In those years it has lain there
I grew different, and my change,

All unknowingly, made it strange.
The image that it lay in me
Was subject as I was to all
Shocks that made my soul grow ill,
Took account of every sorrow,
And of my body did so borrow
Till I think that what was it
Is now, surely, only me.

Still, it has such separate power
It forbids all I would touch
And takes away the life from what
Is living, though it is not.
Perhaps it is my tomb as well,
For both of us without conjunction
Lie prison stones on recollection.
But thought, despite such memory,
Yet tears the soul from the body.
I love and do not love
And indifference and fidelity
Between their greeds fast with me,
My bones plucked dry to satisfy
That double eternity.

THEODORE ROETHKE

The Lost Son

I. THE FLIGHT

At Woodlawn I heard the dead cry:
I was lulled by the slamming of iron,
A slow drip over stones,
Toads brooding in wells.

All the leaves stuck out their tongues;
I shook the softening chalk of my bones,
Saying,
Snail, snail, glister me forward,
Bird, soft-sigh me home,
Worm, be with me.
This is my hard time.

Fished in an old wound,
The soft pond of repose;
Nothing nibbled my line,
Not even the minnows came.

Sat in an empty house
Watching shadows crawl,
Scratching.
There was one fly.

Voice, come out of the silence.
Say something.
Appear in the form of a spider
Or a moth beating the curtain.

Tell me:
Which is the way I take;
Out of what door do I go,
Where and to whom?

Dark hollows said, lee to the wind,
The moon said, back of an eel,
The salt said, look by the sea,
Your tears are not enough praise,
You will find no comfort here,
In the kingdom of bang and blab.

Running lightly over spongy ground,
Past the pasture of flat stones,
The three elms,
The sheep strewn on a field,

Over a rickety bridge
Toward the quick-water, wrinkling and rippling.

Hunting along the rivers,
Down among the rubbish, the bug-riddled foliage,
By the muddy pond-edge, by the bog-holes,
By the shrunken lake, hunting, in the heat of summer.

The shape of a rat?
It's bigger than that.
It's less than a leg
And more than a nose,
Just under the water
It usually goes.

Is it soft like a mouse?
Can it wrinkle its nose?
Could it come in the house
On the tips of its toes?

Take the skin of a cat
And the back of an eel,
Then roll them in grease,—
That's the way it would feel.

It's sleek as an otter
With wide webby toes
Just under the water
It usually goes.

II. THE PIT

Where do the roots go?
Look down under the leaves.
Who put the moss there?
These stones have been here too long.
Who stunned the dirt into noise?
Ask the mole, he knows.
I feel the slime of a wet nest.

Beware Mother Mildew.
Nibble again, fish nerves.

III. THE GIBBER

At the wind's mouth,
By the cave's door,
I listened to something
I had heard before.

Dogs of the groin
Barked and howled
The sun was against me
The moon would not have me.

The weeds whined,
The snakes cried,
The cows and briars
Said to me: Die.

What a small song. What slow clouds. What dark water.
Hath the rain a father? All the caves are ice. Only the snow's here.
I'm cold. I'm cold all over. Rub me in father and mother.
Fear was my father, Father Fear.
His look drained the stones.

What gliding shape
Beckoning through halls,
Stood poised on the stair,
Fell dreamily down?

From the mouths of jugs
Perched on many shelves,
I saw substance flowing
That cold morning.

Like a slither of eels
That watery cheek

As my own tongue kissed
My lips awake.

Is this the storm's heart? The ground is unstilling itself.
My veins are running nowhere. Do the bones cast out their fire?
Is the seed leaving the old bed? These buds are live as birds.
Where, where are the tears of the world?
Let the kisses resound, flat like a butcher's palm;
Let the gestures freeze; our doom is already decided.
All the windows are burning! What's left of my life?
I want the old rage, the lash of primordial milk!
Goodbye, goodbye, old stones, the time-order is going.
I have married my hands to perpetual agitation,
I run, I run to the whistle of money.

Money money money
Water water water

How cool the grass is.
Has the bird left?
The stalk still sways.
Has the worm a shadow?
What do the clouds say?

These sweeps of light undo me.
Look, look, the ditch is running white!
I've more veins than a tree!
Kiss me, ashes, I'm falling through a dark swirl.

IV. THE RETURN

The way to the boiler was dark,
Dark all the way,
Over slippery cinders
Through the long greenhouse.

The roses kept breathing in the dark.
They had many mouths to breathe with.
My knees made little winds underneath
Where the weeds slept.

There was always a single light
Swinging by the fire-pit,
Where the fireman pulled out roses,
The big roses, the big bloody clinkers.

Once I stayed all night.
The light in the morning came slowly over the white
Snow.
There were many kinds of cool
Air.
Then came steam.

Pipe-knock.

Scurry of warm over small plants.
Ordnung! Ordnung!
Papa is coming!

A fine haze moved off the leaves;
Frost melted on far panes;
The rose, the chrysanthemum turned toward the light.
Even the hushed forms, the bent yellowy weeds
Moved in a slow up-sway.

V

It was beginning winter,
An in-between time,
The landscape still partly brown:
The bones of weeds kept swinging in the wind,
Above the blue snow.

It was beginning winter
The light moved slowly over the frozen field,
Over the dry seed-crowns,
The beautiful surviving bones
Swinging in the wind.

Light traveled over the wide field;
Stayed.

The weeds stopped swinging.
The wind moved, not alone,
Through the clear air, in the silence.

Was it light?
Was it light within?
Was it light within light?
Stillness becoming alive,
Yet still?

A lively understandable spirit
Once entertained you.
It will come again.
Be still.
Wait.

I Knew a Woman, Lovely in Her Bones

I knew a woman, lovely in her bones,
When small birds sighed, she would sigh back at them;
Ah, when she moved, she moved more ways than one:
The shapes a bright container can contain!
Of her choice virtues only gods should speak,
Or English poets who grew up on Greek
(I'd have them sing in chorus, cheek to cheek.)

How well her wishes went! She stroked my chin,
She taught me Turn, and Counter-turn, and Stand;
She taught me Touch, that undulant white skin:
I nibbled meekly from her proffered hand;
She was the sickle; I, poor I, the rake,
Coming behind her for her pretty sake
(But what prodigious mowing we did make.)

Love likes a gander, and adores a goose:
Her full lips pursed, the errant note to seize;
She played it quick, she played it light and loose;
My eyes, they dazzled at her flowing knees;

Her several parts could keep a pure repose,
Or one hip quiver with a mobile nose
(She moved in circles, and those circles moved.)

Let seed be grass, and grass turn into hay:
I'm martyr to a motion not my own;
What's freedom for? To know eternity.
I swear she cast a shadow white as stone.
But who would count eternity in days?
These old bones live to learn her wanton ways:
(I measure time by how a body sways.)

Elegy for Jane

(My student, thrown by a horse)

I remember the neckcurls, limp and damp as tendrils;
And her quick look, a sidelong pickerel smile;
And how, once startled into talk, the light syllables leaped for her,
And she balanced in the delight of her thought,
A wren, happy, tail into the wind,

Her song trembling the twigs and small branches.
The shade sang with her;
The leaves, their whispers turned to kissing,
And the mould sang in the bleached valleys under the rose.

Oh, when she was sad, she cast herself down into such a pure depth,
Even a father could not find her:
Scraping her cheek against straw,
Stirring the clearest water.

My sparrow, you are not here,
Waiting like a fern, making a spiney shadow.
The sides of wet stones cannot console me,
Nor the moss, wound with the last light.

If only I could nudge you from this sleep,
My maimed darling, my skittery pigeon.
Over this damp grave I speak the words of my love:
I, with no rights in this matter,
Neither father no lover.

REUEL DENNEY

The Connecticut River

(*For Sidney Cox*)

I

This land whose streams seem as the lives of men,
Birched with the Indian blood and pale with snow
Whose random sheens of spring beneath the sun
Rise in a hilly glitter like words of Emerson;

Land of the barn handhewn, and firmly made
Of some such silent form where hope may stay
Not lush in heat like grapes of sun-warmed towns
But short of season as sweet mountain hay;

Dictionary maker, schoolroom of the Iowa town,
The shining coast turned toward the Opium Wars,
The churched hills and the cotton mills,
And the nasal A's of tottering country stores;

It is the province honored and mistrusted,
Much spoken of in Cleveland, but not understood,
Taking the country home and the summer tourist
As if they knew it—though they never could.

As made for a museum its blades of water
Call and enclose the temper of its skies
Whose chanting blue from the tempestuous mountains
Sharpens the view where charming pasture lies.

And the ladies making tea in governors' mansions
Speak soft the Indian names, the adulteries.
Honey and rum, the captain's nightly bottle,
Are sunk at last in the oriental seas.

2

When commerce sailed a well-clewed gleaming yardarm,
Drove drunken privateers and reeled the foam,
They smoothed the highway for the bonded blackman
And brought the fans but not the hold-stench home.

Nothing they did salt failed to purify,
Making the son forget the sultry trade
That sent the congo gods to dream on cotton
And sing so sad all since have been afraid.

Night. The fortieth parallel. The stars.
The bark lies singing on a tack long held from dawn
Whose pace derives the beneficent westerlies
Still scented with the Azores, spiced and warm.

Or morning, and the horrid Horn behind them
Like gateways where the oceans lean to plunge,
And under the bows the urgent dolphin's fins
Fly frothing, and the Massachusetts towns
Die in the past like words forgot in hymns.

Farmer and herder did not bow to train,
To rail and steel more painful than the crows.
Tea and the supper light were all they needed
Of China, and the surge where right whale blows.

Those mountains blessed with rigid loneliness
And duties hardly said but always known,

And the early dawns of those dissenters showed
Farms all their own, and righteously alone.

3

What hope now in the country and the towns
Whose sons lie in Chicago and whose words
Hover a steel-grey plumage, sober song,
On western towns, whose ears are not on birds?

Blood of jurist and parson, shouting Webster,
The proper people properly tight at fairs,
The stars that J. Q. Adams held in sight,
The strength withheld, the shy and powerful airs;

Are they the hostage of the village mansion
Whose mill-bred beauties ape the former times,
While enterprise is wary, and the bedroom
Fastens the madness of the ancient crimes?

Those things that made a people all themselves
Fight terror in the rooms where madmen lie.
The manias for collection and dissipation
Point out an identical way for men to die.

Neurosis and division feed upon
Aristocrat and the people of the town,
Whether it is known or whether still unknown.
The awful smile of some deserted farm.

4

Milk sold by monopoly, feed at higher prices,
The cost of machinery on farms not made for it,
The west beyond its boom and yet still fruitful,
Closed mills, and a crazier history yet.

Luther and Calvin knew the difficult way
And ships taught others of a wilder kind

How men whose priests held back the western day
Could wake and know, and measure, seek and find.

Now that the order's broken and the hill
Lies curving shadow to the bomber's wing,
Concrete bursts through in rivers fit for wheels
And song delays to hear what air may sing,

What's left to teach a people how, together,
Land and the factory might shake hands,
Not war, as at the edge of rivers, cities
Die slumward where the workless fisher stands?

Hawthorne's fear found, traveling in the mountains,
In hemlock passes Salem-drunk with spice,
The silent girls who knitted at machines
Whose turning wheel drove from the melting ice;

He saw beyond congruities fantastic
Made out of books by Alcott and some others,
And heard what glacial silence would be pressed
On tongues that meant these men should act as brothers.

5

Or, in the spring, it's time to bring our hatred
And sympathy for those granite banks and laws
Our fathers quarried deep from the mothering hill
As children walk in the thunders of divorce.

Led by the rain gone ghosting down the valley,
Our sorrow follows, hovering on the roads
That married once the landscape and the man,
Past streams expressed in reeds and singing toads;

We find the spring shine pale on cellar-holes
And shells of ice along the upland waters;
Husband and child at once of the glistening pasture,
We breathe above the poisons of the motors.

Some dream combines the climber's respiration
With grassy sounds, and motions underhill
As if, where factory chimneys are not seen,
Man and the birch sucked at some single will,

Or, in the liquid voices of that season,
Green ocean greys, wet whisperings of birth,
Both shuddered in the shock of generation
When lifting fogs disclosed both man and earth.

Our bride is the river in the valley
And all the hills around that did not die
When father moved his office into death
In the grey vault in the slope where pheasants fly.

McSorley's Bar

Mac had a place to drink and talk downtown
Where only men were welcome, or grown boys.
When the grey snow flew, there was the forum stove
Where arguments were slow, and out of noise.
The dust was old as Sumter, and the talking
Had never stopped since Dixie went to war;
And all the men from Grant to Hayes to now
Had lived beside, been buried from that bar.
There, in the evening, the city carpenter
Bumped up a drink with one of Croker's men
And politics and poetry were one
From supper-time until it closed at ten.
The grey-haired men considered from their chairs
How time is emptied like a single ale;
Their china eyes saw tabby woo the fire
As men their recollections, at the rail.
Here, among blackened walls, men's time
Flowed past like peaceful dreams of Chinamen
Who sat in temples thinking of those flowers
That die, and live, and close their blooms again.
Here the day's passions, after dusk,

Would, while the children called beneath the L,
Draw in like coals in pipes to gleam a silence
Between the words that cursed or wished them well.
Privilege, and extortion, and corruption,
Or the wreck of the city, or some newer way to power,
Described the moving lives of living men
In voices where each hero had his hour.
And sorrow that rendezvoused in here
Flowed like a stellar scheme whose dying ions
Cascade toward night, when orders somewhere else
Gather the suns like a summer's dandelions.

JOHN BERRYMAN

Homage to Mistress Bradstreet

1

The Governor your husband lived so long
moved you not, restless, waiting for him? Still,
you were a patient woman.—
I seem to see you pause here still:
Sylvester, Quarles, in moments odd you pored
before a fire at, bright eyes on the Lord,
all the children still.
'Simon . .' Simon will listen while you read a Song.

2

Outside the New World winters in grand dark
white air lashing high thro' the virgin stands
foxes down foxholes sigh,
surely the English heart quails, stunned.
I doubt if Simon than this blast, that sea,

spares from his rigour for your poetry
more. We are on each other's hands
who care. Both of our worlds unhanded us. Lie stark,

3

thy eyes look to me mild. Out of maize & air
your body's made, and moves. I summon, see,
from the centuries it.
I think you won't stay. How do we
linger, diminished, in our lovers' air,
implausibly visible, to whom, a year,
years, over interims; or not;
to a long stranger; or not; shimmer & disappear.

4

Jaw-ript, rot with its wisdom, rending then;
then not. When the mouth dies, who misses you?
Your master never died,
Simon ah thirty years past you—
Pockmarkt & westward staring on a haggard deck
it seems I find you, young. I come to check,
I come to stay with you,
and the Governor, & Father, & Simon, & the huddled men.

5

By the week we landed we were, most, used up.
Strange ships across us, after a fortnight's winds
unfavouring, frightened us;
bone-sad cold, sleet, scurvy; so were ill
many as one day we could have no sermons;
broils, quelled; a fatherless child unkennelled; vermin
crowding & waiting: waiting.
And the day itself he leapt ashore young Henry Winthrop

6

(delivered from the waves; because he found
off their wigwams, sharp-eyed, a lone canoe
across a tidal river,
that water glittered fair & blue
& narrow, none of the other men could swim
and the plantation's prime theft up to him,
shouldered on a glad day
hard on the glorious feasting of thanksgiving) drowned.

7

How long with nothing in the ruinous heat,
clams & acorns stomaching, distinction perishing,
at which my heart rose,
with brackish water, we would sing.
When whispers knew the Governor's last bread
was browning in his oven, we were discourag'd.
The Lady Arbella dying—
dyings—at which my heart rose, but I did submit.

8

That beyond the Atlantic wound our woes enlarge
is hard, hard that starvation burnishes our fear,
but I do gloss for You.
Strangers & pilgrims fare we here,
declaring we seek a City. Shall we be deceived?
I know whom I have trusted, & whom I have believed,
and that he is able to
keep that I have committed to his charge.

9

Winter than summer worse, that first, like a file
on a quick, or the poison suck of a thrilled tooth;
and still we may unpack.
Wolves & storms among, uncouth

board-pieces, boxes, barrels vanish, grow
houses, rise. Motes that hop in sunlight slow
indoors, and I am Ruth
away: open my mouth, my eyes wet: I would smile:

10

vellum I palm, and dream. Their forest dies
to greensward, privets, elms & towers, whence
a nightingale is throbbing.
Women sleep sound. I was happy once . .
(Something keeps on not happening; I shrink?)
These minutes all their passions & powers sink
and I am not one chance
for an unknown cry or a flicker of unknown eyes.

11

Chapped souls ours, by the Spring's strong winds swelled,
Jack's pulpits arched, more glad. The shawl I pinned
flaps like a shooting soul
might in such weather Heaven send.
succumbing half, in spirit, to a salmon sash
I prod the nerveless novel succotash—
I must be disciplined,
in arms, against that one, and our dissidents, and myself.

12

Versing, I shroud among the dynasties;
quaternion on quaternion, tireless I phrase
anything past, dead, far,
sacred, for a barbarous place.
—To please your wintry father? all this bald
abstract didactic rime I read appalled
harassed for your fame
mistress neither of fiery nor velvet verse, on your knees

13

hopeful & shamefast, chaste, laborious, odd,
whom the sea tore.—The damned roar with loss,
so they hug & are mean
with themselves, and I cannot be thus.
Why then do I repine, sick, bad, to long
after what must not be? I lie wrong
once more. For at fourteen
I found my heart more carnal and sitting loose from God,

14

vanity & the follies of youth took hold of me;
then the pox blasted, when the Lord returned.
That year for my sorry face
so-much-older Simon burned,
so Father smiled, with love. Their will be done.
He to me ill lingeringly, learning to shun
a bliss, a lightning blood
vouchsafed, what did seem life. I kissed his Mystery.

15

Drydust in God's eye the aquavivid skin
of Simon snoring lit with fountaining dawn
when my eyes unlid, sad.
John Cotton shines on Boston's sin—
I ám drawn, in pieties that seem
the weary drizzle of an unremembered dream.
Women have gone mad
at twenty-one. Ambition mines, atrocious, in.

16

Food endless, people few, all to be done.
As pippins roast, the question of the wolves
turns & turns.
Fangs of a wolf will keep, the neck

round of a child, that child brave. I remember who
in meeting smiled & was punisht, and I know who
whispered & was stockt.
We lead a thoughtful life. But Boston's cage we shun.

17

The winters close, Springs open, no child stirs
under my withering heart, O seasoned heart
God grudged his aid.
All things else soil like a shirt.
Simon is much away. My executive stales.
The town came through for the cartway by the pales,
but my patience is short.
I revolt from, I am like, these savage foresters

18

whose passionless dicker in the shade, whose glance
impassive & scant, belie their murderous cries
when quarry seems to show.
Again I must have been wrong, twice.
Unwell in a new way. Can that begin?
God brandishes. O love, O I love. Kin,
gather. My world is strange
and merciful, ingrown months, blessing a swelling trance.

19

So squeezed, wince you I scream? I love you & hate
off with you. Ages! *Useless*. Below my waist
he has me in Hell's vise.
Stalling. He let go. Come back: brace
me somewhere. No. No. Yes! everything down
hardens I press with horrible joy down
my back cracks like a wrist
shame I am voiding oh behind it is too late

20

hide me forever I work thrust I must free
now I all muscles & bones concentrate
what is living from dying?
Simon I must leave you so untidy
Monster you are killing me Be sure
I'll have you later Women do endure
I can *can* no longer
and it passes the wretched trap whelming and I am me

21

drencht & powerful, I did it with my body!
One proud tug greens Heaven. Marvellous,
unforbidding Majesty.
Swell, imperious bells. I fly.
Mountainous, woman not breaks and will bend:
sways God nearby: anguish comes to an end.
Blossomed Sarah, and I
blossom. Is that thing alive? I hear a famisht howl.

22

Beloved household, I am Simon's wife,
and the mother of Samuel—whom greedy yet I miss
out of his kicking place.
More in some ways I feel at a loss,
freer. Cantabanks & mummers, nears
longing for you. Our chopping scores my ears,
our costume bores my eyes.
St. George to the good sword, rise! chop-logic's rife

23

& fever & Satan & Satan's ancient fere.
Pioneering is not feeling well,
not Indians, beasts.
Not all their riddling can forestall

one leaving. Sam, your uncle has had to
go fróm us to live with God. 'Then Aunt went too?'
Dear, she does wait still.
Stricken: 'Oh. Then he takes us one by one.' My dear.

24

Forswearing it otherwise, they starch their minds.
Folkmoots, & blether, blether. John Cotton rakes
to the synod of Cambridge.
Down from my body my legs flow,
out from it arms wave, on it my head shakes.
Now Mistress Hutchinson rings forth a call—
should she? many creep out at a broken wall—
affirming the Holy Ghost
dwells in one justified. Factioning passion blinds

25

all to all her good, all—can she be exiled?
Bitter sister, victim! I miss you.
—I miss you, Anne,
day or night weak as a child,
tender & empty, doomed, quick to no tryst.
—I hear you. Be kind, you who leaguer
my image in the mist.
—Be kind you, to one unchained eager far & wild

26

and if, O my love, my heart is breaking, please
neglect my cries and I will spare you. Deep
in Time's grave, Love's, you lie still.
Lie still.—Now? That happy shape
my forehead had under my most long, rare,
ravendark, hidden, soft bodiless hair
you award me still.
You must not love me, but I do not bid you cease.

27

Veiled my eyes, attending. How can it be I?
Moist, with parted lips, I listen, wicked.
I shake in the morning & retch.
Brood I do on myself naked.
A fading world I dust, with fingers new.
—I have earned the right to be alone with you.
—What right can that be?
Convulsing, if you love, enough, like a sweet lie.

28

Not that, I know, you can. This cratered skin,
like the crabs & shells of my Palissy ewer, touch!
Oh, you do, you do?
Falls on me what I like a witch,
for lawless holds, annihilations of law
which Time and he and man abhor, foresaw:
sharper than what my Friend
brought me for my revolt when I moved smooth & thin,

29

faintings black, rigour, chilling, brown
parching, back, brain burning, the grey pocks
itch, a manic stench
of pustules snapping, pain floods the palm,
sleepless, or a red shaft with a dreadful start
rides at the chapel, like a slipping heart.
My soul strains in one qualm
ah but *this* is not to save me but to throw me down.

30

And out of this I lull. It lessens. Kiss me.
That once. As sings out up in sparkling dark
a trail of a star & dies,
which the breath flutters, sounding, mark,

so shorn ought such caresses to us be
who, deserving nothing, flush and flee
the darkness of that light,
a lurching frozen from a warm dream. Talk to me.

31

—It is Spring's New England. Pussy willows wedge
up in the wet. Milky crestings, fringed
yellow, in heaven, eyed
by the melting hand-in-hand or mere
desirers single, heavy-footed, rapt,
make surge poor human hearts. Venus is trapt—
the hefty pike shifts, sheer—
in Orion blazing. Warblings, odours, nudge to an edge—

32

—Ravishing, ha, what crouches outside ought,
flamboyant, ill, angelic. Often, now,
I am afraid of you.
I am a sobersides; I know.
I *want* to take you for my lover.—Do.
—I hear a madness. Harmless I to you
am not, not I?—No.
—I cannot but be. Sing a concord of our thought.

33

—Wan dolls in indigo on gold: refrain
my western lust. I am drowning in this past.
I lose sight of you
who mistress me from air. Unbraced
in delirium of the grand depths, giving away
haunters what kept me, I breathe solid spray.
—I am losing you!
Straiten me on.—I suffered living like a stain:

34

I trundle the bodies, on the iron bars,
over that fire backward & forth; they burn;
bits fall. I wonder if
I killed them. Women serve my turn.
—Dreams! You are good.—No.—Dense with hardihood
the wicked are dislodged, and lodged the good.
In green space we are safe.
God awaits us (but I am yielding) who Hell wars.

35

—I cannot feel myself God waits. He flies
nearer a kindly world; or he is flown.
One Saturday's rescue
won't show. Man is entirely alone
may be. I am a man of griefs & fits
trying to be my friend. And the brown smock splits,
down the pale flesh a gash
broadens and Time holds up your heart against my eyes.

36

—Hard and divided heaven! creases me. Shame
is failing. My breath is scented, and I throw
hostile glances towards God.
Crumpling plunge of a pestle, bray:
sin cross & opposite, wherein I survive
nightmares of Eden. Reaches foul & live
he for me, this soul
to crunch, a minute tangle of eternal flame.

37

I fear Hell's hammer-wind. But fear does wane.
Death's blossoms grain my hair; I cannot live.
A black joy clashes
joy, in twilight. The Devil said

'I will deal toward her softly, and her enchanting cries
will fool the horns of Adam.' Father of lies,
a male great pestle smashes
small women swarming towards the mortar's rim in vain.

38

I see the cruel spread Wings black with saints!
Silky my breasts not his, mine, mine to withhold
or tender, tender.
I am sifting, nervous, and bold.
The light is changing. Surrender this loveliness
you cannot make me do. *But* I will. Yes.
What horror, down stormy air,
warps towards me? My threatening promise faints—

39

torture me, Father, lest not I be thine!
Tribunal terrible & pure, my God,
mercy for him and me.
Faces half-fanged, Christ drives abroad,
and though the crop hopes, Jane is so slipshod
I cry. Evil dissolves, & love, like foam;
that love. Prattle of children powers me home,
my heart claps like the swan's
under a frenzy of *who* love me & who shine.

40

As a canoe slides by on one strong stroke
hope his hélp not I, who do hardly bear
his gift still. But whisper
I am not utterly. I pare
an apple for my pipsqueak Mercy and
she runs & all need naked apples, fanned
their tinier envies.
Vomitings, trots, rashes. Can be hope a cloak?

41

for the man with cropt ears glares. My fingers tighten
my skirt. I pass. Alas! I pity all.
Shy, shy, with mé, Dorothy.
Moonrise, and frightening hoots. 'Mother,
how *long* will I be dead?' Our friend the owl
vanishes, darling, but your homing soul
retires on Heaven, Mercy:
not we one instant die, only our dark does lighten.

42

When by me in the dusk my child sits down
I am myself. Simon, if it's that loose,
let me wiggle it out.
You'll get a bigger one there, & bite.
How they loft, how their sizes delight and grate.
The proportioned, spiritless poems accumulate.
And they publish them
away in brutish London, for a hollow crown.

43

Father is not himself. He keeps his bed,
and threw a saffron scum Thursday. God-forsaken words
escaped him raving. Save,
Lord, thy servant zealous & just.
Sam he saw back from Harvard. He did scold
his secting enemies. His stomach is cold
while we drip, while
my baby John breaks out. O far from where he bred!

44

Bone of moaning: sung Where he has gone
a thousand summers by truth-hallowed souls;
be still. Agh, he is gone!
Where? I know. Beyond the shoal.

Still-all a Christian daughter grinds her teeth
a little. This our land has ghosted with
our dead: I am at home.
Finish, Lord, in me this work thou hast begun.

45

And they tower, whom the pear-tree lured
to let them fall, fierce mornings they reclined
down the brook-bank to the east
fishing for shiners with a crookt pin,
wading, dams massing, well, and Sam's to be
a doctor in Boston. After the divisive sea,
and death's first feast,
and the galled effort on the wilderness endured,

46

Arminians, and the King bore against us;
of an 'inward light' we hear with horror.
Whose fan is in his hand
and he will thoroughly purge his floor,
come towards mé. I have what licks the joints
and bites the heart, which winter more appoints.
Iller I, oftener.
Hard at the outset; in the ending thus hard, thus?

47

Sacred & unutterable Mind
flashing thorough the universe one thought,
I do wait without peace.
In the article of death I budge.
Eat my sore breath, Black Angel. Let me die.
Body a-drain, when will you be dry
and countenance my speed
to Heaven's springs? lest stricter writhings have me declined.

48

'What are those pictures in the air at night,
Mother?' Mercy did ask. Space charged with faces
day & night! I place
a goatskin's fetor, and sweat: fold me
in savoury arms. Something is shaking, wrong.
He smells the musket and lifts it. It is long.
It points at my heart.
Missed he must have. In the gross storm of sunlight

49

I sniff a fire burning without outlet,
consuming acrid its own smoke. It's me.
Ruined laughter sounds
outside. Ah but I waken, free.
And so I am about again. I hagged
a fury at the short maid, whom tongues tagged,
and I am sorry. Once
less I was anxious when more passioned to upset

50

the mansion & the garden & the beauty of God.
Insectile unreflective busyness
blunts & does amend.
Hangnails, piles, fibs, life's also.
But we are that from which draws back a thumb.
The seasons stream and, somehow, I am become
an old woman. It's so:
I look. I bear to look. Strokes once more his rod.

51

My window gives on the graves, in our great new house
(how many burned?) upstairs, among the elms.
I lie, & endure, & wonder.
A haze slips sometimes over my dreams

and holiness on horses' bells shall stand.
Wandering pacemaker, unsteadying friend,
in a redskin calm I wait:
beat when you will our end. Sinkings & droopings drowse.

52

They say thro' the fading winter Dorothy fails,
my second, who than I bore one more, nine;
and I see her inearthed. I linger.
Seaborn she wed knelt before Simon;
Simon I, and linger. Black-yellow seething, vast
it lies fróm me, mine: all they look aghast.
It will be a glorious arm.
Docile I watch. My wreckt chest hurts when Simon pales.

53

In the yellowing days your faces wholly fail,
at Fall's onset. Solemn voices fade.
I feel no coverlet.
Light notes leap, a beckon, swaying
the tilted, sickening ear within. I'll—I'll—
I am closed & coming. Somewhere! I defile
wide as a cloud, in a cloud,
unfit, desirous, glad—even the singings veil—

54

—You are not ready? You áre ready. Pass,
as shadow gathers shadow in the welling night.
Fireflies of childhood torch
you down. We commit our sister down.
One candle mourn by, which a lover gave,
the use's edge and order of her grave.
Quiet? Moisture shoots.
Hungry throngs collect. They sword into the carcass.

55

Headstones stagger under great draughts of time
after heads pass out, and their world must reel
speechless, blind in the end
about its chilling star: thrift tuft,
whin cushion—nothing. Already with the wounded flying
dark air fills, I am a closet of secrets dying,
races murder, foxholes hold men,
reactor piles wage slow upon the wet brain rime.

56

I must pretend to leave you. Only you draw off
a benevolent phantom. I say you seem to me
drowned towns off England,
featureless as those myriads
who what bequeathed save fire-ash, fossils, burled
in the open river-drifts of the Old World?
Simon lived on for years.
I renounce not even ragged glances, small teeth, nothing,

57

O all your ages at the mercy of my loves
together lie at once, forever or
so long as I happen.
In the rain of pain & departure, still
Love has no body and presides the sun,
and elfs from silence melody. I run.
Hover, utter, still,
a sourcing   whom my lost candle like the firefly loves.

JAMES MERRILL

The Octopus

There are many monsters that a glassen surface
Restrains. And none more sinister
Than vision asleep in the eye's tight translucence.
Rarely it seeks now to unloose
Its diamonds. Having divined how drab a prison
The purest mortal tissue is,
Rarely it wakes. Unless, coaxed out by lusters
Extraordinary, like the octopus
From the gloom of its tank half-swimming half-drifting
Toward anything fair, a handkerchief
Or child's face dreaming near the glass, the writher
Advances in a godlike wreath
Of its own wrath. Chilled by such fragile reeling
A hundred blows of a boot-heel
Shall not quell, the dreamer wakes and hungers.
Percussive pulses, drum or gong,
Build in his skull their loud entrancement,
Volutions of a Hindu dance.
His hands move clumsily in the first conventional
Gestures of assent.
He is willing to undergo the volition and fervor
Of many fleshlike arms, observe
These in their holiness of indirection
Destroy, adore, evolve, reject—
Till on glass rigid with his own seizure
At length the sucking jewels freeze.

The Greenhouse

So many girls vague in the yielding orchard,
None at my pausing but had seemed therefore

To grow a little, to have put forth a tentative
Frond, touch my arm and, as we went,
Trailingly inquire, but smilingly, of the greenhouse
—One had heard so much, was it never to be seen?
So that it would always have appeared possible
To be distinguished under glass
Down ferned-faint-steaming alleys of lady-slipper,
Camellia, browning at the fingertip,
Yet always to find oneself, with a trace of humor,
In perhaps the least impressive room.
It was hotter here than elsewhere, being shadowed
Only by bare panes overhead,
And here the seedlings had been set to breeding
Their small green tedium of need:
Each plant alike, each plaintively devouring
One form, meek sprout atremble in the glare
Of the ideal condition. So many women
Oval under overburdened limbs,
And such vague needs, each witlessly becoming
Desire, individual blossom
Inhaled but to enhance the fiercer fading
Of as yet nobody's beauty—Tell me (I said)
Among these thousands which you are!
And I will lead you backwards where the wrench
Of rifling fingers snaps the branch,
And all loves less than the proud love fastened on
Suffer themselves to be rotted clean out of conscience
By human neglect, by the naked sun,
So none shall tempt, when she is gone.

Who Guessed Amiss the Riddle of the Sphinx

In the night my great swamp-willow fell.
I had run home early, dark by five,
To find the young sphinx and the hearth swept bare
By the lazy thrashing of her tail.

A scraping on my window woke me late.
Circling those roots aghast in air
I asked of wind, of rottenness, the cause,
As yet unaware of having forgotten

Her yellow gaze unwinking, vertical pupil,
Stiff wing, dark nipple, firelit paws
—All that the odor of my hand brings back
Hiding my face, beside the boughs

Whose tall believed exuberance fallen,
Bug goes witless, liquors lack,
Profusion riddled to its core of dream
Dies, whispering names.

She only from the dead flames rose,
Sniffed once my open palm, but disdained cream,
Civilities of the aftermath.
Now even the young tree branching in that palm

Is gone, as if for having blocked a path.

Mirror

I grow old under an intensity
Of questioning looks. *Nonsense,*
I try to say, *I cannot teach you children*
How to live.—If not you, who will?
Cries one of them aloud, grasping my gilded
Frame till the world sways. *If not you, who will?*
Between their visits the table, its arrangement
Of Bible, fern and Paisley, all past change,
Does very nicely. If ever I feel curious
As to what others endure,
Across the parlor *you* provide examples,
Wide open, sunny, of everything I am
Not. You embrace a whole world without once caring
To set it in order. That takes thought. Out there
Something is being picked. The red-and-white bandannas
Go to my heart. A fine young man

Rides by on horseback. Now the door shuts. Hester
Confides in me her first unhappiness.
This much, you see, would never have been fitted
Together, but for me. Why then is it
They more and more neglect me? Late one sleepless
Midsummer night I strained to keep
Five tapers from your breathing. *No,* the widowed
Cousin said, *let them go out.* I did.
The room brimmed with gray sound, all the instreaming
Muslin of your dream . . .
Years later now, two of the grown grandchildren
Sit with novels face-down on the sill,
Content to muse upon your tall transparence,
Your clouds, brown fields, persimmon far
And cypress near. One speaks. *How superficial*
Appearances are! Since then, as if a fish
Had broken the perfect silver of my reflectiveness,
I have lapses. I suspect
Looks from behind, where nothing is, cool gazes
Through the blind flaws of my mind. As days,
As decades lengthen, this vision
Spreads and blackens. I do not know whose it is,
But I think it watches for my last silver
To blister, flake, float leaf by life, each milling-
Downward dumb conceit, to a standstill
From which not even you strike any brilliant
Chord in me, and to a faceless will,
Echo of mine, I am amenable.

HOWARD NEMEROV

Dandelions

These golden heads, these common suns
Only less multitudinous

Than grass itself that gluts
The market of the world with green,
They shine as lovely as they're mean,
Fine as the daughters of the poor
Who go proudly in spangles of brass;
Light-headed, then headless, stalked for a salad.

Inside a week they will be seen
Stricken and old, ghosts in the field
To be picked up at the lightest breath,
With brazen tops all shrunken in
And swollen green gone withered white.
You'll say it's nature's price for beauty
That goes cheap; that being light
Is justly what makes girls grow heavy;
And that the wind, bearing their death,
Whispers the second kingdom come.
—You'll say, the fool of piety,
By resignations hanging on
Until, still justified, you drop.
But surely the thing is sorrowful,
At evening, when the light goes out
Slowly, to see those ruined spinsters,
All down the field their ghostly hair,
Dry sinners waiting in the valley
For the last word and the next life
And the liberation from the lion's mouth.

The First Leaf

Here is one leaf already gone from green
To edged red and gold, a Byzantine
Illumination of the summer's page
Of common text, and capital presage
For chapters yet to fall. An old story,
How youth may go from glory into glory
Changing his green for a stiff robe of dry
Magnificence, taking the brilliant dye
From steeped oblivion; going, near a ghost,

Become a lord and captain of the host;
Or cardinal, in priestly full career,
Preach abstinence or at the most small beer.

Success is doubtful, you may be perplexed,
Reaching it rich, and old, and apoplexed
To bloody innocence, teaching the green
One of the things at least that life must mean,
And standing in the book of days a splen-
did summary, rubric, index of the end,
Commerced with time to great advantage, high
And singular with instruction how to die—
And immortality, though life be cheap,
For the early turncoat and the Judas sheep.

The Ecstasies of Dialectic

Her laughter was infectious; so, some found,
Her love. Several young men reasonably
Regret inciting her to gratitude
And learning of her ardent facility.

She has gone, back it may be to the world,
To ply her silken exercise elsewhere.
Now is occasion for the medication
(As possible) of ills not all of the heart,

And certain hints, conveyed in sermon or
By private word, are reasoning the weight
Of pleasures, pains. Thus her capable joys
Are debased by her ignominious communications.

"The flesh, the rouged cheekbones of Babylon,
The unclean loins, the thief of legal delight,
O ye generations!" "The spider that eats up
Her mate!" "The test-tube of iniquity!"

Despite the wisdom of Christian Epicures
Many of the affected more regret

Her going than her legacy. They huddle
At street corners, before drugstores, and moon

Over the hour of pestilent delight,
The yellow taste good times will always have.
"The proof of the apple is in the worm," they say,
And hug their new knowledge of life and death.

Praising the Poets of That Country

Many poems may be composed upon the same theme.
The differences between them may be slight
—a comma, or the tilt of an eyebrow—but not
Superficial. Whole traditions existed
For which the strict imitation of the predecessors
And not originality, was the matter of pride.
The poet then is seen as bearing a priestly part
In the ritual, confirming the continuance
Of this that and the other thing, humbly
Refreshing the hearer with his ceremony.
The place of the poet was often hereditary:
Thus, G—— was a learned man, but his grandson,
Left to himself, could not have written a line;
That was no matter. In conversation, however,
Such poets often displayed wit and extravagance
Which they would have thought unworthy
Of the strenuous character of their art.
It was not, that is, a question of "talent,"
But rather of a fanatic and ascetic practice
Of willed submission to the poem existing.
R——'s epitaph read, "The man who placed
The adjective 'calm' in its proper context."
This, a matter of pride, in forty years of work.

Then the beloved face was known to the whole people.
The complexion *white,* the eyes *dark,* and *like*
Twin suns, the lips *like cherries* or
Of the color of rubies, the hair *glorious*
And shiningmost mystery, the shoulders *like cream*

And then the Sestos and the Abydos of it.
These things were well-known, and each man with his doxy
Might make what he might out of the whole business
Nightlong, and daylong if he liked and was able.
Under the cadence of the beat of the common meter
Sustained the matter, and the exact rime
Measured the moment with a considered force.

These not eccentric men were held in honor
Wilder than the expectations of despair;
No valorous excess could mar those characters
That guarded times to time on the baffled drum,
Holding in secret the still-beating victim's heart,
While elsewhere the profane crowds would walk
Unthinking their free and many ways to death.

RICHMOND LATTIMORE

Despair in Seascape

Here is the fix: an hour of time crossed over
a mile of beach to hold disparate
materials, as dunes, boats,
assorted anatomies and almost any amount
of water.

One end of a mile
anchors on those swings, pinwheels, and bannisters a mile
makes into toys; one end smudges off
into soft strokes, haze of dunes and undefined
limit of surf. On feet shoveling
the dry loose hills, on feet (the same) paddles
to smack the wet hard flat
of the afterwave, traverse, loop in, and hold
the scenes of which this mile is composite
in the sightless frame of an hour.

Or try.

Because
any here is elsewhere before you can pin
it to when; because the breaking, the broken, and to-break
wave sucks into itself and wipes
its shine off the sand before the sand
is through shining; because the child's
sea wall, slapped on as slime, is cement, is sand, is wet
no-shape and no-wall; so because
on this material symmetry all moves
except the color of the sand, all sounds
except the silence of the dunes.

Or no? Because
seen gull, shell, leg, spade, chair
escape through holes in that gray envelope of nerve
we pull around them, will not stand and be
anything simple like dimensions?

The child
spading his bucket is that child you thought you knew
how to reshape and hang upon the mind,
and collapses without weight.

Far out, an arc
of marlin, jumping, hanging, clubbed like exclama-
tion points could never be believed
before gone and turned by memory into birds, about
whom nothing is improbable.

Even
a detail of nuns walking against the foam and gray
of breakers seems to fly like fragments
of those bird thoughts that haunt the changes of the sea.

All the most loved and vulgar knees and knobs,
angles of people, posts and piles, also specials
as marlin, nuns, blimps, storms

became as wingless, slipping in fragmentary space,
more gone when they were there than they are now.

Dufy, Grandma, or Alice should have painted
this poem I could not write.

Voyage of Discovery: 1935

Shall we go on with it? Driving ever seaward?
Invisible wings outride this narrow passage.
We see towers golden on the sand. We hear sirens.

The foam flanks widen, the world is split obliquely
after the wind and wings have blessed the burden
of oars swept to the hammer beat no longer,

after the sails were scrapped and the trefoil blades
grind vaster trembling hulls forever forward,
after these and after, the same way always;

the water wrenched astern is a net of wishes,
epitaphs of next years, and the way ahead
tomorrows meeting mortality, imaged islands,

and left and right tomorrows that never happen,
and if you swing the helm and the rudder answers,
sleeve by arm they follow, and still are sidewise.

Maybe the yellow horns quiet the grave water
at Cherbourg, the Solent trodden circumspectly
by giants, the armor and huddle of spears, Manhattan,

San Salvador or Vineland, the northern break
of continent with ice, it hardly will matter.
It will have been a false hope. It will have been

barely the other side of the wings outriding.
They are there, the lovely abstractions, the ifs and maybes,
the forever beyond, the fixed and fugitive,

the not anywhere, the always elsewhere islands.
Shall we go on with it? Driving ever seaward,
the spoke turning and the next spoke turning with it?

A people's purpose is to build its own death,
to be impatient of its youth and remember
that youth completed as a bright grief lost to it,

and break its heart to be young again, and be older,
and build that age in bridges and guns and armor
and meet its death by turning over tomorrow.

It is useless and there is nothing else to do.
The way to recapture is to go ever onward.
It is the only way left though you die of it.

O ever sheathing and seeming always forward
drowned seeming in blue dimension and lost water,
the rocks seaward, the templed capes, the green shallows,

the bright slopes hillward; in your lakes the swans
as by the strand your ships lie ever quiet.
We came there never but remember dying.

ADRIENNE CECILE RICH

Pictures by Vuillard

Now we remember all: the wild pear-tree,
The broken ribbons of the green-and-gold
Portfolio, with sketches from an old
Algerian campaign; the placid three
Women at coffee by the window, fates
Of nothing ominous, waiting for the ring
Of the postman's bell; we harbor everything—

The cores of fruit left on the luncheon plates.
We are led back where we have never been,
Midday where nothing's tragic, all's delayed
As it should have been for us as well—that shade
Of summer always, Neuilly dappled green!

But we, the destined readers of Stendhal,
In monstrous change such consolations find
As restless mockery sets before the mind
To deal with what must anger and appall.
Much of the time we scarcely think of sighing
For afternoons that found us born too late.
Our prudent envy rarely paces spying
Under those walls, that lilac-shadowed gate.
Yet at this moment, in our private view,
A breath of common peace, like memory,
Rustles the branches of the wild pear-tree—
Air that we should have known, and cannot know.

Annotation for an Epitaph

A fairer person lost not heaven.
—Paradise Lost

These are the sins for which they cast out angels,
The bagatelles by which the lovely fall:
A hand that disappoints, an eye dissembling—
These and a few besides: you had them all.

Beneath this cherubed stone reclines the beauty
That cherubs at the Chair will never see,
Shut out forever by the gold battalions
Stern to forgive, more rigorous than we.

Oh, we were quick to hide our eyes from foible
And call such beauty truth; what though we knew?
Never was truth so sweet and so outrageous;
We loved you all the more because untrue.

But in the baroque corridors of heaven
Your lively coming is a hope destroyed.
Squadrons of seraphs pass the news and ponder,
And all their luxury glitters grand and void.

The Celebration in the Plaza

The sentimentalist sends his mauve balloon
Meandering into air. The crowd applauds.
The mayor eats ices with a cardboard spoon.

See how that colour charms the sunset air;
A touch of lavender is what was needed.—
Then, pop! no floating lavender anywhere.

Hurrah, the pyrotechnic engineer
Comes with his sparkling tricks, consults the sky,
Waits for the perfect instant to appear.

Bouquets of gold splash into bloom and pour
Their hissing pollen downward on the dusk.
Nothing like this was ever seen before.

The viceroy of fireworks goes his way,
Leaving us with a sky so dull and bare
The crowd thins out: what conjures them to stay?

The road is cold with dew, and by and by
We see the constellations overhead.
But is that all? some little children cry.

All we have left, their pedagogues reply.

Lucifer in the Train

Riding the black express from heaven to hell
He bit his fingers, watched the countryside,
Vernal and crystalline, forever slide

Beyond his gaze: the long cascades that fell
Ribboned in sunshine from their sparkling height,
The fishers fastened to their pools of green
By silver lines; the birds in sudden flight—
All things the diabolic eye had seen
Since heaven's cockcrow. Imperceptibly
That landscape altered: now in paler air
Tree, hill and rock stood out resigned, severe,
Beside the strangled field, the stream run dry.

Lucifer, we are yours who stiff and mute
Ride out of worlds we shall not see again,
And watch from windows of a smoking train
The ashen prairies of the absolute.
Once out of heaven, to an angel's eye
Where is the bush or cloud without a flaw?
What bird but feeds upon mortality,
Flies to its young with carrion in its claw?
O foundered angel, first and loneliest
To turn this bitter sand beneath your hoe,
Teach us, the newly-landed, what you know;
After our weary transit, find us rest.

Recorders in Italy

It was amusing on that antique grass,
Seated halfway between the green and blue,
To waken music gentle and extinct

Under the old walls where the daisies grew
Sprinkled in cinquecento style, as though
Archangels might have stepped there yesterday.

But it was we, mortal and young, who strolled
And fluted quavering music, for a day
Casual heirs of all we looked upon.

Such pipers of the emerald afternoon
Could only be the heirs of perfect time
When every leaf distinctly brushed with gold

Listened to Primavera speaking flowers.
Those scherzos stumble now; our journeys run
To harsher hillsides, rockier declensions.

Obligatory climates call us home.
And so shall clarity of cypresses,
Unfingered by necessity, become

Merely the ghost of half-remembered trees,
A trick of sunlight flattering the mind?—
There were four recorders sweet upon the wind.

LOUIS O. COXE

Hannah Dustin

(*The Statue in Penacook, N.H.*)

The red veins in the Gravensteins
Started before the frost. I felt
Desire move my blood where vines
And trees hid fruit I only smelt.

That day when windfalls cost me dear
The Indian deviled in his stain
Caught up my solitude. His fire
Ran on my house-eaves dense as rain.

Across the brush he dragged my hate
The miles of Merrimac to north
Where captives stied like pigs were bait
To tempt our kin and vengeance forth.

I would not weep though he splashed out
My child's brains on a beech's root.

God mocks the mockers: with each gout
Bright on the bark I tasted fruit;

And let the red man drink his night,
Myself unfearing. Fear had laced
His liquor had he known how tight
I filled with poison for his taste.

Drunken he pressed me where he heaped
The bed of boughs. When lust griped hard
I felt his knife, unmanned him, reaped
And sickled through his groin like lard.

His heart leapt once. I struck him there.
Blood ran like fire on my breast.
I walked and felt the dark for hair
Sliming my hands. I scalped the rest

And lashing the lids about my thighs
Fled naked to the boat alone:
The years have run me down. I rise
In passion frozen to a stone.

Autumnal

Tell me what shapes your mind. The light grows less
And currents with the lapse of summer fall.
Does crimson stealth bleeding the sumach guess
The end, the death a root alone can call
Promise of new largess?
Speak. Say it all.

Falling, the brutal air weighed down with frost
Thickens the squirrel's coat and blights the vines.
Desire turns migrant, birdsong high and lost
Exhales like color from the peaks of pines,
And autumn to our cost
Speaks fewest lines.

If seasons in the flesh turn with the sun,
Then cold in turning shall engross the hand
Thickening mortal gesture. For this one
Imposture superseding time, command
And tell me all dyes run
To take a stand.

We make that so being grafted at our source,
Not sure of leaf or branch but root alone:
Weather comes over us by foil and force
And thickening first then flays us to the bone,
For killing is its course
And our love our own.

The Old Lecher

All day long I glance against
Girls in the street who glance away:
The rare blood dances in my head
For curve of breast and thigh. It danced
Before my world. When I am dead
Lust shall gambol the world away.

Stiffening of joints when I stoop down
Calcines my age. Yet must I sweat
For this girl bouncing high on heels,
Liquid as love in moving. Drown
In such a liquor! Lust that feels
Still moist is a lust inveterate.

Has she no shame to warm old loins
Tossing that flesh she thinks she saves?
The purse that empty hangs held much
And the lover thrives forever: coins
Are dearer for the wear of touch
And come up shining, dug from graves.

DANIEL BERRIGAN

The Aunt

With eyes a dying candle
with voice telling the years awry
my aunt at her high window
counts the seasons by—
bird-wedges or air of snow
or red leaves of a leaning sky.

Eighty-one years have whittled her hands
white coals have whitened her sweet mouth:
Christ has fountained in her eyes
and crumpled her face to drought:
flood and drought, He entered once—
in and never out.

It was all gardens then: young winds
tugging her trees of cloud.
At night His quiet lay on the quiet
all day no bird was loud:
under His word, His word, her body
consented and bowed.

And what is love, or what love does
looks from a knot of face
where marching fires could but leave
ruin and gentleness in place:
snatched her away, and left her Self:
Christ to regard us, Face to face.

Everything That Is

is not something other:
a ridiculous pablum for the poet's mind
until the wind sing it, or star bring it
ringing its name through the astonished night:

or on a March day, the selfsame crocus struggle
wildly into air, because its roots, through all winter's leveling,
remembered their own name.
Or the maple that shook its glory down
puzzle strollers with its identical
and lovely form, four months later assumed again
gradually as a morning.
Such things somersault the mind
backward, inward:
I wonder who knew the stars
from flowers, before flowers were not stars:
before trees spread between one and other, a growth
by night starlike, by day a flowering, and yet itself?

Here the Stem Rises

deflowered forever.

the bird is wise only
in ways of quiet

time is a lithe fruit
bending above us

too old for comfort
too raw for falling

here no slim morning
steps out of the sea

no season of snow
no hear-ye of thunder

no chameleon crawling
of youth or of age

not even a now
nor an I nor a you

how many the folded
hands. O how lovely

the words never spoken

Haydn: The Horn

Now that compelling silver throat
breathes its own form on the air:

first a green world all renewed,
then with a more knowledgeable and piercing cry

hunter and hunted leaping
tangible, but also into air.

Turn, turn the green vase—
an obbligato raises at the spire
a further angel and his dizzy trump:

or into a roadside mart descends
of children tricked and marched out endlessly
at the pieman's airy heels:—

in and out of mountains
bearded and fresh of face

all the grandfathers step, all the
grandchildren, rubbing their eyes

so purely looking toward
even us

They are filled, vein and throat
with music, they lightly stand

as long as music.
Diminuendo, sweet end of phrase,

all are gone: that impossible
lovely vase they dwelt upon:
gone, gone

JOHN CIARDI

Elegy Just in Case

Here lie Ciardi's pearly bones
In their ripe organic mess.
Jungle-blown, his chromosomes
Breed to a new address.

Was it bullets or a wind
Or a rip-cord fouled on Chance?
Artifacts the natives find
Decorate them when they dance.

Here lies the sgt.'s mortal wreck
Lily-spiked and termite-kissed,
Spiders pendant from his neck
And a beetle from his wrist.

Bring the tic and southern flies
Where the land crabs run unmourning

Through a night of jungle skies
To a climeless morning.

And bring the chalked eraser here
Fresh from rubbing out his name.
Burn the crew-board for a bier.
(Also Colonel what's-his-name.)

Let no dice be stored and still.
Let no poker deck be torn.
But pour the smuggled rye until
The barracks threshold is outworn.

File the papers, pack the clothes,
Send the coded word through air—
"We regret and no one knows
Where the sgt. goes from here."

"Missing as of inst. oblige,
Deepest sorrow and remain—"
Shall I grin at persiflage?
Could I have my skin again

Would I choose a business form
Stilted mute as a giraffe,
Or a pinstripe unicorn
On a cashier's epitaph?

Darling, darling, just in case
Rivets fail or engines burn
I forget the time and place
But your flesh was sweet to learn.

Swift and single as a shark
I have seen you churn my sleep;
Now if beetles hunt my dark
What will beetles find to keep?

Fractured meat and open bone—
Nothing single or surprised.

Fragments of a written stone,
Undeciphered but surmised.

MAY SWENSON

The Centaur

The summer that I was ten—
Can it be there was only one
summer that I was ten? It must

have been a long one then—
each day I'd go out to choose
a fresh horse from my stable

which was a willow grove
down by the old canal.
I'd go on my two bare feet.

But when, with my brother's jack-knife,
I had cut me a long limber horse
with a good thick knob for a head,

and peeled him slick and clean
except a few leaves for the tail,
and cinched my brother's belt

around his head for a rein,
I'd straddle and canter him fast
up the grass bank to the path,

trot along in the lovely dust
that talcumed over his hoofs,
hiding my toes, and turning

his feet to swift half-moons.
The willow knob with the strap
jouncing between my thighs

was the pommel and yet the poll
of my nickering pony's head.
My head and my neck were mine,

yet they were shaped like a horse.
My hair flopped to the side
like the mane of a horse in the wind.

My forelock swung in my eyes,
my neck arched and I snorted.
I shied and skittered and reared,

stopped and raised my knees,
pawed at the ground and quivered.
My teeth bared as we wheeled

and swished through the dust again.
I was the horse and the rider,
and the leather I slapped to his rump

spanked my own behind.
Doubled, my two hoofs beat
a gallop along the bank,

the wind twanged in my mane,
my mouth squared to the bit.
And yet I sat on my steed

quiet, negligent riding,
my toes standing the stirrups,
my thighs hugging his ribs.

At a walk we drew up to the porch.
I tethered him to a paling.
Dismounting, I smoothed my skirt

and entered the dusky hall.
My feet on the clean linoleum
left ghostly toes in the hall.

Where have you been? said my mother.
Been riding, I said from the sink,
and filled me a glass of water.

What's that in your pocket? she said.
Just my knife. It weighted my pocket
and stretched my dress awry.

Go tie back your hair, said my mother,
and *Why is your mouth all green?*
Rob Roy, he pulled some clover
as we crossed the field, I told her.

The Red Bird Tapestry

Now I put on the thimble of dream
    to stitch among leaves the red node of his body
and fasten here the few beads of his song.

Of the tree a cage of gilded spines
    to palace his scarlet, cathedral his cry,
and a ripple from his beak I sew,
    a banner bearing seven studs,
this scarf to be the morning that received his stain.

I do with thought instead of actuality
    for it has flown.
With glinting thimble I pull back, pull back
    that freak of scarlet to his throne:

To worship him, enchanted cherry to a tree
    that never bore such fruit—
who tore the veil of possibility
    and swung here for a day,

a never-colored bird, a never-music heard,
    who, doubly wanded then, looped away.

To find, in hollow of my throat, his call,
    and try his note on all the flutes of memory,
until that clear jet rinses me
    that was his single play—
for this I wear his daring and his royal eye.

Now perfected, arrested in absence—
    my needle laid by and spread my hand—
his claws on stems of my fingers fastened,
    rooted my feet and green my brow,
I drink from his beak the seven beads dropping:
    I am the cage that flatters him now.

The School of Desire

Unloosed, unharnessed, turned back to the wild by love,
the ring you cantered round with forelock curled,
the geometric music of this world
dissolved and, in its place,
alien as snow to tropic tigers, amphitheatric space,
you will know the desert's freedom, wind and sun
rough-currying your mane, the plenitude
of strong caresses on your body nude.

Released to run from me. Then will I stand
alone in the hoof-torn ring,
lax in my hand
as wine leaked out the thin whip of my will,
and gone the lightning-string
between your eye and mine.

Our discipline was mutual and the art
that spun our dual beauty. While you wheeled
in flawless stride apart,
I, in glittering boots to the fulcrum heeled,

need hardly signal: your prideful head
plunged to the goad of love-looks sharper than ice.

I gloated on the palomino of your flanks, the nice
sprightliness of pace,
your posture like Apollo's steed. I stood my place
as in a chariot,
held the thong of studded light, the lariat
that made you halt, or longer leap, or faster.
But you have bridled me, bright master.

On wild, untrampled slopes you will be monarch soon,
and I the mount that carries you to those high
prairies steeped in noon.
In the arena where your passion will be spent
in loops of speed, sky's indigo unbounded
by the trainer's tent,
instead of oboes, thunder's riddle,
rain for the racing fifes, I will be absent.

When orchestras of air shall vault you
to such freedom, joy and power,
I will cut the whip that sent you there, will put
away the broken ring, and shut
the school of my desire.

JAMES WRIGHT

The Avenger

She—the woman whom I loved
Longer than her beauty lasted,
Loved as long as starlight moved

Carefully around the earth—
Lies behind me, old in death,
All her quiet patience wasted.

Now I walk beneath the night,
Having watched her die all day.
Rain veils soft the bedroom light
Where I held her in my arms.
What blind movers of the storms
Steal the living heart away?

Greek avengers used to cry
Of three women in the air.
Deaf to that religion, I
Leave my barren house and seek
Forces of my own to speak
Simple reasons for despair.

Waiting for the rain to fall,
Waiting for the air to slice
Lilies' heads along the wall;
Knowing soon enough the wind
Strikes the bee and rabbit blind,
Blows the sparrow out of eyes,

How should I begin to say
Everything I should have said?
Why should winter blow away
Fleshes bodied up in summer?
Hushed up like a silly rumor,
In the house my love is dead.

Had I caught her in the dark
Snarled in an alien lover's hair,
Murdered him, and left her stark
Wandering among the trees,
I could go to bed in peace,
Knowing I had done my share.

Had some human murderer
Beaten her to death alone,
Knowing I had done my share
Hunting him and cursing him,
I could let her face and name
Fade into a nub of stone.

She, however, loved me so,
I must seek her killers out.
I, who wonder where they go;
Follow faces through a door,
Slip along the river shore,
Leap, and echo every shout.

They who scatter down the rain,
Lop the lilies' heads away,
Spill a saucer, blow the pane
Open as I sit and stare,
Stitch a cobweb in the air,
Blind the rabbit, blind the bee:

What have I to do with such,
Whether they be here or gone?
Let them crumble at a touch
Continents, suck up the sea,
Level a blind mountain down;
Let me alone, let me alone.

Elegy in a Firelit Room

The window showed a willow in the west,
But windy dry. No folly weeping there.
A sparrow hung a wire about its breast
And spun across the air.

Instead of paying winter any mind,
I ran my fingerprints across the glass,

To feel the crystal forest sown by wind,
And one small face:

A child among the frozen bushes lost,
Breaking the white and rigid twigs between
Fingers more heavenly than hands of dust,
And fingernails more clean.

Beyond, the willow would not cry for cold,
The sparrow hovered long enough to stare;
The face between me and the wintered world
Began to disappear;

Because some friendly hands behind my back
Fumbled the coal and tended up the fire.
Warmth of the room waved to the window sash,
The face among the forest fell to air.

The glass began to weep instead of eyes,
A slow gray feather floated down the sky.
Delicate bone, finger and bush, and eyes
Yearned to the kissing fire and fell away.

Over the naked pasture and beyond
A frozen bird lay down among the dead
Weeds, and the willow strode upon the wind
And would not bow its head.

Lament for My Brother on a Hayrake

Cool with the touch of autumn, waters break
Out of the pump at dawn to clear my eyes;
I leave the house, to face the sacrifice
Of hay, the drag and death. By day, by moon,
I have seen my younger brother wipe his face
And heave his arm on steel. He need not pass
Under the blade to waste his life and break;

The hunching of the body is enough
To violate his bones. That bright machine
Strips the revolving earth of more than grass;
Powered by the fire of summer, bundles fall
Folded to die beside a burlap shroud;
And so my broken brother may lie mown
Out of the wasted fallows, winds return,
Corn-yellow tassels of his hair blow down,
The summer bear him sideways in a bale
Of darkness to October's mow of cloud.

On the Skeleton of a Hound

Nightfall, that saw the morning-glories float
Tendril and string against the crumbling wall,
Nurses him now, his skeleton for grief,
His locks for comfort curled among the leaf.
Shuttles of moonlight weave his shadow tall,
Milkweed and dew flow upward to his throat.
Now catbird feathers plume the apple mound,
And starlings drowse to winter up the ground.
Thickened away from speech by fear, I move
Around the body. Over his forepaws, steep
Declivities darken down the moonlight now,
And the long throat that bayed a year ago
Declines from summer. Flies would love to leap
Between his eyes and hum away the space
Between the ears, the hollow where a hare
Could hide; another jealous dog would tumble
The bones apart, angry, the shining crumble
Of a great body gleaming in the air;
Quivering pigeons foul his broken face.
I can imagine men who search the earth
For handy resurrections, overturn
The body of a beetle in its grave;
Whispering men digging for gods might delve
A pocket for these bones, then slowly burn
Twigs in the leaves, pray for another birth.

But I will turn my face away from this
Ruin of summer, collapse of fur and bone.
For once a white hare huddled up the grass,
The sparrows flocked away to see the race.
I stood on darkness, clinging to a stone,
I saw the two leaping alive on ice,
On earth, on leaf, humus and withered vine:
The rabbit splendid in a shroud of shade,
The dog carved on the sunlight, on the air,
Fierce and magnificent his rippled hair,
The cockleburs shaking around his head.
Then, suddenly, the hare leaped beyond pain
Out of the open meadow, and the hound
Followed the voiceless dancer to the moon,
To dark, to death, to other meadows where
Singing young women dance around a fire,
Where love reveres the living.

I alone
Scatter this hulk about the dampened ground;
And while the moon rises beyond me, throw
The ribs and spine out of their perfect shape.
For a last charm to the dead, I lift the skull
And toss it over the maples like a ball.
Strewn to the woods, now may that spirit sleep
That flamed over the ground a year ago.
I know the mole will heave a shinbone over,
The earthworm snuggle for a nap on paws,
The honest bees build honey in the head;
The earth knows how to handle the great dead
Who lived the body out, and broke its laws,
Knocked down a fence, tore up a field of clover.

W. S. MERWIN

White Goat, White Ram

The gaiety of three winds is a game of green
Shining, of grey-and-gold play in the holly-bush
Among the rocks on the hill-side, and if ever
The earth was shaken, say a moment ago
Or whenever it came to be, only the leaves and the spread
Sea still betray it, trembling; and their tale betides
The faintest of small voices, almost still.
A road winds among the grey rocks, over the hill,
Arrives from out of sight, from nowhere we know,
Of an uncertain colour; and she stands at the side
Nearer the sea, not far from the brink, legs straddled wide
Over the swinging udder, her back and belly
Slung like a camp of hammocks, her head raised,
The narrow jaw grinding sideways, ears flapping sideways,
Eyes wide apart like the two moons of Mars
At their opposing. So broadly is she blind
Who has no names to see with: over her shoulder
She sees not summer, not the idea of summer,
But green meanings, shadows, the gold light of now, familiar,
The sense of long day-warmth, of sparse grass in the open
Game of the winds; an air that is plenitude,
Describing itself in no name; all known before,
Perceived many times before, yet not
Remembered, or at most felt as usual. Even the kids,
Grown now and gone, are forgotten,
As though by habit. And he on the other side
Of the road, hooves braced among spurge and asphodel,
Tears the grey grass at its roots, his massive horns
Tossing delicately, as by long habit, as by
Habit learned, or without other knowledge

And without question inherited, or found
As first he found the air, the first daylight, first milk at the tetter,
The paths, the pen, the seasons. They are white, these two,
As we should say those are white who remember nothing,
And we for our uses call that innocence,
So that our gracelessness may have the back of a goat
To ride away upon; so that when our supreme gesture
Of propitiation has obediently been raised
It may be the thicket-snared ram that dies instead of the son;
So even that we may frame the sense that is now
Into a starred figure of last things, of our own
End, and there by these beasts know ourselves
One from another: some to stay in the safety
Of the rock, but many on the other hand
To be dashed over the perilous brink. There is no need
Even that they should be gentle, for us to use them
To signify gentleness, for us to lift them as a sign
Invoking gentleness, conjuring by their shapes
The shape of our desire, which without them would remain
Without a form and nameless. For our uses
Also are a dumbness, a mystery,
Which like a habit stretches ahead of us
And was here before us; so, again, we use these
To designate what was before us, since we cannot
See it in itself, for who can recognize
And call by true names, familiarly, the place
Where before this he was, though for nine months
Or the world's full age he housed there? Yet it seems
That by such a road, arriving from out of sight,
From nowhere we know, we may have come, and these
Figure as shapes we may have been. Only, to them
The road is less than a road, though it divides them,
A bit of flat space merely, perhaps not even
A thing that leads elsewhere, except when they
Are driven along it, for direction is to them
The paths their own preference and kinds have made
And follow: routes through no convenience
And world of ours, but through their own sense
And mystery. Mark this; for though they assume

Now the awkward postures of illustrations
For all our parables, yet the mystery they stand in
Is still as far from what they signify
As from the mystery we stand in. It is the sign
We make of them, not they, that speaks from their dumbness
That our dumbness may speak. There in the thin grass
A few feet away they browse beyond words; for a mystery
Is that for which we have not yet received
Or made the name, the terms, that may enclose
And call it. And by virtue of such we stand beyond
Earthquake and wind and burning, and all the uncovenanted
Terror of becoming, and beyond the small voice; and on
Another hand, as it were a little above us
There are the angels. We are dumb before them, and move
In a different mystery; but may there be
Another road we do not see as a road: straight, narrow,
Or broad or the sector of a circle, or perhaps
All these, where without knowing it we stand
On one side or another? I have known such a way
But at moments only, and when it seemed I was driven
Along it, and along no other that my preference
Or kind had made. And of these others above us
We know only the whisper of an elusive sense,
Infrequent meanings and shadows, analogies
With light and the beating of wings. Yet now, perhaps only
A few feet away in the shaking leaves they wait
Beyond our words, beyond earthquake, whirlwind, fire,
And all the uncovenanted terror of becoming,
And beyond the small voice. Oh we cannot know and we are not
What we signify, but in what sign
May we be innocent, for out of our dumbness
We would speak for them, give speech to the mute tongues
Of angels. Listen: more than the sea's thunder
Foregathers in the grey cliffs; the roots of our hair
Stir like the leaves of the holly bush where now
Not games the wind ponders, but impatient
Glories, fire: and we go stricken suddenly
Humble, and the covering of our feet
Offends, for the ground where we find we stand is holy.

Blue Cockerel

Morning was never here, nor more dark ever
Than now there is; but in the fixed green
And high branch of afternoon, this bird balances,
His blue feet splayed, folding nothing, as though
The too-small green limb were ground; and his shout
Frames all the silence. Not Montezuma nor all
The gold hills of the sun were ever so plumed
As the blue of his neck, his breast's orange, his wings'
Blazing, and the black-green sickles of his tail.
It seems to be summer. But save for his blue hackles
And the light haze of his back, there is no sky,
Only the one tree spreading its green flame
Like a new habit for heaven. It seems to be summer;
But on the single tree the fruits of all seasons
Hang in the hues of ripeness; but on the ground
The green is of spring, and the flowers
Of April are there. And he suspended, brilliant and foreign,
His wings as though beating the air of elsewhere,
Yet if he is not there, the rest is not either.
A cry must be painted silent: the spread red hand
Of his comb thrown back, beak wide, and the one eye
Glaring like the sun's self (for there is no other),
Like the sun seen small, seen rimmed in red secret,
May be the shape of jubilation crowing,
Or the stare and shriek of terror. And whose body
Is this in the foreground lying twisted sideways,
Eyes glazed, whose stiff posture would become
The contorted dead? Though its face gleams white
It might be the self of shadow we have not seen,
Night who was never here, or the hour itself
There to be sung unmoved. Surely it is
The eye's other centre, and upon this,
This only, the bird stares, and for this cause
Cries, cries, and his cry crashes
Among the branches, the blades of great leaves

Looming like towers, the fruits and petals, green
Thickets of light deeper than shadows, the moon-white
Ears of that body lying, and makes
And lends echo and moment to all that green
Watery silence. But does he scream
In joy unfading that now no dark is,
Or what wakening does he herald with all terror?

Two Horses

Oh in whose grove have we wakened, the bees
Still droning under the carved wall, the fountain playing
Softly to itself, and the gold light, muted,
Moving long over the olives; and whose,
Stamping the shadowy grass at the end of the garden,
Are these two wild horses tethered improbably
To the withes of a young quince? No rider
Is to be seen; they bear neither saddle nor bridle;
Their brute hooves splash the knee-high green
Without sound, and their flexed tails like flags float,
Whipping, their brows down like bulls. Yet the small tree
Is not shaken; and the broken arches
Of their necks in the dim air are silent
As the doorways of ruins. Birds flit in the garden:
Jay and oriole, blades in the hanging shadows,
Small cries confused. And dawn would be eastward
Over the dark neck a red mane tossed high
Like flame, and the dust brightening along the wall.
These have come up from Egypt, from the dawn countries,
Syria, and the land between the rivers,
Have ridden at the beaks of vessels, by Troy neighed,
And along the valley of the Danube, and to Etruria;
And all dust was of their making; and passion
Under their hooves puffed into flight like a sparrow
And died down when they departed. The haze of summer
Blows south over the garden terraces,
Vague through the afternoon, remembering rain;
But in the night green with beasts as April with grass

Orion would hunt high from southward, over the hill,
And the blood of beasts herald morning. Where these have
passed,
Tramping white roads, their ears drinking the sword-crash,
The chariots are broken, bright battle-cars
Shambles under earth; whether by sharp bronze
Or the years' ebbing, all blood has flowed into the ground;
There was wailing at sundown, mourning for kings,
Weeping of widows, but these went faint, were forgotten,
And the columns have fallen like shadows. Crickets
Sing under the stones; and beyond the carved wall
Westward, fires drifting in darkness like the tails
Of jackals flaring, no hounds heard at their hunting,
Float outward into the dark. And these horses stamp
Before us now in this garden; and northward
Beyond the terraces the misted sea
Swirls endless, hooves of the gray wind forever
Thundering, churning the ragged spume-dusk
High that there be no horizons nor stars, and there
Are white islands riding, ghost-guarded, twisted waves flashing,
Porpoises plunging like the necks of horses.

RICHARD WILBUR

Mind

Mind in its purest play is like some bat
That beats about in caverns all alone,
Contriving by a kind of senseless wit
Not to conclude against a wall of stone.

It has no need to falter or explore;
Darkly it knows what obstacles are there,
And so may weave and flitter, dip and soar
In perfect courses through the blackest air.

And has this simile a like perfection?
The mind is like a bat. Precisely. Save
That in the very happiest intellection
A graceful error may correct the cave.

Exeunt

Piecemeal the summer dies;
At the field's edge a daisy lives alone;
A last shawl of burning lies
On a gray field-stone.

All cries are thin and terse;
The field has droned the summer's final mass;
A cricket like a dwindled hearse
Crawls from the dry grass.

Love Calls Us to the Things of This World

The eyes open to a cry of pulleys,
And spirited from sleep, the astounded soul
Hangs for a moment bodiless and simple
As false dawn.
Outside the open window
The morning air is all awash with angels.

Some are in bed-sheets, some are in blouses,
Some are in smocks: but truly there they are.
Now they are rising together in calm swells
Of halcyon feeling, filling whatever they wear
With the deep joy of their impersonal breathing;

Now they are flying in place, conveying
The terrible speed of their omnipresence, moving
And staying like white water; and now of a sudden
They swoon down into so rapt a quiet
That nobody seems to be there.
The soul shrinks

From all that it is about to remember,
From the punctual rape of every blessèd day,
And cries,
"Oh, let there be nothing on earth but laundry,
Nothing but rosy hands in the rising steam
And clear dances done in the sight of heaven."

Yet, as the sun acknowledges
With a warm look the world's hunks and colors,
The soul descends once more in bitter love
To accept the waking body, saying now
In a changed voice as the man yawns and rises,

"Bring them down from their ruddy gallows;
Let there be clean linen for the backs of thieves;
Let lovers go fresh and sweet to be undone,
And the heaviest nuns walk in a pure floating
Of dark habits,
keeping their difficult balance."

Beasts

Beasts in their major freedom
Slumber in peace tonight. The gull on his ledge
Dreams in the guts of himself the moon-plucked waves below,
And the sunfish leans on a stone, slept
By the lyric water,

In which the spotless feet
Of deer make dulcet splashes, and to which
The ripped mouse, safe in the owl's talon, cries
Concordance. Here there is no such harm
And no such darkness

As the selfsame moon observes
Where, warped in window-glass, it sponsors now
The werewolf's painful change. Turning his head away

On the sweaty bolster, he tries to remember
The mood of manhood,

But lies at last, as always,
Letting it happen, the fierce fur soft to his face,
Hearing with sharper ears the wind's exciting minors,
The leaves' panic, and the degradation
Of the heavy streams.

Meantime, at high windows
Far from thicket and pad-fall, suitors of excellence
Sigh and turn from their work to construe again the painful
Beauty of heaven, the lucid moon
And the risen hunter,

Making such dreams for men
As told will break their hearts as always, bringing
Monsters into the city, crows on the public statues,
Navies fed to the fish in the dark
Unbridled waters.

An Event

As if a cast of grain leapt back to the hand,
A landscapeful of small black birds, intent
On the far south, convene at some command
At once in the middle of the air, at once are gone
With headlong and unanimous consent
From the pale trees and fields they settled on.

What is an individual thing? They roll
Like a drunken fingerprint across the sky!
Or so I give their image to my soul
Until, as if refusing to be caught
In any singular vision of my eye
Or in the nets and cages of my thought,

They tower up, shatter, and madden space
With their divergences, are each alone

Swallowed from sight, and leave me in this place
Shaping these images to make them stay:
Meanwhile, in some formation of their own,
They fly me still, and steal my thoughts away.

Delighted with myself and with the birds,
I set them down and give them leave to be.
It is by words and the defeat of words,
Down sudden vistas of the vain attempt,
That for a flying moment one may see
By what cross-purposes the world is dreamt.

The Death of a Toad

A toad the power mower caught,
Chewed and clipped of a leg, with a hobbling hop has got
To the garden verge, and sanctuaried him
Under the cineraria leaves, in the shade
Of the ashen heartshaped leaves, in a dim,
Low, and a final glade.

The rare original heartsblood goes,
Spends on the earthen hide, in the folds and wizenings, flows
In the gutters of the banked and staring eyes. He lies
As still as if he would return to stone,
And soundlessly attending, dies
Toward some deep monotone,

Toward misted and ebullient seas
And cooling shores, toward lost Amphibia's emperies.
Day dwindles, drowning, and at length is gone
In the wide and antique eyes, which still appear
To watch, across the castrate lawn,
The haggard daylight steer.

Potato

for André du Bouchet

An underground grower, blind and a common brown;
Got a misshapen look, it's nudged where it could;
Simple as soil yet crowded as earth with all.

Cut open raw, it looses a cool clean stench,
Mineral acid seeping from pores of prest meal;
It is like breaching a strangely refreshing tomb:

Therein the taste of first stones, the hands of dead slaves,
Waters men drank in the earliest frightful woods,
Flint-chips, and peat, and the cinders of buried camps.

Scrubbed under faucet water the planet skin
Polishes yellow, but tears to the plain insides;
Parching, the white's blue-hearted like hungry hands.

All of the cold dark kitchens, and war-frozen gray
Evening at window; I remember so many
Peeling potatoes quietly into chipt pails.

"It was potatoes saved us, they kept us alive."
Then they had something to say akin to praise
For the mean earth-apples, too common to cherish or steal.

Times being hard, the Sikh and the Senegalese,
Hobo and Okie, the body of Jesus the Jew,
Vestigial virtues, are eaten; we shall survive.

What has not lost its savor shall hold us up,
And we are praising what saves us, what fills the need.
(Soon there'll be packets again, with Algerian fruits.)

Oh, it will not bear polish, the ancient potato,
Needn't be nourished by Caesars, will blow anywhere,
Hidden by nature, counted-on, stubborn and blind.

You may have noticed the bush that it pushes to air,
Comical-delicate, sometimes with second-rate flowers
Awkward and milky and beautiful only to hunger.

HY SOBILOFF

Painting of a Lobster by Picasso

This claw remains alive,
Stands aside and swings on fantasy;
It hangs from a drapery rod
Against the wall of a room
And near the window.
This claw seizes the sunlight,
Lies in a crib of muscle
Tied to a string.
The claw surrounds the egg
As in the room the whole lobster sleeps
On a cracked plate,
Lobster eaten by a butterfly
On a checkered table cloth, blue and white.

My Mother's Table

My mother's table was round like a face
Round and covered with fingerstains
And crumbs that stuck to my fingertips.
At that table each child wanted everything:
My father gave everything, emptied himself

Into the pockets round my mother's table.
We ate hard crust and made a hatbrim of hard crust,
Ate each other around my mother's table.
Ashamed to age alone,
My sister cried for too many dresses,
Grabbed for my dessert,
But I hid my chocolate under my pillow,
Stalked about the bedpost
Disappeared among the beams in our attic.
I counted my fingers and toes like a miser
Shouted to myself in my own language.
I grew by making promises to myself;
In lonely baths the fear of love became my religion.
Then one year they erected new fences for me to climb,
Prepared sticks and stones to destroy me
And I flew off at a tangent from my mother's round table.
The hobby horses were playing
And my childhood carrousel
Was still a familiar wonderland,
But when I crossed out chimneys and attics
The world became a strange neighborhood
Where I climbed a ladder of birthdays,
Reading my father's face.

Little Girl Cat

Little girl cat, made for me,
Her long ears listening to street noises,
Her sharp teeth smiling.

My cat, molded on a stand,
A carved spider,
Alert at my fireplace.

I held her paw three times,
And she began to dance,
Began to dress, my cat,

A firefly in spurts of whiskers;
Danced in the outside air,
Bruised her ear, my cat,

Was sent to a wood hospital
On a pillow . . . poor pussy willow,
Pranced away, my practiced cat.

My cat has a wire tail and wooden ears,
A sylph-like animal with a zig-zag spring,
Standing on woman's legs.

My cat has wings for fuzz,
She purrs at my artificial fireplace,
My wild bird, my lady cat.

Family Screams

Compare a stick with the wood
    Bent or round
Wound around a branch, or wet from a morning.
A stick is shaped, curved or rhythmic
Rolling like a stone,
    It sleeps like the wind.

Hear a stick
    It sings like a man
    Or hides in a basket.
Watch a stick
    In the hands of a devil it makes sounds of hallelujah.

Compare a stick with the wood
Compare a stick to the wind
    To a flower stalk half bruised by wind.
Compare a man to his child
    Yourself to yourself
Compare a stick to memory.

RUTH STONE

In an Iridescent Time

My mother, when young, scrubbed laundry in a tub,
She and her sisters on an old brick walk
Under the apple trees, sweet rub-a-dub.
The bees came round their heads, the wrens made talk.
Four young ladies each with a rainbow board
Honed their knuckles, wrung their wrists to red,
Tossed back their braids and wiped their aprons wet.
The Jersey calf beyond the back fence roared;
And all the soft day, swarms about their pet
Buzzed at his big brown eyes and bullish head.
Four times they rinsed, they said. Some things they starched,
Then shook them from the baskets two by two,
And pinned the fluttering intimacies of life
Between the lilac bushes and the yew:
Brown gingham, pink, and skirts of Alice blue.

In a Liberal Arts Building

Someone has idly set a record turning,
And a dead pianist jumps out of the grave.
In the halls his limpid-sounding masteries of bone
And ivory, metal thread and sinew echo.
And in a room where scraping chairs signal adjourning,
He breaks upon dissolution and fatigue with an inbound wave
As the first departure leaves the door ajar. Alone
Among fretting voices, his forehead sweats and slow
Beads form along his lips. He has no smile
For dull papers and all this harmless nonsense,
But he plays it out for them in his brilliant style,

He and the dead composer, until the disc is done,
As the room empties, and wax relents.

Orchard

The mare roamed soft about the slope,
Her rump was like a dancing girl's.
Gentle beneath the apple trees
She pulled the grass and shook the flies.
Her forelocks hung in tawny curls;
She had a woman's limpid eyes,
A woman's patient stare that grieves.
And when she moved among the trees,
The dappled trees, her look was shy,
She hid her nakedness in leaves.
A delicate though weighted dance
She stepped while flocks of finches flew
From tree to tree and shot the leaves
With songs of golden twittering;
How admirable her tender stance.
And then the apple trees were new,
And she was new, and we were new,
And in the barns the stallions stamped
And shook the hills with trumpeting.

The Pear

There hangs this bellied pear, let no rake doubt,
Meat for the tongue and febrile to the skin,
Wasting for the mildew and the rot,
A tallow rump slow rounded, a pelt thin
And for the quickest bite; so, orchard bred,
Heaviest downward from the shaking stem.
Whose fingers curve around the ripened head
Lust to split so fine a diadem.

There is the picker, stretches for the knife,
There are the ravening who claw the fruit,
More, those adjuring wax that lasts a life,
And foxes, freak for cunning, after loot.
For that sweet suck the hornet whines his wits,
And husbandman will dry her for the pits.

DAVID WAGONER

Murder Mystery

After the murder, like parades of Fools,
The bungling supernumeraries come,
Sniffing at footprints, looking under rugs,
Clasping the dead man with prehensile tools.
Lens against nose, false beard down to his knees,
The Hawkshaw enters, hoists his bag of tricks,
And passes out suspicion like lemonade:
"Where were you when the victim—" "In my room."
"Didn't you ask him whether—" "Double locks."
"Who switched the glasses on the—" "Crippled legs."
"Why were the ballroom curtains—" "Mad for years."
Then, tripping on clues, they wander through the house,
And search each other, frighten themselves with guns,
Ransack the kitchen and the sherry bins,
And dance in the bushes with the cats and dogs.

"Where is he?" says the Captain. "Nobody cares."
"We did it!" scream the butler and the maid.
"I did it too!" the jolly doctor cries.
And all join in—detective, counterfoil,
Ingénue, hero, and the family ghosts—
And, flapping like tongues, the trapdoors babble guilt,
The window-boxes, closets understairs,

Whatnots and chandeliers, grandfather clocks,
The sealed-up attic with its litter of bones—
All of them shake, and pour their secrets out.
And the happy party, bearing aloft the dead,
Handcuffed and drunk, go singing towards the jail;
Stage-hands roll up their sleeves, fold up the lawn,
Dismantle the hedges and the flowerbed,
Then follow, hauling the mansion, to confess.

Meanwhile, in another place—their figures cold,
Both turned to shadows by a single pain,
Bloodless together—the killer and the slain
Have kissed each other in the wilderness,
Touching soft hands and staring at the world.

To My Friend Whose Parachute Did Not Open

Thrown backwards first, head over heels in the wind
Like solid streamers from the wing to tail,
You counted whatever pulses came to mind—
The black, the bright—and at the third, you pulled,
Pulled savagely at the ring clenched in your hand.

Down the smooth slope of your trajectory,
Obeying physics like a bauble of hail,
Thirty-two feet per second per second hurled
Toward treetops, cows, and crouching gravity
From the unreasonable center of the world,

You saw the cords trail out from behind your back,
Rise up and stand, tied to a piece of cloth
Whose edges wobbled, but would not spread wide
To borrow a cup of air and hold you both.
O that tall shimmer whispered you were dead.

You outraced thought. What good was thinking then?
Poor time—no time for plunging into luck

Which had, like your whirling, weightless flesh, grown thin.
I know angelic wisdom leaped from your mouth,
But not in words, for words can be afraid:

You sang a paean at the speed of sound,
Compressed miraculous air within your head
And made it fountain upward like a cowl.
And if you didn't, then you struck the ground.
And if you struck the ground, both of us died.

NED O'GORMAN

L'Annunciazione

from Bellini

An angel stepping through her window said:
I come to you, a sign from him who sent me.
And leaving then her unbelief she told
the incident from off the sill
and bade it sit before her on the floor.

There was nothing like the fear she felt;
to have a winged and sudden thing
appear to her with not a trumpet or
a trace of wind. She bade him come and say,
if anything would say it well, the news.

He said: I bring you barns and donkeys,
satraps and camel humps, one dozen sheep,
their shepherds and their smell, a star,
a raging king, his sharp knife and a man
who cuts out windows, doors and chairs.

She said: I am used to walking and no grand
folderol of yours will still the flying wind
nor feign trumpets out of silence; connive away,
there's breach enough in any God
to answer you. I have no truck with incidents.

He said: I bring you meadow and winter,
cypress and river, white oxen in the sun,
a boy whose eyes scare dolphins high
as kites; the beautiful mirror of the incessant
zero; I bring you contradiction.

She said: I'll leave you now, you incident,
and from my sight you'll fly, leaving
your wing's shadow caught on that shutter,
your spine breaking the light. I must get
off the dream and back to filling jars.

He said: I bring you flaring squares, circles,
perpendiculars, and trapezoids; I bring you
color from the sun. I bring you
folderol. You'll be Jehovah's honeycomb.
I bring you caravans, a burglary.

She said: I will behave as filling jars were
all my life; I will decide to have a walk,
and incident, I shall not dance again
nor tremble when some doubtful thing steps on my sill.
And fell from heaven then a dominion in her womb.

Myth

I knew a man with a terrible obsession
who thought that he was fire
who would tramp the fields in hob-nail boots
turning all the timothy into ash
and all the wild geese into funerary jugs.
He had no fit so terrible as one I saw

at high noon when he turned a page
of Jeremiah and scorched the sands of Gideon
to glass. He was terrible another time
and cypresses curled like shavings at his touch;
roots yielded up their syrups and the sun
rocked in the oven of his eye. He moved
through the world, burning rivers from their beds,
tottering the centers of hoops, galvanizing
snowmen into juggernauts, and pulled up to boiling
the streams of spring. O terrible this booted colossus
this hooting flame who saw all the world
in his obsession and made it do for tinder, flint
and furnace. Hulking in the sun, rattling
among poppies he contended for dominion
in the flaring orbit of his terrible obsession.

ROBERT BAGG

Ronald Wyn

Inscriptions on Greek tombstones intrigued him,
The way stones spoke to the dead with sure words.
'This little stone, good Sabinus, records
Our great friendship, which I still need. Leave the numb
Waters of Lethe alone, and remember me.'
Sometimes the dead answer, 'Please don't worry
Long over me. Do your work, be happy. At nineteen
Cancer killed me, and I leave the sweet sun.'

We both had strong Platonic appetites.
Three pound symposiums of grapes and plums
Gnawed bare to their Aristotelian pits
He pocketed. 'Logic thrives on a peach blossom's
Troubles,' he said, and when a calm mirror

Lake reflected us, we dove underwater,
Blew out mouthfuls, and swam until the honey
Of exhaustion filled every cell in the body.

From a frame normally tense and careless
A tennis ball exacted gracefulness
By skipping on the tip of the net's tongue.
The dust kicked from our reflexes in long-
Winded rallies. Sharp satisfying plocks,
Both of us bent on keeping play alive,
We'd silence with a winning forehand drive,
Let sweat cool, and drink harsh gulps from our Cokes.

His death ten seconds in my ears, I shook
Off sorrow, walked out in a cool downpour
And drank rain from my palms. I had no power,
So thirsty for his slippery life, to make
Anything but absurdity of that bath.
I wandered Amherst in drenched shame
Because I had let weather drive the same
Wonder from my feelings as a man's death.

This Spring, at Epidaurus, dying of poems,
I stood tired and sweaty in a great cloudburst.
Only for honest, singleminded thirst
Will sense be made from the skies by cupped palms,
Said the acoustics in the theater, where
Greek speech lives cupped in the worn marble's care.
I shall drink many palmfuls of my friend's life
In your presence, laurel and myrtle leaf;

Then set these stones speaking to each other.
'I am Ron Wyn, promising philosopher,
I pledged myself to music, calculus
And Greek, but mastered none, since my last promise,
To death, was the one I fulfilled first.'
'Rest easy, Ron. Although our friendship was killed
To metaphor by the illiterate world
I grave these rocks with love, in which you are versed.'

'Laine

I

Where Lackawanna's tracks graze our backyards
An elm opens toward its leaves. Slight wooden slats
Climb its trunk crazily like vertebrae
To my old tree house, house of three girls, all
Named 'Laine.
'Laine unafraid listened for diesels
Scaring 4:39 out of our watches,
Diesels rattling our wrists, the elm tree's slats,
And a half mile of track. Faces flicked past
Like faces on a riffling deck of cards.
Our eyes wrinkled after a college girl
Sipping gin in the club car, "Your wife for sure,"
'Laine said, thumbtacking the Black Queen of Spades
(Pulled deftly from the deck on her first try)
Beside DiMag. "You'll marry her on Friday
And spend the morning swimming to Bermuda,"
She whispered, spreading down cards like sandwich halves,
Perhaps shuffling herself deeper in the deck.
She looked in my eyes as if they led somewhere,
Then spread my palm, and until dinnertime
Ran her ball-point pen down my life's blue rivers.

II

Two nights before school ended, wondering if
The elm house still would hold us, we climbed there,
Twisting uncomfortably close together
Since there was truly only room for one.
"This is how lovers stretch," she said, arranging
Copper hairpins like fireflies in her hair,
"Their twin hearts click as tracks click beneath trains,
Their eyelids whir out of sight in no time."
She counted three times over my twelve wild ribs.
Soft felt roosters crowing in her green dress

Folded away, trackless and white her thighs
Lay side by side, her lips closed over mine,
Closed bitterly, then opened by my ear:
"You've followed me where all the meagre rivers
Overflow my eyes, sailed so far downstream
That ocean when you reach it, is a wide lie.
If you think schooners beach on gentle islands
You'll surely founder in my furious hair."
She curled toward nonexistent blankets, and her
Arms cooled as winds breathe gooseflesh over water.
"When you and Charles go overseas this summer
Other girls will beckon from their speeding berths,
Their sheets will rise like crests, but I'll stay here
Traveling warm nights on waves that never break."
A spring of woven roosters settled on
Her ankles, as she alighted from the elm.

III

Though the vast church is draughty, though the pews
Absorb these vows, organ music will insist
Oaken doors swing open on the same spring
That's flourished since the ceremony began.
Skin that once held her breasts high as her bra
Now holds them, cools below her wedding gown,
And later on tonight will shiver at
The first disastrous passing of the diesel,
Will search old trails blazed through civilized
Flesh, itch for woolen summers when shrill roosters
Sang from green fences piled past waking waists.
How shall her voice close over our whole lives?

"Our wedding night was several falls ago,
Now spring comes wearily on a cold scent
With perfect confidence, that foxes bleed,
That snow will find its way to waterfalls,
That if our eyes soak blurring skies with love
Invisible ink will draw taut warriors

And kitchenware from stars."
                    Tonight, dear 'Laine
Mysterious threads draw headlong birds to sleep,
The blood flies home by sweetly charted courses.

CHARLES PHILBRICK

New England Suite

I

I hear in my brain all New England echoing down and around me,
And in the colony of my heart away. My land is a factory now,
Or a suburb, a parking-lot liquid in sun on the level tar.
Below local histories, markers and chartered ground, beneath brick,
Bright cemented disclaimers, lie crushed and still Indian-
Haunted rock, lie the bones of hard people often uncomely and cold,
Lie swatches of hair, and commodes, lie mirrors and lobster-pots, letters
In palimpsest, arrowheads, fish-knives, and ropes now all mummied in tar;
Good familied books and chipped jugs, penwipers, samplers and useful shells;
Whalebones and beads, genealogy, sweetgrass and old uphill passions;
Birchbark and dimity, cracked leather straps and shrunk iron, denials;
And spyglasses empty of eye, the salted-green brassbound recallers
Of the masted-in-intricate-pride, of the widowing seas, and the land

Sea defines: the tides of the mind leave this rack on the memory's shore.

II

The regional bird is the gull, protected by law, protecting
And proctoring, fouling and scavenging all our most visited shores:
Able, unlovely, raucous, persistent, at home in the storm;
Friendless, eternal, yellow of eye and whitely aware;
Undiscouraged if dun, a clown to the camera, famishers' food.
The southering bird on whose feather has fallen the rumor of snow,
The flier afflicted with instinct and warned by the touch and the go
Of a soft geometric—that sniff and that sift in the needling air—
He leaves. All the birds know by the cold, and believe in the sun,
Slant as he may.
(And you watch. When last did a bird of this world
Seize a child from your bloody town, mar a woman, accuse or unmake
Any man?)
To the birds who ensky many myths they would scorn—
Who high-bracket New England—New England is only a flat like a map,
With the waters precise in the infinite inlets, a visible ground
Laid out for their feeding, is neither to nest on nor haply to fall.
For themselves, the seen birds, whether migrants or natives, have never
Been known to give names to the curious people, to count and report
All the tourists or label the ankles of strangers like herons who stalk
The emptying estuaries, quiet, with glass to the questing eye.

III

Musselled, sea-lavendered shores throwing beaches, low dikes
To put sand between salt of the wave and the salt of the meadowing marshes
Where silt waves have grained into grasses of silver and green, are unpeopled
Like the beaches that run under gull-foot, below eagled cliffs and the headlands
Inspected by whales, and the uplands patrolled by the bear overhill
And the horsy, high-shouldered moose with antlers of ossified kelp.
From mountain to shore, through hills, rises, valleys and rivers, odd ponds
In their pockets, the bent stands of scrub and the hungry foundations, all acres,
The regional beast is no proudfoot, deep in his chest, nor a brightmane;
No flasher of eyes, nor bayonet-brandisher frightful of man;
The regional beast is a trinity noxious to dogs, knowing men;
The muskrat, the skunk and the woodchuck, all drab in defiance, all near.

IV

The regional fish is the mackerel, or else the low pastoral cod
In the market; but over the eyelid's horizon goes swimming away,
Like a barrel of anguish, the great whale trailing his stintless blood
In a moonpath of red across the Pacific savannas, and huge
Green valleys down, below the white sails and crisp oars,
The sharp intentions, going under and down. Both whaler and whale,
Pursuit and profit, loss and return of the voyagers, now
Read as history's blow; and the strike and the flurry, the sounding,
The flensing, the reek of the try-out recede to a region

Of rowboats for rent and of dories agap and awash with petunias,
Of seafood at roadside, clean restrooms and gas. The regional fish
Is the clamcake announced in electrical script; the seasonal fish
Is the sucker.
And all New England echoes down and away.

V

Violet, daisy, sweet-william and blackeyed susan, sea-rose,
Queen-anne's-lace, the goldenrod, sumac and orient hydrangea
Unbelieved, but brought home by new-bearded son with new judgment in eyes—
Like lilac, no bride was declared in the cargo; columbine, laurel
And honeysuckle, trumpet-vine, buttercup—all these combine
To make the regional flower: with fireweed and Indian-pipe, paintbrush
Of devils, the gentian, the jewelweed, milkweed, the poison-bright ivy:
These, and more, are given to see. The good herbs are left to discover.
The flowers were pressed between leaves of the books—the few books and good—
And the books were impressed on the brains; on a continent brains were then sown.

VI

Whole graveyards on hillsides are stone-fledged with beards up-ended
To heaven and frozen at chin to the flint of the soil; whole hillsides
Are graveyards unhallowed, perimeters nubile with birches like hopes
Of young serious virgins, all clean and surrounded by sentinel cedars:
Dark daggers at wrong, evergreen like original sin. Planted here

In this undulant underground churchyard, are the hopes of New England,
Unique in their angles and white in their morals, unique in their bite
On the sky; these fears are redeemed by their force, which made and still makes
But metaphor of winter weather. The wind frays the flags and shrivels
The wreaths that sag onto urns eroded, under stiff wings
In the moving air over earth of such coffined rectitude,
Cold regard of recording stones, generations of marbled woe.

VII

Our tree is ubiquitous pine—possibly spruce or the tamarack,
Maple whose blood bespeaks sugar in veins—but the bark is of birch,
And the leaf is the loyal hard brown old man's hand of the oak.
Sweet groundpine or juniper, wild grape or bayberry, brambles —all run
Like the nerves of this ground whose berries taste tart as an apothegm.
But the tree that the colonists planted as badge of their towns was another—
And this is their reason—: the reach and the slendering height of the straight,
Academic, imperious elm, like the aim of New England in art,
Lurks in the crook of the root gripping soil, in its thirst among rocks.

VIII

The regional colors are wilder by contrast and subtler than Mexico.
The urge of the autumn, the accent of frost, makes the primary chords:
The scarlets and oranges, yellows and purples, the high exclamations

In leaf, and the firmer, full statements in fruit. Brown earth
and pale sand,
And impossible snow make the canvas. The sky and the sea do
the rest:
All the blue, gray and silver, all greens not alive that can change;
All the changes among them, and sunsets in season, all weather-
ing motions.
The regional hues that are minor are man's: the glosses of
lanterns
And tar, the dulled ictus of rust and the glint of the hair-thin
ring,
Wedding-gold.
The regional colors dream under neon, and wait.

IX

The life of New England in centuries gone is a guess, or pro-
verbial guff.
Lust could wear homespun and wonder on calico, sun sweeten
sweat
On the skin, or skin get the alternate ache of dry salt from the
sea;
Love could walk barefoot and brown with the dust of the sun,
or go booted,
And berried in cheek and bright lip by the hollying frost. The
life
Of the regional youth was no glimpse between headstones of
wives early gone
From the childbed and footstones of children stillborn or but
shown for a season
Or two. The life of the youth of this country was not just a
summer
Following thaw, before blizzard, a sun between snows. The
youth
Of this region was everything strong, little easy: if hard, yet it
shone.
—Cleaning and bleaching, mending and patching, painting with
paint,

Oil or varnish, with whitewash or tar; the quilting and candling,
preserving
And saving, here making and there making do—but they made!
To mend
Is a form of *to make,* and to paint is a shaping, an outward
approval;
Doing without is an aspect of using: the use of each thing is to
wear
It utterly out, as loving old couples have done of their bodies,
Yet live and apparently love; as thinkers have whittled their
brains
Into words, and still see things and laugh as the poets I know
From this region can go to the antarctic ice-cap, alone with a
pen,
And there make New England of nothing, or scrimshaw whole
Indies of ice.

X

These states are my mind, and my blood with their history flows
all down
And away, bleeding west in an empire and south in a passion;
these states
Are the map of my intricate heart, and no orderly page and no
print
Can reduce them to handbook. The mind flows away to begin-
nings in water,
Past sand, over rocks and rock-pools, to the rising of hills
through the pines
And the pine-heavy air of all lands, and across the whole cloud
of the sky.
Yet my mind is this country of slower than tropical, longer,
more passionate
Growth, and this ocean contains my imaginings; mountains
suggest
My haphazard projects; astonishing snows are my silences, gales
My level declaring of Autumn. In August untended wild roses
That overwhelm silvering shingles of cedar amount to my
tenderness.

Quite like a monument, steepled and peeling of paint, worth preserving
By the civic of mind, I am nothing alone without gift of this ground
To grow in and give in the double-bed dark to my boys in the sacrament
Love before driving the seed of my being, long warm with a wife
And all green with a poem, under the quilt of this eldering earth.

GEORGE STARBUCK

Poems from a First Year in Boston

To Jonathan Edwards, d. 1758

I. New Year: View West over Storrow

Boston. Lord God, the ocean never to windward,
never the sweet snootful of death a West Coast
wind on its seven-league sea-legs winds its wing-ding
landfalling up by upheaving over you.
Wonders.
Streetsful of San Francisco my thirst still wanders.
Head still heavy with harvests of rot winrowed
on beaches, hands with a haul of fishes weed-wound
in jetsam of nets, throat with a rise of white-winged
wallowing sea birds, I dream that city, the once-loved
weight of those seas, and the sea-sucked girl I waylayed
through deserts who sours here, a sick wife.
With land wind.
Nothing but land wind hot with steel, but lint-white
bundles of daily breath hung out over textile

towns, but the sweat sucked from mines, but white smokestacks
soaring from hospital workyards over grassplots
of pottering dotards. Life. Life, the wind whispers;
crouch to its weight: three thousand miles, three hundreds-
of-years of life rolled up in a wind, rolled backwards
onto this city's back, Jonathan Edwards.

And never the full sea wind. Lord God, what wonder
kids go skinny and pale as ale down one-way
pavements to pitch pinched pennies onto the subway's
eyes, his cast-iron eyes.
                    Jonathan Edwards,
funny old crank of Social History lectures,
firm believer in hell and witches, who knows whether
you of all witnesses wouldn't watch this wayward
city with most love?
                    Jonathan, while prim Winter
bustles with steam and batting, bundling the wind-torn
birth of your death's two-hundredth year—while internes,
sober as bloody judges, clean the downtown
haul of the mercy-fleet—while rearing and sounding
through panicked traffic the sacred scows come horns-down
and huge with woe—while heavy-headed thousands
of bells nod off to sleep like practiced husbands
propped in high corners of their lady Boston's
white-laid and darkened room—while worst- and best-born,
Beacon and Charlestown, clench, giving this stubborn
year nineteen hundred fifty-eight its birth-bath
of blood, I turn to you as to a sabbath—
turn, as the drugged dawn deadens, to the solace
of your staid rage.
                    At least no wretch went soulless
when you had damned him Man. Nor would you sell us
that Freedom-to-end-Freedoms that the self-sold
crow about: Freedom from Guilt, they name it, shiftless
for any other shrift. Yachtsmen, their footloose
legatees fitting reefers into faultless
features with febrile wrists, protest: some leftist
restlessness threatens them in brittle leaflets;

some angry boy, some undiscovered artist
has put soot whiskers on their public statues.
They wring their strange left hands that every-whichways
scatter the khakied corpses onto elsewhere's
turbulent waters to save oil. The world-wise
rage at the world—
                                        where you, Jonathan Edwards,
wise to the same sad racket, bore some inward
wisdom, some inward rage. There and there only,
letting this city sicken me and own me,
knowing the grief there is, taking it on me,
may I hope (having not your Christ for bondsman)
to earn these hearts, their paradise, this Boston.

II. Outbreak of Spring

Stirring porchpots up with green-fingered witchcraft,
insinuating cats in proper outskirts,
hag Spring in a wink blacks the prim white magic
of winter-wimpled Boston's every matesick
splinter of spinster landscape.
                                                        Under the matchstick
march of her bridgework, melting, old lady Mystic
twitches her sequins coyly, but the calls
of her small tugs entice no geese. Canals
take freight; the roads throw up stiff hands, and the Charles
arches. Spring's ón us: a life raft wakes the waters
of Walden like a butt-slap.
                                                And yet she loiters.
Where is song while the lark in winter quarters
lolls? What's to solace Scollay's hashhouse floaters
and sing them to their dolls? and yet—
                                                            strange musics,
migrant melodies of exotic ozarks,
twitter and throb where the bubble-throated jukebox
lurks iridescent by these lurid newsracks.
Browser leafing here, withhold your wisecracks:
tonight, in public, straight from overseas,
her garish chiaroscuro turned to please

you and her other newsstand devotees,
the quarter-lit Diana takes her ease.

So watch your pockets, cats, hang onto your hearts,
for when you've drunk her glitter till it hurts—
Curtain.
Winds frisk you to the bone.
Full-feasted
Spring, like an ill bird, settles to the masthead
of here and there an elm. The streets are misted.
A Boston rain, archaic and monastic,
cobbles the blacktop waters, brings mosaic
to dusty windshields; to the waking, music.

III. Surfeit and Hot Sleep

Heavy on branch, on tight green knuckles heaves
the Spring. Cumulus, thick as broodhens, thieves
green from the earthy bark like worms, like leaves,
like dollars from up sleeves.
Outbreak of billfolds,
bellbottoms, burleycue babes. Musical billboards
join the parade. And deep in bars the railbirds
listen: "They selling something?" "Can't tell, traffic."
On corners cats bounce once or twice: "Hey frantic."
"Yeah." and they stop. Flared forward like an intake
the lips lurch on. DISASTER OUTLET, NATICK
BEHEMOTH BARGAINS MONSTER DEALS TITANIC
the soundtruck reads; but what it says is "Mine.
You're my obsession. No I can't resign
possession. I'm confessin' that you're mine
mine mine mine mine click." Da Capo. Move on.

Slowly the moon, that shifty chaperone,
performs her preconcerted wink, but none
are quite prepared. Hag Spring's had it: she's made
her bed of faggots and goes up in jade
flame like the tough old bird she is. Green, green
upon green, hips the store windows—I mean

it's summer now, that lolloping large mother,
comes puttering about some spell or other
among her brats the beasts.
                                        But back streets trammel
her traipse with tracks and snood her up in metal;
she smiles from Fenway's temple walls too madly
to matter much, and though admission's free,
few worship, fewer dance, and none with glee.

What then? Her bouncing boy—that honeyed wonder's
hernia'd ruiner Love—has aged no tenderer:
portly he paces the parks, poking under
odd scraps of news his forcible reminder
what buds had best be at. They mull it over.

Rest, Mr. Edwards, not a Boston voter
calls him paisan: save your grave pocket veto;
for if they still make time in Waltham's drugstores,
if ladies see new light on Beacon's backstairs,
the fault's not Venus's, it's not the Dog Star's;
if Cupid's in, he's not the deepest prankster;
for spring and fall and all, the hapless hustler
cries her undoubted wound in rouge past picture
palaces; winter long her helter-skelter
sisters go squealing to the marriage-smelter:
the tin-pan Moon, the Moon's to blame!
                                                        for throngs
follow the bouncing ball and sing along,
"Moon, salivary Moon, won't you please be
around, Moon, silv'ry dollar Moon so's we
can go to town, Moon: ain' no one aroun'
to get us high, O, Dionysian Moon,
like to die . . ." Moon. Lubricious spinster. Crone.
A pox!—
            Powder with stardust. And the bride's
the broad's the broodmare's Moon at a cloud's side
poses, while slowly the light is hers. She glides,
golden, an apple of eyes, and so cold, only
heart at its heaviest can join the lonely

circle in emptiness that is her dance.
Yet she is Love, our Love, that frantic cadence.
Listen:

O Love, Love, but I had such dreams!
The wood was thick but knived with light, and streams
from a warm spring tangled about my feet.
Behind me the single pair of hooves beat
and shaggy hands played in the splash of my heels.
"Sister!" I cried, "Diana . . ." and the squeals
of the magpie bushes, ricochet of stones
struck from his hooves like sparks, impertinence
of woodmice in the leaves, and all sound, stopped.

Far and treeless away the gray plain steeped
to blackness. I leapt far—but slow, through heavy
moonlight, so slow in a long falling the very
land seemed to cringe from me, and that blue moon
—Earth—to reach out for me—(O Love be bone,
be burning flesh, be weight and heat and breath,
bear me beneath your bodysweight of earth
to earth) I woke and dreamed I was alone.

Crying. Poor creatures tying across the torn
spilt-milk grin of a sheet their sweating knot—
while at the westward window see with what
aplomb the round haunch of the Moon hangs through,
and far back in the dark she truckles to,
stoppling her champagne giggles, what dark crew . . .

IV. Autumn: Progress Report

Becalmed in old Back Bay's dead water sulk
the square four-storey barges, hulk to hulk.
These increments, so brusquely set aside
by the busy longshore muscle of the tide,
nurse the cut glint of chandelier and cup
like geodes: here Cathay lies silted up,
where tides of trade once moved: old weather eyes
look from the mansard portholes sans surmise.

Sans tooth, sans claw, late blood-competitors
hold in the faces of inheritors
a tight precarious old man's embrace.

Whaddaya do for action in this place?
Taxicabs scuttle by on the wet streets.
I weave with two sweet ladies out of the Ritz,
stare at the Garden pond.

Old pioneer,
Jonathan Edwards, did you stop off here
where marsh birds skittered, and a longboat put
its weed-grown bones to pasture at the foot
of Beacon, close on Charles Street? And see then,
already sick with glut, this hill of men?
And even there, see God? And in this marsh,
and in the wood beyond, grace of a harsh
God? And in these crabbed streets, unto the mid-
mire of them, God? Old Soul, you said you did.

It's still the same congested spit of land—
Dry Heaven's devil's-island, where the banned
gods of the blood's regime still play at court
in the stripped palatial prisons of the heart.
Poor pagan spooks, so gently spoken of
in Boston—brainwashed beggar-ghosts of love
so painfully, as if we knew such gods,
trying our neoclassical façades—

Prayer without praise. Glut in the atrium.

Jonathan, praise may be when the blood's drum
carries from camp to camp through jungles of
an entwined dark flesh, and the beat of love,
forcing that forest, overflows the sky.

Vegetal flesh, huge-bosomed, fills the eye
on Washington Street. Portly drummers croak,
their clotted hearts into their hands, no joke,

unsounded and unsung. You had your grand
God at your heart—could tremble in his hand—
could stare the cold stars through and find his voice
cupped in your ear by farthest space: "Rejoice
that you know not!"—could know, curled like God's spit
in dust, his meanest Incarnation: it
can be State Street and Monday Noon: it may
be drunk as a Lord: a guy might well say
"Christ!" scooting by.
And Christ why bleed about
some Kingdom we can never know, cast out
with all our flesh and blood before our birth?
Why not take stock of this stone island, earth,
and dig for its downed gods? Christ I could laugh,
so many pray; and yet—
I have seen half
the sculpted heads of Boston make the face
of one caged lion of a man their place
of weary battle: every day again
he must survive them all—the lettered men,
the men of means, the men of parts and shares—
and if he seeks God's peace instead of theirs,
God rest him for it: though I no more can
stomach your God than you my faith in man,
I too must worship blindly, Jonathan.

THEODORE WEISS

Barracks Apt. 14

All must be used:

this clay whisky jug, bearing
a lamp-shade; the four brown pears,

lying ruggedly among each other
in the wicker basket; the cactus
in its pot; and the orange berries,
old now as they dangle from their twigs
as though badly hung there.

These as well as the silence,
the young woman reading Aristotle
with difficulty, and the little girl
in the next room, voluble in bed:
"I'm talking in my sleep . . . laughing
in my sleep . . . waking in my sleep"

all are parts hopeful, possible,
expecting their place in the song;
more appealing because parts
that must harmonize into something
that rewards them for being, rewards
with what they are.

Do this and do,
till suddenly the scampering field
you would catch, the shiny crows
just out of reach, the pears
through which a brown tide breaks,
and the cactus you cannot cling to
long like that thorny Aristotle
suddenly, turning, turn on you

as meaning, the ultimate greenness
they have all the time been seeking
in the very flight they held
before you. No matter what you do,
at last you will be overwhelmed,
the distance will be broken,

the music will confound you.

Hayseed

The by-ways
of my oaten straw? Toot
as I will, the fruits do not
respond; the tension in the room
does not twang forth
a catalog
of ships and heroes, the clustered
dooms between them, wreaths hung
on a tree at dinner. My music
is more modest.
Still its reedy
pipings resound a time that might,
with leaning like a face, survey
some courtyard or a clearing
under an arc-light
where action
is not completely shamed.

II

Straw,
making up a meadow once, remarked
the passing of many positive fates.
Now, no less, when night comes down
like kindness—
the fleet god,
his bow still shaking on his back,
the quiver already quick with arrows
rustling flight—straw echoes
unforgettably
lovers gasping
out their burdened air: the heroes,
harbored here, a fleet enroute, sail-
in-sigh-winged, for its saltier
waterings.

Homecoming

I

Like that oldtimer who has kept by me
I know the place of danger and of change
and most, most tellingly, when they jut forth
their avid face, the moments that deny me
a staple of the place.
                              That oldtimer—
rope bloody through his hands, coursing
as the cordage sings: dog's lope and grace
of the deer, faun like a woman's love,
meat-scent fattening whatever air;

that song also like his chambered bow,
twenty years' music coiled waiting within,
catching on comrades, harnessed together,
winter and summer caught in the toils,
driving the sun, from east to west
one wheaten swath, his goddess winged
in this weather;
                              love likewise enduring
(twenty years not able to take its measure,
not chimerae, not orgies, able to make it
forget) its own lulls and forgettings,
surges of hunger the sea shrinks away in—

that oldtimer, buffeted as he was,
gripping twisted planks in a rampant sea,
clutching the last shreds of his wits
against rock and brackish brutality,
saw still this was his native element.

II

This and not sea-nymphs, not floating
islands centered in a season made of wish;
not noon with air the tissue of a voice

winsome at its loom,
                                    spinning out
along the ample warp of boughs a spell
that tangles men like thrushes in a net,
knots them, fawning claws or bristle set,
in one appetite.
                              Like him mast-pinioned,
flung by stormy words out of the sea,
hot blood in the lungs of a blinded cry
or grist for a bird song they become;
but only his ears open to homespun hunger—

"feasts and vistas of love, the struggle's
gaiety: her voice in all its changes,
in division strongest, ranging over peaks
and losses, leaf-tossed island in her voice"

(like him golden liar she was, lyre
strummed for their amusement by the gods,
loom too in its weaving night and day,
spinning him nearer home)
                                          "in our room
the changes come, zodiac in its restless
pride, its creatures here to suck selfhood
from our interbreeded breath;
                                            she the sea
under me, dolphins arch a sleek summer
by our side, the poplar and the birch
whirled in their autumn"—

III

                                          rooted, yes,
as his old tree, but flowering in open love,
in boughs that branch a household, season
air and crown, as it is crowned, sky-
high change.
                          In the top-greenery
the gods, looking down, dumbfounded,

at our strangeness with vast unblinking
incredulous eyes,
                                        envy us that we forever
change and, by our changing, settle
in this whirling place.
                                                    Better driftwood
swirling in the sea, an olive's litterings
over a battered body, than the ample warp
of boughs that snags us—thrushes in a net—
out of the complicated, mortal text.

DONALD JUSTICE

The Poet at Seven

And on the porch, across the upturned chair,
The boy would spread a dingy counterpane
Against the length and majesty of the rain,
And on all fours crawl in it like a bear
To lick his wounds in secret, in his lair;
And afterwards, in the windy yard again,
One hand cocked back, release his paper plane
Frail as a May fly to the faithless air.
And summer evenings he would whirl around
Faster and faster till the drunken ground
Rose up to meet him; sometimes he would squat
Among the foul weeds of the vacant lot,
Waiting for dusk and someone dear to come
And whip him down the street, but gently, home.

Southern Gothic

for W.E.B. & P.R.

Something of how the homing bee at dusk
Seems to inquire, perplexed, how there can be
No flowers here, not even withered stalks of flowers,
Conjures a garden where no garden is
And trellises too frail almost to bear
The memory of a rose, much less a rose.
Great oaks, more monumentally great oaks now
Than ever when the living rose was new,
Cast shade that is the more completely shade
Upon a house of broken windows merely
And empty nests up under broken eaves.
No damask any more prevents the moon,
But it unravels, peeling from a wall,
Red roses within roses within roses.

Tales from a Family Album

How shall I speak of doom, and ours in special,
But as of something altogether common?
No house of Atreus ours, too humble surely,
The family tree a simple chinaberry
Such as springs up in Georgia in a season.
(Under it sags the farmer's broken wagon.)
Nor may I laud it much for shade or beauty,
Yet praise that tree for being prompt to flourish,
Spite of the worm and weather out of heaven.

I publish of my folk how they have prospered
With something in the eyes, perhaps inherent,
Or great-winged nose, bespeaking an acquaintance
Not casual and not recent with a monster,
Citing, as an example of some courage,

That aunt, long gone, who kept one in a bird-cage
Thirty-odd years in shape of a green parrot,
Nor overcame her fears, yet missed no feeding,
Thrust in the crumbs with thimbles on her fingers.

I had an uncle, long of arm and hairy,
Who seldom spoke in any lady's hearing
Lest that his tongue should light on aught unseemly,
Yet he could treat most kindly with us children
Touching that beast, wholly imaginary,
Which, hunting once, his hounds had got the wind of.
And even of this present generation
There is a cousin of no great removal
On whom the mark is printed of a forepaw.

How shall I speak of doom and not the shadow
Caught in the famished cheeks of those few beauties
My people boast of, being flushed and phthisic?
Of my own childhood I remember dimly
One who died young, though as a hag most toothless,
Her fine hair wintry, from a hard encounter
By moonlight in a dark wood with a stranger,
Who had as well been unicorn or centaur
For all she might recall of him thereafter.

There was a kinsman took up pen and paper
To write our history, whereat he perished,
Calling for water and the holy wafer,
Who had, ere that, resisted much persuasion.
I pray your mercy on a leaf so shaken,
And mercy likewise on these other fallen,
Torn from the berry-tree in heaven's fashion,
That there was somewhat in their way of going
Put doom upon my tongue and bade me utter.

Ladies by Their Windows

I

They lean upon their windows. It is late.
Already it is twilight in the house;
Autumn is in their eyes. Twilit, autumnal—
Thus they regard themselves. What vanities!
As if all nature were a looking-glass
To publish the small features of their ruin!

Each evening at their windows they arrive
As in anticipation of farewells,
Though they would be still lingering if they could,
Weary, yet ever restless for the dance,
Old Cinderellas, hearing midnight strike,
The mouse-drawn coach impatient at the door.

2

The light in going still is golden, still
A single bird is singing in the wood,
Now one, now two, now three, and crickets start,
Bird-song and cricket-sigh; and all the small
Percussion of the grass booms as it can,
And chimes, and tinkles too, *fortissimo.*

It is the lurch and slur the world makes, turning.
It is the sound of turning, of a wheel
Or hand-cranked grinder turning, though more pomp
To this, more fiery particles struck off
At each revolve; and the last turn reveals
The darker side of what was light before.

Six stars shine through the dark, and half a moon!
Night-birds go spiralling upwards with a flash
Of silvery underwings, silver ascendings,

The light of stars and of the moon their light,
And water-lilies open to the moon,
The moon in wrinkles upon the water's face.

To shine is to be surrounded by the dark,
To glimmer in the very going out,
As stars wink, sinking in the bath of dawn,
Or as a prong of moon prolongs the night—
Superfluous curve!—unused to brilliancies
Which pale her own, yet splurging all she has.

3

So ladies by their windows live and die.
It is a question if they live or die,
As in a stone-wrought frieze of beasts and birds,
The question is, whether they go or stay.
It seems they stay, but rest is motion too,
As these old mimicries of stone imply.

Say, then, they go by staying, bird and beast,
Still gathering momentum out of calm,
Till even stillness seems too much of haste
And haste too still. Say that they live by dying,
These who were warm and beautiful as summer,
Leaning upon their windows looking out,

Summer-surrounded then with leaf and vine,
With alternate sun and shade, these whom the noon
Wound once about with beauty and then unwound,
Whose warmth survives in coldness as of stone,
Beauty in shadows, action in lassitude,
Whose windows are the limits of their lives.

GALWAY KINNELL

Rain over a Continent

Rain over a continent, the train
From Washington to Washington plunged
In the sowing rain. He slept with
His nurse on the voyage, she was rough,
Scarred with transcontinental love,
She was his all-guessing heart when he died.
Raise the blind, he commanded. Under
The rain the continent wheeled, his own land
Electric and blind, farmlights and cities'
Blazes—points and clusters and chains—
Each light a memory and the whole of darkness
Memory. In the seedfall of a continent
The majesty of a man rendered himself home:
His death was across the land when he died.

Promontory Moon

The moon: she shakes off her cloaks,
Her rings of mist and circle of blurred light,
And shines without chemistry or heat
Upon us. Milky blue in her influence
The sea rises dabbing at the tiers of rock.
A few shadowy rabbits dash feinting
Over the grass and paths. In sunlight
Men will sprawl generating on the grass;
But the rabbits ask nothing of the moon,
And run at midnight for delight alone.

Half rabbits, half rabbits' shadows,
They are like the night roistering fairies
For whom as children we set banquets
In the dusk, of bits of bread and honey,
That we explored for in the dawn and found
Untouched, the one trace of fairies being
The dew glistening on the moss and grass
At daybreak, which they shed for sorrow
Their weightless bodies have no appetite,
Being woven by the night of moonlight.

The sun makes the grass increase, feeding
The things it can corrupt. The moon
Holds her purer watches on the night,
Mirroring on that fairest time of day
Only the subtlest miracles of light;
And that within ourselves too straight to bend
In agonies of death and birth—as now
The blue-white sea swirls at the moonbeams
And keeps on winding on the shining clew—
Dissolves at her touch and is weaved anew.

The Supper after the Last

for Anne Buchanan

I

The desert moves out on half the horizon
Rimming the illusory water which, among islands,
Bears up the sky. The sea scumbles in
From its own inviolate border under the sky.
A dragon-fly floating on the sand on six legs
Lifts its green-yellow tail, declines its wings
A little, flutters them a little, and lays

On dazzled sand the shadow of its wings. Near shore
A bather wades through his shadow in the water.
He tramples and kicks it; it recomposes.

2

Outside the open door
Of the white washed house,
Framed in its doorway, a chair,
Vacant, waits in the sunshine.

A jug of fresh water stands
Inside the door. In the sunshine
The chair waits, less and less vacant.
The host's plan is to offer water, then stand aside.

3

They eat *rosé* and chicken. The chicken head
Has been tucked under the shelter of the wing.
Under the table a red-backed, passionate dog
Cracks chicken bones on the blood and gravel floor.

No one else but the dog and the blind
Cat watching it knows who is that bearded
Wild man guzzling overhead, the wreck of passion
Emptying his eyes, who has not yet smiled,

Who stares at the company, where he is company,
Turns them to sacks of appalled, grinning skin,
Forks the fowl-eye out from under
The large, makeshift, cooked lid, evaporates the wine,

Jellies the sunlit table and spoons, floats
The deluxe grub down the intestines of the Styx,
Devours all but the cat and the dog, to whom he slips scraps,
The red-backed accomplice busy grinding gristle.

4

When the bones of the host
Crack in the hound's jaw
The wild man rises. Opening
His palms he announces:
I came not to astonish
But to destroy you. Your
Jug of cool water? Your
Hanker after wings? Your
Lech for transcendence?
I came to prove you are
Intricate and simple things
As you are, created
In the image of nothing,
Taught of the creator
By your images in dirt—
As mine, for which you set
A chair in the sunshine,

Mocking me with water!
As pictures of wings,
Not even iridescent,
That clasp the sand
And that cannot perish, you swear,
Having once been evoked!

5

The witnesses back off; the scene begins to float in water;
Far out in that mirage the Saviour sits whispering to the world,
Becoming a mirage. The dog tuns into a smear on the sand.
The cat grows taller and taller as it flees into space.

From the hot shine where he sits his whispering drifts:
You struggle from flesh into wings; the change exists.
But the wings that live gripping the contours of the dirt
Are all at once nothing, flesh and light lifted away.

You are the flesh; I am the resurrection, because I am the light.
I cut to your measure the creeping piece of darkness
That haunts you in the dirt. Steps into light—
I make you over. I breed the shape of your grave in the dirt.

ANNE SEXTON

Kind Sir: These Woods

For a man needs only to be turned around once with his eyes shut in this world to be lost. . . . Not til we are lost . . . do we begin to find ourselves.

Thoreau, Walden

Kind Sir: This is an old game
that we played when we were eight and ten.
Sometimes on The Island, in down Maine,
in late August, when the cold fog blew in
off the ocean, the forest between Dingley Dell
and grandfather's cottage grew white and strange.
It was as if every pine tree were a brown pole
we did not know; as if day had rearranged
into night and bats flew in sun. It was a trick
to turn around once and know you were lost;
knowing the crow's horn was crying in the dark,
knowing that supper would never come, that the coast's
cry of doom from that far away bell buoy's bell
said *your nursemaid is gone*. O Mademoiselle,
the rowboat rocked over. Then you were dead.
Turn around once, eyes tight, the thought in your head.

Kind Sir: Lost and of your same kind
I have turned around twice with my eyes sealed

and the woods were white and my night mind
saw such strange happenings, untold and unreal.
And opening my eyes, I am afraid of course
to look—this inward look that society scorns—
Still, I search in these woods and find nothing worse
than myself, caught between the grapes and the thorns.

Said the Poet to the Analyst

My business is words. Words are like labels,
or coins, or better, like swarming bees.
I confess I am only broken by the sources of things;
as if words were counted like dead bees in the attic,
unbuckled from their yellow eyes and their dry wings.
I must always forget how one word is able to pick
out another, to manner another, until I have got
something I might have said . . .
but did not.

Your business is watching my words. But I
admit nothing. I work with my best, for instance,
when I can write my praise for a nickel machine,
that one night in Nevada: telling how the magic jackpot
came clacking three bells out, over the lucky screen.
But if you should say this is something it is not,
then I grow weak, remembering how my hands felt funny
and ridiculous and crowded with all
the believing money.

Her Kind

I have gone out, a possessed witch,
haunting the black air, braver at night;
dreaming evil, I have done my hitch
over the plain houses, light by light:

lonely thing, twelve-fingered, out of mind.
A woman like that is not a woman, quite.
I have been her kind.

I have found the warm caves in the woods,
filled them with skillets, carvings, shelves,
closets, silks, innumerable goods;
fixed the suppers for the worms and the elves:
whining, rearranging the disaligned.
A woman like that is misunderstood.
I have been her kind.

I have ridden in your cart, driver,
waved my nude arms at villages going by,
learning the last bright routes, survivor
where your flames still bite my thigh
and my ribs crack where your wheels wind.
A woman like that is not ashamed to die.
I have been her kind.

Where I Live in This Honorable House of the Laurel Tree

I live in my wooden legs and O
my green green hands.
Too late
to wish I had not run from you, Apollo,
blood moves still in my bark bound veins.
I, who ran nymph foot to root in flight,
have only this late desire to arm the trees
I lie within. The measure that I have lost
silks my pulse. Each century the trickeries
of need pain me everywhere.
Frost taps my skin and I stay glossed
in honor for you are gone in time. The air
rings for you, for that astonishing rite
of my breathing tent undone within your light.

I only know how this untimely lust has tossed
flesh at the wind forever and moved my fears
toward the intimate Rome of the myth we crossed.
I am a fist of my unease
as I spill toward the stars in the empty years.
I build the air with the crown of honor; it keys
my out of time and luckless appetite.
You gave me honor too soon, Apollo.
There is no one left who understands
how I wait
here in my wooden legs and O
my green green hands.

CLAIRE MCALLISTER

Mystery

Having squandered my years to follow that wake beyond the elm
Where cold the moon wheels carefully on unfurling cloud;
Having bartered any wit for a light not sold, except, except for a song,
Staked midnights like chips on a number not there
For a sum (O where? Not here, I hear now) not here to be won
Willing stillness stretch tight the veins that they might
Plucked by no earthly hand, someday render true one, one sound—
Wits as twanging away, I have this much to say: Do not stop
When the whisper among the leaves of quiet says "Listen!"
Not stop. No, that murmur, though than green of leaf clearer,
Deeper ringing, more bitter, a mockery of eardrum,
Of iris, of tastebud, O say now, it was perhaps but

But the burring of the heavy moths gold at the edge of the
copse,
But the stirring of woodfern searching the dark night of earth.
Turn away! This say, this. Or let pressed be, as first clustered
grapes,
Let pressed be the braincells, staining all sight inside,
Pressed until body but a goatskin hold much heady wine,
Till Time like the Ice Sheet begin, melt thin,
Old legend pushed young into sun,
Frozen mystery to roll, there to lie before the eye
Seeming one day simple, sound, warm.
No, no; that tone of leaf taller than height sending where? O
Had but for barter, all bartered
And freely giving only, as April air, but for the breathing
Freely giving more than all in return,
Will take every once shed salt tear in the chest,
Will break every not yet shed tear in the head
And drink those drops all with one sip, imperceptible sip.

Go, go your ways. Be not dazed. Do not praise, but in ageless
old ways
Like the waves of the sea, salt or grass, that repeat, sweet repeat.
For walking the wood O what do I see but unfoldings each
moment more strange,
Tricking the lane, the brain, and the pain;
Weeds wild as beasts and never the same
Expression gestured from bough.
A spruce growing bluer in the rain saying, "Gaze! Graze, love,
now! Now
Give tongue to my wonder-numbed ways, for Tomorrow is
Never."
It taught me, it tossed me my thought (fallen cone—
And all thought a slow falling to the floors, lying low like those
cones)
Taught O quiet as a pinecone in shade I might learn how to
praise;
All still as a stone in a valley I might learn firm praise.
But stop, stilled by growths in a woodlight and, crazed,

The fool brain shall fool dervish and downdrop.
Stand sighting the woodlily that tells you not toil—
But, Lord, not to toil is to coil unto death
Unless unless like the cobra clever
Love roll away like old skin.

Do not, I advise you, (my charming ambitions in a heap
As robes after revelry, and the wine-flasks dry) Do not pray;
But gaily sing away, gay and loud sing the night blue to dawn.
Forget the one crown to be wished is yours all for the willing;
Nor think to catch glimpse of the only Face. Nor follow that
 streak in the sky.
It belongs to the Grail, and you will, unaware,
All failing succeed like the day-
Break of day, break of once black heart.
And the once wooden twigs leasing tears, tossing pearls, drop-
 ping
Rain on the head become chrism. . . .
What return can the beggar brain render but shedding of blood?
What give but that wish: to shed its loved blood.
Face. Grail. Ghost. Before the very eye, in the Host, in the Flesh
On the linen-spread tombstone table a stonethrow away
Waiting waiting waiting waiting
To melt in the head, set crown right.
But O not, do not alter your pauper-proud dusty steps. Do not
Believe it! O sleepwalker, sleepwalker, No! Sleep,
Sleep, sleep. . . .

Daphne

From a hillslope I look on the wet fields flattening before me,
Mud holding mirrors, and the withered twigs alive with rain;
I would pick my way down through the darkness and straining
 bramble
But I'd only be stumbling to that weather-rank tomb, my true
 name—

A name never meant for men's mouths, that to no man I'd answer.
And what paths would I step but the small ways down my own ear?
Since the day that I fled them along the fields of my pride
Every tree says, Stand, tall in your silence, till blood return from fear.

But Lord if I stand so I feel my human limbs taking root
And the glint on the ground from a lichened twig might stare me blind,
And the Apollo of my Imagination pursuing . . . his arms, O the arms almost about me,
Would he leave me there forever, with my love branching stiff from the spine?

Yet a form has walked in the broken sun of the wood,
Has hunted with the arrows of prayer where the wild boars drip red.
O him let me see! if mistaking but a birch for his gestures;
Those hands could change my sad flesh which change to Body the bread.

Or the terrible secret, is it lodged in the rings of a tree?
That I, slowed as Laurel, had else ambled wilder than most
Did I not know He walked, the Christ, sounding all depths from those eyes,
Cry, why should he so please my soul? Half blessed is half cursed.

That out of the corner of my eye, only, dare I now look.
To have followed a love to its lonely throne in the wood
Sees me struck clutching earth, slow leaves of my brain brought to light,
Speechless with rustling: God is now Body and Blood.

If the rude wood I rambled were my own empty loving, he pitied.

Lord, among these leaves, O now let Your sun toss a few coins.
See a thing stilled staring into distances reflecting You, in his eyes;
Lord, unless You breathe on me now, let rot shroud my loins . . .

A Dedication

For Father D'Arcy

Lucilla, saved from shipwreck on the seas,
Dedicates to those who bade her live—
The ocean deities—
Her wringing hair. There's nothing else to give.

Dedicates to those who bade her live
And told her walk on the tall waves with pride,
Her wringing hair. There's nothing else to give
Except the hoar sea-fruit at her side.

Walk out over the black waves with pride.
No sea was ever crossed not crossed in fear.
Her heart that talked to men died;
Who, but the sea gods, hear?

No sea was crossed but crossed in fear.
From a land of slime and shard she gives what is left.
Then may blind love see, so brought ashore,
And she beg, wringing out her hair: Accept.

What from all the flotsam had she kept?
Forgetting salt-stung eyes and tired arms
She entreats: My seaweed hair, accept.
He goes his way, with fishing-nets, and psalms.

Stung eyes, tired arms,
The dark divinities
Go their way, with fishing-nets, and psalms,
Plucking lovers from shipwreck on the seas.

INDEX OF POETS

INDEX OF FIRST LINES

MODERN LIBRARY GIANTS

A series of sturdily bound and handsomely printed, full-sized library editions of books formerly available only in expensive sets. These volumes contain from 600 to 1,400 pages each.

THE MODERN LIBRARY GIANTS REPRESENT A SELECTION OF THE WORLD'S GREATEST BOOKS

G76 Andersen & Grimm: *Tales*
G74 Augustine, St.: *The City of God*
G58 Austen, Jane: *Complete Novels*
G70 Blake, William & Donne, John: *Complete Poetry*
G2 Boswell, James: *Life of Samuel Johnson*
G17 Browning, Robert: *Poems and Plays*
G14 Bulfinch: *Mythology* (Illustrated)
G35 Bury, J. B.: *A History of Greece*
G13 Carlyle, Thomas: *The French Revolution*
G28 Carroll, Lewis: *Complete Works*
G15 Cervantes: *Don Quixote* (Illustrated)
G33 Collins, Wilkie: *The Moonstone* and *The Woman in White*
G27 Darwin, Charles: *Origin of Species* and *The Descent of Man*
G43 Dewey, John: *Intelligence in the Modern World: John Dewey's Philosophy*
G70 Donne, John & Blake, William: *Complete Poetry*
G36 Dostoyevsky, Fyodor: *The Brothers Karamazov*
G60 Dostoyevsky, Fyodor: *The Idiot*
G51 Eliot, George: *Best-Known Novels*
G41 Farrell, James T.: *Studs Lonigan*
G82 Faulkner, William: *The Faulkner Reader*
G39 Freud, Sigmund: *The Basic Writings*
G6, G7, G8 Gibbon, Edward: *The Decline and Fall of the Roman Empire* (Complete in three volumes)
G25 Gilbert & Sullivan: *Complete Plays*
G76 Grimm & Andersen: *Tales*
G37 Hawthorne, Nathaniel: *Complete Novels and Selected Tales*
G78 Holmes, Oliver Wendell: *The Mind and Faith of Justice Holmes*
G19 Homer: *Complete Works*
G3 Hugo, Victor: *Les Miserables*
G18 Ibsen, Henrik: *Eleven Plays*
G11 James, Henry: *Short Stories*
G52 Joyce, James: *Ulysses*
G24 Lamb, Charles: *The Complete Works and Letters*
G4 Keats & Shelley: *Complete Poems*
G20 Lincoln, Abraham: *The Life and Writings of Abraham Lincoln*
G84 Mann, Thomas: *Stories of Three Decades*
G26 Marx, Karl: *Capital*

G57 Melville, Herman: *Selected Writings*
G38 Murasaka, Lady: *The Tale of Genji*
G30 Myers, Gustavus: *History of the Great American Fortunes*
G34 Nietzsche, Friedrich: *The Philosophy of Nietzsche*
G55 O'Neill, Eugene: *Nine Plays*
G68 Paine, Tom: *Selected Work*
G86 Pasternak, Boris: *Doctor Zhivago*
G5 Plutarch: *Lives* (The Dryden Translation)
G40 Poe, Edgar Allan: *Complete Tales and Poems*
G29 Prescott, William H.: *The Conquest of Mexico* and *The Conquest of Peru*
G62 Pushkin: *Poems, Prose and Plays*
G65 Rabelais: *Complete Works*
G12 Scott, Sir Walter: *The Most Popular Novels* (Quentin Durward, Ivanhoe & Kenilworth)
G4 Shelley & Keats: *Complete Poems*
G32 Smith, Adam: *The Wealth of Nations*
G61 Spaeth, Sigmund: *A Guide to Great Orchestral Music*
G75 Stevenson, Robert Louis: *Selected Writings*
G53 Sue, Eugene: *The Wandering Jew*
G42 Tennyson: *The Poems and Plays*
G23 Tolstoy, Leo: *Anna Karenina*
G1 Tolstoy, Leo: *War and Peace*
G49 Twain, Mark: *Tom Sawyer* and *Huckleberry Finn*
G50 Whitman, Walt: *Leaves of Grass*
G83 Wilson, Edmund: *The Shock of Recognition*

MISCELLANEOUS

G77 *An Anthology of Famous American Stories*
G54 *An Anthology of Famous British Stories*
G67 *Anthology of Famous English and American Poetry*
G81 *An Encyclopedia of Modern American Humor*
G47 *The English Philosophers from Bacon to Mill*
G16 *The European Philosophers from Descartes to Nietzsche*
G31 *Famous Science-Fiction Stories: Adventures in Time and Space*
G85 *Great Ages and Ideas of the Jewish People*
G72 *Great Tales of Terror and the Supernatural*
G9 *Great Voices of the Reformation*
G87 *Medieval Epics*
G48 *The Metropolitan Opera Guide*
G46 *A New Anthology of Modern Poetry*
G69 *One Hundred and One Years' Entertainment*
G21 *Sixteen Famous American Plays*
G63 *Sixteen Famous British Plays*
G71 *Sixteen Famous European Plays*
G45 *Stoic and Epicurean Philosophers*
G22 *Thirty Famous One-Act Plays*
G66 *Three Famous Murder Novels*
Before the Fact, Francis Iles
Trent's Last Case, E. C. Bentley
The House of the Arrow, A. E. W. Mason
G10 *Twelve Famous Plays of the Restoration and Eighteenth Century* (1660–1820)
(Congreve, Wycherley, Gay, Goldsmith, Sheridan, etc.)
G56 *The Wisdom of Catholicism*
G59 *The Wisdom of China and India*
G79 *The Wisdom of Israel*